Understanding the Gender Gap

NBER SERIES ON LONG-TERM FACTORS IN ECONOMIC DEVELOPMENT

EDITORS
Robert W. Fogel and Clayne L. Pope

Also in the series

Roderick Floud, Annabel Gregory, and Kenneth Wachter
Height, Health and History: Nutritional Status in the United Kingdom, 1750–1980
(Cambridge University Press, 1990)

Samuel Preston and Michael Haines
Fatal Years: Child Mortality in Late-Nineteenth-Century America
(Princeton University Press, 1990)

In preparation (tentative titles)

Robert W. Fogel
The Escape from Hunger and Early Death: Europe and America, 1750–2050

Robert A. Margo
Race and Schooling in the American South, 1880–1950: A Quantitative History

Kenneth L. Sokoloff
In Pursuit of Private Comfort: Early American Industrialization, 1790 to 1860

'Understanding the Gender Gap /

An Economic History of American Women

CLAUDIA D. GOLDIN

New York   Oxford
OXFORD UNIVERSITY PRESS
1990

Oxford University Press

Oxford New York Toronto
Delhi Bombay Calcutta Madras Karachi
Petaling Jaya Singapore Hong Kong Tokyo
Nairobi Dar es Salaam Cape Town
Melbourne Auckland

and associated companies in
Berlin Ibadan

Published by Oxford University Press, Inc.,
200 Madison Avenue, New York, New York 10016
Oxford is a registered trademark of Oxford University Press

Library of Congress Cataloging-in-Publication Data
Goldin, Claudia Dale.
Understanding the gender gap : an economic history
of American women / Claudia Goldin.
p. cm. Bibliography: p. Includes index.
ISBN 0-19-505077-0
1. Women—Employment—United States—History.
2. Sex discrimination in employment—United States—History. I. Title.
II. Title: Economic history of American women.
HD6095.G65 1990 331.4'0973—dc20 89-33502

The following appear in this book by permission:

Figures 2.1 and 2.2 reprinted with minor changes from Goldin, "The Economic Role of Women: A Quantitative
Approach," *Journal of Interdisciplinary History*, XIII (1983), 707–733, with the permission of the editors of the
Journal of Interdisciplinary History and The MIT Press, Cambridge, Massachusetts. © 1983 by The Massachusetts
Institute of Technology and the editors of the *Journal of Interdisciplinary History*.

Figure 2.4 and Table 2.10 reprinted with minor changes from Goldin, "The Economic Status of Women in the Early
Republic: Quantitative Evidence," *Journal of Interdisciplinary History*, XVI (1986), 375–404, with the permission of
the editors of the *Journal of Interdisciplinary History* and The MIT Press, Cambridge, Massachusetts. © 1986 by The
Massachusetts Institute of Technology and the editors of the *Journal of Interdisciplinary History*.

Tables 2.1, 2.2, 2.3, 2.4, 2.9, 3.2, and Appendix to Chapter 2 with changes from Goldin, Ch. 10 in S. L. Engerman
and R. E. Gallman, *Long-Term Factors in American Economic Growth,* © 1986 by the National Bureau of Economic
Research, all rights reserved. Reprinted by permission of The University of Chicago Press.

Tables 2.5, 2.6, 2.7, 2.8 with minor changes from Goldin, "Life-Cycle Labor Force Participation of Married Women"
Journal of Labor Economics, 7 (1989): 20–47. © 1989 by The University of Chicago, all rights reserved.

Table 3.1 excerpted from Goldin, "The Gender Gap in Historical Perspective, 1800 to 1980." Copyright © 1987 by
Wesleyan University. Reprinted from *Quantity and Quiddity* edited by P. Kilby by permission of Wesleyan University
Press.

Tables 3.4 and 4.3 with minor changes from Goldin, "Monitoring Costs and Occupational Segregation by Sex," *Journal
of Labor Economics,* 4 (1986): 1–27. © 1986 by The University of Chicago, all rights reserved.

9 8 7 6 5 4 3 2 1

Printed in the United States of America
on acid-free paper

PREFACE

Our generation is constantly reminded that it is undergoing significant change in the economic role of women. The percentage of American women at work has just exceeded 60%, nearly 50% of all workers are women, and more than 50% of women with newborns are back at work within one year. The share of women doctors, lawyers, and other professionals is at an all-time high. Women drive buses and work on construction sites; one ran for vice president; and another made a bid for president. Women's employment milestones fill the press. Yet each generation of Americans, at least since the mid-nineteenth century, has claimed to be on the verge of an unprecedented and momentous change in the economic position of women.

I explore in this volume the process of change and continuity in the economic history of American women that has led so many generations to believe each was at a turning point in women's economic position. Despite the perception that there has been little meaningful change in the past, my work demonstrates that crucial foundations have been instituted by many past generations. But I emphasize, as well, the reasons for the tenacity of gender differences in the workplace. The progress of women's work is like none other in the labor market. It cannot be understood as an isolated market responding to economic factors, as most other economic variables can. Rather, it is tied, as is each woman, to the home, the family, and the process of socialization, and is linked by each woman to her past and her future through the life cycle. Consequently, my volume is fundamentally interdisciplinary research.

I offer a simple explanation for the apparently contradictory perception that each generation is unique. Significant progress in the economic sphere was achieved by many generations—female employment increased, women's earnings rose, and their occupations expanded in number. Yet, despite these advances, gender distinctions in society and in the workplace eroded slowly, and in the minds of many the advances were rapidly incorporated into a status quo. At the turn of this century, for example, young women moved from manufacturing to office jobs, a shift that would have important consequences for their employment in future decades. But clerical jobs soon became feminized, and most were dead-end, stereotypically female positions. Later generations would associate office employment with the unjust treatment of women in the economic marketplace rather than with progress. Thus each generation could view its own era as unique in undergoing substantial and meaningful change because so little of consequence was apparent from the past.

It may come as a surprise to many that economists, generally the most conservative of all social scientists, have long been interested in women's participation in the economy and in gender differences in pay and occupations. Their concern, since the

1920's, has been with the determinants of hours, days, and years worked, and their focus was on women whose lifetime work contains more variation than men's. With increased female labor force participation in the post–World War II era, economists turned their attention to why women entered the labor market and the relationship between these changes and the large swings in fertility dating from the 1920's. More recently, economists have focused on the reasons for differences between men and women in earnings and occupations, and the role of legislation, among other factors, in the recent narrowing of gender differences.[1] Economists have largely emphasized the more progressive and equalizing aspects of the history of women's work.

In stark contrast, historians have highlighted the stability of gender differences in the social and economic spheres, the frequent struggles for equality in the economic and political arenas, and the past achievements of remarkable women.[2] Those who read history carefully are aware of the long period of time the process has taken.

Thus historians have emphasized barriers to equality and the manner in which the market reinforces the gender distinctions of a patriarchal society. Economists have shown how economic progress fosters equality and have contended that the competitive market ameliorates, not accentuates, the consequences of social prejudice. Both disciplines, like all generations, can be correct: there has been meaningful change in women's role in the economy, yet much constancy in gender distinctions.

I began this study more as an economist but have ended with a fuller appreciation of how the distant past affects the present, how norms and expectations impede change, how discrimination can survive in even highly competitive markets, and how slow genuine change can be. My sense of the appropriate balance between continuity and change in the economic history of women was altered in the process of researching the book. At the end of the project, I realized I could resolve only some of the paradoxes and fully grasp only some of the contradictions in this complex history. Indeed, the study of women's changing role in the American economy is sustaining and intriguing because of its enormous complexity.

This project has taken many more years to complete than I first envisioned. An initial complication was the absence of evidence for many key variables. No consistent series for the female labor force existed, the ratio of female to male earnings was available only since the 1950's, and historical evidence on work experience, hours, and wages, among other variables, was scanty. I soon realized that the economic history of American women could not be told until various data series were constructed. Archival sources, state and federal reports, city and business directories, census manuscripts, and a variety of other sources allowed me to assemble time series on the labor force, work experience, earnings, hours, part-time work, education, and fertility.

A thorough reworking of the published population census figures from 1890 to the present produced a consistent time series. But because the locus of production shifted from the home to the market, and because women were undercounted in the labor force, I also produced an augmented female labor force figure for the period around 1890. I explored the origins of the paid labor of single women using the manuscripts of the manufacturing censuses, and examined the work of women in the late eighteenth century with city and business directories. Because the concept of the "labor force participation rate" cannot yield a measure of work experience crucial to understanding women's economic position, I sought evidence from longitudinal studies. But the only readily available longitudinal data covered too recent a period. I discovered precisely the records I needed in the National Archives—a large-scale survey of women's work histories for cohorts born from 1880 to 1915.

The findings from these labors produced a new view of women's work in America. A more comprehensive measure of labor force participation indicates that it probably fell sometime before its more celebrated rise. Market production of married women in cities was high even in the late eighteenth and early nineteenth centuries. Perhaps the greatest surprise was that the average work experience of married working women increased little from the 1920's to the 1980's, yet was substantial even when participation rates were low.

I next turned to a study of gender differences in earnings and occupations and set out to extend a time series of female and male earnings available only since the mid-1950's back to the early nineteenth century. I pieced together a wage series from a variety of archival and published sources that demonstrates a significant increase in the ratio of female to male earnings at two times in American history, one during the Industrial Revolution and the other during the early twentieth century. A more recent increase in the ratio, since 1981, may in the future be considered a third period of narrowing in the gender gap in earnings. The finding that the ratio of female to male earnings increased at several points in American history overturned the usual presumption that it was as constant in the past as it had been from the 1950's to the early 1980's.

Given the two changes in the economic status of women—that in the labor force and that in the wage series—I then set out to examine the reasons for both. Various features of the economic development process greatly altered the economic role of women. Changes in female labor force participation were effected mainly by advances in education, the growth of sectors such as clerical work and sales, and the shorter workday. The secular decline in fertility and its cyclical aspects that affected cohorts differentially, as well as a host of well-known advances in household production, also altered female employment. Although the advances in participation occurred primarily in the post–World War II period, the preconditions for the increase had been set between 1900 and 1930.

The issue, in the case of earnings differences between men and women, was whether differences in attributes or a concept termed "wage discrimination" was to blame.[3] Data for manufacturing occupations from various state and federal reports published around the turn of this century indicate that while earnings and occupations differed substantially between men and women, so did the productive attributes of workers. A rather different result was uncovered for office workers somewhat later in the century; productive attributes of female and male workers began to converge by the 1940's, yet earnings converged less so. The original, individual-level schedules of a Women's Bureau bulletin, found in the National Archives, enabled an exploration of the origins of "wage discrimination." The firm-level schedules for the same bulletin indicated that firms' policies segregated women into particular occupations. Firms had occupations for which no males would be hired and those for which no females would be hired. Furthermore, many firms fired women who married in service, and many more would not hire married women. Such "smoking gun" evidence in our current litigious environment is quite extraordinary. But the officials of the hundreds of firms in the 1940 sample were often proud of their policies, which not only maximized firm profits but also were consistent with prevailing social attitudes.

The reasons for "wage discrimination" and the firm-level policies that excluded women from certain occupations and married women from many types of work are complex. One element is that most women, at the time, exited the labor force at marriage, and the jobs deemed appropriate for all women suited the majority. The complexities involve the supporting roles of social consensus, norms, and prejudices, all of which were reinforced by these policies. Discrimination in the labor market survived even a highly competitive environment because it was bolstered by various norms that circumscribed the behavior of male and female workers and employers alike.

Real change in the political economy of gender was also impeded by the manner in which the past influenced the present. The female labor force was, in the early twentieth century, a young, transient, apparently exploitable group perceived by social reformers as needing protection. Even though women workers eventually became older, were more stable in their employment, and were less likely to be exploited, the protective legislation passed in the early twentieth century impeded future legislation guaranteeing true equality for at least a half-century.

Many of the ideas and the data series in each of the chapters were originally parts of 18 published papers (4 with co-authors) and 1 working paper listed in the references. The Data Appendix describes the 11 quantitative data sets (and 1 qualitative source) that I have compiled over many years while working on the project. The research that produced these papers and the data series could never have been accomplished without the support of various institutions.

The University of Pennsylvania provided several generous leaves. The first was taken during 1982 to 1983 at the Institute for Advanced Study at Princeton, where many of the ideas in this volume first took form. The manuscript was written five years later at the Industrial Relations Section of Princeton University, which housed me during a Guggenheim Fellowship leave, 1987 to 1988. The National Science Foundation funded my research on the evolution of the female labor force during the full period of the project. A Mellon Foundation grant to the PARSS program at the University of Pennsylvania supported several graduate students whose research endeavors complemented mine. The University of Pennsylvania library funded the microfilming of various Women's Bureau schedules from the National Archives. The staff of the National Archives, particularly Jerry Hess and Jerry Clark of the Industrial and Social Branch, kindly and ably filled my many requests over the years. I thank all these institutions and individuals for their generous support and assistance.

Numerous research assistants were involved on the project, and I am grateful to them all. Nadja Zalokar, among the first, left meticulous notes on the labor force estimates that I have depended on for many years; Robert Whaples worked on the hours data; Judith Hunter assisted on the 1790 to 1860 project; Kathy Snead collected the 1957/64 College Graduate Survey, through a grant from the PARSS program, for his dissertation; and Laura Huntoon and Daniel Kinney helped with myriad final chores.

My colleagues have added immeasurably to my work. Without demeaning the contributions of the rest, I would like to express my sincere gratitude to Stanley Engerman and Robert Margo, who commented on the entire manuscript. I thank my Penn colleagues Jere Behrman, Jerry Jacobs, Lynn Lees, Walter Licht, Janice Madden, Ann Miller, Robert Pollak, Paul Taubman, and Susan Watkins, and my Princeton colleagues Joshua Angrist, Orley Ashenfelter, Kevin Barry, Dwayne Benjamin, Becky Blank, David Card, Ann Case, Alan Krueger, Peter Kuhn, Janet (Neelin) Currie, Sharon Smith, and Richard Lester, who recounted to me his experiences on the President's Commission on the Status of Women. National Bureau of Economic Research summer-institute participants Lance Davis, Stanley Engerman, Peter Lindert, Clayne Pope, Kenneth Sokoloff (who also served as a co-author), Richard Sutch, and Peter Temin commented on early versions of some chapters. Many others have shared their own research and data and have offered helpful suggestions. I will never be able to recall everyone, but among them are Jeremy Atack, Barbara Bergmann, Francine Blau, David Buffum, Susan Carter, Sam Cohn, Barry Eichengreen, Stefano Fenoaltea, Randy Filer, Nancy Folbre, Gerald Friedman, Michael Haines, James Heckman, M. Ann Hill, Linda Kerber, Michael Leeds, June O'Neill, Elizabeth Pleck, Sol Polachek, and Elyce Rotella. I thank them all.

Robert William Fogel, always my mentor, encouraged me from the very start of the project to write a book-length manuscript. Richard Easterlin, once my colleague at Penn, provided intellectual guidance that he may not have realized. The project coincided with my four-year term as editor of the *Journal of Economic History,* and I could never have accomplished any research during my tenure without a most able assistant editor, Carol Petraitis. Carol also edited my manuscript as she did the *Journal,* with her fine eye, understanding mind, and sensitive nature. Selig L. Sechzer read some of this manuscript; more often he listened to ideas in their roughest form. He shared much with me during its years of creation, and I thank him for his patience and understanding.

There must be a moment when all projects terminate, at least long enough to write the book that summarizes the available information. As I worked on this project, new data sets became available that I have not been able to use. The recently issued public use sample of the 1910 census will fill many gaps in Chapter 2, that for the 1940 census could have been used for Chapter 5, and the original schedules from Gladys Palmer's (1954) study of job mobility between 1940 and 1950, just uncovered at Penn by Ann Miller, will help resolve the role played by World War II discussed in Chapter 5. Various statistics in the book differ from those in the many articles that preceded it. The occasional error was found and new methods were used. There will, it is hoped, be further work with these and other data sets that might support or supersede my conclusions. That is the essence of scholarly endeavor.

Philadelphia   C. G.
April 1989

CONTENTS

LIST OF TABLES

LIST OF FIGURES

Understanding the Gender Gap

1

Women's Experience
in the American Economy

The number of women in the paid labor force has advanced steadily since the early 1800's, and from World War II its climb has been rapid. In 1900 fewer than one in five workers were women, while almost half are today. Yet occupational segregation by sex has diminished only slightly since 1900, and the ratio of female to male earnings remained stable from the 1950's to the early 1980's. To many observers, women have entered the labor force in unprecedented numbers but have not been treated as equals to men.

This book is a history of the female labor force and of gender differences in occupations and earnings. It focuses on the historical roots of present inequalities and why real progress in the economic position of women has seemed slow to emerge. Much of the growth in the female labor force over the last two centuries has been the result of long-run changes in the economy—the Industrial Revolution, the rise of white-collar work, advances in education, the decline in fertility, and the decreased workday, among others. In many cases, change was brought about by the aging of cohorts whose education, job training, early socialization, and fertility differed from those of previous generations. Thus progress has frequently seemed prolonged.

But a genuine integration of women into the American economy has often been impeded. Past conceptions of female workers as marginal and transient led employers to bar women from many occupations. Social norms have often dictated which jobs were appropriate. Change in the workplace has both helped women and served to widen gender differences. White-collar work, for example, led to a narrowing in the gender gap in earnings and an increase in women's participation and work experience. But it produced restrictions on women's jobs and barriers to many with the greatest promotion possibilities. The history of women in the economy appears filled with contradictions. Many can be resolved through quantitative study, such as the resolution of the apparent paradox between the increase in participation rates in the post-1950's period and stability in the gender gap in earnings. In all cases, however, they point to the importance of history in the study of current gender distinctions in the economy.

Within the twentieth century and much of the nineteenth, women's paid labor outside the home advanced from decade to decade. From 1820 to 1920 the participation of young, unmarried women increased considerably with America's industrial activity and urbanization. The history of the paid labor of adult and married women is less easily summarized. It is complicated by the existence of unpaid work in the home and on the farm and by the undercounting of paid work in and outside the home. An inclusive measure of their labor force participation indicates that it probably decreased from the nineteenth century until the early twentieth century, when it began its more celebrated rise. And although increases in married women's participation are discernable in the 1920's among young women, the increases are most striking from the 1950's to the present. Despite various complications concerning the definition of paid and unpaid labor, and the distinction between the home and the workplace, the labor force activity of all women advanced in a more or less continuous fashion from the early nineteenth century to the present (Chapter 2).

But an absence of progress has marked various measures of equity in the labor market and paradoxical evidence has been revealed for yet others. Occupations were nearly as segregated by sex in 1900 as they were in 1970, and although occupational segregation has decreased since 1970, it still remains substantial (Chapter 3). The ratio of female to male earnings was virtually constant from the mid-1950's to the early 1980's. But new findings presented in Chapter 3 indicate the ratio of female to male earnings increased from 1815 to the 1930's. In the absence of such evidence, many had presumed the ratio was as constant before 1950 as it had been since. Rather, it rose in two distinct periods. It increased substantially in the early nineteenth century with the Industrial Revolution in America and again a half-century later with a revolution that marked the growth of clerical and other white-collar work. The episodes enhanced the productive abilities of women relative to men through the use of machinery, a greater division of labor, and, in the case of the second event, increased returns to education. Both episodes also served to break down various customs and traditions that had circumscribed women's work.

The narrowing of the gender gap in earnings occurred prior to advances in adult, married women's participation and was not accompanied by meaningful social change. It neither was produced by a social revolution nor did it effect one. And even though the gap between male and female earnings narrowed before the 1930's, the ability to explain the difference, as shown in Chapter 4, diminishes with time. Economic discrimination can be interpreted as a difference in earnings between two groups that cannot be accounted for by differences in the average productive attributes of the groups, such as job experience, education, and tenure with a firm. According to the estimates in Chapter 4, therefore, discrimination on the basis of sex actually increased from the late nineteenth century to the mid-twentieth century. "Wage discrimination," as the measure will be called, increased while the gap between male and female earnings narrowed. Why this seemingly paradoxical result occurs has much to do with the movement from manufacturing to white-collar jobs, expanded schooling, and the increased returns to education in the marketplace. Increased schooling and the growth of the clerical sector enhanced the earnings of female workers relative to male workers. But the replacement of brawn by brainpower also meant that women could enter most entry-level jobs, and firms responded by barring women from jobs with long promotional ladders.

Thus historical evidence on the experience of women in the economy provides a conflicting picture. Some of the contradictions are more easily resolved than others. Many owe to the slow nature of change in the labor market, which is often accomplished by the movement of individual cohorts through time. Cohorts carry through life their early socialization, schooling, work experience, and attitudes toward paid work, and may be differentially influenced by contemporaneous factors, such as increased wages, unemployment, and social advancements. Because different cohorts exist simultaneously, real progress may take several generations to fully emerge.

Cohorts of women born in the early 1900's, for example, experienced an increase in schooling and were employed in the clerical sector to a greater extent than cohorts born before 1900. They also had relatively low levels of marital fertility, and a substantial proportion never had children. As they aged, these cohorts altered various features of the labor market. They were, for example, the older married women in the 1950's who experienced large increases in their labor force participation rates after World War II. Cohort effects often prolong the period of change because they require substantial time to work through the economy and society.

Further, the impact of cohort effects is often obscured by contemporaneous changes. The extraordinary increase in the participation of married women in the American labor force dates with the post–World War II period. Yet many of its preconditions originated earlier in the twentieth century with increased education, decreased fertility, and an increased demand for female workers in the clerical and sales sectors. Older married women in the 1950's were able to respond to an increase in the wages offered them by entering the labor force because their cohort was better prepared to do so. Social change was, no doubt, unleashed during World War II. But advances in the female labor force in the 1950's were more likely produced by cohort effects than by shifting social attitudes. Indeed, the increased participation of women over the long run resulted more from a changed nature of jobs, such as the decrease in hours of work and the rise of white-collar work, than from shifts in social norms and attitudes.

Progress may be slowed by the formation of expectations concerning future labor force participation. Young women in periods of rapid change may be unable to forecast accurately their future labor force participation and may misjudge future occupational requirements. They may be guided more by the experiences of their mothers' generation than by those of intervening cohorts. Young women should have been capable of making rather accurate forecasts had they extrapolated on the basis of past cohort variables. But survey evidence, presented in Chapter 5, shows their forecasts were extremely poor in the 1960's, yet became more accurate in the 1970's. Why their expectations suddenly became more realistic remains an open question, and one cannot dismiss the possibility that the feminist revival gave young women a wider vision of their future.

Despite increases in participation rates from the 1950's to the early 1980's, the ratio of female to male earnings did not rise. Many have claimed that this paradox is strong evidence of increasing economic discrimination against women. But the two facts need not be contradictory. As shown in Chapter 2, increased participation rates need not result in increased labor market experience. The relationship between participation and work experience depends on whether working women remain in the labor force over time. Empirical evidence suggests that the work experience of employed women did not greatly increase during periods of rising participation. Therefore, it is not surprising that the ratio of female to male earnings did not advance along with participation rates. These findings, however, do not dismiss the charge that labor market outcomes reflect discrimination. Indeed, my estimates of women's work experience from 1930 to 1950 underscore findings from various cross sections that economic discrimination was substantial. The evidence does serve to sort out true paradoxes in the economic history of women from more explicable phenomena.

Many of the impediments to equality in the labor market concern the peculiar relationship between the workplace and society. In Chapter 6, I explore the institution of "marriage bars," the policies that many firms and school districts initiated from 1900 to the 1930's not to hire married women and to fire single women when they married. The policies may be similar to those that, until recently, mandated retirement at a particular age. Marriage bars originated in certain personnel policies of firms and local school districts that made the retention of married women workers costly. The marriage bar was associated with tenure-based salary scales, written or implied contractual obligations of employers, paternalistic policies of firms, and other modern personnel practices.

Although the marriage-bar policy may not have been founded in the prejudices of workers and employers, it was fueled by these prejudices. Social consensus had been formed on the necessity for married women to remain at home with their children and on the need for their husbands to support them. Without such consensus, these policies could never have been established, nor could they have been expanded during the Great Depression as a means of rationing jobs. When few married women worked for pay, marriage bars did not greatly restrict labor supply and thus were not very costly. But as cohorts of educated and trained women increased in size, the bars involved greater sacrifices by firms. Only with the "labor squeeze" of the 1950's, when demographic change led to a sharply decreased supply of young single women, were marriage bars abolished by the majority of firms and school districts. Social consensus, therefore, reinforced the dictates of the marketplace and probably prolonged the period of real change.

Further evidence of how past conceptions of female workers produce later inequalities is found in the history of protective legislation. The movement for equality by sex from the 1920's to the 1960's was severely handicapped by the notion that female workers were young, transient, marginal, and exploited laborers. Maximum hours laws and other forms of protective legislation were passed by almost every state from the mid-1800's to the mid-1900's. Protective legislation was viewed by social reformers in 1920, and for almost a half-century later, as more valuable to women than was legislation to ensure equality. Even as late as the 1960's, prominent liberals opposed the Equal Rights Amendment on the ground that it would jeopardize protective legislation. The campaign for equal treatment by sex under the law, discussed in Chapter 7, is a case study in the role of institutions and historical precedent in impeding progressive change.

How occupations become segregated by sex and the forces that sustain sex segregation are perhaps the most complex of the topics addressed (Chapter 3). Sex segregation is often founded on the initial skill requirements for an occupation. But these differences are reinforced by society and the marketplace. Norms that define the appropriate behavior of women through various sanctions, such as public disapproval and the specter of spinsterhood, often maintain gender distinctions. Manufacturing industries in the nineteenth and early twentieth centuries were highly segregated by sex. Certain industries, such as iron and steel, carriages, and agricultural implements, never hired women despite the fact that women were considerably cheaper to employ. Other industries, such as foundries and meatpacking, were eventually integrated but only to the extent that women worked in separate rooms and at different tasks from the majority of men.

Some of the differences among industries owes to their initial requirements of strength and the hazardous and dirty nature of the work. But the physical capital and work organization initially put in place worked together with the "aura of gender" that pervades the marketplace to reinforce the original reasons for sex segregation. It is, therefore, difficult and probably impossible to determine whether a clearly discriminatory policy originated from the biases of agents in the marketplace or from the dictates of efficient production. Another example, discussed in Chapter 4, concerns the origins of "wage discrimination."

Before 1940, more than 80% of all married women had exited the labor force at marriage, and the majority never returned to work. But among married women who did remain at work, a substantial fraction worked for much of their lifetime. Employers, however, may have been unable, ex ante, to discern who among the single women would remain employed and who would not. And workers themselves may have been uncertain early in their working lives whether or not they would remain employed. Employers, therefore, channeled the vast majority of women into rather dead-end jobs involving little job training and skill acquisition. Women were excluded by company policy from many jobs, at both entry-level and more senior positions. The uncertainty concerning who would remain employed was less serious in the manufacturing sector around the turn of this century. Not only were almost all women employed for a rather brief duration, but many jobs and industries were fashioned for male workers in terms of physical capital, custom, long apprenticeships, and so on.

With the institution of white-collar work from the early twentieth century, not only did women extend the period of their employment, but most had the skills to enter any beginning job. With the replacement of intellect for strength and the increase in education, starting salaries between males and females achieved equality. The ratio of beginning wages in office work for males to that of females was one by 1940, but the ratio in manufacturing around 1900 exceeded two. Many of the new white-collar jobs had long promotional ladders, unlike those in manufacturing, and most women, despite their increase in work experience, would not remain on the job long enough to receive promotions. Employers therefore instituted policies to bar women from certain jobs and men from others. Women's jobs were of two types: dead-end positions, such as typist and stenographer, and positions that involved promotion but relatively short ladders. Although most men began at rather low-level jobs, such as mail boy and messenger, their earnings increased with time more than women's did because they were promoted to considerably higher positions. The denial of access to these ladders, despite the long tenure for many women, produced the large measures of "wage discrimination" found in the data. The gender gap in earnings between men and women narrowed because of increased returns to education and decreased returns to strength, but the residual difference in earnings is harder to explain on the basis of differences in attributes.

The explicit policies to segregate the workplace and to fire married women that I have uncovered in the historical records of hundreds of firms would be clearly illegal today. Not surprisingly, such "smoking gun" evidence is extremely rare now. Many of these discriminatory policies, at least as the written procedures of firms, were abandoned sometime after 1950. Some were changed in the 1950's as a response to tighter labor supply conditions, while others were altered only later when the policies became clearly illegal. But their impact remained long after. If few women worked for extensive periods of time, even fewer would remain when jobs were dead end and when women were barred from promotional ladders. When virtually no woman was an accountant, for example, few would train to be accountants. And if women's work was defined in one way and men's in another, few individuals would choose to be the deviant, for deviance might cost one dearly outside the workplace. Thus change in the economic sphere is slowed not only by the necessity for cohorts to effect change, but also by the institutionalization of various barriers and by the existence of social norms maintained by strong sanctions.

Despite real advances since the early 1980's in the earnings ratio and in measures of occupational segregation, many women have become frustrated with the fairness of the labor market and have supported a campaign to alter the rules that govern it. At the time of this writing, about 20 states and several localities have passed legislation that guarantees equity in pay by sex in a manner that greatly extends the doctrine of equal pay for equal work. Public-sector unions, and even many private firms, have embraced the controversial concept of comparable worth, discussed in Chapter 7. Comparable worth serves to guarantee equal pay on the basis of the content of jobs, not the dictates of the marketplace. If successful, it will increase the earnings of women in largely female-intensive occupations, such as those in the clerical and sales sectors, as well as teachers and nurses. In times of progressive change, young women, just entering the labor force, may be able to pursue careers in male-dominated occupations, but older women remain hampered by their previous choices and the constraints they faced when young. Comparable worth is a mechanism to redistribute income to a group that, according to many, has been subjected to economic discrimination. The success of comparable worth in various states, localities, public-sector unions, and firms is a tribute to the growing political power of women, particularly the older group.

Over long periods of time, economic progress has furthered the economic position of women. Progress often appears to have been thwarted because individual cohorts require the passage of time to effect meaningful change. But change is often stymied by institutions, norms, stereotypes, expectations, and other factors that serve to impose the past on the present. My reading of history, therefore, is a guardedly sanguine one. It is buoyed by the increase since 1981 in the ratio of female to male earnings, by the narrowing of differences in occupations since 1970, and by the closing of the gender gap in areas outside the economic sphere. Yet history also teaches one to be suspicious of claims that unprecedented change has occurred in one's lifetime. A past president of the American Economic Association, for example, proclaimed,

> Our age may properly be called the Era of Woman, because everything which affects her receives consideration quite unknown in past centuries . . . [she] is valued as never before . . . and . . . it is perceived that the welfare of the other half of the human race depends more largely upon the position enjoyed by woman that was previously understood. (Campbell, 1893, p. v)

These are not the words of John Kenneth Galbraith, who as president of the AEA in the early 1970's supported a movement to make the status of women in the profession of economics an internal issue in the association. They are instead those of its sixth president, Richard T. Ely, who wrote the passage in 1893.

2

The Evolution of the Female
Labor Force

Adult women are the only demographic group whose paid labor outside the home advanced continually over this century. Older men, teenagers, and, more recently, middle-aged men decreased their employment rates at one time or another. In 1987, 66% of all Americans older than 15 years were in the civilian labor force; 52% had been in 1890. Had the female labor force not expanded during the past century, the civilian participation rate would have declined to 46% in 1987.[1] Therefore, a declining male participation rate by itself would have caused a decrease in aggregate participation from 52% to 46%; the rising female participation rate overcame the decline and led to an increase from 46% to 66%. Census estimates indicate that while 19% of all women were in the labor force a century ago, 60% are today, and, more strikingly, while 5% of all married women were in the labor force in 1890, nearly 60% are today. Women now constitute 45% of the nation's workers, but were about a third that figure in 1890. The increase in the paid employment of women is easily demonstrated. How precisely the female labor force evolved is considerably more complex and is the subject of this chapter.

The transformation of women's employment occurred in several phases. The period to 1920 witnessed the expansion of single women's employment and that after, the growth of married women's paid work. From the 1920's to the 1940's, the paid employment of married women rose slowly, but the increase accelerated after World War II. For every decade since 1940, the percentage of married women in the labor force has increased by about 10 percentage points. The broad outlines of female employment, particularly across the last century, are well known to the specialist and to many others. But various details examined in this chapter are unanticipated, and many have startling implications.

The key findings, from among the newer results, concern differences in employment among cohorts of married women born since the 1860's and employment increases by cohorts of married women. Work experience among employed married women was extensive, but did not grow much over time. Other findings concern labor market activity among married women before 1890 and a more inclusive measure of employment for the past that suggests female employment was considerably greater than had been thought. Finally, the evidence points to important changes within the family, such as the substitution of young, single women's employment for married women's.

The emphasis on work for pay, specifically that outside the home, is often dictated by an interest in how economic development affects standards of living. But here the motivation is more a concern for how economic development affects social relations in general and those within the family, in particular. Work within and outside the home have each accorded individuals a particular status, a set of social contacts, and, more recently, a different ability to proclaim independence from the family unit.

In her highly influential treatise, Betty Friedan surmised that women could find an "identity only in work that is of real value to society—work for which, usually, our society pays" (1963, p. 334). Friedrich Engels, among others, equated "the reintroduction of the entire female sex into public industry" with their emancipation (1978, p. 744; orig. publ. 1884). And from considerably more mundane testimony, a husband, in Lillian Rubin's classic study of working-class families, complained that his wife "doesn't know how to give respect. . . . Because she's working and making money, she thinks she can argue back whenever she feels like it" (1976, pp. 176–77; cited in Matthaei, 1982, p. 308). The point is, in the words of a noted historian of the family, that "work for money, as opposed to work for family, generates different attitudes and relationships among family members" (Degler, 1980, p. 362). Work for pay outside the home alters power relationships between husband and wife, and thus the division of goods within the family.

The distinction between work for the market and work for family is increasingly blurred as one moves farther back in time. It is possible, as will be detailed later, to construct labor force estimates that are relevant and consistent over the past century. A participation rate for 1890 that includes the paid and unpaid labor of farm wives and boardinghouse keepers, among others excluded from census estimates, is approximately equal to that achieved by 1940. Further, data on occupations in the late eighteenth and early nineteenth centuries indicate that women's market-oriented work in cities may have been more extensive even at that time than early in the twentieth century. Thus women on farms and in cities were active participants when the home and workplace were unified, and their participation likely declined as the marketplace widened and the specialization of tasks was enlarged. The more comprehensive measure of participation, therefore, probably declined sometime before its more celebrated and studied period of increase, that directly following World War II. To put it another way, the married women's labor force participation rate is vaguely U-shaped over our history. Much emphasis has been placed on the rising portion, considerably less on the initially declining segment previously hidden from view. But participation rates, however defined, still rose considerably from the first decades of this century to the present.

Specialization and division of labor steadily became prominent features of family life, mirroring changes in the broader economic marketplace. In the nineteenth century when the market-oriented, home-based work of married women was slowly being reduced, the paid work of young, single women was expanding. Factory goods, such as textiles, clothing, soap, and canned goods, replaced those made in the household; but generally just unmarried women were employed in factories.[2]

Thus the market-oriented work of one group declined, while that of the other increased. In the late nineteenth and early twentieth centuries, the vast majority of employed white women were unmarried. Marital status, more than any other characteristic save race—and more on that later—determined a woman's economic role. The difference between the participation rates of married and single women appears to have been most pronounced sometime just after World War I.

The specialization of some women in market employment and others in family-oriented tasks affected women doubly. For most of our history, women exited the labor force at the time of marriage, rather than with pregnancy, and their exit was, more often than not, final. Their economic status and function were fundamentally altered at the time of marriage. Changes in the marketplace would have wide-ranging repercussions on the social context of household work. Daughters were to spend less time in the household performing chores alongside their mothers and under their tutelage. Wives and mothers were to become increasingly isolated during the workday. From 1850 to 1950, the working time of married women within the household was separated first from their spouses and other workers, next and most ironically from their own children, and finally from other married women who had entered the work force. Their value, as producers of market goods and as instructors in household skills, would become steadily diminished over that century. The data presented support a revisionist view that the discontented housewife was likely a phenomenon of the 1920's, rediscovered in Friedan's influential 1963 monograph (Cowan, 1983a).

Although the precise timing is unclear, the 1920's appear to mark a turning point in the declining employment of married women and in the specialization of economic function by marital status. Conventionally measured participation rates among married women rise with every subsequent decade. Arraying the data by cohort, instead of time, reveals how economic change affected the experiences of individual women rather than those of cross sections.

Among those who were married, employment advanced in the last century for specific cohorts at particular times. Cohorts born around 1910, for instance, were employed to a far greater extent in the 1950's, when they were in their forties, than they were earlier, and their participation rates were considerably greater than were those of older cohorts. Women born since 1940 also experienced significant increases in their employment, but for these cohorts the change took place when they were in their twenties and thirties, in the 1970's and 1980's. Further, among all cohorts of white married women participation rates have increased steadily over the life cycle. The proportion of married women in the labor force, therefore, has risen with age for all cohorts.

A more surprising and rather significant finding is that married women who were in the labor force, even when participation rates were low, had substantial attachment to their jobs and to paid work in general. Data on the life cycle of female employment reveal considerably more continuity of employment than has been presumed. Work experience among those currently employed, therefore, was high, not low. Women have been depicted as working when young and single, then for a brief period after marriage, and again later in their lives. But for most cohorts, this characterization is simply inaccurate. Married women were either in the labor force or out; the majority did not engage in much intermittent labor force activity.

Yet until recently, few married women were to remain in the labor force for most of their lives. Among white, urban women born around 1895 and married by 1939, only about 10% at age 45 had spent over three-quarters of their years since beginning work in the labor force, and, as a lower-bound figure, at least 40% had been in the labor force less than one-quarter of the total years since they began work.[3] In 1939, of all married women not currently working, but who had worked prior to marriage, more than 80% exited the workplace at the precise time of marriage.

These findings, taken together, have important implications for the relationship between changes in participation rates and gender inequality in earnings. Knowledge of intermittency and work experience will help resolve why earnings between men and women have differed and continue to differ and what determines both change and stability in the ratio of their earnings from 1900 to the present (discussed in Chapters 3 and 4).

Although the process of change regarding the work of married women was set in motion in the 1920's, it was not until the 1950's that labor force participation rates increased greatly. Initially, older married women's participation advanced most, but by the late 1960's and 1970's, the participation of younger married women began to accelerate. The reasons for the increases, and the various constraints that stood in the way of change, are the subjects of Chapters 5 and 6. Many constraints—for example, bars against the employment of married women and the virtual absence of part-time work—resulted from the initially large numbers of young, unmarried women workers. The definition of female laborers as young and unmarried lasted well beyond actual change. As late as the 1960's, the legacy of an earlier female labor force impeded the enactment and performance of equal rights and antidiscrimination legislation, as will be discussed in Chapter 7.

There is much ground to cover in this chapter—two centuries of change across many demographic groups. The beginning point is the more recent, and thus apparently more relevant, experience of married women's participation in the twentieth century. I then work back to the rise of single women's participation in the nineteenth century and change in married women's market work since the eighteenth century.

The Measure of Market Work

In charting employment changes, a necessary and significant distinction will be made between work for one's family, for which neither money nor barter is exchanged, and work that is generally compensated within or outside the home. The distinction between trade among family members and trade with what is called the market is central to the economist's, and most governments', concept of labor force participation. The concept has considerably more meaning today than in the past, when goods produced in the home, such as textiles, butter, and clothing, were used by family members as well as sold or traded.

A wide-ranging controversy has developed over excluding from national income goods produced by family members solely for themselves, such as housekeeping and child-care services. For some, the exclusion from national income of home production has devalued women's work and has had profound political and social consequences, such as the differential treatment of wives and husbands in the American Social Security system.[4] The issue for most economists, however, is less controversial and concerns whether the nation's real income increases when an individual leaves unpaid work in the home and enters the labor force. The resolution of that issue will depend, in part, on what goods and services are included in the national income.[5] Because most home production is excluded from national income, an increase in the nation's labor force participation rate is normally accompanied by an increase in measured national income.

The concern here, however, is not political. Instead, it is to evaluate the impact that economic development has had over long periods on the economic and social roles of women. Two procedures are adopted in this chapter. One relies on existing census estimates. The other adjusts the earliest available data, those for the late nineteenth century, to account for work performed in the home and on the farm, as well as for possible undercounts in the more usual labor market.

To construct a labor force series that is comparable over time and consistent with modern national income estimates, I adopt existing national income accounting procedures. These entail measuring the labor force according to the type of work done, not necessarily whether it is performed for pay outside the home. Detailed revisions of the existing census estimates are made to account for unpaid family workers on farms and in the home and for those whose work has often been hidden from view and from census takers. But before these estimates are presented, the unrevised census data since 1890 are explored. These data implicitly use a more narrow definition of employment—generally whether the work was compensated—but one that can be easily defended. The distinction between work for one's family, for which pay is not received, and work for pay, generally outside the home, is central to various social and economic concerns.

Of the various measures of market work, the labor force participation rate is the most frequently used indicator of economic function and is the most convenient and informative single statistic summarizing the economic role of women. But the concept of labor force participation is not without ambiguity and is beset with measurement problems. The labor force participation rate today is computed by the Department of Commerce and gives the proportion of the population employed or seeking employment during a particular survey week.[6] The definition is only one of several that could be used and is generally called the "labor force" construct. It was not always the measure used. Before the U.S. government had an official labor force construct, data on occupations were collected by the U.S. population census. These data have been used to compute a labor force participation measure called the "gainful worker" construct of participation. The gainful worker construct measures the proportion of individuals who claimed to have had an occupation during the year just prior to the census. The current definition, the labor force measure, was initiated in 1940 and transformed the rather subjective question of the previous definition—did the individual have an occupation?—into an objective question—did the individual work for pay during the survey week? But even gainful worker estimates, using published census data, can be constructed only since 1890. Data for the earlier period must be culled from census manuscripts and less comprehensive sources, such as city directories and manufacturing censuses.

Although the two definitions—that of gainful worker and that of labor force—differ, they can, under particular circumstances, produce similar estimates. Two factors will determine whether the definitions are comparable: the distribution of days worked by all workers and the number of days worked in the pre-1940 period that caused individuals to list an occupation. It is fortunate that circumstances existed to produce consistent estimates of female participation rates from 1890 to the present, at least for those sectors in the economy accurately covered in each of the censuses.[7] Consistent estimates for these sectors, however, may not be representative of all in the economy. The population census may have undercounted employed individuals, particularly women, in 1890 more so than today, resulting in too large an increase in female participation over the century. Furthermore, the movement of production from the home to the economic marketplace may demand a complete reassessment of the census definition of participation.

Both the labor force and the gainful employment measures attempt to estimate the proportion of the population participating in the market or paid sector of the economy. While participation is a convenient summary statistic, convenience has its price. The measure does not by itself enable one to estimate the time spent working during the day or week and the intermittency experienced over the year and across years. Thus the degree of part-time employment and the turnover of workers over the year and from year to year cannot be computed with labor force participation data alone. These additional aspects of work will be detailed separately using other sources.

Given the importance accorded the statistic of participation, it should come as a surprise that occupational data, on which the measure to 1940 is based, are not available in detail in the printed U.S. population censuses prior to 1890. Furthermore, as already mentioned, it was only in 1940 that data on the labor force were designed to be fully comparable across the decennial censuses. To make matters even more confusing, the inclusion of information on marital status and the age groupings displayed in the printed censuses vary from decade to decade.

It becomes necessary, therefore, to make many assumptions in constructing a time series comparable over long periods. But even then, the revised data extend just a century, from 1890 to the present. Various subgroups will be traced through the preceding century, but these must first be anchored in the data of their counterparts for the post-1890 era. The evolution of the female labor force begins here with the most recent century.

There are many ways of arraying the labor force participation rate data—by age, marital status, race, nativity, and location, to mention a few. The focus will be initially on all women in the economy, arranged by marital status, and then, piece by piece, other layers of detail are explored. The standard and official population data from 1890 to the present are analyzed first. Revisions to the earlier census figures are offered later to account for possible undercounts of working women in particular sectors and because the transition from home production to market work has produced inconsistencies over time.

Labor Force Participation of Married Women Since 1890

For most of American history, marital status provides a clear dividing line for female labor market participation. The majority of women exited the labor force at or just after marriage, as apparent from the low participation rates of married women in Table 2.1 compared with those of single women. By the 1950's, however, this simple comparison breaks down. Looking first at the data for white women, in 1960 49% of all single women were in the labor force, as were 30% of married women, across all age groups. Assuming these were the same women moving across their own life cycles, and ignoring, for the moment, differences in participation by age within marital groups, 39% $[= (49 - 30)/49]$ of these women would have exited the labor force at marriage.[8] The corresponding figure for 1890, produced in an identical manner, is 93%—considerably larger. The results remain essentially intact using the more disaggregated data by age from Table 2.2. The tentative conclusion, to be explored further with actual life-cycle data, is that throughout American history most women left the labor force at or just after marriage. The extreme differences in the participation rates by marital status apparent in Tables 2.1 and 2.2 cannot be explained in any other reasonable manner.

The eventual increase in the participation of married and adult women was the single most important change in the evolution of labor market work of women. Looking first at the rates for the white population, the expansion appears to begin in the 1940's with increases of 10 percentage points for each subsequent decade. From the 1940's to the 1960's, the expansion was greatest for married women older than about 35 years. From the 1960's to the present, it was greatest for younger married women. Both trends are evident in Figure 2.1. The expansion in the employment of older married women in the post–World War II period reflects their life-cycle position at that time. Their children were already grown, while the larger families of the "baby boom" era were being reared by the younger women, as discussed in Chapter 5. These facts concerning the increased participation of women in the American labor force are not new. Change in the economic role of women has been carefully tracked and noted by astute observers such as John Durand, Richard Easterlin, and Clarence Long. What is new is how the increase in participation was accomplished.

This increased participation of women evolved in a particular manner, one that has eluded researchers for some time. From almost the beginning of the increase in married women's participation, certainly by 1940, more educated women were drawn into the labor force than in the aggregate population of married women. Further, these women tended to persist once they began work, and those who remained out tended to stay out. That is, the turnover rate of adult, married women was not particularly high. Why certain women entered the labor force and why this group grew in numbers over the years will be left for Chapter 5. Here I substantiate

TABLE 2.1. Female Labor Force Participation Rates by Marital Status, Race, and Nativity, 1890 to 1988

	≥ 15 Years Old							≥ 16 Years Old		
	1890	*1900*	*1920*	*1930*	*1940*	*1950*	*1960*	*1970*	*1980*	*1988*
Total	18.9	20.6	23.7	24.8	25.8	29.5	35.1	41.6	51.1	
Married	4.6	5.6	9.0	11.7	13.8	21.6	30.6	39.5	50.1	
Single	40.5	43.5	46.4	50.5	45.5	50.6	47.5	51.0	61.5	
White	16.3	17.9	21.6	23.7	24.5	28.5	34.2	40.9	50.9	
Married	2.5	3.2	6.5	9.8	12.5	20.7	29.8	38.5	49.3	55.8
Single	38.4	41.5	45.0	48.7	45.9	51.8	48.5	52.1	64.2	68.6
Nonwhite	39.7	43.2	43.1	43.3	37.6	37.8	42.7	47.3	52.1	
Married	22.5	26.0	32.5	33.2	27.3	31.8	40.5	50.0	59.0	64.4
Single	59.5	60.5	58.8	52.1	41.9	40.0	39.7	43.6	49.4	56.4
Foreign born	19.8			19.1						
Married	3.0			8.5						
Single	70.8			73.8						

Notes: The 1910 labor force figures have been omitted. See Appendix to Chapter 2 for a discussion of the overcount of the agricultural labor force in that year. For various years, the data assume that all 14 and 15 years olds are unmarried.

Sources: 1890: U.S. Census Office, *Eleventh Census of the U.S.: 1890.* Parts I and II (Washington, DC: Government Printing Office, 1895c, 1897).

1900: U.S. Bureau of the Census, *Twelfth Census of the U.S.: 1900. Supplementary Analysis and Derivative Tables* (Washington, DC: Government Printing Office, 1906).

1920: U.S. Bureau of the Census, *Fourteenth Census of the U.S.: 1920.* Vol. IV, *Occupations* (Washington, DC: Government Printing Office, 1923).

1930: U.S. Bureau of the Census, *Fifteenth Census of the U.S.: 1930. Occupational Statistics, Abstract Summary of the U.S. Census* (Washington, DC: Government Printing Office, 1932).

1940, 1950: U.S. Bureau of the Census, *U.S. Census of Population: 1950.* Vol. IV, *Special Reports*, Part 1, Chapter A, "Employment and Personal Characteristics" (Washington, DC: Government Printing Office, 1953b).

1960: U.S. Bureau of the Census, *Census of Population: 1960. Subject Reports: Final Report PC(2)-6A. Employment Status and Work Experience* (Washington, DC: Government Printing Office, 1963b).

1970: U.S. Bureau of the Census, *Census of Population: 1970. Subject Reports: Final Report PC(2)-6A. Employment Status and Work Experience* (Washington, DC: Government Printing Office, 1973).

1980: U.S. Department of Labor, Bureau of Labor Statistics, *Marital and Family Patterns of Workers: An Update*, Bulletin 2163 (Washington, DC: Government Printing Office, May 1983).

1988: U.S. Department of Labor, Bureau of Labor Statistics, unpublished data from May 1988, Current Population Survey.

these new facts concerning the increase over time and that for individual birth cohorts.

Cohorts of White Married Women

The best method to explore participation of adult women is by arraying the rates by age and grouping them over time according to birth cohort. Thus the participation rate for 25- to 34-year-old women in 1920 is linked to that for 35- to 44-year-old women in 1930 to yield part of the cohort profile for women born from 1886 to 1895. Because the U.S. decennial population censuses provide the only data for much of the past and because the age groups in these censuses are often wide, the resulting cohort profiles will be somewhat gross, as in the example just given. The

Year	Age 15–19	(16–19)	15–24	(16–24)	25–34
	Never Married (Single), White				
1890			35.0		53.1
1900			37.5		56.7
1910			n.a.		n.a.
1920			46.6		67.7
1930	27.8		42.6		75.4
1940	n.a.		40.8		79.4
1950	28.1		42.9		80.6
1960	28.9		40.0	(45.9)	81.9
1970	30.1		40.9	(47.9)	81.5
1980	n.a.	(52.7)	n.a.	(62.6)	87.8

Year	15–24	25–34	Age 35–44	45–54	55–64
	Currently Married, White				
1890	2.9	2.6	2.5	2.3	1.8
1900	3.0	3.1	3.1	2.6	2.3
1910	n.a	n.a.	n.a.	n.a.	n.a.
1920	8.2	7.7	6.3	(4.9)	(4.9)
1930	13.3	11.5	9.8	7.8	5.1
1940	14.7	16.7	13.8	10.1	6.4
1950	24.9	21.0	25.3	22.2	12.6
1960	30.0	26.7	35.4	38.6	24.6
1970	44.1	36.2	44.4	46.7	34.1
1980	60.1	56.0	59.1	53.4	36.8
	Currently Married, Nonwhite				
1890	24.5	23.3	22.4	21.0	19.1
1900	25.0	27.6	26.2	23.9	21.1
1910	n.a.	n.a.	n.a.	n.a.	n.a.
1920	30.4	33.7	34.5	(30.4)	(30.4)
1930	29.9	35.9	35.8	30.1	27.6
1940	23.7	31.4	30.5	25.5	19.3
1950	23.7	34.8	38.7	32.9	22.3
1960	31.8	40.7	48.9	47.3	33.7
1970	48.0	54.8	57.5	54.5	41.2
1980	60.2	71.4	72.0	61.3	42.0
	Widowed and Divorced, White				
1890	37.2	45.8	42.6	31.4	21.0
1900	32.3	52.7	53.5	38.1	23.8
1910	n.a.	n.a.	n.a.	n.a.	n.a.
1920	47.6	(63.9)	(63.9)	(37.5)	(32.5)
1930	56.7	(63.9)	(63.9)	45.1	24.8
1940	49.3	63.2	59.3	44.1	25.2
1950	52.0	60.9	65.2	55.7	35.4

TABLE 2.2.   (*Continued*)

1960	49.5	60.7	68.4	57.1	47.8
1970	58.5	66.8	71.0	71.5	54.9
1980	73.2	77.2	77.7	73.8	54.0

Notes: Single includes unknown marital status for 1890, 1900, and 1920; for 1970, the ratio of 14-year-old participants to those (14 + 15) is given by that in 1960. Widowed and divorced includes only widowed for 1890 and 1900; unknown and widowed and divorced for 1920 and 1930; and widowed and divorced and other for 1940, 1950, and 1960.

1920 figures in parentheses refer to 25–44 year olds for single and married groups; 1920 figures in parentheses for widowed and divorced refer to 25–44 year olds in 24–35 and 35–44 categories and 45+ and 45–54 and 55–64 categories.

1930 figures in parentheses for widowed and divorced refer to 25–44 year olds in 24–35 and 35–44 categories.

Married spouse present for 1940 to 1980.

Sources: See Table 2.1, and *1960:* U.S. Bureau of the Census, *Census of Population: 1960. Detailed Characteristics, U.S. Summary: Final Report PC(1)-1D* (Washington, DC: Government Printing Office, 1963a).

term "cohort" means a group born within some time interval and refers here to various constructed measures, rather than to the actual movements of individuals over time. Individuals who die, for example, cannot be removed from the earlier data. Nevertheless, these profiles are extremely revealing of cohort experiences. The profiles can be arrayed in a manner that holds marital status constant across the cohorts or in a manner that by aggregating marital statuses implicitly allows the composition by marital status to vary over the life cycle.

As is evident in both Tables 2.1 and 2.2, participation rates have varied substantially by marital status. The question, therefore, is whether marital status should be held constant in the cohort profiles or whether population averages are more appropriate. The population averages tell the story of a group but cannot reveal the experiences of any one individual. Individual women generally spend only part of their lives single, married, divorced, or widowed; an entire population is proportionally weighted by the time it spends in each of these marital statuses.

A cohort profile arrayed by marital status reveals the experience of the average woman within each marital status. But to trace the average woman as she moves across marital transitions requires connecting various cohort profiles. Thus if one believes that the average woman marries at age 24 and is widowed at 55, it might be appropriate to connect three cohort profiles. The profile for single women would then be used up to age 24, the married profile would be applicable to age 55, and the widowed profile would be relevant after.

There may, however, be interconnections among these profiles. The labor force participation rate of individuals is often contingent on their subjective probability of making life-cycle transitions. Women who marry late, for example, may have higher participation rates when single and when married; women who get divorced may have higher participation rates just prior to separation. Those who marry late will enter the data for married women with higher than average participation rates for their cohort; those who get divorced, as opposed to those who exit because of death or widowhood, will leave the data for married women with higher participation rates than average for their cohort.[9] These interconnections are still only poorly understood, and data requirements for their study cannot be met for all cohorts in the past. Further complications arise in using the cohort data over time because it is

Percent in Labor Force
25–34 years old

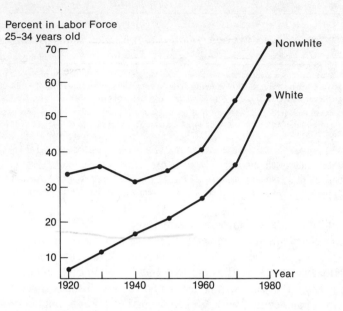

Percent in Labor Force
45–54 years old

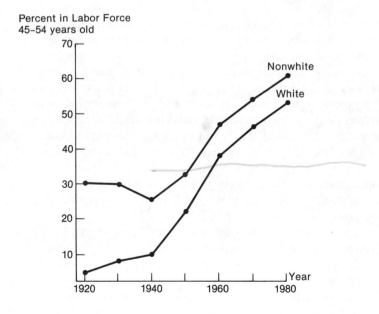

FIGURE 2.1. Female Labor Force Participation Rates for Two Age Groups of Married Women by Race, 1920 to 1980. *Source:* Table 2.2.

not possible to stratify all profiles by place of residence. Thus differences across region and by level of urbanization will not be evident.[10]

Despite possible biases in using cohort data by marital status, the benefits of the approach far outweigh its disadvantages. By focusing on the average individual, rather than on the average of the group, there is a better sense of how participation rates change over the life cycle and the manner in which individual expectations of future work experience have been formed. The results of the procedure will provide a startlingly new view of the evolution of the female labor force.[11] It is, as well, a view that cannot be overturned by correcting the data for its minor defects.

The new account is apparent in Figure 2.2. In the left-hand panel of the graph, labor force participation rates are drawn for cohorts of white, native-born (with native-born parents) married women. Each line represents a different birth cohort (the birth-year intervals are given for each) as it ages and thus moves across its life cycle. Age is the horizontal axis, and labor force participation is the vertical axis. The census years corresponding to each of the segments are not given, with the exception of that for 1970.

COHORTS VERSUS CROSS SECTIONS

The most important aspect to note in the left-hand portion of Figure 2.2 is that participation rates increase for all cohorts as they age, up to a peak reached generally around 55 to 60 years. The increase over the life cycle of these cohorts is in direct contrast to the cross-section data, given by the dotted line. The cross-section line for 1970 does not increase with age. Instead, it first declines, then rises, and finally declines again, possessing more of a double-peaked form than the continuous upward trend of the cohort functions. The cross sections cannot represent the actual life-cycle experiences of individuals but are instead the experiences of (married, white) women of all ages alive during some year.

The differences between the cohort and the cross-section lines have significant policy implications. The cohort data indicate that for most of the twentieth century the majority of married women who reentered the labor market, say in their late thirties, had not worked for pay since marriage. Rather than having numerous interruptions in paid employment during marriage, these women had left the labor force at the precise time of marriage. Of course, there are exceptions to this characterization among these cohorts, and some women's working lives were interrupted during marriage, as is the pattern for most women in recent cohorts. Some work interruption is hidden in the figure by the broad age groupings. But the cohort lines indicate that the standard account, that women's work careers are frequently interrupted by pregnancy and other family-related responsibilities, cannot be valid for the majority of women throughout American history. The standard account of high turnover was inferred from recent cross-section data but is an improper extrapolation of cross-section results to time series and of current notions to the past. All cohorts, however, had considerably higher participation rates before marriage, although these cannot be observed in Figure 2.2. (See, instead, Table 2.2.)

An example of life-cycle labor force participation using the cohort born between 1916 and 1925 is instructive. That cohort had a participation rate of 41% when it was 15 to 24 years old and single, but only 15% when it was married and in the

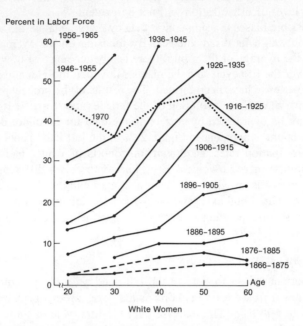

FIGURE 2.2. Labor Force Participation Rates by Cohort and Race for Married Women, 1890 to 1980, for Cohorts Born 1866 to 1965. *Notes and Source:* Table 2.2; white data for 1890 to 1920 are for native-born women with native-born parents (not included in Table 2.2).

same age bracket. The rate for married women in the cohort rose to 21% when it was 25 to 34 years old and then exceeded 35% when it was 35 to 44 years old. Only had there been very high labor force turnover among those in the youngest age group during marriage (15 to 24 years) could the majority of those working later in life have had any employment experience when young and married. That is, most older women in the labor force could not also have been working when they were younger and married. Further, the data suggest that many could not have reentered the labor force until their children were considerably older. Data on actual work histories, presented later in the chapter, will substantiate these presumptions.

The distinction between the employment transition at the time of marriage and the transition while married is central to understanding changes in the work of women and the constraints facing them in the labor market. Figure 2.2 demonstrates that for most of American history, white women progressively entered the labor force within their married years over their life cycles. Their participation rates were lower when they were young and married than when they were older and married. They had, however, far higher labor force participation rates prior to marriage. Thus their work in the labor market was interrupted in the sense that marriage itself, not necessarily pregnancy, childbirth, or other family duties, altered their economic status.

It should be emphasized that because the cohort-participation lines in Figure 2.2 are conditioned on marital status, one cannot observe the substantial participation

Percent in Labor Force

Nonwhite Women

Observations are the midpoints of five age groups: 15–24, 25–34, 35–44, 45–54, and 55–64. Dashed lines denote missing data. *'s for nonwhite cohorts denote Depression period, 1930 to 1940. Dotted line is the 1970 cross section.

rates for single women in the diagram. Recall that these participation rates were well over 40% since 1890, and an even higher proportion of all single women had worked sometime before marriage. Several microlevel studies reveal that few married women had not worked at all before they married, and even those not presently in the labor force had worked for pay sometime before they married.[12]

IMPLICATIONS OF COHORT CHANGE

Married working women who entered the labor force in their middle years had, by and large, entered a rather new world. They were not returning to a labor force they had left a short while before, as would be the case if the cross-section lines told the entire story. For the cohort born around 1910, the participation rate (among those who were married) was 13% in 1930. But it was 25% in 1950 and increased by 14 percentage points between 1950 and 1960, becoming 39% when this cohort was, on average, 50 years old.

The implication is that the labor force experiences of older women entering the labor market were rather distant and brief. They were not bringing to the labor market recently acquired skills. Many were, instead, reentering occupations they had left many years, or possibly decades, before, and most were inadequately prepared for their new labor market roles. Not only do already acquired skills depreciate with disuse over many years, but modern technologies require investments in new skills. The problems that faced this emerging labor force were well understood by contemporaries. In 1956, during the initial expansion in the employment of older married women, a manager of a large retail establishment remarked that "anyone over 30 has great difficulty in learning to cope with the elaborate cash registers" but also added that "this difficulty is secondary to the better selling ability which the older women generally show."[13]

Because cross-section data are more readily available than cohort data, it had not been at all evident that the actual experiences of cohorts deviated so substantially from the cross-section data. In the absence of actual work histories of various cohorts, we have been unable to understand the adjustment problems of recent labor market entrants. It is no wonder, therefore, that the earnings gap between men and women, and that between older and younger women, has failed to narrow during periods of rapidly increasing labor force participation, particularly among older, married women. This increased participation has drawn the less experienced into the work force. But only data on actual cohort experiences can reveal the accumulation of work experience over the life cycle, and that is the topic of the next section.

The primary reason each cohort line in Figure 2.2 increases with age is because of an increase in participation over time for women of all ages and in all cohorts. At the same time, aging by itself, up to some point, increases participation; women in their late thirties and forties have fewer home responsibilities than married women in their twenties and early thirties. Therefore, as each cohort has aged, two effects altered its participation—one relating to time and the other to age.

The larger stimulus of the two has been the first factor—the increase in participation over time—which is common to all birth cohorts at each date. For various reasons, explored in Chapter 5, all cohorts have experienced increases in participation over time. Thus each of the cohort lines lies above the previous one.

Another feature of Figure 2.2 is that certain cohorts have experienced increases in participation over their life cycle that have been considerably larger than those of other cohorts. What is less obvious from the manner in which the diagram has been drawn is that certain periods have provided a stimulus to vastly increased participation rates. The cohort born around 1910, for example, experienced a remarkable advance in its participation rate in the 1950's, when its members were in their forties. The largest increase for the cohort born around 1900 was in the 1940's, when its members were, coincidentally, also in their forties. As can be seen in Figure 2.2, the shape of the life-cycle participation line for the cohort born around 1900 is mimicked in all succeeding lines, but is not apparent before.

The cohort born around 1940 experienced a rather large increase in its labor force participation rate during the 1970's, when its members were in their thirties. The previous cohort, that born around 1930—one of the "baby boom"-parent cohorts—also experienced a rather large increase when it was in its thirties, during the 1960's.

It might be claimed that both the cohort experiences and the time series graphed in Figures 2.1 and 2.2 reflect in large measure the long-run movement of the population out of agricultural and nonfarm rural areas. Similarly constructed data for urban areas only, given in Table 2.3, demonstrate that the general trends in participation rates for married women in Figures 2.1 and 2.2 are upheld and can even be extended. The somewhat small rise in the participation of young married women in the 1920's, apparent for white women in both figures, is increased for the

TABLE 2.3.   Labor Force Participation by Age and Nativity for Married
White and Nonwhite Women in Urban Areas, 1890 to 1970

Age	1890			1920			1930	1940	1950	1960	1970
	NN	NF	F	NN	NF	F	NF+NF	All	All	All	All
White Women											
15–19	5.5	4.2	5.9	15.4	15.5	15.3	17.8	20.1	26.1	29.5	37.6
20–24				12.2	12.9	11.2	20.9		31.2	33.2	47.9
25–34	4.3	3.4	4.2	9.6	10.5	8.5	15.8	19.5	23.3	27.3	36.7
35–44	4.3	3.7	4.0	9.0	10.0	7.8	12.8	15.4	27.5	36.5	44.9
45–64	4.0	4.0	3.3	n.a.	n.a.	n.a.	n.a.	9.2	20.1	35.2	43.8
45+	3.8	4.0	3.2	6.4	7.3	5.4	8.4	n.a.	17.5	29.8	36.7
Nonwhite Women											
15–19		39.2			28.0		30.6	28.6	19.7	26.5	35.6
20–24					36.5		39.0		30.4	37.0	54.1
25–34		27.7			37.0		43.4	37.1	40.1	43.5	57.8
35–44		28.8			39.4		43.8	33.9	45.1	52.2	60.2
45–64		35.0			n.a.		n.a.	25.4	34.3	46.2	51.4
45+		35.0			36.5		36.7	n.a.	31.7	41.8	45.2

Notes: NN is native-born white with native-born parents; NF is native-born white with at least one foreign-born parent; F is foreign born; Nonwhite is Negro in 1970.

1890 to 1940: Urban includes cities of more than 100,000 population.

1950 to 1970: Urban includes cities of more than 2,500 population.

1890 to 1930: Married is married spouse present or absent.

1940, 1960, 1970: Married is married spouse present.

1950: Married is wife of the head of household.

Procedure used to derive 1890 data: The census data are aggregated by nativity, age, and marital status separately for cities over 100,000 persons. The number of women in each cell was constructed from the number of women for each nativity under the assumption that the age–marital status distribution was the same as that of the nonagricultural female labor force, which is available from the 1890 population census.

Sources: See Table 2.1, and *1940*: U.S. Bureau of the Census, *Sixteenth Census of the United States: 1940. Population: The Labor Force, Employment and Family Characteristics of Women* (Washington, DC: Government Printing Office, 1943b).

urban areas alone. Increased participation of young married women in the 1920's suggests they were beginning to exit the labor force sometime after marriage instead of directly with marriage. As the Lynds noted in one of their Middletown studies, "there is . . . some tendency for a young wife to retain a clerical job until her husband begins to get established."[14]

The increased participation of married women in the economy also affected the marital composition of the female labor force, given in Table 2.4. This manner of expressing the information presented in the previous tables adds another dimension to the social and political implications of economic change. Even though participation rates of married women were low for most of American history, married women composed a substantial percentage of the female labor force because the majority of adult women are married. In 1930, when the participation rate of married white women was less than 10%, one in four female labor force participants was currently married. Even in 1920, when the participation rate of married white women was a mere 6.5%, one in six female labor force participants was married.

It is no wonder that even as early as the 1920's, social commentators shifted

TABLE 2.4. Marital Composition of the Female Labor Force, 1890 to 1988

	1890	1900	1910	1920	1930	1940	1950	1960	1970	1980	1988
					Percent Single						
NN	69.0	69.1	n.a.	66.4							
NF	89.9	86.4	n.a.	74.3	61.0						
F	74.3	71.1	n.a.	54.1	49.6						
White	76.2	74.7	n.a.	63.6	59.5	52.3	33.6	24.3	23.4	24.3	24.4
Black	50.8	49.0	n.a.	33.3	30.6	29.1	20.1	18.8	22.5	30.1	n.a.
					Percent Married						
NN	10.0	11.3	n.a.	19.0							
NF	4.5	5.8	n.a.	11.6	24.6						
F	9.4	11.6	n.a.	19.8	31.3						
White	8.3	9.7	n.a.	17.0	25.5	29.2	46.9	56.3	58.0	57.4	57.4
Black	27.7	28.6	n.a.	42.2	43.2	34.4	43.6	47.4	47.7	39.4	n.a.
					Percent Other (Widowed, Divorced, Unknown)						
NN	21.0	19.6	n.a.	14.6							
NF	5.6	7.8	n.a.	14.1	14.4						
F	16.3	17.3	n.a.	26.1	19.1						
White	15.5	15.6	n.a.	19.4	15.0	18.5	19.5	19.4	18.6	18.3	18.2
Black	21.5	22.4	n.a.	24.5	26.2	36.5	36.3	33.8	29.8	30.5	n.a.

Notes: NN is native-born white with native-born parents: NF is native-born white with at least one foreign-born parent; F is foreign-born. 1930 data are for all native-born white. Percent married includes only married spouse present 1940 to 1980. Percent single includes "unknown marital status" 1890 to 1900.

Sources: See Table 2.1

their attention from the plight of the single working woman to that of the married woman. From the mid-1800's to 1920, policy issues regarding working women centered on the unmarried—their conditions of work, hours, wages, and independent life apart from their families. But around 1920, monographs about working women began to perceive the problem as one of working married women and mothers. "We have known, vaguely enough, that in the gray stream of women pouring into our industries at dawn there are many married women, and here and there is a mother of little children," began one such volume (Hughes, 1925, p. xiii).

Another consequence of the increased participation of older women was the aging of the female labor force. Around 1890, the median female manufacturing worker was only 20 years old while the median female in the population, among those over 14 years, was 30.2 years old.[15] By 1960, the median female worker was 40.4 years, slightly older than the median female among those older than 14 years in the population.[16] Both the female labor force and the female population aged over time, although the labor force aged more rapidly.

In sum, participation rates of married white women, calculated from census data, advanced from 1890 to the present, but accelerated during certain decades and for certain cohorts. Why certain cohorts experienced increased rates of participation during particular periods of time will provide the clues to why participation rates of adult, married women expanded at all during American history, the central issue to be addressed in Chapter 5.

Cohorts of Nonwhite Married Women

I alluded earlier to the fact that participation rates of black and white women differed greatly throughout American history. The participation rate for nonwhite, married women in 1890 was almost 10 times that for white women; in 1930, it was more than 3 times that for white women; and in 1970, it was 1.3 times (see Table 2.1). Even by 1980, only the youngest cohorts of married women have identical participation rates by race. Various factors might account for the greater participation of black women in the labor force. Black families have had lower incomes, in part because black men have had higher unemployment rates and lower educational levels than white men. Yet numerous studies conclude that differences in participation between black and white women cannot be explained just by differences in family and individual characteristics. Black women, it has been shown, participate more than white women even when both have the same family income, education, and number of children, among other factors (see Goldin, 1977, for a summary of the studies). Some have argued that black men face more discrimination than black women, and that black families often substitute the labor of the wife for that of the husband. My own research on the issue has concluded that slavery may have left a double legacy. Black Americans were less educated, and had lower incomes and fewer job opportunities, than white Americans, in part because of slavery's direct effects. Yet slavery may have left an indirect legacy by making paid work less socially stigmatized among black than white married women throughout history (Goldin, 1977).

In the right-hand panel of Figure 2.2, cohort lines for nonwhite women rise throughout the life cycle only for those born after 1916 to 1925. The lines for white women, in contrast, rise for all cohorts, with the obvious exception of the lower rates for many of the oldest groups in both diagrams. The cohort lines for nonwhite and white married women are similar for women born after 1920, although the lines for nonwhite women are uniformly higher and rise more steeply at younger ages.

Differences between the two groups are more readily apparent in Figure 2.1, which graphs participation rates by age rather than birth cohort. The lines for nonwhite women are always above those for white women, but they decline from 1920 to 1940 rather than rising continuously over the 60-year period shown. In other respects, however, the two sets of lines are similar. In both cases, there is an acceleration for the younger group in the post-1960's period and another for the older group in the post-1940's period.

Until the last few decades, black women have held jobs almost exclusively in agriculture and the service sector. In 1890, 92% of all employed black women were agricultural workers and servants; in 1930, 90% were; and even by 1970, 44% were. (Occupational differences between black and white women are examined in more detail in Chapter 3.) It might be presumed, therefore, that the movement out of agriculture served to reduce the participation of black women. Although it is likely that sectoral shifts affecting agriculture, and to a lesser extent a reduced demand for household servants, lowered the participation rate of black married women, much of the decrease was due to the depressed economic conditions of the 1930's. In fact, all the anomalous cohorts in Figure 2.2 experienced decreased employment during the 1930's (see the asterisks in the diagram) that was not fully restored in later decades. The role of the Depression in reducing incomes of black Americans through the decreased paid labor of wives must be left for further study.

Life-Cycle Labor Force Participation and Work Experience

Increased participation rates would seem to imply that women born in, say, 1930 remained in the labor force for considerably longer portions of their lifetimes than women born in, say, 1910. That inference might be drawn from the rise in cohort participation rates over the lifetime of each cohort, and the increase across successive cohorts. But the inference is not necessarily correct in theory and, as will be shown below, is only partially correct in fact. Years of experience since marriage have increased only slightly across all birth cohorts examined.

The implications of the labor force data for the accumulated lifetime work experience of women are not as transparent as they first appear. Although the data may suggest that working women of all ages must have accumulated more years in the labor force over time, work experience for currently employed women need not rise during periods of rapid increase in participation rates. Indeed, work experience can even fall as participation rates climb. The reason for this apparent anomaly is found in the definition of participation and its relationship to the life cycle of work.

An increase over time in the labor force participation of a cohort does not necessarily mean that more of its cohort members are employed. It could mean that each cohort member increases the number of weeks she works during the year. This perplexing aspect of the participation rate is a direct result of its somewhat ambiguous definition.[17] Since 1940, the participation rate has been constructed from data that capture individuals working during a particular week in the year.[18] An individual working 26 weeks randomly distributed over the year stands a 50% probability of being counted in the labor force. An individual working 13 weeks has a 25% probability of being counted. Therefore, an increase in the participation rate from 25% to 50% could mean that while all women work at some time during the year, each doubled the number of weeks she works. Rather than working 13 weeks, each now works 26 weeks. But that scenario is only one of many.

At the other extreme, a participation rate of 25% could mean that 25% of all individuals were in the labor force for a full 52-week year and that 75% were not working at all that year. An increase in the participation rate from 25% to 50% would then mean that an additional 25% of the population was drawn into the labor force, all working the full 52-week year.

The two extreme cases point to an ambiguity in the definition of labor force participation. Call the first of the cases that of "complete homogeneity," in which each individual—possibly differentiated by sex, birth year, and so on—works an identical number of weeks per year, however small. Because the labor force participation rate is equivalent to the expected number of weeks an individual works, the rate will be the number of weeks each individual works divided by 52. Therefore, in the case of a 25% participation rate, each woman is in the labor force 13 weeks out of the year and stands a 25% probability of being found in the labor force in any one week by census enumerators.

Call the other extreme case that of "complete heterogeneity," in which some individuals are in the labor force for the entire year, while the others are not employed at all.[19] Therefore, when the participation rate is 25%, exactly 25% of the population is in the labor force for 52 weeks, whereas those in the other 75% are never in. It is likely that neither of the two extreme scenarios is ever observed. The truth will lie somewhere between the cases of complete homogeneity and complete heterogeneity and will be some mixture of the two.

The point I am making is that the meaning and implications of work will depend on which of the two extremes dominates. The degree to which women have been homogeneous or heterogeneous, in the manner just defined, will determine the average work experience of employed women. For any given labor force participation rate now and in the past, a group of working women from a homogeneous population will have a lower level of accumulated work experience than a group from a heterogeneous population. Thus the consequence of the same history of labor force participation rates will be different amounts of work experience embodied in the currently employed group.

Work experience generally indicates the training and seniority of an individual, and accumulated experience is a good indicator of earnings. Working women from a population that is heterogeneous in its labor supply will have greater accumulated work experience and higher earnings than a population of women who are homogeneous. They will, more likely, include women who are considered "career" workers, those who have worked for a considerable portion of their lifetimes. The distinction determines more than just the number of years of work experience. It also affects the continuity of work over the year and the precise nature of work.

The more heterogeneous the population, the more women will remain in an occupation during the year and in future years. Their occupations will tend to differ from those of women who experience rapid turnover for reasons concerning the cost of training and the maintenance of skills. Thus a particular woman from a homogeneous population with a labor force participation rate of 25% is not likely to be a physician. She would spend only 25% of each year in the labor force. But among a group of heterogeneous women with the same labor force participation rate of 25%, those in the labor force might be highly skilled. An extremely low participation rate—even one as low as 5%—could still be consistent with low turnover and high persistence in the labor force and in an occupation. A low participation rate, however, would mean that a married working woman would be a rare individual, and, despite her persistence in the labor force, her work might not meet with social approval.

More important for the material in Chapter 4 on economic discrimination, a low participation rate among married women, especially among a group of heterogeneous women, will mean that a large portion had dropped out of the labor force at the time of marriage. Recall that even though a small fraction of married women were in the labor force across most of the cohorts studied, a far greater number had been in the labor force when they were single. As I will demonstrate later, in 1940 more than 80% of all married women had dropped out of the labor force at the approximate time of marriage, and most never returned. An employer, ex ante, might find it difficult to predict which of the unmarried women would remain in, and thus might discriminate on the basis of sex in job assignment and training.

In a dynamic context, the relationship between an increase in labor force participation and the change in the average work experience of working women will also depend on the degree of homogeneity or heterogeneity in the population. As noted before, an increase in participation can, paradoxically, lead to a decrease in the average work experience of working women. In the heterogeneous case, individuals must be drawn into the labor force from the nonworking population. When participation rates climb very rapidly, a substantial fraction of working women will be recent entrants, with little job training to prepare them for skilled jobs, and they will depress the average work experience and skill level of those already employed.

The interpretation of labor force data, such as those in Figure 2.2, will depend heavily on the degree to which the population of women is homogeneous or heterogeneous. The distinction has implications for the type of occupations women will want and will be offered, for their earnings absolutely and relative to those of men, for differences across the populations of working and nonworking women, and for the dynamic consequences of increases in participation. The extreme that is most relevant is an empirical matter that can be answered only with data on life-cycle labor force participation.

It may seem a bit curious to approach the topics of work experience, the nature of work, job turnover, and the earnings of women relative to those of men using the somewhat contrived concepts of homogeneity and heterogeneity. It would simplify matters considerably to use data that directly measure accumulated work experience and job turnover. The problem is that such data exist only for recent cohorts of women, those born after 1920 who were sampled by various longitudinal surveys such as the NLS and the PSID.[20] But these surveys were initiated in 1967 and consequently give only limited retrospective information on work experience prior to that date.

DIRECT MEASURES OF LIFE-CYCLE WORK

Various archival sources suggest that even when participation rates among married women were low, accumulated experience of currently working women was substantial. Original schedules from a Women's Bureau bulletin on clerical work, discussed further in Chapters 4 and 6, reveal that in 1940 the average married female office worker was 33 years old and had accumulated 13.7 years of work experience in office jobs since beginning work. Almost all these years of work experience, fully 10.5 years, were achieved in her current job. Further, she had 11.3 years of education, had only 1.3 jobs prior to the current one, and spent just 1.1 years out of the labor force since beginning work.[21] The schedules from another Women's Bureau bulletin confirm these findings for a cross section of urban women in 1939. Among married women currently in the labor force and between the ages of 40 and 49, mean experience was an astounding 15.5 years. Among the group between the ages of 30 and 39, mean experience was 12.2 years (Table 2.5). The participation of married women, therefore, must have been considerably more continuous than previously believed. And although the data just reported give only the accumulated experience of currently working women, they suggest that the entire population of women must have been more heterogeneous than homogeneous.

TABLE 2.5. Life-Cycle Labor Force Participation of Married Women, at Work and Not at Work in 1939

Year of Birth Age	1900–1909 30–39		1890–1899 40–49		1880–1889 50–59	
	At Work	Not at Work	At Work	Not at Work	At Work	Not at Work
Part A: Distribution of the Proportion of Years Worked Since Work Began, by Age						
0	0.0%	0.0%	0.0%	0.0%	0.0%	0.0%
0 ≤ 0.125	0.0	11.7	0.0	21.6	0.0	29.8
0.125 ≤ 0.250	2.6	21.9	1.6	27.0	5.1	35.1
0.250 ≤ 0.375	3.3	29.1	5.5	19.8	2.6	21.1
0.375 ≤ 0.500	4.0	13.8	6.3	12.6	18.0	3.5
0.500 ≤ 0.625	8.4	9.2	11.8	9.9	7.7	7.0
0.625 ≤ 0.750	12.1	6.6	11.8	4.5	15.4	1.5
0.750 ≤ 0.875	13.2	4.6	8.7	2.7	10.3	0.0
0.875 ≤ 1.000	56.4	3.1	53.5	1.8	41.0	1.8
Part B: Mean Years Worked by Proportion of Years Worked Since Work Began and Age						
0 ≤ 0.125	—	1.5 years	—	2.0 years	—	1.6
0.125 ≤ 0.250	2.5 years	3.6	5.0 years	4.9	7.5 years	6.5 years
0.250 ≤ 0.375	6.9	5.4	8.2	7.7	7.5	11.3
0.375 ≤ 0.500	7.5	7.8	10.6	11.9	16.1	11.3
0.500 ≤ 0.625	9.5	9.7	14.8	13.8	20.0	18.5
0.625 ≤ 0.750	12.3	11.2	15.2	14.4	22.9	24.0
0.750 ≤ 0.875	14.0	11.0	21.1	13.9	25.0	—
0.875 ≤ 1.000	13.2	14.8	16.6	27.5	18.9	36.0
Mean experience in 1939	12.2	6.0	15.5	7.6	19.0	7.6
Mean age at which work began	19.3	17.1	22.2	18.7	23.6	20.5
Number of observations	273	195	127	111	39	57

Notes: Married women include only married, spouse present. All intervals exclude lower bound and include upper bound. Means for the age at which work began and average experience also include observations having missing variables for the percent of time worked since work began. The small number of observations in the oldest age group implies that means within that age group are measured imprecisely. — indicates there are no observations.

Source: 1939 Retrospective Survey. See Data Appendix.

Fortunately, various historical and current sources have been located that contain retrospective and longitudinal data on work experience on both working and nonworking women. By using relationships between labor force participation and the concepts of homogeneity and heterogeneity, data from just a few cohorts can produce information about the entire period from 1920 to the present.

Two sources will provide the historical material. The first is a survey taken by the Women's Bureau in 1939 and called here the 1939 Retrospective Survey (see Data Appendix). The original schedules from the survey were uncovered in the treasure trove of the National Archives and have yielded information on the work experience and job turnover of women born from around 1880 to 1910. The schedules contain what I believe is the first large-scale retrospective data set on work histories. Work histories of individuals born from the early 1900's are also contained in a second source, the Social Security Administration records linked to the Retirement History Study. This source, however, can yield relatively complete information only for the period since 1951. Information on more recent cohorts has been assembled by other researchers from data on current job experience in the Current Population Survey and those on continuous time out of the labor force in the Social Security Administration records.[22]

Taken together, inferences from these data have produced a new view of the life cycle of work of American women over the course of the twentieth century. The new view accords with the findings on years of experience—that married women's labor supply has been rather continuous and, in consequence, that current participants have rather extensive work experience. Women who are in the labor force tend to remain in for long periods of time, while those out of the labor force tend to remain out. The labor force of married women has expanded, therefore, through the entrance of individuals whose prior labor market work was rather distant and brief. The behavior of the female labor force accords more with the theoretical notion of heterogeneity, as defined above, than with that of homogeneity.

The earliest retrospective data on work experience I have been able to locate are contained in a large-scale longitudinal study of work conducted by the Women's Bureau in 1939, *Women Workers in Their Family Environment*. To counter public disapproval of working women during the Great Depression, the Women's Bureau sought to demonstrate that "married women have the right to work" (U.S. Department of Labor, 1941, p. 1) by showing that their earnings went to support dependents. To accomplish the task, they interviewed thousands of women in several cities about their current earnings, financial contributions to their families, education, and work histories, including previous occupations and reasons for entrance and exit. Some women were currently working in 1939, while others were not. Information on work histories was taken for both groups, but because of the curious history of the survey, somewhat different and more detailed information exists for those working in 1939 than for those not working (see Data Appendix). For some of the analyses, therefore, the two groups must be presented separately. The emphasis for both will be on married women whose husbands were present in the household. All women sampled were white and were living in a large midwestern metropolitan area in 1939.

The persistence of women in the labor force is clear from the data in Tables 2.5

TABLE 2.6. Labor Force Transitions of Married Women, 1939

Part A: Women Currently Working in 1939

Mean Birth Year	1904	1894	1884
Age	30–39	40–49	50–59
Continuous experience in similar occupations	35.8%	30.9%	35.9%
Broken experience in similar occupations	31.4	31.7	33.3
Broken experience in different occupations	32.9	37.4	30.8
Number of observations	271	123	39

Part B: Women Not Currently Working in 1939

Mean Birth Year	1914	1904	1894	1884	1874
Age	20–29	30–39	40–49	50–59	60–69
Exit with marriage	49.3%	60.7%	62.1%	56.1%	57.1%
Work only after marriage	5.0	1.5	4.5	8.8	14.3
Work before and after marriage	25.0	31.1	26.1	24.6	17.9
Not indicated	20.7	6.6	7.2	10.5	10.7
	(45.7)	(37.7)	(33.3)	(35.1)	(28.6)
Number of observations	140	196	111	57	28

Notes: The women in Part B who worked prior to marriage but did not list an occupation on the schedule have been included in the "work only after marriage" category. Figures in parentheses group the "work before and after marriage" and "not indicated" cases because it is most probable that those who did not indicate when they worked actually did work before and after marriage.

Source: 1939 Retrospective Survey. See Data Appendix.

and 2.6. The first part of Table 2.5 gives the distribution of time worked, since work began, for women at work in 1939 as well as for those not at work, across three age groups. Among those at work in 1939, more than 60% who were 40 to 49 years old—those born around 1895—had been in the labor force for more than 75% of the years since they began work, and 54% had participated for more than 87% of the time since they first worked. Fully 70% of those born around 1905 had been in the labor force more than 75% of the years since beginning work.[23]

Among the women not at work in 1939, all sampled had worked sometime in the past,[24] but very few had persisted in the labor force for anywhere approximating the averages found for the currently working group. Looking again at the top half of Table 2.5, among those born around 1895, who were about 45 years old at the time of the survey, about 50% had worked fewer than 25% of the years since beginning work and more than 80% had worked fewer than 50% of the years since beginning work. Only 4.5% had worked more than 75% of the years since work began. The comparable figures for women at work in 1939 are 1.6%, 13%, and 62%. Because almost all the women not currently working had worked prior to marriage, an even lower percentage had persisted in the labor force for substantial durations when married than the data in Table 2.5 indicate.[25] The differences between the two groups could hardly be more extreme.

The bottom half of Table 2.5 gives average work experience for each group, those at work and those not at work, by the three cohorts and eight categories of years-worked percentages. The average number of years worked within each category does not vary markedly by work status in 1939. But average years of work experience across the entire distribution for currently working women exceeds twice the number for those not at work in 1939. Currently working women, between 40 and 49 years old, logged 15.5 years of job experience, while those not at work accumulated only 7.6 years. For those nearing the end of their working lifetimes, those at work had 19.0 years of experience, while those not at work had only 40% the amount.

Even though working women in the cohorts shown persisted in the labor force, it might be claimed that they changed their occupations with sufficient rapidity to have garnered little experience in any one job. Table 2.6 contains additional data from the same Women's Bureau survey that dispute the assertion. For women working in 1939 (see Table 2.6, Part A), more than one-third had been working continuously in the same occupational group since they began work.[26] Somewhat less than one-third had broken experience in a similar occupation, and the remaining third switched occupations at least once since work began. These data also reveal the degree to which women exited the labor force at the time of marriage among women not in the labor force in 1939. For those between the ages of 30 and 50, at least 60% had left the labor force at the precise time of marriage and had not yet returned by 1939 (see Table 2.6, Part B). An additional group may have exited the labor force at marriage yet returned later.

Further computations using the data that underlie Table 2.6 indicate that among those 40 to 49 years old in 1939, more than 80% exited the labor force at the precise time of marriage, although some eventually returned.[27] Therefore, even though average years of work experience among employed married women was substantial, the vast majority of all women exited the labor force at marriage. Employers may have been unable to discern who would persist in the labor force, and may have restricted the job opportunities of all young women.

Whichever cohort one looks at and whatever measure is used, women working in 1939 had extreme persistence in the labor force, and those not working in 1939 had far less work experience than those currently working. One might wonder, however, about the particular circumstances that women workers faced during the Depression and the role of economic conditions in fostering continuity among those currently working and preventing those out of the labor force from entering. Because even the oldest cohort in Table 2.5 remained in the labor force for a substantial proportion of their working lives, the possible role of the Depression in biasing the results toward continuity seems slender.

The Depression, if anything, should have reduced persistence. Married women entering the labor force temporarily when their husbands became unemployed would have lowered the measures of job continuity. Further, many firms faced with labor cutbacks during the Depression instituted policies to fire married women. But other aspects of the Depression labor market may have encouraged continuity. Employed married women, who might otherwise have left the labor force, may have chosen to retain their jobs for added security.

The most compelling evidence concerning the validity of the 1939 survey comes from an independent source—Social Security data for the 1950's and 1960's covering identical and slightly younger cohorts. These data demonstrate that the persistence of married women in the 1920's and 1930's was sustained in the rather different economic conditions of the 1950's and 1960's.

Records of the Social Security Administration have been linked to several data sets, and among them the Retirement History Study contains the largest number of women from the cohorts covered in the 1939 Women's Bureau sample.[28] Social Security data contain information on employment histories by quarter for workers covered by Social Security. Because this coverage changed over time and because employment information is by quarter, and not in terms of annual labor force participation, the linked data set presents numerous problems.[29] Despite them, the results of the analyses below will indicate conclusively that women in the labor force tended to remain in during the 1950's and 1960's, as they had in the decades before. Because these were times of rather large increases in the participation rate of married women, the finding implies that recent entrants had little prior labor force experience. Years of job experience for the working population may have been stable or even have fallen over these years, even though the experience of the entire female population must have risen.

The distribution of years worked since 1951 is given in Table 2.7, Part A, and covers all women in the sample who were between 54 and 63 years old in 1969 or equivalently 36 to 45 years old in 1951.[30] The first group coincides with the youngest cohort in the Women's Bureau sample, and the second is about 10 years younger. The distribution of years worked among all women is similar to that from a labor force weighted average of the 1939 Women's Bureau data, which can be derived from Table 2.5, and to that from the NLS for somewhat younger women (Heckman and Willis, 1979). A substantial mass forms around no years of work during 1951 to 1969, and a slight upturn occurs at the maximum possible in the sample—19 years' experience. The distributions of work experience among all women, in Part A, seem to offer little of interest, but their significance lies in comparison with those in Part B, for women who worked in a particular year.

Working in any of the years 1953, 1960, or 1965 radically alters the distribution of years worked since 1951 for both cohorts.[31] Among women in the younger birth cohort (1911 to 1915) who worked in 1960, 69% would eventually work nearly 70% of the years covered (13 of the 19 years), and for those in the older birth cohort (1906 to 1910), the figure is 72%. Almost 50% of those in the older cohort who worked in 1953 would eventually work 90% of the years from 1951 to 1969; more than 40% of those working in 1965 would eventually work 90% of the 19 years considered. Similar percentages hold for the younger cohort. These data attest to the considerable continuity of employment among women workers who ranged in age from 36 to 63 years between 1951 and 1969. The data are to be contrasted with those of the same age group who were not in the labor force in any of the years chosen. Of those not working in 1960, 85% would eventually work fewer than 5 years out of 19, and 64% would never be in the labor force, defined here as participating in two quarters in any one year.[32]

Both surveys, that from the 1939 Women's Bureau bulletin (the 1939 Retrospective Survey) and that from the Retirement History Study–Social Security records, attest to the heterogeneity of women's labor supply. Married women currently

TABLE 2.7. Life-Cycle Labor Force Participation of Married Women, 1951 to 1969, for Cohorts Born 1906 to 1915

Years Worked During 1951–69	Cohort Born 1906–10	Cohort Born 1911–15
Part A: Distribution of Years Worked Since 1951, for Women 54 to 63 Years Old in 1969		
0	44.0%	37.7%
1 < 3	9.5	10.2
3 < 5	5.5	6.3
5 < 7	5.5	6.5
7 < 9	4.8	4.7
9 < 11	4.0	4.7
11 < 13	3.6	5.1
13 < 15	5.6	5.9
15 < 17	4.7	5.2
17 < 19	5.4	4.6
19	7.5	9.2
Number of observations	1568	2065

	1906–10 Cohort If Work = 1 in Year			1911–15 Cohort If Work = 1 in Year		
	1953	1960	1965	1953	1960	1965
Part B: Distribution of Years Worked Since 1951, Conditional on Working in 1953, 1960, or 1965						
0	0.0%	0.0%	0.0%	0.0%	0.0%	0.0%
1 < 3	1.8	1.0	0.8	2.1	1.3	0.8
3 < 5	9.1	1.4	0.8	5.2	3.1	1.4
5 < 7	5.1	4.1	8.4	7.8	3.2	6.7
7 < 9	7.8	4.1	6.3	6.2	3.9	7.2
9 < 11	6.3	7.5	8.1	6.2	7.2	8.6
11 < 13	6.3	9.5	6.9	6.1	12.3	10.9
13 < 15	9.1	17.0	13.2	8.4	15.8	12.9
15 < 17	6.3	14.0	14.5	9.6	14.2	13.2
17 < 19	18.7	17.0	17.1	14.8	12.4	12.5
19	29.6	23.7	23.8	33.6	26.6	25.8
Number of observations	396	494	491	562	710	734

Note: Work = 1 defined as ≥ 2 quarters of (covered) paid employment during the year.

Source: Retirement History Study–Social Security Administration exact match tapes.

in the labor force tend to stay in, and married women out of the labor force tend to stay out.

The meaning of the rising cohort participation rates in Figure 2.2 should be more transparent at this point. Recall that the increase over time could have signaled one of two extreme cases, or possibly some combination of the two. If women move in and out of the labor force over time, the increase in cohort participation would mean that the degree of intermittency declined. But if working women have substantial continuity of employment, the increase in cohort participation would mean that new entrants increased participation rates. The data just assembled point to the latter interpretation.

Rather than reflecting a decrease in the turnover rate among married women, the increase in participation rates over the life cycle of each and every cohort reveals an expanded proportion of married women in the labor force. Each year a greater fraction of a cohort enters the labor force, and of these entrants few could have been in the labor force in recent years. It is more likely that a new entrant had not been employed for pay since she was single. I have already established that the majority of married women in the past left the labor force at marriage; therefore, the expanded participation in these cohorts must come from women who had not worked since before they were married.

WORK EXPERIENCE, 1930 TO 1950

These findings have several significant implications for the experience of married women in the labor market of the post–World War II period and earlier. Through the use of a rather simple framework, the information in the two longitudinal studies enables the estimation of the average work experience of women after marriage; the exact procedure is described in Goldin (1989). The data in the two reports yield estimates for the experience of married women in birth cohorts from 1875 to 1925 and for cross sections from 1930 to 1950. It is fortunate that other researchers, using different methods and data sources, have computed comparable data for the period from 1940 to 1980, and the numbers for the period of overlap are remarkably similar.

The simulated life-cycle labor force experiences of cohorts of working, married women generated are given in Table 2.8. The extrapolations reveal first that accumulated experience for the working population of married women was extremely high in all years. Particularly interesting is that accumulated experience was high even for the earliest periods and among the oldest cohorts. For example, a group of married women born in 1895 and working in 1940 had accumulated almost 15 years of experience since they were married. These data are, and should be, consistent with those in Table 2.5, which were computed directly from the 1939 Retrospective Survey, although Table 2.8 gives only work experience accumulated since marriage.[33] But the procedure that has produced them is also capable of producing estimates for cohorts not covered by the sample and for a national, not an urban, sample of women.

One can also read from Table 2.8 how the experience of the cohort born around 1895 changed as it aged—by following the line of the 1895 cohort birth year across the page from 1920 to 1950. Alternatively, one can observe how the work experience of women 40 to 49 years old changed over time. Here one is keeping the age of the group constant, but varying the time period. Finally, one can look at work experience in cross section, as is done for three years in the bottom of Table 2.8.

Although work experience since marriage of all working married women was exceptionally high, it did not advance much over time even as participation rates soared. Take, for example, a group of women 45 years old and born around 1875. The data in Table 2.8 indicate that these women had accumulated 13.8 years of post-marriage work experience in 1920. The cohort born around 1915 when it was age 45 had accumulated 15.4 years—only 1.6 more years—some 40 years later in 1960. During that 40-year period, the female labor force had been fundamentally

TABLE 2.8.   Simulated Years of Work Experience Since Marriage for
Cohorts of Working Married Women, 1900 to 1980

Cohort Birth Year	Age			
	20–29	30–39	40–49	50–59
1875	3.63	9.53	13.78	16.06
1885	3.73	9.98	14.56	17.11
1895	3.77	10.16	14.95	17.86
1905	3.79	10.16	15.10	18.50
1915	3.82	10.25	15.38	19.29
1925	3.85	10.36	15.69	20.04

Year	Age				Weighted Average
	20–29	30–39	40–49	50–59	
1930	3.79	10.16	14.56	16.06	9.11
1940	3.82	10.16	14.95	17.11	9.88
1950	3.85	10.25	15.10	17.86	10.52

Notes: The homogeneous case is constructed from: $\alpha(A_n - A_b) + (\beta/2)(A_n^2 - A_b^2)$, where A_b is the age at first marriage, assumed here to be 20 years, and A_n is the mean of the age group. The parameters α and β are computed from labor force participation rates (ℓ) by age (A) for each of the cohorts, where $\ell = \alpha + \beta A$. They are estimated from the cohort participation lines for white women in Figure 2.2. The heterogeneous case is computed by dividing the homogeneous work experience figures by $(\alpha + \beta A_n)$. The computation of total work experience assumes that the percentage of women who are heterogeneous by age is given by those working $\geq$ 65% of the years since beginning work, or from the data underlying Table 2.5: 20–29 years, 80%; 30–39 years, 80%; 40–49 years, 75%; and 50–59 years, 65%. The precise equations for each of the cases are derived in C. Goldin, "Life-Cycle Labor Force Participation of Married Women: Historical Evidence and Implications," *Journal of Labor Economics* 7 (January 1989): 20–47.

Source: 1939 Retrospective Survey, see Data Appendix.

altered by the increase of married and adult women. Yet there was little change in accumulated experience for any of the cohorts, among any of the age groups, and for any of the cross sections in Table 2.8.

Neither of the two major findings—substantial levels of work experience and low growth of work experience with increased participation—should be surprising. The concept of substantial heterogeneity, as it was termed above, implies these findings by definition. Because women in the labor force remain in for substantial periods of time, the accumulated experience of current participants can be and was high. Even when participation rates of married women were very low, as in the 1920's and 1930's, the work experience of employed women was significant, because those in the labor force had persisted in it for a long time. Work experience is particularly high when labor force participation is not expanding rapidly. As the labor force expands, women enter with little prior work experience. Their addition to the labor force tends to bring down the average work experience of all workers. The more rapid the increase in participation, the greater the proportion of new entrants among the current working group and the greater the dilution of work experience for the existing working group.

Therefore, periods of very rapid expansion of the female labor force—particularly that after World War II—are associated with slow growth in the work experience of working women. As a corollary, the variance in work experience across individuals will also expand as participation rises. Note that although average work experience of employed women need not rise, and can even fall, when participation rates climb, the average work experience of all women, working and not working, will rise. But because occupations and earnings are observed for only currently employed women, the work experience of the employed, not the population, is most relevant.

As might be obvious, the new view presented here of the work experience of married women contains two related, but opposite, findings. Work experience of married women has been substantial from the earliest years and birth cohorts being considered here. Even in 1920, for example, married working women labored for pay during substantial periods of their lives. Therefore, differences in earnings and occupations between men and women will be difficult to explain solely on the basis of differences in accumulated work experience. But—and here is where the two related findings may seem contradictory—work experience will not increase much over time and could even decline. Thus a stable ratio of female to male earnings and an unchanging distribution of occupations among women could be consistent with an increase in their participation. Even though years of work experience of married women were substantial around 1940, few of the working women in the 1939 survey could be termed "career women." They had persisted in the labor force in terms of years, but had not advanced within firms, as had men with equal experience. The reasons for this asymmetry will be explored in Chapter 4, when these data are used to address issues concerning the gender gap in earnings and occupations.

Cross-section levels of work experience for employed married women in 1930, 1940, and 1950 are in the bottom part of Table 2.8. Aggregate data for each year can be obtained by weighting each of the age groups for a particular year by the age distribution of the (married) female labor force. Work experience since marriage rose from 9.11 in 1930, the first year for which all age groups appear in Table 2.8, to 9.88 in 1940, and reached 10.52 in 1950, the last year for which all age groups are given.[34] Therefore, during the 20-year period from 1930 to 1950, the work experience of women after marriage increased by 1.4 years or 15%, and their total experience since work began may have increased even less.

These results are consistent with those of Smith and Ward (1984), who estimate life-cycle labor force participation by a different, but related, indirect procedure.[35] According to their estimates, the labor market experience of all working women aged 45 remained roughly constant at almost 17 years from 1950 to 1980 and that for women aged 35 rose by about 1 year from 1950 to 1960 and then remained below 12 years to 1980.[36] At the same time, the work experience of the entire population of women aged 35 or 45 rose by 3.5 years. Because the Smith and Ward estimates of experience also include that garnered when women were single, they are about 2 years higher than my figures of 10.2 years for those 30 to 39 years and 15.0 for those 40 to 49 years.[37]

Scatter plots of work experience by age in 1939 and the fitted regression lines are given in the three graphs that compose Figure 2.3.[38] For single women, each year of age adds over eight-tenths of a year of work experience, and nine-tenths when younger women, who likely were in school while at work, are excluded. For married women, the coefficient is just below one-half. Not surprisingly, widowed and divorced women have demonstrated the least continuity of work over their entire life cycles, and the coefficient is four-tenths for this group.

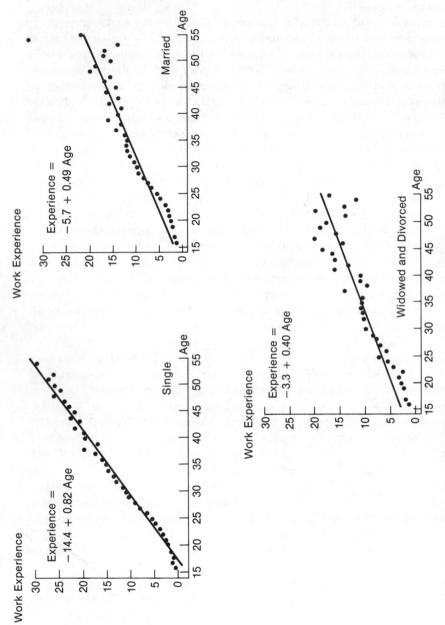

FIGURE 2.3. Work Experience by Age and Marital Status, 1939. *Note and Source*: 1939 Retrospective Survey. Mean work experience by age (for age < 56 years) was regressed on age for each marital status using a GLS procedure.

The data indicate that the average work experience of single women (using national labor force weights) was 8.9 years in 1939 and that for the category of widowed, divorced, and married, spouse absent was 13.8 years. The comparable figure for married women, obtained directly from the study, is 12.1. Thus average work experience for the 1939 cross section was 10.7 years.[39]

Around 1890 average experience for a cross section of women working for pay was between five and seven years.[40] Thus the aggregate level of experience among working women rose considerably over the first half of this century, even though that for married women rose far less. Mean work experience across all working women may well have doubled from 1890 to 1940. The increased participation of married women caused the female work force to age, and as it aged the aggregate experience of working women rose.

Comparable estimates for the 1950 to 1980 period by Smith and Ward (1984) indicate virtual stability in average work experience despite the continued aging of the female work force extending to 1960. Their data imply that years of work experience across all working women was 11.57 in 1950, 13.25 in 1960, 12.97 in 1970, and 12.22 in 1980.[41] The increase from 1950 to 1960 and subsequent decrease in work experience are produced by changes in the age distribution of the employed female population rather than by changes in work experience at each age.

In sum, my evidence on years of work experience reveals a small increase of 15% among working married women from 1930 to 1950 but a large increase of about 65% among all women from 1900 to 1940. Complementary evidence from the work of Smith and Ward (1984) suggests an increase of only 6% among all working women from 1950 to 1980.

The evidence compiled on life-cycle work reveals surprising aspects of women's role in the economy. From the late nineteenth century to the present, married female participants have had relatively low labor market turnover during their life cycles. The persistence is apparent even when participation rates among married women were very low and is evident among both those with high and those with low levels of education. Stability of employment among single women can also be demonstrated and will be examined further in Chapter 4.

Had these findings been inferred from only the Women's Bureau 1939 Retrospective Survey, they would be highly suspect because that survey was taken during the Great Depression and is only one sample. But the findings of that rich source have been confirmed by a national sample covering similar birth cohorts and by other researchers who have used different methods and data sources.

There is a double-edged significance to the fact that female workers tend to remain in the labor force. Persistence, it can easily be shown, produces considerable work experience among the employed. High levels of work experience among adult and married women ought to be reflected in their occupations and earnings, and when they are not, the fairness of the marketplace must be questioned. But the persistence of already employed women means as well that when participation rates increase, work experience need not increase and can even decline. Recent entrants will be considerably less prepared in the workplace than are those already employed. As the female labor force expands, therefore, many of the currently employed will be in entry-level positions. It should also be emphasized that when participation rates of married women are low, even if many persist in the labor force, a large fraction of all working women will have left the labor force around the time of marriage. Employers, therefore, might discriminate by sex in jobs and training because they cannot discern who will remain at work. The implications of these findings for gender distinctions in occupations and earnings are explored further in Chapters 3 and 4.

Economic Development and the Life Cycle of Work

The altered involvement of married women in the economy is a story in two parts. That concerning the rise of married women's paid work since 1890 has just been recounted and will be further elaborated in Chapter 5. The other is a distinctly opposite tale. It is a story of the decreased participation of married women in unpaid work for their families, and in paid and unpaid work in their homes. It is also the story of the increase in the paid labor of single women. Evidence from a wide variety of sources points to the significant contribution of married women to economic activity in the eighteenth and nineteenth centuries. Their involvement was sufficiently great that the paid employment of women, when viewed over the very long run, must have displaced much of their unpaid (or undercounted) employment, not just homemaking activities. As families left farms and as work moved from the home to the factory, married women's employment must have decreased. The augmented measure computed here for 1890 is about equal to that actually achieved in 1940. It is likely, therefore, that a trough in the economic activity of married women was reached sometime between 1910 and 1920.

When viewed across the past two centuries, the participation of married women in the American economy underwent change that was not always increasing. It began rather high, declined over the nineteenth century, and then rose, first gradually and then rapidly. While existing data do not enable precise employment numbers and dates for these changes, it is clear that the historical record of paid employment and wage labor must necessarily omit a significant part of women's work.

One may rightly wonder whether the evidence on changes in unpaid employment over time will call into question the material just presented on paid employment. Each time series, however, provides its own complementary testimony to the social consequences of economic change. Recall that many commentators, ranging from Friedrich Engels to Betty Friedan, have connected the significance of women's entry into the labor force to the role of paid labor outside the home. It seems clear that work done intermittently and without direct compensation did not revolutionize social roles, and that power within the home and the polity is based more on paid than unpaid labor.

The reliance on paid employment data, however, has arisen for less compelling reasons. Such data are easier to compile and are more readily available than are those for unpaid employment, and, somewhat more justifiably, there is the need to construct series consistent with modern definitions of the labor force. For whatever reasons, time series on paid employment have exposed only one portion of the change in the economic role of women. I turn now to the other part of the story, the substantial involvement of married women in unpaid family labor and in what I term "hidden market work."

Corrections to the c. 1890 Data

Participation rates for married white women calculated from the 1890 census—the first that can be used to produce labor force rates stratified by various character-istics—were extremely low. Nationwide the level was less than 3%; it was equally low in cities and rural areas, and for native- and foreign-born women alike. But official census data for the late nineteenth century need not be entirely accurate, particularly if interest centers around a more inclusive definition of market work. The large increase in participation rates among married white women over the past century has been predicated on the accuracy of census data for the period around 1890, but these data were questioned at the time of their collection and sporadically since.

Numerous criticisms have been lodged against census procedures in the pre-1940 period and against various aspects of national income accounting that give rise to the labor force data. Three sources of bias can be explored: that due to the change in definition, that due to the omission of workers in the census count, and that due to the change in the locus of production in the economy. My focus will be primarily on the first two. Because these corrections use quantities of additional information and employ a multitude of assumptions, the detail is reserved for an appendix. It should be emphasized at the outset that my intention is to construct a defensible estimate of a revised labor force participation statistic and that such an estimate provides a lower bound to the actual one.[42]

Rates computed from the census may be artificially low in comparison with the data for the post-1940 period, which employ a different employment construct, that of the labor force. But the change in definition, it turns out, has no effect on the participation rates of women. Applying the labor force concept to the pre-1940 data produces approximately the same numbers as obtained by the gainful worker procedure.

The movement of production from the household to the marketplace, the third potential source of bias, artificially lowers the measured productive value of women in 1890, in the absence of a fully consistent set of national income accounting rules. Adjustments here are both complicated and controversial, requiring numerous the-oretical assumptions. Under one set of assumptions, detailed in an appendix, fully 14% of the value of household production in 1890 ought to be added to the 1890 market production of women to create a consistent set of national income account-ing estimates over time. The 14% includes tasks performed in the home in 1890 that later moved to the market and are therefore now included in estimates of national income. The correction lowers the addition to economic growth from the increased employment of women over the last century. It is not clear, however, whether it is appropriate to incorporate the figure into a labor force participation rate.[43]

It is the second source of bias, the omission of workers, that results in the largest

TABLE 2.9.   Adjustments to the 1890 Female Labor Force Participation Rates

Corrections Due to	Percentage Point Adjustments		
	Married[a]	Widowed	All[b]
Change in definition[c]	n.c.	n.c.	n.c.
Omission of workers			
(1) Boardinghouse keepers			
In urban areas with ≥ 25,000 persons[d]	1.0 (2.7)	1.3 (3.4)	0.69 (1.84)
In nonfarm rural areas with < 25,000 persons[d]	2.2 (5.9)	2.4 (6.4)	1.47 (3.94)
(2) Agricultural laborers, unpaid family farm			
Cotton farms	1.33		1.24
All other farms	5.40		3.14
(3) Manufacturing workers[e]			0.50
Total omission of workers	9.93		7.04
Omission of household production from national income	14% of 1890 household production value to be added to 1890 market production due to women workers		

[a]The figure for cotton workers is adjusted for white women only; all other adjustments are implicitly for all races.
[b]"All" refers to 15 to 64 years olds. In constructing the "all" column from the other two, the proportion of the adult female population that was married (widowed) in 1890 is assumed to be .582 (.079).
[c]The change in definition refers to that from "gainful worker" in the pre-1940 period to the "labor force" definition. See text.
[d]The estimates in parentheses include the total number of wives or widows who kept boarders, unweighted by the number of days employed. See Appendix to Chapter 2.
[e]The adjustment to manufacturing workers cannot distinguish among marital statuses.
n.c. = no correction needed
Source: See Appendix to Chapter 2.

and least controversial correction. Here the bias is not caused by a simple change in the definition of work or the more complicated reassignment of goods on the basis of the current locus of production. Rather, the bias arises simply from the under-counting of workers. The correction due to the omission of workers considers three activities: boardinghouse keepers, unpaid family farm workers, and manufacturing workers in homes and in factories. In all three cases, the undercount was greatest for white, married, and adult women working within their homes and on family farms. The potential undercount was well understood by census officials as early as 1870, and it was their attempt in 1910 to count all unpaid family workers that has enabled some of the revisions in the appendix.[44] It is ironic that their attempt led to the wholesale rejection of the female employment figures in the published 1910 census.

A summary of the adjustments to the 1890 participation rate figure is presented in Table 2.9. The inclusion of boardinghouse keepers adds about 3.2 percentage points for married women and, not surprisingly, somewhat more for widowed women. That for unpaid family farm laborers is considerably higher—adding to the married figure 1.33 percentage points for cotton farms and 5.40 percentage points for all others.

Taken together, the inclusion of these activities increases the participation rate of married women across the entire economy by about 10 percentage points. Most of the adjustments apply only to white married women, and the revised figure of 12.5% is five times the official one of 2.5% given in Table 2.1.[45] Further, the revised estimate for 1890, constructed for consistency with the labor force construct first used in 1940, is approximately equal to that achieved by white married women in 1940.

Both boardinghouse keeping and family farm labor were casual occupations in the sense that they were done occasionally throughout the day and the year. In constructing the estimates, care was taken to adjust for the amount of time women spent in these activities and to treat the work in approximately the manner the census would treat it today. A boardinghouse keeper, for example, who worked 40% of a full-time year, was counted as having a 40% probability of being in the labor force. The adjustments were made to replicate the modern concept of the labor force, not to produce an upper- or a lower-bound estimate. But no matter how resourceful the economic historian, surviving historical data cannot reveal the complete extent of hidden production for the market. By inference, the adjustments in Table 2.9 are lower bounds.

The conclusion from all adjustments is that the census did not severely undercount the paid labor of married women outside the home but did severely understate their paid and unpaid labor within the home and on the family farm. The largest adjustments to the census figures stem from widespread boarding in late-nineteenth-century cities and from the employment of family members in agriculture.

The obvious implication is that the labor force activity of adult and married women must have reached a minimum point sometime just after the turn of this century, falling before that time and rising after. Thus the participation of married women in the labor force may well be somewhat U-shaped over the course of economic development. Participation was initially high in family-farm regions and in cities with small retail establishments and substantial boarding. With the growth of the market, the progressive separation of home and work, and the movement of families from farms to cities, the participation of married women fell. Eventually, the trend reversed, and the participation of married women gradually rose with increased white-collar employment, education, and changes in other factors detailed in Chapter 5. The U-shape in female labor force participation over the course of economic development is evident in several countries and is most apparent in those undergoing substantial economic development and a shift in the locus of production from the home to the market.[46]

The corrections to the participation rate figures suggest rather substantial economic activity of married women in the nineteenth century. Most of the difference between the official census figures and the adjusted figures of Table 2.9 is found in omissions to the unpaid work of women on farms. That correction alone adds almost two-thirds of the total percentage point adjustment. The precision of the estimates in Table 2.9 owes to a wealth of data that exist for the period from 1890 to about 1920. The data sources, detailed in an appendix, include time-budget studies of farm wives and large-scale government surveys of family income and time worked. These sources cannot be duplicated for the preceding century, when the farm work of women must have been even more extensive (Jensen, 1980, 1986; see also Stansell, 1986, on antebellum urban employment). But other, more subtle information from 1790 to 1860 reveals an added dimension to the economic role of women and further change over the process of economic development.

Substantial hidden market work of married women can be inferred from information contained in city and business directories for the late eighteenth and early
nineteenth centuries. And for the same time period, manufacturing censuses suggest
that industrial employment for single women emerged just as the hidden market
work of married women began to decline. I turn now to examine extant evidence on
the economic activity of American women during the period of early industrialization and before the census collected information on their occupations.

Participation Rates Before 1890: Married and Adult Women

Labor force participation rates, such as those for the period since 1890, cannot be so
easily constructed for the century before. In only three census years prior to 1890
were the marshals requested to obtain the occupations of women. The manuscripts
of the censuses for 1860 to 1880 have been used to compute participation rates in
certain regions and cities, and these scattered data suggest that reported participation rates of married women were no higher than in the 1890 census and that those
of single women were substantial in most industrial and urban areas but much lower
elsewhere. No national estimates exist for these two years. Yet had they been
calculated, they would be subject to the same undercounts that afflict the estimates
for 1890. No attempt will be made here to reconstruct participation rates for the
pre-1890 period. Rather, key periods in the development of the American economy
since independence will be examined.

The era of early industrialization was a critical juncture in American economic
growth, and its study reveals the changing economic role of women from the
colonial period to the mid-nineteenth century. The evidence amassed points to two
related changes; one concerns the economic role of married women, and the other
reveals the origins of the paid labor of single women.

The previous section suggested that unpaid female labor must have been substantial in certain farm, urban, and industrial areas around the turn of this century.
Evidence for the period of the early republic reveals yet other aspects of unpaid
labor within the home. Adult women engaged in considerably more atypical trades
in the 1790's than during the first few decades of the nineteenth century. Married
women were often drawn into their husbands' work when home and workplace were
physically unified, and women were more frequently employed in retail trades when
the store and house were one unit. Benjamin Franklin, for example, recounted in his
autobiography that his wife, Deborah, assisted "cheerfully in my business, folding
and stitching pamphlets, tending shop, purchasing old linen rags for the papermak-
ers, etc." (Franklin, 1961, p. 92). Despite her duties as mother of many Franklin
children, Deborah was able to relieve Benjamin from the everyday chores of printing and allow him to become the editor and statesman he is remembered as. Not
surprisingly, their print shop was an integral part of their house.

Early industrialization and the expansion of cities rapidly led to the specialization of tasks within the home and within the lives of women. Married women in an
era of high fertility could be engaged in family labors only if work were done at
home, and the progressive separation of home and work made their paid and unpaid
labor less feasible. At the same time, industrialization increased the wages of the

young relative to those of the old, and of females relative to males (see Chapter 3; also Goldin and Sokoloff, 1982, 1984). Young women and young men were drawn from the home to the marketplace, and their paid labor often replaced that of adult members of the household, particularly their mothers. Thus the trends noted earlier in the chapter, concerning the progressive isolation of married women in the home, culminate a process set in motion a century before.

The history of women's economic role in the early republic is revealed here in two sets of documents. The first set consists of city and business directories for the city of Philadelphia from 1791 to 1860 and the manuscripts of the U.S. censuses of population for 1790, 1820, and 1860, also for Philadelphia.[47] City and business directories are lists of household heads and business persons, and yield information on the occupations of all heads of household, female and male.[48] They are used here primarily to reveal the market work of married women through the occupations of widows and their late husbands. The second set of records are the manuscripts of the censuses of manufacturing for 1820 and 1832 (known as the McLane Report), and the published returns for 1850 and 1860. They show the extensive employment of young, single women wherever manufacturing activity spread in the American Northeast.

A sample of 12,000 female heads of household was drawn from 26 city and business directories for Philadelphia from 1791 to 1860. For the years 1791 and 1820, the data were matched to the U.S. census manuscripts for Philadelphia, and for the year 1860 a large sample from the manuscripts was already available.[49] These data have been used to produce estimates of the labor force participation rate of female heads of household over the 1790 to 1860 period and a distribution of occupations. This extensive body of evidence was collected to examine the possible decline in the status of women during the period of the early republic.[50]

Participation rates among female heads of household averaged about 44% and declined modestly over the 70-year period (Figure 2.4).[51] Comparable figures for the turn of this century are even lower, suggesting a downward trend over the entire century in the participation rate of female heads of household. Over the same period, the occupational distribution of women shifted toward sewing trades and domestic service and away from various proprietorships. It was a shift discernible as well in the male occupational distribution, which moved toward industrial jobs and away from proprietorships.

Female heads of household were primarily widows and unmarried adult women, living with other adult relatives.[52] Because city directories were compiled virtually every year, it is possible to link the occupations of widows to those of their deceased husbands. In this manner, one can infer the existence of hidden market activity of married women. While it might be useful to also have information directly on the occupations of married women, the city and business directories generally did not list wives separately. But if they did, it is likely that married women would not have listed an occupation even if they were involved in hidden market work.

The period of the 1790's was selected for the record linking. The 1790's mark a high point in the proportion of female heads having occupations, and their occupations contain a disproportionate number that were atypical by the standards of the early nineteenth century. Women in the 1790's were listed as turner, tallow

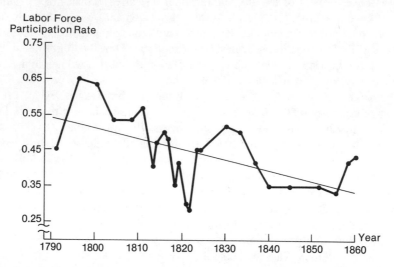

FIGURE 2.4. Labor Force Participation Rates for Female Heads of Household in Philadelphia, 1790 to 1860. *Source:* C. Goldin, "The Economic Status of Women in the Early Republic: Quantitative Evidence," *Journal of Interdisciplinary History* 16 (Winter 1986a): 375–404.

Note: Fitted line is: *Labor Force Participation Rate* =   0.539 − 0.0028 *Time*
                                                          (16.3)   (3.20)

where absolute values of *t*-statistics are in parentheses, R^2 = .31, and *Time* is 1790 = 1.

chandler, shoemaker, pewterer, cooper, tinplate worker, glass engraver, sieve maker, and ironmonger. Although some of these titles could signify the seller of a product (an ironmonger, for example, was precisely that), proprietorships of this nature were rare for women later in the century. Late-eighteenth-century Philadelphia provides a rare opportunity for record linkage because a virulent yellow-fever epidemic in 1793 produced an abundance of recently widowed women.

Of the entire sample of 1,019 female household heads listed in the 1796 Philadelphia city directory, 83% could be traced back in time to an earlier directory, and of those who could be located at all during the 1791 to 1795 period, 26% had husbands who were listed in at least one earlier directory. Some of the initial 1,019 women never had husbands; a great many others had entered the city already widowed; and still others may have split off from larger households in the city too recently to be traced to earlier directories. None of these considerations affects the main finding of the linkage: widows in 1796 had a high probability of assuming their deceased husbands' businesses and craft positions. The second column of Table 2.10 gives the diagonal elements of a cross tabulation of the occupations of widows and of their husbands, when alive. The numbers of couples having a similar trade as a percentage of all husbands and, alternatively, of all wives are given in the last two columns.

TABLE 2.10. Occupations of Widows and Their Husbands, 1791 to 1796

Widow's Occupation (Husband's)	Number of Widows, Husbands[a]		Number of Couples with Same Occupation	Percent of Husbands	Percent of Widows
Grocer and shopkeeper	33,	29	23	79%	70%
Boardinghouse keeper	32,	8	8	100	25
Innkeeper	7,	11	6	55	86
Baker	5,	9	4	44	80
Seamstress (tailor)	15,	6	3	50	20
Artisan	15,	71	14	20	93
Washer and huckster (low-status occupation)	30,	33	14	42	47
Gentlewoman (gentleman and high-status occupation)	40,	33	21	64	53
Other	40,	17			
Total	217,	217			

[a]The number of widows (husbands) listed with the occupation.

Source: C. Goldin, "The Economic Status of Women in the Early Republic: Quantitative Evidence," *Journal of Interdisciplinary History* 16 (Winter 1986a): 375–404.

Of the 217 husbands who could be located in the directories from 1791 to 1794, for example, 11 had been innkeepers and 6 of their wives were innkeepers in 1796. Virtually all widowed boardinghouse keepers had had husbands who had been boardinghouse keepers. There were 29 husbands who were shopkeepers or grocers from 1791 to 1794, and 23 of their widows were similarly employed in 1796. Of the 33 husbands on the lower end of the income distribution who had been laborers, mariners, carters, or skindressers, about half their wives became hucksters or washers when widowed. There were 12 cases of anomalous or atypical trades taken over by a wife: tallow chandler, bottler, shoemaker, turner, cooper, stationer, ironmonger, tea merchant, sieve maker, tinplate worker, brewer, and a pewterer who was enumerated separately even when her husband was alive and was one of the very few married women who were listed as employed. An upholsterer, two butchers, and four bakers, uncommon but not rare positions for women, also passed their trades to their wives or commonly shared them when alive. Almost all 15 women occupying craft positions in 1796 were the widows of men who had been artisans.[53]

The conclusion that trades and businesses were overwhelmingly carried on by widows should not be surprising, but it does raise an issue about the amount of practical knowledge these women had of their husbands' occupations. It is likely that many women in the 1796 directory were actively engaged in hidden market work when they were married, and that the decrease over time in proprietorships and occupations of a craft nature among widows is linked to the progressive separation of home and work.[54] Other studies have also found evidence of numerous "silent partnerships" between husbands and wives during the 1750 to 1850 period and of "deputy wives" for the century before (Ulrich, 1980; Waciega, 1985).[55]

The implication of the material on female heads of household is that the contribution of women to national income was substantial when the home and workplace were unified. Home and work never completely separated over the next two centuries. My grandparents, for example, lived in the rear of a grocery store they jointly operated, and work has, more recently, been reintroduced into the home by the advent of computer technology. But the process of specialization was accelerated by the rise of wage labor and industrialization.

The Industrial Revolution affected the work of women not only by the separation of home and work. The relative price of many home-produced goods, such as textiles, clothing, shoes, soap, and candles, declined in the nineteenth century, and the wage and opportunities of young workers increased greatly in the brief period from 1820 to 1850. Families in both rural and urban areas were able to take advantage of the emerging market in wage labor by having their sons and daughters work in industry. In 1860 Philadelphia, a female head of household having a daughter over 19 years old living at home had a decreased labor force participation rate of 8.5 percentage points; one with a son over 19 years old had a decreased rate of 10.1 percentage points; and one with a son between 15 and 19 had a decreased rate of 6.2 percentage points. There is evidence, therefore, that the increase in the paid labor of adult children reduced the necessity of widows to labor, and it may have had a similar impact on married women.[56]

Participation Rates Before 1890: Single Women

The role of industrialization in vastly increasing the employment of young women can be studied through the manuscripts of the early censuses of manufacturing. Many authors have commented on the extensive and early use of child and female labor in American manufacturing (e.g., Abbott, 1910). But until recently, there were no precise estimates of the proportion of women and children in the manufacturing labor force and the proportion of the population of young women employed in the industrial labor force. The use of the manuscripts of the federal manufacturing censuses and that for Massachusetts has demonstrated that women and children were about 40% of the entire industrial labor force around 1840. Further, the percentage was higher in 1840 than it was before or after.

More to the point of this chapter, the proportion of all young women in the northeastern states employed in the industrial sector was considerable as early as 1832 and rose rapidly wherever significant industrial development spread (Goldin and Sokoloff, 1982). Because the only evidence for this period comes from the manufacturing censuses, I have constructed a "manufacturing labor force participation rate," which is the number of women in the industrial labor force divided by the number in the population. This variant of a true participation rate is a lower-bound estimate, because single women were also employed in other sectors. But the data for the industrial counties of the Northeast indicate that even this lower bound was substantial in the period of early industrialization.

In the early industrializing state of Massachusetts, where the reporting of firms was most complete in the early censuses of manufacturing, 33% of all young women 10 to 29 years old were employed in industry in 1850. Even in 1832, at the dawn of industrialization in America, the figure was 18.7% among firms and 27.1% among firms and (reported) home workshop production; in 1837, for which a special state manufacturing census exists, the figure was 29.7% among firms and

40.2% among firms and home workshops.[57] On a county-by-county basis, even more can be discerned. The industrialized counties of Essex and Middlesex had manufacturing labor force participation rates for firms in excess of 25% in 1832 and 40% in 1837, and crude migration rates suggest that only after the 1830's was there a movement of young women from surrounding counties and states. In other words, local industry was attracting an enormous proportion of local youth. Evidence for the other industrial states of the Northeast confirms the notion that the manufacturing labor force participation rate of young women was high by 1850, if not before.

Because the population data prevent a calculation of the proportion between 15 and 29 years old, these figures should be considered high in comparison with participation rates of about 40% for single white women 15 to 24 years old around 1900 (see Table 2.2). Of greater importance in making such comparisons, it should be recognized that young women were also employed as teachers and household servants, among other occupations, and that these data are lower bounds to a true labor force participation rate.

The young women who worked in manufacturing during the period of the early republic were often daughters of native-born farmers. Factory employment enabled them to purchase clothes and, ironically, to enjoy various freedoms and independence. I say ironic because factory work, particularly in textiles (about which a considerable amount is known), consumed nearly the entire day and week. The bells that called factory girls to work rang between 5:00 and 6:00 A.M., depending on the season, and those that freed them rang around 7:00 P.M.; the bells rang six days a week (Dublin, 1981, p. 12). It is revealing of the working hours of agricultural and servant workers that Lucy Larcom, the celebrated textile operative, noted that country girls preferred factory work to being a servant because "at this new work the few hours they had of every-day leisure were entirely their own" (Cott, 1977, p. 49).

Letters written and received by female factory operatives from 1830 to 1860 suggest that their independence was achieved not only by having their own time, but also by being able to support themselves and at times their families. Luther Trussell advised his adopted daughter Delia Page that the mill town is "a good place to earn money and a very good place to spend it" (Dublin, 1981, p. 156). For most factory girls, earnings were used for necessities, such as the clothes Mary Paul noted in 1845 she needed and could not "get if I stay about here" (p. 100). Grander purchases also brought young women to the mill. Mary Knowlton Trussell wrote Delia that she would "go to the mill sometime in [the] course of a year to two and get some money to buy a piano" (p. 159). Factory girls knew they were earning substantially more than they could in servant work, and even more, as Luther wrote to Delia, "than any man gets this season of the year who works on a farm" (p. 178).

They knew as well, and perhaps with greater force, that this was their last opportunity before marriage to attain personal and economic independence. Luther wrote to Delia, "You now feel & enjoy independence trusting to your own ability to procure whatever you want, leaning on no one no one depending on you" (p. 166). Although the nineteenth-century workday was long and strenuous, marriage was often seen as more confining by those who toiled in the factories.[58]

There is considerable evidence that the age at first marriage among white women increased secularly throughout the nineteenth century, as did the proportion of women who never married. Both probably peaked for cohorts born in the 1870's, those who would come of age in the 1890's. Although the secular rise in both demographic indicators is not in doubt, the precise timing of the peak and the reasons for the increase require further investigation. There is considerable evidence that both increases might have been fostered by the expansion of labor force participation among young women.[59] Increased paid work among young women may have led them to delay marriage for several years, and the delay could have produced an increase in the age at first marriage and an increase in the proportion who would never marry.[60]

Some contemporary commentators saw as an added benefit of the paid labor of single women that it would enable them to find more suitable mates. In one of the many advice books to young women written in the late nineteenth century, the "bread-winning girl, the independent one" was respected for "her power to be sure that she is taking the right step, and can give more careful thought to the matter [of marriage], than the one who is hurried into it from motives of convenience" (Willard, 1897, p. 489).

Mill girls in 1830 were most often daughters of native-born Americans. Beginning in the 1840's and continuing to the first decades of this century, waves of immigrant daughters—first from Canada and Ireland and later from all parts of the globe—entered the factories. Much has been made of the transition from native-born mill girls to immigrant workers, and of the possibility that a reduced social status was accorded female laborers. In a highly influential article, Gerda Lerner (1969) investigated the role of immigrant factory labor in degrading women's work. Prior to the influx of immigrant female labor, the mill girl, it has been claimed, was a respected member of American society, and the paid labor of women of all ages was sanctioned. But, according to Lerner, the poverty of the immigrant worker irrevocably altered the status of working women and led to the withdrawal of native-born women from the factory work force. Work in the factory, to Lerner, was degraded by the presence of immigrant workers, and the paid labor of all women became synonymous with indigence.

Immigration did vastly alter the work force, its hours, wages, and conditions of work, but the role Lerner gives to the immigrant worker in lowering the status of women's work is probably too extreme. Although the children of immigrants were more likely to work for pay than were those of native-born Americans, differences between the labor force participation rates of young, single women are substantially reduced when urbanization is considered.

Participation rates of urban women 15 to 24 years old in 1890 are 43% among native born with native parents and 54% among those with at least one foreign-born parent. Among young women 16 and 20 years old, living in large cities in 1900, 39% of those with native-born parents were in the labor force, 54% of those with at least one foreign-born parent were, and 66% of the foreign born were. About 28% of all working daughters of the native born (16 to 24 years old) were in manufacturing jobs in 1900, while 40% of those of foreign-born parents were. Fully 58% of all white female manufacturing workers 16 to 24 years old in 1900 had native-born parents. The differences in participation are considerably less than are those between the groups in the entire population. And although participation rates are lower for daughters of the native born, the difference is insufficient to demonstrate that their work had become socially unacceptable. Further, in analyzing the labor force decisions of immigrant and native families, I have elsewhere shown that differences in labor force participation among single women were due primarily to the lower income and wealth of immigrant families (Goldin, 1980), rather than to cultural difference. Therefore, the daughters of the native born were not removed from the labor force to any greater degree than were those of foreign-born parents of equal income and wealth.

It is more likely, as noted by Edith Abbott, that unemployment, not immigration, changed the rhetoric of the workplace: "There was in the early days of the factory system no feeling of prejudice against the industrial employment of women, no jealous fear that they would 'drive out the men,' or that domestic life and the home would be ruined" (1910, p. 490). But massive industrial unemployment, particularly in the 1870's and 1890's, led many to question women's right to labor, as was the case again in the 1930's.

At the inception of industrial development in America, many factories, most notably textile mills, were built at water sites, far removed from cities. The factories drew their labor forces from the surrounding area and built boardinghouses to accommodate workers. As industry became progressively urbanized and as mill towns aged, working girls were more likely to live at home; surely a higher proportion did in 1900 than in 1830. Increased urbanization and immigration had an important impact on young, unmarried female workers. They were far more likely to be living at home and therefore more likely to be working for their parents rather than themselves. Mill girls in the antebellum period may have purchased gifts for their families and sent funds home on occasion, but most did not routinely remit their pay to their families.[61]

Young workers who lived at home in the late nineteenth century gave their earnings to their families, while those who boarded generally retained all. Several large-scale surveys of female workers around the turn of this century reveal the connections among earnings, age, nativity, place of residence, and the proportion earned that was retained by the worker.

Two types of workers were surveyed: those living at home and those living away from home, or "adrift," as social reformers termed female migrants. Among those living at home, 86% remitted their entire earnings to their families, and the mean percentage remitted for the full sample is 93%. Of the 14% who did not remit their entire earnings, the mean percentage remitted was 50%. The percentage remitted is a decreasing function of age and earnings, as might be expected if children who are able to leave their parents' homes wield more power than those who cannot. But the relationships are not very large. There is no relationship between the percentage remitted and nativity, occupation, and industry.[62] The results reverse when the sample includes only those living away from home. Women "adrift" retained virtually all their earnings. More than two-thirds retained 100%. The mean percentage remitted among those who gave a positive amount was 33%, and remittances are not a function of the woman's age. Some of the difference between the percentage remitted in the two samples may be due to the initial reasons for the woman's residency. But much, as in the case of the earlier mill girls, has to do with the fact that young women who lived at home generally remitted most of their earnings, while those who migrated, either permanently or temporarily, generally did not.

Young working daughters living with their parents, it would be fair to say, gained very little from their employment. Although there is only scant evidence concerning the material treatment of these workers within the home, social reformers of the day were probably correct in viewing their plight as they viewed child labor. Because they gained little from their work, they would probably be better off at school or home. This view of the young working girl encouraged the passage of protective legislation and, in a complex manner to be discussed in Chapter 7, delayed the equal treatment of women in the work force. The origins of single women in the pre-1890 labor force lead back to the beginning of this chapter and to the data on the labor force participation rates of single women in the 1890 to 1930 period.

Single Women in the Labor Force, 1890 to 1930

Table 2.2 indicates that the trend in the proportion of single (white) women in the labor force (15 to 24 years old) rose gradually over the last hundred years, along with urbanization and, for the earlier period, immigration. It began at a level of 35% in 1890, rose to 47% in 1920, and then fell somewhat to 43% by 1950. But the data in Table 2.2 are for the entire United States and by necessity aggregate rural and urban areas. When urban areas alone are considered, the percentage of white single women who worked for pay was 55% in 1890 and declines by about 12 percentage points by 1960. An even clearer trend can be discerned by holding yet more variables constant. The participation rate among the 15- to 24-year-old white, native-born group in cities was 43% in 1890, at the same time the national rate for that group was just 24%; the post–World War II rate for 15 to 24 year olds nationwide was just over 40%.[63] Thus by holding urbanization and nativity constant, the participation rate of young single women appears relatively stable over the period from 1890 to 1960.

This relative constancy of the labor force participation rate among groups of single women is curious because their schooling levels increased substantially over the last century. The 1890 to 1930 period, in particular, witnessed the emergence of the American high school across the entire United States.[64] Increased education among young single women should have served to decrease their time spent in other activities, including paid employment.

But the labor force data for single women conceal other changes in their lives and in those of their family members. Individuals who are not in the labor force can be engaged in a variety of activities. The most obvious and usual of these are attending school and staying at home, presumably engaged in leisure or household activities. Young single women, who in the aggregate had a relatively stable labor force participation rate over this period, greatly altered the structure of these other activities.

Because the participation rates of single women remained virtually constant while their school attendance rates increased sharply, they must have altered their time in yet another activity. That activity was time spent at home, helping their mothers with household chores, caring for younger siblings, and training for their future role as housewife.

Direct and indirect evidence on time allocation among the three activities—home, work, and school—has been compiled to produce the estimates in Table 2.11 on the percentage of single young women "at home" over the 1880 to 1930 period. Among the five cities chosen for study, the percentage at home declined steadily over the period, dropping by at least a third from 1900 to 1930. By 1930, the variant I estimates in the table indicate that virtually no young women were solely occupied at home; that is, very few were either not at school or not at work. The variant II estimates, which account for the possibility that young women were enumerated in both the school and the work categories, yield a figure of about 10% occupied at home in 1930. The variant II estimates were constructed to produce an upper-bound estimate and yet are considerably lower than the 1900 estimates, which are around 35%. The 1880 figures are from the census manuscripts and reflect the direct statement of individuals that they were "at home." The data, computed for only Philadelphia, indicate a decrease from 1880 to 1900 in the proportion spending time at home among all nativities, with the greatest decline, of about 22 percentage points, for daughters of native-born parents.

The change in time allocation had dual significance because it affected both daughters and mothers. For daughters, the expanded time in school came during a period of increased labor demand in the clerical and sales sectors. Their schooling prepared them for the new menu of occupations in the white-collar sector of the economy. The coincidence of increased schooling and job opportunities altered the nature of women's work for generations to come. The role of these critical changes in the subsequent expansion of married women's paid work will be examined in Chapters 4 and 5.[65]

The reduction of time spent at home among young women severed, to some extent, the method by which norms and ideals were reinforced within the family. Mature, single daughters were spending a far smaller amount of time doing those home-bound activities expected of wives and mothers. Their help with usual household chores and with younger siblings was needed less in the twentieth century, with increased mechanization in the home and with smaller families. In this manner, their paid work time may have substituted for their mothers', as was shown above in a case study for 1860 Philadelphia, and could thereby have delayed even further the increased labor force participation of adult women.

Summary: The Work of Women, 1790 to 1988

From our late-twentieth-century perspective, increases in the labor force participation of married, adult women, particularly those with young children, are of greatest interest. The movement of women from the home to the workplace is seen as emancipating, an indicator of equality by sex in society. Yet this chapter has shown that the increase in married women's paid work over the last half-century is only the

TABLE 2.11. Percent "At Home" Among Single Women, 16 to 24 Years Old, in Five Cities, 1880 to 1930

City and Nativity	1880	1900 Variant I	1900 Variant II	1930 Variant I	1930 Variant II
Boston					
NN		32.6%	37.6%		
NF		26.0	27.1		
NN + NF				0.0%	8.6%
Chicago					
NN		33.9	37.6		
NF		31.4	32.2		
NN + NF				1.1	9.6
New York					
NN		37.3	38.5		
NF		30.7	31.1		
NN + NF				1.7	8.7
Philadelphia					
NN	57.4%	33.8	34.6		
NF[a]	32.6	27.8	28.2		
NN + NF[a]	44.6			5.0	11.2
St. Louis					
NN		39.0	39.7		
NF		37.2	37.6		
NN + NF				4.5	11.1

[a]Irish and German only for 1880.

Notes: NN is native-born white with native-born parents; NF is native-born white with at least one foreign-born parent.

1900 Variant I: Described in procedure below.

1900 Variant II: Variant I minus school attendance for those ≥ 21 years.

1930 Variant I: Described in procedure below.

1930 Variant II: Variant I minus school attendance for those ≥ 21 years and minus 20% of school attendance for those 16 to 20 years old.

Sources: 1880: C. Goldin, "Household and Market Production of Families in a Late Nineteenth Century City," *Explorations in Economic History* 16 (April 1979), table 2. All ages are weighted equally; data for ≥ 20 years olds are used for 21–24 year olds.

1900 NN: Labor force (*LF*) and total population (*T*) for all marital groups 16 to 24 years old from U.S. Bureau of the Census, *Statistics of Women at Work: Based on Unpublished Information Derived from the Schedules of the Twelfth Census: 1900* (Washington, DC: Government Printing Office, 1907a), table 10, pp. 148ff. School attendance (*S*) 15 to 20 years old and ≥ 21 years from U.S. Census Office, *Twelfth Census of the United States, 1900.* Vol. II, *Population,* Part II (Washington, DC: Government Printing Office, 1902), table 50, pp. 388ff. Number of married women (*M*) 15 to 24 years old from table 32, pp. 310ff.

1900 NF: Identical to 1900 NN except λ is relevant for the group of NF, 15 to 20 year olds, and $\beta = 0.15$. School attendance (*S*) is from U.S. Bureau of the Census (1902), table 51, pp. 390ff.

The 1900 Public Use Sample yields an estimate for the "at home" proportion of single women (NN) in cities (≥ 25,000 persons) of 0.42. The figure is consistent with the data derived as above. Although it is slightly higher than the derived data, it includes small cities in which the proportion was larger.

$$1900 \ Variant \ I = 1 - \frac{LF_{16-24} + S_{15-20} + S_{\geq 21} - \lambda(S_{15-20}) - \beta(M_{15-24})}{T_{16-24} - M_{15-24}}$$

where λ = percentage of 15 year olds in the group of NN, 15- to 20-year-old females attending school in the relevant state in 1910 (U.S. Bureau of the Census, *Thirteenth Census of the United States, 1910.* Vol. I, *Population, General Report and Analysis* [Washington, DC: Government Printing Office, 1913a], table 26, pp. 1130ff), and β = labor force participation rate of married women 15 to 24 years old, assumed to be 0.1 for NN.

1900 Variant II = same as Variant I but excluding $S_{\geq 21}$.

rising portion of a U-shaped process that extends across the last two centuries. It is likely that the market activity of adult women declined sometime before its more celebrated rise. At the same time, the paid labor of young women rose during the nineteenth century, with the spread of industrial and urban activity. The period to about 1920 can be viewed as the era of single women's work, while that from 1920 can be depicted as the era of married women's work. I have stressed the complex interrelationships between the paid work of the young and that of older women, in terms of the substitution between them within the home and the acquisition of norms. I have alluded here to the fact that increased participation of adult, married women occurred in a particular manner, in terms of cohorts, years, persistence, education, and so on. The increase for certain cohorts at certain times, emphasized in the discussion of married women's participation, will be used in Chapter 5 to reveal why participation advanced.

The finding that the market work of women probably declined before its recent rise came from various revisions to the census estimates of the labor force. Yet the census estimates still contain valuable information, and I contend there are really two ways of measuring economic change in the role of women. In one, the measure of work encompasses more activities; in the other, the social and political implications of work are stressed and the measure is more limited. These are complementary, not conflicting, views of work.

Changes in labor force activity, however important, do not fully reveal the work experience of women, their occupations, their earnings, their treatment in the labor market, and the eventual social implications of their work. The relationship between the participation rate and work experience was explored in this chapter. The result was a rather surprising finding that work experience has been substantial among working women since the turn of this century, but that work experience among married women did not advance significantly over the last half-century. I turn in Chapter 3 to the occupations and earnings of women over the last century, and then in Chapter 4 to their treatment in the labor market.

1930 NF + NN: Labor force (*LF*) for single women 15 to 24 years from U.S. Bureau of the Census, *Fifteenth Census of the United States: 1930, Population.* Vol. II, *General Report, Statistics by Subject* (Washington, DC: Government Printing Office, 1933a), table 26, pp. 951ff. School attendance (*S*) 16 to 20 years and $\geq$ 21 years from U.S. Bureau of the Census, (1933a), table 24, pp. 1143ff. The number of 15 years olds in the labor force (LF_{15}) is from U.S. Bureau of the Census, *Fifteenth Census of the United States: 1930, Population.* Vol. V, *General Report on Occupations* (Washington, DC: Government Printing Office, 1933b), table 23, pp. 390ff. T_{15} is assumed to be one-half the total female population 14 to 15 years old from U.S. Bureau of the Census (1933a), table 24, pp. 1143ff.

$$1930 \quad Variant\ I \ = \ 1 - \ \frac{LF_{15-24} - L_{15} + S_{16-20} + S_{\geq 21}}{T_{15-24} - T_{15}}$$

$$1930 \quad Variant\ II \ = \ 1 - \ \frac{LF_{15-24} - L_{15} + (0.8)S_{16-20}}{T_{15-24} - T_{15}}$$

3

The Gender Gap in Earnings
and Occupations

Recent research on gender differences in earnings and occupations has produced a discouraging set of findings. The ratio of female to male earnings among full-time workers was roughly constant from the 1950's to the early 1980's, and the segregation of occupations by sex is substantial and has declined only slightly across the last century. Only since the early 1980's has the ratio of female to male earnings begun to rise. One might have hoped and expected economic progress to have narrowed differences in earnings and occupations between men and women. Gender differences in earnings and occupations appear impervious to the broad social and economic changes that have operated in other spheres, such as labor force participation and the political arena.

In this and the next chapter, I hope to clarify the long-term aspects of the stability and persistence of gender differences and point to changes in some indicators that have been hidden from view. At other points, I discuss features of the historical record that appear discouraging and even paradoxical, such as the apparent lack of a relationship between the ratio of female to male earnings and female labor force participation. Some of these features are, in reality, easily explained. Rather than being an apologist for the historical record and for the treatment of women in the labor market, I am trying here to separate true demonstrations of past inequity from evidence that actually disguises how change over time is revealed. Whether or not economic progress has fostered a real economic emancipation of women is a rather difficult issue that I cannot hope to answer definitively. There is, however, much in the historical record that will be surprising and heartening, yet much, unfortunately, that will remain discouraging.

The examination of the historical record, presented in this chapter, reveals that the ratio of female to male full-time earnings was not as constant before 1950 as it has been since. Rather, it rose from the early nineteenth century to the 1930's. The reliance on the last three decades of earnings data owes not to their greater relevance, but to their greater availability. Earnings data for the more distant past must be constructed from surviving documents on specific occupations and for particular sectors. Occupational data from the manufacturing sector suggest that occupational segregation may have declined across the last century somewhat more than other estimates indicate.

58

But there is little solace to be gained from the narrowing in the gender gap in earnings from 1815 to 1930, or from the possible decline in occupational segregation by sex. "Wage discrimination"—and by that I mean a statistical concept developed in Chapter 4 to measure the degree to which earnings differences between men and women are not accounted for by differences in their productive attributes—increased over time. "Wage discrimination" emerged sometime between 1890 and 1940 and has remained at roughly the same level since. How the gender gap in occupations and earnings changed over time is the subject of this chapter. The reasons for differences in earnings by sex, the degree to which these differences reflect discrimination, and the possible reasons for change or stability in the earnings ratio over time are taken up in Chapter 4.

The Gender Gap in Earnings over the Long Run, 1815 to 1987

Economic progress over the long run ought to reduce differences between the earnings of men and women. By economic progress, I mean the use of machinery, the reliance on mental as opposed to physical power, the increase in schooling for all, the general expansion of the market for goods and services, and the breakdown of norms and ideologies that have constrained both women and men. The labor market's rewards to strength, which made up a large fraction of earnings in the nineteenth century, ought to be minimized by the adoption of machinery, and its rewards to brainpower ought to be increased. Formal education, supplied by the employee, should replace on-the-job training possibly denied individuals who, as a group, have brief life-cycle employment. As more women enter and remain in the labor market, their experience in jobs and with firms should approach that of the male labor force. With the broadening of markets in goods and services, there is less gain to specialization by men and women in the home and to household production. Economic progress, it seems, should narrow and eventually eliminate differences in the earnings of females and males.

The Ratio of Female to Male Full-time Earnings

Recent trends in the gender gap appear to contradict the hypothesis that economic progress brings with it a narrowing in the differences between the sexes. Current as well as historical trends are given in Table 3.1 and are illustrated in Figure 3.1. The ratio of female to male full-time, year-round earnings has hovered around 0.60, and that for full-time weekly earnings has been around 0.62 (0.68 adjusted for hours of work among full-time workers) for the 30 years since 1955. Young women earn closer to parity with young men (the value for 25 to 34 year olds is given), and the ratio declines at all ages, except among the very oldest, at least since 1971 (O'Neill, 1985, table 3). Although the ratio of female to male earnings increases after 1981 and has continued its slow creep up to the time of this writing, there have also been periods of decrease in the ratio, particularly in the late 1950's.[1]

Data for the past three to four decades do not appear consistent with the notion

TABLE 3.1. Ratios of Female to Male Full-time Earnings in Agricultural and Manufacturing Employment and Across All Occupations, 1815 to 1987

(Except where noted, these ratios are based on full-time, year-round employees.)

Agriculture

1815	0.288

Manufacturing

1820	0.371–0.303
1832	0.441–0.432
1850	0.460–0.509
1885	0.559 (0.552)
1890a	0.539
1890b	0.537 (0.553)
1900	0.554
1905	0.556

	Full-time, NICB	
	Weekly	*Hourly*
1914	0.568 (0.592)	0.592 (0.622)
1920	0.559 (0.573)	0.645 (0.666)
1921	0.617	0.653
1922	0.612	0.677
1923	0.607	0.672
1924	0.593	0.664
1925	0.592 (0.592)	0.657 (0.658)
1926	0.585	0.662
1927	0.587	0.652
1928	0.573	0.645
1929	0.575 (0.570)	0.637 (0.635)
1930	0.578	0.635
1931	0.612	0.621
1932	0.653	0.618
1933	0.661	0.656
1934	0.688	0.704
1935	0.653 (0.646)	0.700 (0.688)

	Manufacturing		All Occupations		
			Median Year-Round	Median, Weekly Wage and Salary Income	
	Full-time	*Total*	*Earnings*	*Actual*	*Hours–Adjusted (25–34 year olds)*
1939	0.539	0.513			
1950		0.537			
1951		0.532			
1952		0.558			
1953		0.512			
1954		0.497			
1955	0.580	0.526	0.639		
1957	0.554	0.496	0.638		
1959	0.580		0.613		
1961	0.534		0.592		
1963	0.544		0.589		
1965	0.532		0.599		
1967	0.563		0.578		
1969	0.544		0.605		
1971			0.595	0.617	0.68 (0.73)

TABLE 3.1.　(*Continued*)

| | All Occupations | | |
| | Median Year-Round Earnings | Median, Weekly Wage and Salary Income | |
		Actual	Hours–Adjusted (25–34 year olds)
1973	0.566	0.617	0.68 (0.72)
1975	0.588	0.620	0.68 (0.73)
1977	0.589	0.619	0.67 (0.72)
1979	0.596	0.625	0.68 (0.73)
1981	0.592		
1982	0.617	0.654	0.71 (0.79)
1983	0.636	0.667	0.72 (0.80)
1984	0.637	0.678	0.71 (n.a.)
1985	0.646	0.682	0.74 (n.a.)
1986	0.643	0.692	0.75 (n.a.)
1987	0.655	0.700	0.76 (n.a.)

Notes and Sources: 1815–1850: C. Goldin and K. Sokoloff, "Women, Children, and Industrialization in the Early Republic: Evidence from the Manufacturing Censuses," *Journal of Economic History* 42 (December 1982), table 5. The range is for New England and the Middle Atlantic, respectively. The (b) results from table 5 are given and use Lebergott's male common-laborer wage as the base.

1885: C. Long, *Wages and Earnings in the United States: 1860–1890* (Princeton, NJ: Princeton University Press, 1960), p. 146, from First Report of the U.S. Commissioner of Labor, daily wage for adult males and females. Figure in parentheses is hourly wages for adult males and females.

1890a: Long (1960), p. 148, from Dewey Report, median hourly wages for men and women ≥ 16 years across 31 industries.

1890b: U.S. Census Office, *Report on Manufacturing Industries in the United States at the Eleventh Census: 1890.* Part I, *Totals for States and Industries* (Washington, DC: Government Printing Office, 1895a), actual wages used for operatives and piece-rate workers, males > 16 and females > 15 years. Figure in parentheses is for operatives only.

1900: U.S. Census Office, *Twelfth Census of the United States, 1900, Census Reports.* Vol. VII, *Manufactures,* Part I, *United States by Industries* (Washington, DC: Government Printing Office, 1902). Includes wage-earning men and women ≥ 16 years. Because both the 1890 and the 1900 census asked employers for the average number of employees during the year (in 1900 for each month), average earnings are presumably for year-round workers, although not necessarily for full-time workers. Because the question concerning the number of employees differs between 1890 and 1900, there may be differences between the years particularly in industries with extreme seasonality. The Dewey Report (U.S. Census Office, *Twelfth Census of the United States, 1900, Special Reports: Employees and Wages* by Davis R. Dewey [Washington, DC: Government Printing Office, 1903]), was an attempt to correct for the problem of variation in days and hours worked.

1905: U.S. Bureau of the Census, *Manufactures, 1905.* Part I, *United States by Industries* (Washington, DC: Government Printing Office, 1907b), p. lxxi. Includes wage-earning men and women ≥ 16 years.

1914–1935: M. Beney, *Wages, Hours, and Employment in the United States, 1914–1936* (New York: National Industrial Conference Board, 1936), table 3, pp. 48–51. Figures in parentheses reweight the 21 separate industries in the NICB data using data in the manufacturing censuses of 1914, 1919, 1929, and 1939 and the population censuses of 1930 and 1940. The basic procedure is to use the percentage female by industry from the population census data but the total employment by industry from the manufacturing census to allocate across industries.

1939–1983: Manufacturing. *Historical Statistics,* series G 372-415, pp. 304–5. Female earnings for operatives are multiplied by 1.02 to adjust for craft and supervisory positions when such data are unavailable. Male earnings are weighted by the labor force proportions in craft and operative positions.

ALL OCCUPATIONS: J. O'Neill, "The Trend in the Male-Female Wage Gap in the United States," *Journal of Labor Economics,* 3 (January 1985), tables 1 and 3, and data provided to me by the U.S. Bureau of the Census.

1984–1987: U.S. Department of Labor, Bureau of Labor Statistics, Employment and Earnings series, January issues, for weekly data, and data provided to me by the U.S. Bureau of the Census. Median, year-round for 1987 from Current Population Report, P-60 series, March 1988.

Both the year-round and the weekly data are from the Current Population Surveys, but the former is produced by the Bureau of the Census and latter by the Department of Labor. The differences in the two series may be due to a number of factors. The most likely explanation is that men who work fewer than 50 weeks during the year report lower earnings relative to all men, compared with women who work less than year-round. It is also possible that male self-employed workers, excluded from the weekly data, earn more, relative to the average male, than female self-employed workers.

From 1955 to 1980 only odd-numbered years are presented.

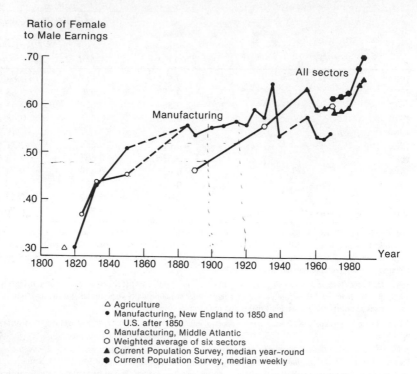

Ratio of Female
to Male Earnings

FIGURE 3.1. Ratio of Female to Male Earnings, 1815 to 1987. *Notes and Sources:* Tables 3.1 and 3.2. The unweighted, weekly NICB (Beney) manufacturing data are used for 1914 and 1920 to 1935, at five-year intervals. Data are for full-time workers where available. Dashed lines link manufacturing data series separated by many years.

that economic progress has been emancipating, but data reaching back to the early nineteenth century present a more sanguine view. Comprehensive national earnings data were initiated late in the history of the American labor force. The first population census to request information on earnings was that in 1940, and the P-60 series of the Current Population Reports, which continued the reporting of earnings on an annual basis, was initiated in the 1950's. There are no corresponding figures for earlier periods.[2]

Numerous data sources can be used to piece together a nearly two-century history of the earnings of female and male workers, and Tables 3.1 and 3.2 show the results of that effort. In brief, the constancy of the earnings gap from the 1950's to the 1980's is a short-run phenomenon; it cannot be extrapolated into the more distant past. The ratio of female to male earnings in the economy as a whole rose from 0.46 to 0.56 during the period 1890 to 1930, but was virtually stable from 1950 to around 1980. The increase in the ratio from 1890 to 1930 can be traced primarily to an increase in the ratio of female to male earnings within broad occupational groupings and, to a lesser extent, to the increase in the employment of women in high-paying sectors. Economic progress, it will be shown in Chapter 4, narrowed the earnings gap from 1890 to 1930 by increasing the returns to schooling, by expanding the labor market experience of women, and by decreasing the returns to physical strength.

The economy-wide series cannot be extended before 1890, but a history of male and female earnings can be constructed for certain sectors, manufacturing and agriculture being the most quantitatively important. The gender gap in both these sectors narrowed from around 1815 to the turn of this century, but, with the exception of various ups and downs over the business cycle, has remained virtually constant since. The early narrowing was likely produced by the enhanced division of labor in manufacturing, the use of machinery, and the resulting increase in demand for relatively unskilled labor. The virtual stability in the gap after 1900 may be rooted in the growing heterogeneity of the female labor force. The manufacturing sector in 1890 employed the median female worker in terms of skill, education, and age. But by 1960, the sector employed some of the least educated female workers, working the fewest hours and weeks per year. More educated and skilled women workers were increasingly drawn into the clerical and professional sectors, where returns to education were the highest, leaving the manufacturing sector with lower skilled, and therefore lower paid, workers.

MANUFACTURING AND AGRICULTURE, 1815 TO 1970

The history of gender differences in earnings can begin almost two centuries ago with data from the agricultural and manufacturing sectors. The ratio of female to male earnings for the entire economy, however, can be constructed for only the last century. It should be emphasized at the outset that the earnings and wage data in Tables 3.1 and 3.2 are, unless otherwise indicated, for full-time, year-round workers.[3] The data have been adjusted, where possible, for differences in weeks worked per year between full-time male and female workers, but not necessarily for differences in hours of work per day among full-time workers.

The ratio of female to male earnings was exceptionally low in the northeastern states prior to industrialization but rose quickly wherever manufacturing activity spread (Goldin and Sokoloff, 1982, 1984). Around 1815, the ratio of female to male wages in agriculture and domestic activities was 0.288, but rose to about 0.303 to 0.371 among manufacturing establishments at the very inception of industrialization in America around 1820. By 1832, the average ratio in manufacturing was about 0.44, and it continued to rise to just below 0.50 in the northeastern states by 1850. Early industrialization, therefore, increased the wage of females relative to males by over 70% (from 0.288 to 0.50), and the ratio in the industrial sector expanded by 43% (from about 0.35 to 0.50). In a mere two decades, the gender gap in manufacturing narrowed by about 15 percentage points, its greatest narrowing in so short a period of time.

It should not be surprising that events during the period of the Industrial Revolution in America, 1820 to 1850, should have substantially increased the ratio of female to male earnings. The substitution of machinery for human strength and the increased division of labor also enhanced the relative productivity of young boys compared with adult men.

Nationwide, the ratio of female to male earnings in manufacturing rose slowly

TABLE 3.2. Full-time Earnings and Occupational Distributions
of the Female and Male Labor Forces: 1890, 1930, and 1970

Part A: Full-time Earnings in Current Dollars (w_m, w_f)

	1890		1930		1970	
	Male	Female	Male	Female	Male	Female
Professional	1391	366	3713	1428	12250	8700
Clerical	943	459	1566	1105	8750	6000
Sales	766	456	1580	959	10150	4450
Manufacturing	587	314	1532	881	8891	4950
Service	445	236	1220	730	7100	3965
Agricultural	445	236	1220	730	7050	4151

Part B: Occupational Distribution (ϕ_m, ϕ_f)

	1890/1900		1930		1970	
	Male	Female	Male	Female	Male	Female
Professional	10.2%	9.6%	13.6%	16.5%	24.9%	18.9%
Clerical	2.8	4.0	5.5	20.9	7.6	34.5
Sales	4.6	4.3	6.1	6.8	6.8	7.4
Manufacturing	37.6	27.7	45.2	19.8	48.1	17.9
Service	3.1	35.5	4.8	27.5	8.2	20.5
Agricultural	41.7	19.0	24.8	8.4	4.5	0.8

Part C: Ratio of Female to Male Earnings Within Occupations (w_f/w_m)

	1890/1900	1930	1970
Professional	0.263	0.385	0.710
Clerical	0.487	0.706	0.686
Sales	0.595	0.607	0.438
Manufacturing	0.535	0.575	0.557
Service	0.530	0.598	0.558
Agricultural	0.530	0.598	0.589

Part D: Ratios of Female to Male Earnings Across All Occupations[a]

(1) $\Sigma\phi_f w_f / \Sigma\phi_m w_m$	0.463	0.556	0.603
	ϕ_m, ϕ_f: 1890	ϕ_m, ϕ_f: 1930	ϕ_m, ϕ_f: 1970
(2) w_m, w_f: 1890	0.463	0.489	0.455
(3) w_m, w_f: 1930	0.534	0.556	0.507
(4) w_m, w_f: 1970	0.571	0.610	0.603

[a]Row (1) is the weighted average ($\Sigma w_{fi}\phi_{fi}/\Sigma w_{mi}\phi_{mi}$), where w_i is earnings from Part A for occupational group i, ϕ_i is the occupational share from Part B, expressed as a proportion, and the wages and occupational weights are for the same year. In rows (2) to (4) ϕ varies across the rows while w is for the year given. Thus ϕ is constant down each column and w is constant across each row.

Sources: OCCUPATIONAL DISTRIBUTION: Historical Statistics, series D 182-232, pp. 139–40. The 1900 occupational distribution was used for 1890. Professional category includes professional, technical, and kindred workers, and managers, officials, and proprietors (lines 218 + 219).

EARNINGS: All earnings are annual, full-time, and in current dollars.

1890, Male, Professional: Weighted average of professional (34%) and managerial (66%) workers. Professional earnings for six categories, representing over 75% of all professionals, were obtained from: S. Lebergott, Manpower in Economic Growth: The American Record Since 1800 (New York: McGraw-Hill, 1964), p. 500, gives $1,662 for first- to third-class postal workers (government officials); Historical Statistics, series D 793, p. 168, gives $731 for ministers (clergy); a value of $460 for male teachers was derived from Historical Statistics series D 763, p. 167, given the assumption that the ratio of female to male teacher salaries was 0.8 and a value of $1,505 for the 5% who were college teachers); the figures for physicians ($2,540), lawyers ($2,691), engineers ($2,108), and college teachers ($1,505) were derived from Historical Statistics, series D 913-920, p. 176, for 1929, extrapolated back to 1900 on federal employee earnings, Historical Statistics, series D 764, p. 167. Managerial earnings were derived from U.S. Census Office, Report on Manufacturing Industries in the United States at the Eleventh Census: 1890. Part II, Statistics of Cities (Washington, DC: Government Printing Office, 1895b), table 6, using the category "officers or firm members actively

TABLE 3.2. (*Continued*)

engaged in the industry or in supervision." A figure of $1,264 was converted into a 1900 figure of $1,285, based on nonfarm money (when employed) earnings, *Historical Statistics*, series D 735, p. 165. The final estimate of $1,391 ($1,414 for 1900) was constructed by weighting by the actual occupational distribution, and it is consistent with the notion that the ratio of full-time earnings in manufacturing jobs to those in professional occupations must have been smaller in 1890 than it was in 1930; J. Williamson and P. Lindert, *American Inequality: A Macroeconomic History* (New York: Academic Press, 1980).

Clerical: U.S. Census Office (1895b), p. 10, yields data for urban clerical workers excluding salaried personnel.

Sales: Data for dry-goods salesmen in U.S. Commissioner of Labor, *Eleventh Annual Report of the Commissioner of Labor, 1895–96: Work and Wages of Men, Women, and Children* (Washington, DC: Government Printing Office, 1897) for 11 states yield a mean of $13.58/week or $706/year for 1895, and conversion to 1890 based on nonfarm money (when employed) earnings gives $766.

Manufacturing: P. F. Brissenden, *Earnings of Factory Workers, 1899 to 1927: An Analysis of Pay-roll Statistics* (Washington, DC: Government Printing Office, 1929), p. 94; full-time manufacturing earnings are used. Although these are given for 1899, the accompanying actual figures are identical to those for 1890. See also E. Rotella, *From Home to Office: U.S. Women at Work, 1870–1930* (Ann Arbor, MI: UMI Research Press, 1981), pp. 197–212, appendix B, on the 1890 figures. The implied ratio of full-time to actual earnings is 1.18.

Service and Agricultural: Lebergott's (1964) common laborer wage × 310 days. The figure for service is almost identical to that in L. M. Salmon, *Domestic Service* (New York: Arno Press, 1972; orig. publ. 1897), p. 96, of $6.93/week, given 52 weeks and $100/year board. Conversion was made to 1890 based on full-time annual earnings. The farm figure poses problems because no data are readily available for owner-operator farmers in 1890, and those for more recent periods indicate lower earnings for operators than for farm laborers. Farm wage laborers received less than the wage for common laborers, but owner-operators earned far more. The ratio of female to male farm wages for yearly contracts in 1909 was 0.578 and those for seasonal contracts (with board) was 0.538; G. Holmes, *Wages of Farm Labor*, Bulletin No. 99 (Washington, DC: U.S. Department of Agriculture, 1912). Therefore, the relationship between male and female earnings on farms does not differ significantly from that given by the rate for farm wage laborers.

1890, Female, Professional: Historical Statistics, series D 760, 763, p. 167, for 1900.

Clerical: Rotella (1981), pp. 197–212, appendix B.

Sales: See source for male earnings. The 1895 figure is $421.

Manufacturing: U.S. Census Office (1895a).

Service: Historical Statistics, series D 758, p. 167, for 1900. Salmon (1897) gives an average of $3.23/week or $268/year, including $100 board. Lebergott (1964), p. 542, gives an estimate of $3.14/week in 1900.

1930, Male, Professional: A weighted average of the earnings of lawyers, physicians, engineers, and dentists from M. Friedman and S. Kuznets, *Income from Independent Professional Practice* (New York: National Bureau of Economic Research, 1945); semiprofessionals, clergy, professors, and teachers from *Historical Statistics*, series D 793, D 792, D 913, $4,099. Earnings of proprietors, managers, and officials are from U.S. Bureau of the Census, *Sixteenth Census of the United States: 1940, Population*. Vol. III, *The Labor Force*, Part 1, United States Summary (Washington, DC: Government Printing Office, 1943a), p. 121, for males who worked 12 months in 1939, adjusted to 1929 dollars, $3,500.

Clerical: Rotella (1981), p. 197–212, appendix B.

Sales: U.S. Bureau of the Census (1943a), p. 121, for males who worked 12 months in 1939, adjusted to 1929 dollars.

Manufacturing: The weekly full-time wage from Beney (1936), for 50 weeks; also in *Historical Statistics*, series D 835, p. 172.

Service and Agricultural: Unskilled manufacturing laborers, *Historical Statistics*, series D 841, p. 172, × 50 weeks.

1930, Female, Professional: A weighted average of professors, teachers, nurses, and attendants from *Historical Statistics*, series D 763, p. 167, and U.S. Department of Labor, Women's Bureau, *The Age Factor as It Relates to Women in Business and the Professions*, by H. A. Byrne, Bulletin of the Women's Bureau, No. 117 (Washington, DC: Government Printing Office, 1934a).

Clerical and Manufacturing: The weekly full-time wage from Beney (1936), for 50 weeks; Rotella (1981), pp. 197–212, appendix B gives $868. U.S. Department of Labor, Women's Bureau, *The Employment of Women in Offices*, by E. Erickson, Bulletin of the Women's Bureau, No. 120 (Washington, DC: Government Printing Office, 1934b) gives median clerical earnings for 1931 of between $1,044 and $1,308.

Sales: U.S. Bureau of the Census (1943a), p. 125; see *1930, Male* above.

Service: Historical Statistics, series D 758, p. 167, for 1929.

1970, Male and Female, All Sectors: U.S. Department of Labor, Bureau of Labor Statistics, *Labor Force Statistics Derived from the Current Population Survey: A Databook*, Vol. 1, Bulletin 2096 (Washington, DC: Government Printing Office, 1982), p. 732, table C-23. Median, full-time, weekly earnings for each sex-occupation group. The manufacturing group for males and the service group for females are weighted averages of subgroups. Earnings for the agricultural sector are those of nonfarm laborers. Annual wages are weekly × 50 weeks.

from 1850 to about 1885, when it reached a value of about 0.56 (see Table 3.1 and Figure 3.1). Although the ratio has varied considerably with economic fluctuations over the last century, rising during recessions and wars and falling during peacetime booms, over the long run it has not materially budged from its value in 1885.

The magnitude and implications of the initial advance, from 1820 to 1850, are sufficiently important to warrant further attention. The observations of those who lived through the transitory times of the Industrial Revolution support the fragile quantitative evidence that the wages of females relative to males rose considerably over this period. Many who had observed the factory system in late-eighteenth-century England commented on the possibility of enhancing the relative productivity of females and on their opportunities in manufacturing. Perhaps best known is the prescient remark in 1791 by Alexander Hamilton that "women and children [would be] rendered more useful, and the latter more early useful, by manufacturing establishments than they would otherwise be" (Taussig, 1892, p. 9). Hamilton's assertion was echoed 40 years later by another Secretary of the Treasury, Albert Gallatin, who noted that "female labor employed in the cotton and woollen [sic] manufactures appears from the rate of their wages to be more productive than applied to the ordinary occupation of women" (Taussig, 1892, p. 192). Hamilton's vision of the factory system in 1791 had become reality by 1831. Henry Carey, whose essay on wage rates appeared in 1835, confirmed Gallatin's sense that

> agricultural labor has not varied materially in these forty years [1793 to 1833] in its money price . . . the wages of men having been very steadily about nine dollars per month [with board] . . . [but] the wages of females have greatly advanced being nearly double what they were forty years since. (1835, p. 26)

As Chapter 7 will suggest, Hamilton, Gallatin, Carey, and other industrial nationalists may not have been entirely disinterested observers of the impact that industrial development would have on the nation and on particular groups, such as female laborers. They were powerful supporters of the new industrial system and of any public policy to foster it. The claim that the factory system would employ women and children who were otherwise underemployed may have been a means of building political consensus over a larger set of issues, including the tariff, internal improvements, and other domestic policies.

One need not depend solely on the statements of politically motivated and possibly biased individuals. Additional evidence on the role of manufacturing in changing gender differences in wages is readily available from the rather ordinary folk who were surveyed by the McLane Report of 1832 (U.S. House of Representatives, 1833), an early version of the manufacturing census (see Goldin and Sokoloff, 1982, for a description of the report). This extraordinary document, commissioned by Secretary of the Treasury Louis McLane, includes information on the wages of males and females in areas undergoing the transition from agriculture to manufacturing as well as in those yet untouched by industrial development. One Aaron Tufts in Dudley, Massachusetts, noted in his schedule, "Comparatively nothing is done in the household manufactory: a female can now earn more cloth in a day than she could make in the household way in a week" (vol. I, p. 69). Although

Tufts may have overstated the case for the factory system, a fairly typical McLane Report respondent referred to the factories as affording the employment of "females who had little else to do" (vol. I, p. 819).

Thus the commentary of the exceptional individuals who lived through these transitionary decades is corroborated by the many respondents to the McLane Report whose motives cannot be so easily questioned. All support the quantitative evidence that the ratio of the female to male wage increased from around 1800 to 1830 and increased by an exceptional amount.

Women who labored in manufacturing at the inception of the factory system and throughout the nineteenth century were almost all young and unmarried. As was discussed in Chapter 2, they were often the daughters of local farmers who temporarily left home to work in manufacturing and live in the boardinghouses established by factory owners. Industrial development significantly altered the paid labor and wages of single women, but it left those of married and older women virtually untouched.

The ratio of female to male wages in the manufacturing sector continued to rise slowly across most of the nineteenth century but reached a plateau before 1900. The only major increase in the ratio of hourly wages of females to male after 1900 is for the World War I and postwar recession periods, and the depression years of the 1930's, as seen in the NICB data (Beney, 1936).

The NICB data for 1914 to 1936 also indicate that the ratio of female to male hourly wages in manufacturing was more than 10% higher than the ratio for weekly earnings. Women in the NICB data worked a smaller number of hours per week than did men, and they also work fewer hours in more recent samples (O'Neill, 1985; compare the actual and hours-adjusted data for the post-1971 period in Table 3.1). There is little indication, however, that hours worked were lower for females than for males in the first half of the nineteenth century or that they differed for the period from 1890 to 1914. If anything, there is some evidence that hours of women in manufacturing were greater than those of men in the late nineteenth century (Atack and Bateman, 1988). Thus the ratio of female to male wages in manufacturing corrected for hours worked among full-time workers was about 0.35 in 1820, increased to 0.56 by 1885, and rose to about 0.59 by 1970, when adjusted for hours (0.54 × 1.1). The ratio increases by 60% from 1820 to 1885, but by only 6% from 1885 to 1970, using the hours-adjusted data.

The narrowing of the earnings gap in manufacturing across the nineteenth century resulted from the increasing division of labor and use of machinery, both of which decreased the need for skill and strength. But the degree to which industrialization increased the ratio of female to male wages has depended as well on the initial type of agriculture in a region.[4] Early industrialization need not increase the ratio of female to male earnings to the degree it did in the American North. Certain crops today, and in the past, produce a high ratio of female to male earnings, while others produce a low ratio. Areas with an initially low ratio of female to male earnings, such as the grain-growing regions of North America, have more extensive change in female earnings and labor force participation with industrialization than do those with an initially high ratio, such as the cotton-growing regions of the American South (see Goldin and Sokoloff, 1984).

After the initial narrowing of the gender gap in earnings within manufacturing, change was substantially slower, and the hours-adjusted ratio reaches a plateau sometime around the late nineteenth century. The relative constancy of the ratio of female to male earnings might be explained, at least in part, by the expansion of the female labor force over the course of the twentieth century.[5] As the female labor force became more diverse, in terms of levels of experience, education, desired hours of work, and so on, the manufacturing sector, it seems, attracted those with low levels of human capital, desiring or having to work less than full-time.

Around the turn of the century, more than 80% of all female workers were domestic servants, manufacturing operatives, and farm laborers. The variation in schooling among these workers was small, and although professional and clerical workers were more highly educated, they constituted too small a proportion of the labor force to greatly affect the mean level of education for the average female worker. By 1950, 63% of all employed women were in these three categories, and mean levels of education and hours differed greatly across occupational groupings. Median years of school completed among all female workers was 11.8 years, but was only 8.9 years among manufacturing operatives. The percentage of all female workers who had worked more than 40 hours during the census week was 26.4%, but was only 13.7% among operatives (Kaplan and Casey, 1958). The possibility remains open, therefore, that the constancy of the ratio of female to male earnings in manufacturing results from the changing composition of the female labor force.

Manufacturing data provide nearly two centuries of information on the gender gap in earnings. But because the manufacturing sector hired only one-third of all female employees across the last century, it becomes necessary to construct earnings data for a wider range of occupations. The constructed data cannot easily be extended to the early nineteenth century. They do indicate that the gender gap in earnings when averaged across all sectors narrows from 1890 to 1930.

ALL WORKERS, 1890 TO 1987

Six major occupational groups are used in the construction of the nationwide averages in three benchmark years. Full-time earnings for females and males are given in Table 3.2, Part A, for the six groups of workers—professional, clerical, sales, manufacturing, service, and agricultural—in the three years 1890, 1930, and 1970. Data for the last of these years are readily available; the sources for the other two are detailed in the notes to Table 3.2. Average earnings are constructed by weighting the earnings for each group by the occupational distribution, given in Part B. The ratio of female to male earnings in each of the occupational groups is given in Part C. The nationwide ratios of female to male earnings for the three benchmark years are given in the first line of Part D. Ratios of female to male earnings across all occupations for the post–World War II period, obtained from more conventional sources, are presented in Table 3.1.

Even though the gender gap in manufacturing earnings had stabilized by the turn of this century, the ratio across all sectors continued to increase. The ratio of female to male full-time earnings increased from 0.463 to 0.603 over the 1890 to 1970 period (Part D). Rather than remaining constant, it rose by about 30%.[6]

Further refinements to the data serve to heighten the increase in the ratio of female to male earnings. The figure for 1970, like those in the manufacturing data, is unadjusted for differences among full-time workers in average hours of work per week. It increases from 0.603 to 0.663 when implied earnings per hour are used (0.603 × 1.1). Because data for manufacturing workers in 1890 indicate that scheduled hours per day were approximately the same in female- and male-intensive industries, there is no adjustment necessary for full-time workers in 1890.

Thus the increase in the ratio of female to male earnings is between 30% and 43% over the 80-year period considered, depending on whether the hours-corrected or the uncorrected earnings data are used. The finding distinctly overturns the notion that the economy-wide earnings ratio was stable for a period extending into the distant past. Rather, the gender gap in earnings narrowed to the 1930's. Yet with some ups and downs, it remained virtually stable from then to about 1980. Thus the narrowing by from 30% to 43% extended over only a 40- to 50-year period since 1890.

The ratios of female to male earnings within each occupational group are given in Part C of Table 3.2, and most rise over time, particularly in the period from 1890 to 1930. An exception is the manufacturing sector, as discussed above. Increases were greatest in the professional and clerical categories, for which advances in education appear to have augmented both the ratio of female to male earnings and the number of women employed (Goldin, 1984).

Part D constructs a matrix of female to male earnings ratios in which the occupational structure varies across the rows while the earnings data, by occupation and sex, vary with time down the columns. Thus all the off-diagonal elements in the matrix are hypothetical numbers that would have resulted had either the occupational distribution or the underlying wages been those of different years. The diagonal elements are merely the actual weighted earnings, for which the occupational distribution and the earnings are for the same year.

It is generally presumed that differences in the occupational distribution between men and women are the major determinant of the gender gap, and therefore that changes in the occupational distributions provide the only way of altering relative earnings between men and women. The notion that occupational structure is the primary, if not exclusive, explanation of earnings differences between men and women and that changes can and have occurred only through occupational change is pervasive. The belief remains even though many researchers, often on polar extremes of policy issues regarding gender, have demonstrated that although occupations matter, they may not be the primary determinants of earnings differences. The research on the issue, to be discussed below, has focused on only the period since 1960. Even though the material in Table 3.2 contains just six occupational groups, the change in the occupational distributions over time was substantial. I first replicate analysis of the role of occupational change and of occupation using these data, then review the findings of more comprehensive studies using modern data, and finally look further into the historical data for clerical workers.

If changes in the occupational distribution were of primary importance, then allowing the distribution to change over time but keeping earnings constant for each occupation should account for most of the increase in the ratio of female to male earnings. The matrix of Part D has been constructed to examine the proposition that changes in the occupational distribution have affected the gender gap in earnings.[7] Row (1) gives the actual ratio of female to male earnings for the three years. The next three rows hold female and male wages constant within occupational groups for each of the three years, but vary the occupational distributions across the rows. The ratio of female to male earnings increases going down the columns far more than it does going across the rows. The ratio of female to male earnings rose from 0.463 to 0.556 over the first 40-year period, 1890 to 1930. Had the earnings figures by occupation remained at their 1890 levels, but the structure of occupations changed, the ratio would have increased from 0.463 to 0.489 (row 2, Part D). The remaining difference of 0.067 was due to changes in the structure of earnings, both between the sexes and across all occupations. Similar findings result from holding the structure of earnings at the 1930 and 1970 levels (rows 3 and 4, Part D).

Across the last period, 1930 to 1970, the male labor force moved relatively into the high-paying positions, out of the agricultural sector and into professional activities. The share of the male labor force in the professional category increased from 14% to 25%; that for females increased from 17% to only 19%, but the proportion of female employment in the clerical sector continued to expand. As in the previous 40 years, the ratio of female to male earnings rose during the 1930 to 1970 period but less than in the previous 40 years, from 0.556 to 0.603. But had the earnings figures remained at their 1930 levels, the ratio would have declined, from 0.556 to 0.507. Alternatively, had the 1970 earnings by occupation prevailed, the ratio would have been 0.610 in 1930 but would have declined to 0.603 by 1970. Thus the shift of both males and females across sectors from 1930 to 1970 reduced the relative earnings of women. That the aggregate ratio increased at all was due to the increase in the ratio of female to male earnings for professionals and to the reduction of skill differentials for men (on changes in the skill differential see Keat, 1960; Williamson and Lindert, 1980).

Thus the increase in the relative earnings of females over the past century was due far more to changes in the ratio of female to male earnings within broad occupational groups than to changes in the distribution of these occupational groups between men and women, at least when considering the six occupational categories in Table 3.2. Although the computation in Table 3.2, Part D, is for only six occupational groups, it is still remarkable that occupational change had so little impact on the ratio of female to male earnings and that relative earnings within the broad occupational groups had so much more. The reason for the change in earnings within occupational groups, to be detailed in Chapter 4, is due in large part to the expansion of schooling among all Americans and the rise of occupations that place a high value on education.

A somewhat different way to assess the notion that the occupational distribution was a prime determinant of the ratio of female to male earnings involves giving the female population the male occupational distribution for each date but holding female earnings for each occupational group at the actual levels. If women are relegated to lower paying occupational groupings, then giving them the male occupational distribution should substantially increase relative earnings.

Had females in 1890 the male occupational distribution given in the table for 1890, the ratio of female to male earnings would have been 0.473, but it was actually 0.463; had females in 1970 the male occupational distribution for 1970, the ratio would have been 0.629, but it was 0.603. Six occupational groups, however, are insufficient to assess conclusively whether earnings differences between men and women arise primarily because of differences in occupations or because of differences in earnings within occupations. Various studies have performed the same calculation on an expanded menu of occupations. Yet increasing the number even to about 500 does not overturn the qualitative result found here that differences between men and women in conventional occupational groupings cannot explain a major fraction of the difference in male and female earnings.

Occupational Segregation and the Male–Female Wage Gap

Two studies have used an expanded group of occupations to measure the impact that occupational segregation has had on the earnings gap between male and female workers (Polachek, 1987; Treiman and Hartmann, 1981). The technique used is precisely the one described above. Female earnings by occupation are applied to the male occupational distribution to produce a measure of earnings that would be received by the average female had she the occupational distribution of male workers but the wage per occupation for females. Call this number $\Sigma w_f \phi_m$, representing female earnings by occupation (w_f) times the proportion male in each occupation (ϕ_m). Another number can be produced in a similar fashion. Male earnings by occupation (w_m) can be applied to the female occupational distribution (ϕ_f). Call this number $\Sigma w_m \phi_f$, representing male earnings times the proportion female in each occupation. The actual difference between earnings is $(\bar{w}_m - \bar{w}_f) = (\Sigma w_m \phi_m - \Sigma w_f \phi_f)$, which can be broken into two parts: a portion explained by differences in the occupational distribution and a portion explained by differences in wages within occupations. The partition, moreover, can be computed in two extreme ways, depending on whether male or female weights are used. The degree to which the occupational distribution affects average earnings can, therefore, be measured as either $(\Sigma w_f \phi_m - \bar{w}_f)/(\bar{w}_m - \bar{w}_f)$ or $(-\Sigma w_m \phi_f + \bar{w}_m)/(\bar{w}_m - \bar{w}_f)$, that is, the proportion of the original gap explained by reassigning either all females or all males to the other's occupations. Note that 1 minus either of the two measures is then the proportion that is explained by differences in wages between males and females within occupations, given the occupational distributions.

If the difference between women's and men's earnings were explained entirely by differences in the occupational distribution, then assigning females the male distribution should enable them to reach parity with men. Put another way, $\Sigma w_f \phi_m$ should then equal $\bar{w}_m$, and the first of the measures above would equal 1. Alternatively, if one assigned to men the female occupational distribution, their earnings should equal those of females, if the occupational distribution were the only factor. Using the same notation, this would imply $\Sigma w_m \phi_f$ would equal $\bar{w}_f$, and the second of the measures above would equal 1. No empirical study has found either of the measures to exceed 41%, and most of the measures cluster around 20%.

Polachek (1987) has shown that occupational segregation, measured in the two manners above, explains only 20% to 21% of the 1970 earnings gap using 195 occupations. Similarly, Treiman and Hartmann (1981, table 9) show that occupational segregation explains only 11% to 19% of the differential for 222 occupations and between 19% to 41% for 479 occupations.[8] Occupational classifications would have to be considerably finer to overturn the conclusion that changes in occupational structure matter less than changes in wages for men and women within occupations. It is also of interest that the percentage of the wage difference explained by the occupational distribution is greater in nearly all calculations when the male wage is applied to the female occupational distribution than vice versa. The reason is that the earnings of women tend to have less variance across occupations than do those of men. Part of the greater variance among men is due to their distribution across industries and sectors, holding occupation constant.[9]

How occupations affect the earnings of males and females may require a more precise measure of occupational segregation within sectors and within firms. One of the sources used in Chapters 4 and 6 allows a decomposition by occupations and by occupation-industry classifications for office workers in 1940.

A Women's Bureau bulletin summarizing a large-scale survey of firms hiring clerical workers in 1940 (U.S. Department of Labor, 1942) contains earnings of male and female office employees by 44 detailed occupations, and by 145 detailed occupation-industry groups (e.g., typist in telephone sector, typist in railroad sector). Even though both men and women were hired in 44 occupations, the occupations were highly segregated by industry. Male typists in 1940, for example, were hired by Philadelphia's railroads, telegraph companies, and state and federal government offices, but not in the banks, insurance companies, telephone company, printing and publishing firms, and department stores surveyed. Female hand bookkeepers were hired by nonprofit organizations and manufacturing companies, but not by a single bank, insurance company, or railroad in the survey. Male hand bookkeepers were hired in all the sectors. Occupational segregation was so extreme by industry that fully 114 of the possible 145 occupation-industry groups are empty. Males are not found in 82 cells, and females are not found in 32.

The technique used above to partition the difference in actual earnings requires that there be at least one male and one female within a narrowly defined occupation, and only 31 of these occupation-industry cells meet the criterion. Another technique, therefore, is also used that imputes to males and females their average earnings in the occupation, even when the occupation-industry cell is empty.

Very little of the earnings gap between men and women office workers is explained using the 44 conventional occupations (e.g., typist, bookkeeper, stenographer), −4.6% to 15.6% depending on the weights used. Indeed, the negative figure of −4.6% for the hypothetical female having the male occupation distribution indicates that females were distributed relatively toward occupations in which their wage was highest. Considerably more (16.1% to 55.5%) can be explained when occupations are further divided by industries, but that computation can be performed for only the 31 nonempty occupation-industry cells. If, instead, one imputes wages to the empty cells, a far smaller proportion of the difference in earnings is explained by the occupational distribution (5.2% to 28.1%).[10] The reason the explanatory power of occupation falls is clear from the extreme division of males and females across industries. Males are found in female-intensive occupations (e.g., typists) only in the higher-paying sectors (e.g., railroads, public utilities). Therefore, by imputing wages from these industries to those that do not hire male typists, for example, differences within the occupation-industry cells are made more extreme. The exclusion of the empty cells, therefore, reduces rather than increases the differences within occupations and heightens the differences across occupations.

Surely some of the difference in the occupation-industry distribution is due to work experience, education, job responsibility, hours, and other productivity-related characteristics and choice variables that may differ by sex. But it also seems that another, possibly large, portion is not the result of these characteristics, and that male workers have tended to be overrepresented in high-paying sectors, such as public utilities and railroads.

The conventional groupings of occupations, therefore, even when there are 500 of them, cannot explain a large share of the difference in earnings between male and female workers. This is particularly true when the measure uses the hypothetical case of female workers with the male occupational distribution. Had female workers the male occupational distribution, the increase in their earnings would close the gap by only 19%. Even when occupations are more finely divided into occupation-industry cells, the explanatory power of the occupational distribution is still not as high as many would expect. Differences in earnings for male and female workers within occupations remains an important issue. I have shown, in the case of office workers around 1940, that much of the difference in earnings is due not to the occupational distribution but to the industrial and sectoral distribution of workers, given their occupations.

Sources of Change in the Ratio of Male to Female Earnings

(handwritten margin note: Mens wages are settling and women are catching up.)

The increase in the ratio of female to male earnings, from 0.463 to 0.603 over the period 1890 to 1970 (see Table 3.2), might have been expected. The work experience and education of working women increased relative to men's. Years of job experience among working women doubled over the last century but probably increased trivially for men. Further, the returns to education increased for women with the expansion of the clerical sector. One study (Goldin and Polachek, 1987) has partitioned the change in the ratio of female to male earnings over the past century into its various components. About 90% can be explained by increased work experience and education and by changes in the returns to both factors in the marketplace. Changes in characteristics had a greater impact on the experience variable, while changes in returns had a greater effect on the education variable. It is likely that about half the increase in the ratio of female to male earnings was due to increased returns to education. Even though the narrowing of the wage gap can be explained by changes in various factors, the difference between male and female earnings at any one date need not be explicable by the same or additional factors. Chapter 4 will explore the possibility that much of the gender gap in earnings cannot be explained by conventional factors and that substantial "wage discrimination," as it is termed, exists.

The Gender Gap in Occupations

Occupational Distributions Among White and Black Women

The broad outlines of occupational change among all women was revealed in Table 3.2, Part B. The share of female workers in the clerical and professional sectors expanded over the 1890 to 1970 period, while agricultural, manufacturing, and service employment declined. Despite meaningful change in female employment, male and female differences across the six occupational groups actually widened, rather than narrowed, during the last hundred years. Before the trend in occupational segregation can be examined further with more disaggregated data, differences' among women must be addressed.

Occupational change for white and black women is given in Table 3.3 for the same years—1890, 1930, 1970 (plus 1980)—and occupational groups as in Table 3.2, Part B. For white and black women alike, personal service was the single most important occupation in 1890 and remained so for several decades. More than 35% of all working women were in the service group in 1890; more than 30% of white working women were. Even in 1930, 23% of all white women were in the service group. In 1890 and 1930, fully 90% of all black women who worked for pay were employed in just two sectors, personal service and agriculture, and as late as 1940 fully 60% of all employed black women were servants in private households. For black women, the initial shift in occupations was from farm labor to the service sector, mainly private household work. The extensive differences between the occupational distributions of white and black females began to narrow only in the post-1950 period, and Chapter 5 explores more fully the roles of education and discrimination.

White women moved progressively from service and manufacturing jobs to clerical and professional positions. The movement into the clerical sector was particularly rapid from 1890/1900 to 1930. During the first few decades of this century, the proportion of employed white women in the clerical sector increased by

TABLE 3.3. Occupational Distributions of White and Nonwhite Women: 1890, 1930, 1970, and 1980

	White				Nonwhite			
	1890	1930	1970	1980	1890	1930	1970	1980
Professional	12.5%	19.2%	19.8%	25.5%	0.9%	3.4%	12.2%	19.9%
Clerical	5.2	25.1	36.5	32.2	0.4	0.6	20.5	25.8
Sales	5.7	8.1	8.1	12.0	0.1	0.5	2.6	6.1
Manufacturing	34.7	22.7	17.4	13.1	6.4	6.0	20.3	18.4
Craft, supervisory	(1.9)	n.a.	(1.8)	(2.3)	(0.0)	n.a.	(1.5)	(2.3)
Operative, laborer	(32.8)	n.a.	(15.6)	(10.8)	(6.4)	n.a.	(18.8)	(16.1)
Service	31.3	20.3	17.5	16.3	48.2	62.6	43.0	29.3
Agricultural	10.8	4.6	0.7	1.0	44.0	26.9	1.4	0.5

Sources and Notes: For sources, see Table 2.1. The figures for white women in 1890 are derived from the 1900 figures in *Historical Statistics* (see notes to Table 3.2) by subtracting the implied number of nonwhite women in each category. The occupational distribution for nonwhite women was computed directly from the 1890 census. Thus the white percentages are for 1890/1900; the nonwhite are for 1890. The professional category includes managerial; manufacturing includes nonfarm laborers; service includes that in private households.

almost five times (5.2% to 25.1%). The proportion continued to climb, reaching 37% by 1970 and then decreasing to 32% by 1980. The role of the clerical sector in spurring changes in the labor force participation of cohorts of women is explored in Chapter 5. The percentage in the professional group increased from 1890/1900 to 1930, remained constant to 1970, and increased again from 1970 to 1980.

Occupational changes within the female labor force were, at times, rapid and often heralded further change in participation. But change within the female labor force does not imply a narrowing of the difference between working men and women, and it is to that topic that I return.

Occupational Segregation by Sex, 1900 to 1980

The material on the impact of occupations on earnings presumed that occupational differences by sex were and are substantial. But the occupational classifications used to compute earnings by sex for the three benchmark years are far too broad to form meaningful conclusions about the extent of occupational segregation, its impact, and its change over time. Occupational segregation by sex has been and still is extensive. Although the data remain fragmented, it is likely that occupational segregation by sex was more extensive around the turn of this century than it is today and that it declined at various points, particularly in recent decades.

A commonly used method for evaluating the extent of occupational segregation and its change over time is to construct indices of dissimilarity. One particular measure of dissimilarity is given by $D = \Sigma |f_i - m_i|/2$, where f_i or m_i is the percentage of all female or male workers in occupation i. The index ranges from 0 to 100. The index is 0 when men and women are identically distributed; the index is 100 when segregation is most extreme and there is no overlap in occupations. The value of the index gives the percentage of either all men or all women who would have to change occupations to produce equality in the distribution. There is no a priori reason why men and women should or ought to be distributed identically across occupations. But there is a presumption that movements over time in the index should reflect changes in the attributes of the two groups that make them more alike.

Various estimates of occupational segregation indicate that the index of dissimilarity (D) is virtually identical for 1900 and 1960 but that it declined somewhat during the 1970's. In a much-cited article, Gross (1968) has shown that the index when constructed across over 300 occupations has a value of 66 in both 1900 and 1960. Approximately two-thirds of the female or male labor force would have had to shift occupations to produce occupational equality in either year. Jacobs (1988), in a reworking and an extension of Gross's research, finds that the index across all sectors was virtually stable to 1950 (65 to 67) but declined somewhat from 1950 to 1980 (67 to 60). Excluding the nonfarm labor force in 1900 increases the index in that year and thus heightens the decline from 1900 to 1950 (75 to 67). Beller (1985; see also Beller and Han, 1984; Blau and Hendricks, 1979) demonstrates a decline in the index by 11% from 1972 to 1981. The most plausible course of events from 1900 to 1980, obtained by splicing these various estimates, is that occupational segregation was stable from 1900 to 1950 for the entire labor force but declined by

12% among the nonfarm group over the first half-century. Over the next 30 years, occupational segregation declined further by about 13%, with about 80% of the decrease occurring in the short period from 1970 to 1980.

My own work, below, on occupational differences strongly suggests that the occupational segregation summarized by these figures should be considered a lower-bound estimate. Further, there is some indication that it is most biased in the earliest years computed. As considerable as a dissimilarity index of 66 is, the actual degree of occupational segregation for all years is probably even higher, and an expanded index might increase the value for 1900 more than for 1980.

Refinements to the occupational data can be made for certain sectors, although detailed occupational data, particularly by firm, are not easily obtainable. In the manufacturing sector around 1900, segregation by sex was both industrial and occupational. Almost all female operatives worked in just two large industries, apparel and textiles (Tables 3.4 and 3.5). More than 60% of all male operatives worked in industries in which there were virtually no female operatives. Because occupations were often specific to a particular industry or groups of industries, industrial segregation meant that few male and female operatives could possibly have the same occupational title.

The three categories used in Table 3.4, female-intensive, male-intensive, and mixed, differ also in the method of payment used to compensate operatives. The proportion of operatives in the female-intensive (and mixed) industries that were paid by the piece, independent of sex, is considerably higher than in the male-intensive industries. Female operatives across all industries were paid by the piece far more often than were male operatives; fully 47% of all female operatives were, while only 13% of all male operatives were. Some of the difference in payment was likely due to the greater division of labor in the industries that hired women; some was the result of the role of piece rates in monitoring workers (see Goldin, 1986b). Piece rates, it should be noted, were not only used to pay women for outwork performed in their homes, but also extensively used to remunerate women when the work was performed in a factory.

Virtually all occupations integrated by sex involved piece-rate payment, particularly when male and female workers were employed in the same firm. Not all operatives in integrated occupations were in integrated firms, however. The case of compositors is instructive. Compositors around 1900 typeset handwritten copy often containing numerous idiosyncratic abbreviations; they were skilled workers, often well educated. The occupation was integrated in the 1860's after the union received assurances that women would be brought in at "scale" (Baron, 1982). A sample of compositors in 41 firms is given in Table 3.6. Only 12 firms were integrated by sex, where integration means having at least one male and one female compositor. Most women were paid by piece and worked in integrated firms; most men were paid by time and worked in nonintegrated firms. Piece-rate payment dominated for both in the integrated firms. Within the integrated firms, men were paid about 35% more than women, although piece rates were identical. Because there is no indication that hours of work differed, the only explanation is that men and women produced different amounts, possibly because they worked at different levels of intensity or had different skills.

The industrial segregation apparent in Table 3.4 is also evident when the nineteenth-century industrial headings are mapped into more modern two-digit SIC categories, as done for 1890 and 1960 in Table 3.5. The aggregation into the modern classification indicates that industrial segregation declined considerably over time. An index of dissimilarity among the 20 two-digit SIC industries falls by almost one-half from 1890 to 1960 (61 to 33). Women's relative employment share increased in metals, machinery, and transportation and decreased in the traditionally female-intensive industries of apparel and textiles. By 1960, the female labor force in manufacturing was far more dispersed across industries than it had been in 1890. Although a more equal industrial distribution of the female labor force does not necessarily mean that occupations were more equally distributed, it does mean that women were more evenly represented among the high-paying sectors of the economy. Industrial or sectoral segregation, it may be recalled, accounted for a substantial fraction of the difference in earnings among clerical workers in 1940; males were disproportionately found among high-paying industries and sectors. There is evidence that industrial segregation accounted for some of the difference in earnings as well among manufacturing workers around 1890 (Carter and Philips, 1988; although see Goldin, 1987a).

OCCUPATIONAL SEGREGATION IN MANUFACTURING, 1900

The industrial data suggest an extraordinary degree of occupational segregation around 1890 and a probable decline in segregation over time. A better notion of the degree of segregation for the turn of this century can be obtained from two U.S. Commissioner of Labor Reports published around 1900. Each report is incomplete: one undercounted female and male piece-rate workers, and the second surveyed only female-intensive and mixed industries. But when taken together, the two reports yield an estimated dissimilarity index of sex segregation. The estimate from these reports exceeds 90 and is nearly at the maximum value possible.

The first report is a 1904 survey that included 483 industry-occupational groupings (excluding the category "laborer") across 52 (nonbuilding trades) industries, covering over 2,200 firms (U.S. Commissioner of Labor, 1905). Of these occupations, only 44, or 9%, were integrated to any extent and 35 occupations contained only female workers. Not surprisingly, given the data in Table 3.5, virtually all the integrated or female-only occupations were in the textile, tobacco, clothing, paper, and printing industries. Among male workers, over 90% were in male-only occupations. Because the survey asked questions about hours of work, many piece-rate workers were excluded, and the number of female-only and integrated occupations is probably biased downward. The absolute number of female workers is also too low, as indicated by the proportion of all workers who are female. But because the second report surveyed only workers in integrated industries, these defects can be surmounted.

The second report focused exclusively on female-intensive and mixed industries at the firm level, and yields information on piece-rate workers absent from the first report (U.S. Commissioner of Labor, 1897). Although most industries were highly segregated by sex, the few that were integrated often contained integrated occupations that hired large portions of the industry's labor force. About one-third of all

TABLE 3.4.   Sex Segregation and Piecework Among 48 Industries, 1890

	"Male-Intensive" Industries[a]		
	Percent of Total Manufacturing Labor Force	*Adult Males/ Labor Force (× 100)[b]*	*Percent of Adult Workers on Piece Rates[c]*
Agricultural implements	0.93%	98%	20.59%
Blacksmithing & wheelwrighting	1.08	100	2.65
Boots & shoes, custom work	0.75	98	36.34
Brick, tile, clay, & pottery	2.75	94	3.80
Carpentering	2.97	100	1.62
Carriages, wagons, & cars	3.07	99	10.81
Cooperage	0.52	98	41.26
Flouring & grist mill	1.35	99	2.13
Foundry & machine shop	5.26	99	10.01
Furniture, factory	1.36	95	12.79
Iron & steel	3.24	99	0
Leather, includes morocco	0.90	98	10.89
Liquors, malt	0.74	98	1.27
Lumber & other mill products	6.07	98	3.47
Lumber, planing	1.84	98	1.70
Masonry, brick, & stone	2.30	100	1.76
Painting & paper hanging	1.19	100	4.94
Plumbing & gas fitting	0.90	98	0.74
Saddlery & harness	0.64	95	21.59
Shipbuilding	0.55	100	4.58
Slaughtering & meat packing	0.86	96	3.53
Timber products	0.98	99	21.51
Tin- & coppersmithing	0.82	94	6.38

% of total manufacturing labor force, in these 23 industries   38%
% adult males across all industries   79
% total adult male workers in these 23 industries   54
% adult male workers on piece rates across all industries   12.9[d]

	"Female-Intensive" Industries[a]			
	Percent of Total Manufacturing Labor Force	*Adult Females/ Labor Force (× 100)[b]*	*Percent on Piece Rates[c]*	
			Females	*Males*
Boots & shoes, factory	3.00%	29%	60.0%	53.5%
Boxes	0.40	65	55.6	23.0
Carpets	0.60	45	17.8	14.9
Clothing, men's	3.32	49	68.1	49.2
Clothing, women's	0.09	63	46.8	43.2
Confectionery	0.06	39	16.7	5.8
Corsets	0.02	81	63.5	53.4
Cotton goods	4.70	52	73.4	31.7
Dressmaking	1.43	97	*	*
Fruits & vegetables, canning	1.08	48	49.9	19.8
Furnishing goods, men's	0.05	74	65.7	51.7
Gloves & mittens	0.02	59	78.0	39.7
Hats & caps	0.06	34	70.2	55.3
Hoisery & knit goods	1.30	67	63.0	21.3
Millinery & lace goods	0.03	73	41.4	29.7

TABLE 3.4. (*Continued*)

| | "Female-Intensive" Industries[a] | | | |
| | Percent of Total Manufacturing Labor Force | Adult Females/ Labor Force ($\times 100$)[b] | Percent on Piece Rates[c] | |
			Females	Males
Millinery, custom	0.05	98	*	*
Shirts	0.07	79	69.4	52.6
Silk	1.08	57	75.6	39.8
Woolen goods	1.68	38	76.6	26.3
Worsted goods	0.09	46	*	*
	"Mixed" Industries[a]			
Clothing, men's custom	1.83	23	54.0	56.1
Paper	0.63	23	31.4	0.5
Printing, book & job	1.23	17	15.0	9.3
Printing, newspaper & periodical	1.22	11	19.8	18.4
Tobacco	2.75	27	64.8	65.5

% of total manufacturing labor force, in these 25 industries	27%
% adult females across all industries	18
% total adult female workers in these 25 industries	83
% adult female workers on piece rates across all industries	46.9[d]

[a]Male-intensive, female-intensive, and mixed refer to the actual percentage of males or females in each industry, not to an inherent characteristic of the industry.

[b]Male and female children make up a separate category, not included here, and the figures for percent adult males and females do not exhaust the entire labor force.

[c]The percent of workers on piece rates includes only operatives and nets out clerical workers and other nonoperatives.

[d]Adjusted for the undercount of pieceworkers in the cotton goods, silk, and woolen industries in the 1890 Census of Manufacturing. See notes below for the procedure.

Notes: An asterisk (*) indicates that the figure for the percentage on piece rates is vastly understated. The understated figure was used in the computation of the percentage of all workers on piece rates biasing downward that for females in particular. The data for cotton goods, silk, and woolens are adjusted for the undercount of pieceworkers in these industries using the more detailed firm and occupation-level data in U.S. Commissioner of Labor, *Eleventh Annual Report of the Commissioner of Labor, 1895–96, Work and Wages of Men, Women, and Children* (Washington, DC: Government Printing Office, 1897). Tobacco includes cigars and cigarettes; leather includes morocco; boots and shoes, factory includes rubber. Adult females are > 15 years old, and adult males are > 16 years old.

Source: United States Census Office, *Report on Manufacturing Industries in the United States at the Eleventh Census: 1890.* Part I, *Totals for States and Industries* (Washington, DC: Government Printing Office, 1895a).

operative occupations that employed females (within the female and mixed sectors) had some overlap by sex, but not necessarily within the same firm and not necessarily of any great magnitude.[11] About one-half of these occupations, 15% of the total, contained at least one male and one female hired within the same firm. One may still wonder how important the integrated occupations were within the industries covered.

In apparel, for example, both men and women were sewing-machine operators, and sewing-machine operators were about 50% of all apparel employees, although fully 82% of all female sewing-machine operators worked in firms having no male operators. In printing and publishing, compositors were integrated and constituted

TABLE 3.5.   Male and Female Employment in the Manufacturing Sector
by Two-digit SIC Industries, 1890 and 1960

Two-digit SIC Industries	Percent of All Females		Percent Female		Percent of All Males	
	1890	1960	1890	1960	1890	1960
20 Food	6.17%	10.29%	20.2%	26.8%	7.04%	10.67%
21 Tobacco	4.83	0.98	31.9	48.3	2.62	0.36
22 Textiles	34.30	9.62	40.8	44.8	7.71	4.09
23 Apparel	35.53	19.64	60.2	74.9	6.25	2.30
24 Lumber & wood	0.62	0.92	0.7	5.7	17.93	5.12
25 Furniture	0.56	1.49	4.8	17.8	4.31	2.40
26 Paper	2.72	2.77	39.9	22.0	0.95	3.45
27 Printing & publishing	3.61	6.62	17.5	26.7	4.39	6.33
28 Chemicals	1.05	3.63	15.9	19.5	1.85	5.18
29 Petroleum	0	0.73	0	12.3	0.38	1.84
30 Rubber	1.14	2.45	48.8	28.2	0.34	2.16
31 Leather	5.76	3.96	21.0	49.7	5.94	1.37
32 Stone, clay, glass	1.11	2.22	1.4	16.6	10.42	3.89
33 Primary metals	0.20	1.94	0	7.3	6.79	8.75
34 Fabricated metals	0.31	5.11	3.3	17.7	3.18	8.21
35 Non-electrical machinery	0.24	4.76	0.8	13.9	8.33	10.33
36 Electrical machinery	0.20	11.50	16.8	35.4	0.26	7.36
37 Transportation	0.12	5.07	0.5	12.5	9.11	12.42
38 Instruments	0.29	2.49	n.c.	n.c.	0.17	1.84
39 Miscellaneous	1.23	3.79	n.c.	n.c.	2.03	1.92
Total across all manufacturing	100.0	100.0	19.0	25.8	100.0	100.0
Index of dissimilarity[a]	60.8	33.3				

[a]Index of dissimilarity $= \Sigma\, |f_i - m_i|\, /\, 2$, where f_i, m_i = the percentage of the female (male) labor force in industry i.
n.c. = not computed.
Sources: Computed from the 1890 and 1960 U.S. manufacturing censuses.

about 20% of all employees in the industry. The fact that these workers had the same titles does not ensure that they did precisely the same work, but it does bring the comparison closer than that between workers in entirely different industries.

The information from the first report can be used in tandem with some parameter values obtained from the second to produce an index of dissimilarity. The problem with the first report is that the number of male and female workers in integrated occupations, as well as the number of females in segregated occupations, was undercounted. I assume that the number of males in segregated occupations was not undercounted, and know from the census that 20% of the manufacturing labor force was female (U.S. Census Office, 1902). The percentage of females among all workers in integrated occupations was 56%, from the second report, and the percentage of all female workers who worked in integrated occupations is 72% in the first report, consistent with evidence in the second. Because one of the adjustments involves increasing the number of male workers in integrated occupations, the percentage of male workers in male-only occupations decreases to 86% in the adjusted figures; the percentage of female workers who labored in female-only

TABLE 3.6. Earnings and Employment by Sex, Method of Pay, and Integration of Firm: Compositors, 1896

	Integrated	*Nonintegrated*
Male		
Time	$15.8 (2.9)	$14.4 (1.9)
	[84]	[158]
Piece	$12.2 (2.2)	$16.2 (1.7)
	[72]	[87]
Female		
Time	$9.5 (3.8)	$9.4 (2.2)
	[24]	[21]
Piece	$9.0 (2.3)	$8.1 (0.5)
	[62]	[15]

Notes: Wages are weekly and are weighted by the number of female (male) employees in each firm. Standard deviations of wages are in parentheses; numbers of workers are in brackets. The sample consists of 39 firms, 12 integrated and 27 nonintegrated. An integrated firm is one having at least one female and one male compositor. "Compositors" includes "book," but not "job."

Source: U.S. Commissioner of Labor, *Eleventh Annual Report of the Commissioner of Labor, 1895–96, Work and Wages of Men, Women, and Children* (Washington, DC: Government Printing Office, 1897).

occupations remains at 28%. All that is needed to form the index of dissimilarity is the distribution of workers across the integrated occupations, and it is assumed to be identical to that actually observed in the 1904 survey. The resulting dissimilarity index is roughly 91, a figure that supports the notion that occupational segregation was enormous in the manufacturing sector around 1900.[12]

Therefore, most operatives around 1900 were employed in highly sex-segregated industries. Among industries that were female intensive or mixed, males and females shared very few occupational titles, but these accounted for a nontrivial fraction of the employment in these industries. The extraordinary division of labor by sex may appear to be easily explainable. Many of the male-intensive industries listed in Table 3.4 required substantial amounts of strength, and the particular form of physical capital dictated that men would most often be hired. Other industries may have required long training periods and formal apprenticeships. But the extraordinary degree of segregation along gender lines suggests that more was involved than just differences in strength or training.

IMPLICATIONS OF OCCUPATIONAL SEGREGATION

When an industry was predominantly male, its occupations and its factory setting gained what I will call an "aura of gender." The gender of the occupation was often publicized through the use of rhetoric, such as the notion in meatpacking that women should not be hired because "handling the knife" was not women's work (Abbott and Breckinridge, 1911). Occupations were often termed "men's work" and were considered unsuited for women. Norms often barred women from various occupations within industries long after strength requirements, which may originally have justified a male labor force, could be surmounted. Men may have feared that the introduction of female labor would lead to the deskilling of occupations within their industry and to a reduction in their wages. Less easily assessed is that some men feared that women in the industry, certainly in the occupation, would lead to a degrading of the status or prestige of their occupation in the minds of others (Goldin, 1988b).

Summary: Earnings and Occupations

This chapter has demonstrated that the gender gap in earnings was not as constant in the past as it was from the 1950's to the early 1980's, and that occupational segregation was considerably more severe in 1900 than conventional measures indicate. Yet occupational segregation has been exceedingly high throughout our history, and the stability of the ratio of female to male earnings over the last several decades has been a source of concern. Many see the constancy of the gender gap in earnings as reflecting discrimination against women in the labor market. The narrowing of the gender gap in earnings from 1815 to 1930 might then be greeted as evidence of decreased discrimination. Neither interpretation is appropriate, however. But before that position can be defended, the determinants of earnings for both males and females must be explored and a measure of discrimination defined. These are the subjects of Chapter 4.

4

The Emergence
of "Wage Discrimination"

Even among full-time, year-round workers the ratio of female to male earnings has been far below 1 for all of American history and was about .60 until the early 1980's (see Chapter 3). In the 1970's, the 59 cents on the dollar figure became synonymous with inequality between men and women in the labor market. It symbolized the failure of the marketplace to ensure equal treatment and became a banner for the women's movement.

The reasons for differences in earnings by sex and possible explanations for the periods of change and stability in the earnings ratio over time are the subjects of this chapter. I also explore the possibility that much of the gap in earnings cannot be explained by conventional factors and that substantial "wage discrimination" has existed. "Wage discrimination," it appears, rose with advances in education, with increased job experience among women, and with the shift of the labor force from manufacturing to office work. An explanation for the emergence of "wage discrimination" between 1900 and 1940, of equal magnitude to that in modern studies, is offered in the last section.

It is well known that a simple ratio of earnings is insufficient to establish failure of the labor market to reward workers impartially. Ever since the issue of female earnings was broached in academic journals and the public policy arena of the late nineteenth century, it has been clear that earnings fashioned into ratios may not hold enough factors constant. A 1926 survey of clerical workers lamented that "it is doubtful whether such precise determination of the degree of difference is possible . . . through statistical procedure. It would involve the gathering of parallel cases in which the work was absolutely identical" (NICB, 1926, p. 28). Carroll Wright had attempted that very procedure thirty years earlier in a 1895–1896 study in which he compared the "earnings of women . . . and of men of the same grade of efficiency" in various occupations. From Sidney Webb's article in an 1891 issue of the *Economic Journal* to the recent literature of modern econometric masters, various techniques have been sought to measure the extent to which women are underpaid compared with men.

A Measure of "Wage Discrimination"

A useful and simple statistical technique has been formulated to assess the degree to which individuals with comparable characteristics are paid differently and whether the difference is correlated with sex or race. The technique will be termed "wage discrimination," because it may reflect the prejudices of one group toward another.

Put simply, this technique computes the dollar value of various characteristics in the labor market for each of two groups, say, males and females. It then assesses how much one group, say, females, ought to receive if paid as the male group—that is, by a "sex-blind" market. The difference between the value computed for females and the one actually observed, divided by the difference in male and female earnings, is a measure of "wage discrimination." Thus the technique assesses the difference between male and female earnings had they been remunerated identically for their, possibly dissimilar, characteristics and then compares the result with the actual difference. The measure gives the percentage of the original difference that cannot be explained by tangible, measurable differences between men and women that affect productivity.

Consider first the case of a single characteristic that is rewarded identically, in terms of marginal increments, for males and females but in which earnings, nonetheless, differ between an equally qualified man and woman. The case is depicted in Figure 4.1a. When males and females are rewarded identically for incremental amounts of total experience (E), the only attribute considered, the difference between male and female earnings ($w_m - w_f$), would be due to a difference in their characteristics times the value of the characteristic, $[\beta(E_m - E_f)]$, and to a difference in the intercept, ($a_m - a_f$), of the two lines, m and f. If they had equal characteristics, the difference in the intercepts would measure the "unexplained" or "residual" difference in their earnings. The difference in their actual characteristics times the value of the characteristic (β) is the "explained" portion. Both the residual and the explained differences are shown in Figure 4.1a.

Consider now the more difficult case in which the reward to the characteristic differs by sex. In Figure 4.1b, the f line, now f', has a different slope from the m line, meaning that females and males are now rewarded differently for increments of job experience. Both the different slopes and the different intercepts may be the culprits in causing differences in wages between males and females. There are two extreme ways to assess how much of the gap in earnings results from differences in characteristics. One way, suggested above, is to consider point $w_{f,m}$, a shorthand for the wage of a female had she been paid as a male. The difference ($w_m - w_{f,m}$) is explained by the greater experience level of males than females, while the difference ($w_{f,m} - w_f$) is the residual. The unexplained or residual portion is a measure of how much females are penalized because they begin at a lower earnings level and because they are paid less for each year of experience than are males. As seen in Figure 4.1b, part of the residual portion is due to the intercept difference and part to the different slopes. The measure just proposed weights the difference in characteristics by the value of the characteristic for men (β_m). It values a female as if she were paid as a male. The other extreme uses, instead, the female slope (β_f) as the point of comparison, and is also depicted in Figure 4.1b. There is no necessary

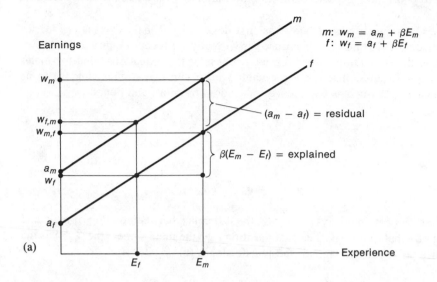

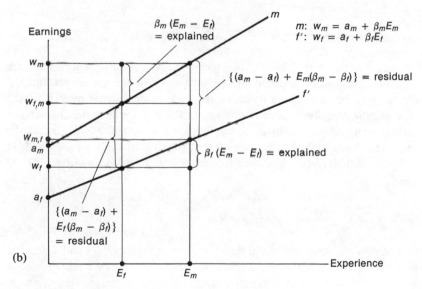

FIGURE 4.1. Earnings Functions and "Wage Discrimination."

(a) Returns to the Attribute Are Equal by Sex ($\beta_f = \beta_m = \beta$)

(b) Returns to the Attribute Differ by Sex ($\beta_f < \beta_m = \beta$)

reason to chose one measure over the other, although they can produce divergent results.

The technique advanced here was first devised by Ronald Oaxaca (1973; see also Blinder, 1973) and has been used in virtually all recent empirical studies of economic discrimination. More formally, consider two equations, one for males and one for females, that relate the natural logarithm of earnings (log W) to its determinants (X), such as experience, education, training, and hours:

$$\log W_f = a_f + \Sigma \beta_f X_f$$

and

$$\log W_m = a_m + \Sigma \beta_m X_m$$

There are two extreme ways of writing the difference between the log of male and the log of female earnings. The first partition uses the male slopes (the β_m's) as the reference point and the second, the female slopes (the β_f's):

$$(w_m - w_f) = [(a_m - a_f) + \Sigma X_f(\beta_m - \beta_f)] + \Sigma \beta_m(X_m - X_f)$$

and

$$(w_m - w_f) = [(a_m - a_f) + \Sigma X_m(\beta_m - \beta_f)] + \Sigma \beta_f(X_m - X_f)$$

where lower case $w = \log W$. The first two terms in each equation, in brackets, are the unexplained portions, composed of the difference in the intercepts and the difference in the slopes multiplied by either the male or the female mean attribute values. The third term is the explained portion, or the difference in the characteristics evaluated using either the male or the female coefficients. Note that if the coefficients are the same but the intercepts differ, the two methods are identical. In the case of one variable, say experience so that $X = E$ as above, we get

$$(w_m - w_f) = [(a_m - a_f) + E_f(\beta_m - \beta_f)] + \beta_m(E_m - E_f)$$
$$= (w_m - w_{f,m}) + (w_{f,m} - w_f)$$

for the first of the equations, written in the shorthand of Figures 4.1a and 4.1b. The first term is the difference between the male wage and the wage of a female who is paid as a male, while the second is the difference between that and the female wage.

"Wage discrimination" means that one group, here females, is paid less than another group, here males, even when the characteristics of each are identical. It measures the degree to which equal characteristics are given a different value by the market. The interpretation of "wage discrimination" and its empirical counterpart, however, are considerably more complicated than the definition.

The concept could measure the extent to which prejudices against women in the labor market lower their earnings compared with those of men. But prejudice could be more extensive than indicated by "wage discrimination" if women are denied job training and education, or if jobs are segregated by sex. It could, alternatively, overestimate the extent of discrimination if the earnings function omits relevant variables such as strength, intensity of work, hours, and responsibility. Even if all relevant variables are included in the estimation, econometric measures of "wage discrimination" can be upwardly biased if the data contain a classic errors in variables problem (see Hashimoto and Kochin, 1980). I address these possible criticisms of the empirical measure of "wage discrimination" toward the end of the chapter.

The U.S. government has recently begun to use the measure of "wage discrimination" in its reporting of male and female earnings differences, and the Equal Employment Opportunity Commission (EEOC) has introduced it as evidence pertaining to discrimination cases brought under Title VII of the 1964 Civil Rights Act.[1] At least one state government has employed the technique to eliminate pay differences between men and women without resorting to a policy of "comparable worth." In April 1988, the University of Connecticut, using a procedure almost identical to that just outlined, calculated how much female faculty members should receive given their qualifications. "An average of $1,700," it was found "could be attributed only to sex discrimination"; that is, it was the unexplained or residual difference in earnings. Earnings between male and female faculty were adjusted by that amount.[2]

"Wage Discrimination" in Recent Studies

The statistical technique of "wage discrimination" requires detailed information for both men and women on individual characteristics that are rewarded in the labor market and others that might indicate individual preferences. Few modern data sets, however, give detailed information on work experience, education, and personal information for both men and women. Most empirical studies of discrimination use either the National Longitudinal Survey (NLS) or the Panel Study of Income Dynamics (PSID), both of which are longitudinal surveys. Several use firm-level data often from actual discrimination cases (e.g., Malkiel and Malkiel, 1973). Two surveys of the literature (Cain, 1986; Madden, 1985) summarize the extensive findings on the percentage of the gender gap in earnings explained by differences in characteristics and the remainder that is unexplained, here termed the measure of "wage discrimination."

In one well-known and oft-cited study, which includes true measures of work experience and corrects for weeks and hours worked, 44% of the difference in the log of (white) male and female earnings is explained by differences in attributes (Corcoran and Duncan, 1979). Put another way, 56% of the difference in earnings cannot be explained by attribute differences and is our measure of "wage discrimination." Other studies have reduced the gap further by introducing variables that could not be incorporated in this otherwise comprehensive study. Differences in the quality of college education, measured by the college majors of men and women, augment the explanatory power of the usual equation by 1.6 to 2.3 times among recent male and female college graduates. If college major were not a variable in the equations, only 28% to 34% would be explained (depending on the weights used); but the inclusion of college major enables 44% to 77% to be explained by attribute differences (Daymont and Andrisani, 1984).

In most studies, but not all, women receive higher returns to years of schooling than do men (0.077 versus 0.059 in the Corcoran–Duncan study among white workers). Returns to total work experience are considerably lower for women, but those to experience with the current employer, a variable usually called tenure, are generally greater. Married men usually receive about 10% more than do single men. There is, however, usually no difference in the earnings of women by marital status, but when there is, it is that single, not married, women earn a premium.

The measures of "wage discrimination" and the coefficients for men and women just presented are from studies using rather modern data. The historical evidence on "wage discrimination" in this chapter afford interesting and perhaps surprising comparisons. Clerical sector data from 1940 yield results that are almost identical to those of modern studies. An exception is that higher education now mitigates "wage discrimination," but served to widen differences in the historical material. Of equal interest is that the results for 1940 and those of the modern samples are vastly different from those of manufacturing workers around the turn of this century. But before the details of these historical studies can be presented, the difficult issue of the relationship between discrimination and the measure of "wage discrimination" must be addressed.

Discrimination and "Wage Discrimination"

The measure of "wage discrimination" and the word "discrimination" are not necessarily the same concepts. By discrimination or prejudice, we often mean a distaste for associating with another person because of some characteristic unrelated to intrinsic aspects of productivity. Alternatively, discrimination can occur because an individual is part of a group—say, all women or all blacks—having average characteristics that differ from those of another group—say, all men or all whites. If there is an inability to discern individual attributes, each individual may be assigned the mean characteristics of the group. The first type of discrimination is generally termed "taste discrimination" and is associated with the economist Gary Becker (1957, rev. 1971), who first formalized a theory of discrimination. The second is called "statistical discrimination" and is connected with the work of Kenneth Arrow (1972, 1973; see also Phelps, 1972).

There are various forms of both general models. In statistical discrimination, for example, the groups need not differ by characteristics related to productivity. They may, however, differ by the ability of others to infer productivity from an attribute such as education (Aigner and Cain, 1977). The groups, if they do differ in ability or education or skill, need not differ by much, but small initial differences can, through feedback effects, lead to large differences over time.[3] The taste discrimination models of Becker allow for employee, employer, and customer discrimination.

They have been extended to include hierarchical forms of discrimination in which men have a distaste for working under the direction of a woman but have no distaste for supervising women.

The presence of discrimination, in either model, need not lead to differences in the earnings of individuals or to differences in occupations, although it can lead to both. Discrimination and prejudice can be rampant in society, but competitive forces may serve to mitigate their influence on earnings. If male employees in one firm do not want to work with women, then women will be undervalued compared with their productivity, and another firm can be profitably constituted with only female employees.[4] But even when firms are established that hire only undervalued workers, prejudice still exists. If a sufficient number of employers or employees do not have prejudicial tastes, wages generated by market forces may not reveal the underlying heterogeneity of tastes. Statistical discrimination, as well, can be reduced or eliminated through the greater ability of employers to discern the able from the less able.

The historical material, however, will indicate the existence of both occupational segregation and "wage discrimination," although each has differed in magnitude over time. Competitive forces have not eliminated the impact of discrimination, whether due to tastes or some statistical differences. Given the extreme occupational segregation by sex that existed in manufacturing in the nineteenth and early twentieth centuries, it is surprising there are virtually no examples of firms in male-intensive industries established with only female employees. Helen Sumner related the only example I have found, and even that is probably apocryphal: "In 1871 . . . a 'lady' saddlery and harness dealer in Chicago is said to have employed more than a hundred women" (U.S. Senate Documents, 1910–1911, vol. 94, p. 229).

Even today, using exceptional empirical data and powerful econometric tools, it is not entirely clear why earnings differ between men and women and what interpretation should be given the residual, our measure of "wage discrimination." The historical evidence, however, will add significantly to our understanding.

I will show that "wage discrimination" emerged sometime between 1890 and 1940 in the white-collar sector of the economy. Even though manufacturing employment was highly segregated by sex, as shown in Chapter 3, wages between men and women were more equal, given the characteristics of the two groups, than they have been since. As women began to extend their time in the labor force and compete directly with men for jobs in the white-collar sector, substantial amounts of "wage discrimination" started to appear. Accounting for unexplained differences in earnings between men and women cannot be precise, but several prime suspects are revealed in the historical evidence.

One is a form of "statistical discrimination." Because most women would leave the labor force at the time of marriage, employers denied them access to various job ladders, and women were tracked into various dead-end positions or ones involving very limited mobility (see also Thurow, 1975). Historical surveys concerning the jobs offered males and females in office employment reveal policies designed to segregate workers in this fashion.

A related reason is that male workers and employers had a distaste for working with or under the direction of women. There was, in other words, simple discrimination against women workers with a multitude of possible origins. Male workers may have feared the introduction of females would lower their earnings and dilute the skills required through the division of labor and increased capital intensity. In the nineteenth and early twentieth centuries, male manufacturing workers knew the impact that mechanization and the division of labor had in the tobacco and canning industries. The molders' union, for example, instituted fines for teaching a woman the trade of core making and did not allow women into the union during World War I (U.S. Department of Labor, 1920b; also Greenwald, 1980). Another possibility is that male workers believed the introduction of females would lower the prestige or status attached to their occupation (Goldin, 1988b).

The search for a monocausal explanation for differences between the earnings and occupations of men and women can only produce frustration. Current distinctions in the labor market affect future distinctions through conceptions of appropriate behavior, through the prejudices of workers, customers, and employers, and through individual expectations. A highly segregated workplace, where pay for women's work is less than that for men's work, will lead men to increase their prejudices against having women work in their occupation; increased prejudice, in turn, reinforces the status quo. A highly segregated work force will render the woman who seeks employment in a man's occupation a deviant, and the stigma could have an impact on other spheres of social interaction, such as marriage.

Explaining Differences Between Male and Female Earnings

The determinants of earnings for both men and women are many. The more schooled, trained, and experienced tend today to be better paid than the usual lot, as do those who are just smarter and more able. But schooling and training amount to little in an economy with low demand for such skills. Education has not always commanded the substantial premium it does today. In the manufacturing sector of the late nineteenth century, strength and stamina were more highly valued traits than the formal skills acquired at school. But in the emerging white-collar sector of the early twentieth century, education became highly rewarded for both men and women. The labor market became transformed in several dimensions from the late nineteenth century to the 1920's, in ways that would have a heavy impact on differences between male and female workers. The manufacturing and clerical sectors are examined here in detail to explore the origins of differences in earnings and occupations between men and women.

Wages serve various purposes in the labor market. In the nineteenth century, they acted primarily to clear the labor market, as prices often do in the goods market. But sometime during the twentieth century, wages, benefits, hours, and other aspects of the earnings package began to serve functions in addition to equating supply and demand. Earnings, occupations, and benefits became management's tool to alter worker behavior. The wage structure, by which I mean the time path of earnings over a worker's lifetime, became, in part, an invention of management. Monitoring, supervising, screening, encouraging, and enticing workers became functions of the earnings package.

There is also mounting evidence of considerable rent-sharing in the labor market and the payment of "fair," rather than competitive, wages (Akerlof and Yellen, 1986). Particular industries tend to pay workers higher earnings than others, and they pay higher earnings across the skill distribution. Further, the industrial wage distribution has been stable for considerable periods of time; high-paying industries in 1900 are often the high-paying industries in 1980.[5] Also of interest is that married men earn more than do single men (Korenman and Neumark, 1987), although the same is not true for women, and the percentage premium to marriage for males has been remarkably stable from 1890 to the present.

Over the extensive period considered here, the demands for various characteristics in the labor force changed, as did their supplies. To determine why earnings differ across individuals with varied characteristics, information on workers, their earnings, and their attributes is needed. To observe how the emergence of various sectors of the economy, such as the growth in manufacturing and later in the clerical sector, affected women's earnings, data on workers in various sectors and at different points in time will be used.

Manufacturing, 1888 to 1907

Several large-scale surveys of female manufacturing and sales workers were undertaken at the federal and state levels from 1884, the date of the Massachusetts report *Working Girls of Boston* (1889), to 1907, that of the U.S. Senate, *Report on Condition of Woman and Child Wage-Earners* (1910–1911). The surveys were designed for a variety of purposes. For some, the original rationale could not possibly have been furthered by the methods used. Carroll Wright, the most famous labor statistician of his age and the first U.S. Commissioner of Labor, was often concerned with the morals of young women workers. The information he collected on earnings, work experience, and contributions to relatives might reveal working girls' industriousness, but could not directly answer whether they engaged in promiscuous and immoral behavior.

Other, less intimate details of working life were better explored by the surveys. The issue confronted in Wright's 1895–1896 report, *Work and Wages of Men, Women, and Children* (U.S. Commissioner of Labor, 1897), provides a good example. Here he turned his attention to whether women were taking jobs from men during periods of economic downturn and, thus, whether women were paid less than men for equal work in general. But the extremely crude means of data processing and the absence of modern modeling and hypothesis-testing methods stymied his efforts. What one generation may have lost, however, has been the gain of another. Unable to process the enormous quantities of raw data collected, they were merely attached to the final document as if their weight alone would support the claims of the brief accompanying text. The text runs to fewer than 20 pages; the data to another 600.

These various surveys are used here to explore the determinants of earnings among working women in the period 1888 to 1907. The principal group is young, single, and employed in the manufacturing sector. Some samples give information on married and widowed women, others surveyed sales workers, and yet others have data on women living apart from their families in the large cities of the

Northeast. The types of questions vary across the surveys. Most asked earnings, occupation, industry, and age. Many contain questions on work experience in general, as well as that at an occupation and with the current firm. Wright and his followers did not need modern economists to lecture them on the importance of job tenure and work experience in determining earnings. But only two of the studies contain direct questions on schooling. Perhaps Wright and his fellow labor commissioners knew that formal education was important in certain sectors of the economy, but recognized, as will be demonstrated below, that it had little impact on the earnings of factory girls.

Several aspects of earnings and its determinants are of importance here. A primary issue is whether the ratio of female to male earnings around the turn of the century can be explained by the relative youth of female workers and their lack of job experience or whether it owes, instead, to differences in pay given equal characteristics—what has been termed "wage discrimination." Also of interest is how education was rewarded in the manufacturing and sales sectors and whether sales positions were more remunerative, particularly for the American born. For married women and others with dependent children, the issue of how the presence of children and the husband's employment status affected earnings is as relevant for the past as it is recently. The resolution of these various issues will influence the measure of "wage discrimination" to be computed later in the chapter. It also reveals some of the reasons why female labor force participation increased over time.

Five different samples are used in the resolution of the determinants of female earnings around 1900, and a full description of all data sets can be found in the Data Appendix. Four come from the U.S. Senate, *Report on Condition of Woman and Child Wage-Earners* (1910–1911), and the other is from a U.S. Commissioner of Labor study, *Working Women in Large Cities* (1889). The largest of the microlevel data sets, termed here 1907 Single Women Workers, consists of 1,796 women older than 15 years working in cotton textile and clothing factories. A related data set from the same source, called 1907 NYC Women Workers, contains information on more than 1,300 women living at home and working in factories and stores in New York City. Another, called 1907 Women Adrift, is similar to that just described, but concerns women living away from home in New York City and Philadelphia and contains nearly 400 observations. A final data set from the Senate report is called 1907 Married Women Workers and contains more than 900 observations on married, widowed, and divorced women working primarily in the cotton textiles and clothing industries. The fifth data set, from Wright's *Working Women in Large Cities*, called 1888 Working Women Report, contains 1,148 city-industry cells on almost 17,500 working women in 22 cities.

The 1888 Working Women Report and the 1907 NYC Women Workers and Women Adrift samples surveyed women of all marital statuses, although of the three, only the 1888 Working Women Report inquired of their marital status. The 1907 Single Women Workers sample and the 1907 Married Women Workers sample are, obviously, stratified by marital status. All samples, except the one on married women, surveyed work experience and earnings; two asked about education; three give the age at which work began; three contain data on days worked; and all have various information on ethnicity and other family variables. The survey of married women includes information on children and husband's work status, and whether the woman did industrial home work. Three of the 1907 samples have information on the amount of earnings working daughters and wives remitted to their families. (See Data Appendix for more detail on all samples.)

FEMALE MANUFACTURING WORKERS

The women in these samples were young, a finding that is to be expected given that in 1900 over three-quarters of the female labor force was unmarried (see Table 2.4), and the percentage of single women was higher in manufacturing employment. The mean age of the workers in the 1888 study, the most comprehensive of the five, is 22.7, and the median age is 20.[6] The mean age in the 1907 NYC Women Workers sample, which surveyed working women living at home of all marital statuses, is 20, while the median is just 18 years old.[7] The women in these turn-of-the-century samples began work at a rather young age. The weighted mean from the 1888 Working Women Report is just 15.4 years, while the median is but 15.1. Most, as will be shown below, would continue to work from the time they entered the labor force until they married.

Many young women working in America's cities lived apart from their families, like the majority of their counterparts earlier in the century who worked in textile mill towns and like many much later in the century who would leave home for college at a somewhat older age. More than one-third of all unmarried, native-born young women who lived and worked in the nation's large cities around 1900 lived apart from their families and relatives. The figure is higher for unmarried women of all races and nativities (38%); both figures, however, are reduced somewhat by omitting servants and waitresses, who frequently boarded with their employers.[8] Still, after omitting servants and waitresses, fully 27% of all native-born, white working women in large cities boarded, lodged, or lived as tenants in 1900. It is no wonder they were the subject of numerous state and federal reports on women "adrift" around the turn of the century.[9] Native-born, working women who lived in rooming houses were the lamentable and pitiable characters in many of O. Henry's stories, such as "The Furnished Room" and "The Green Door."

All these considerations—the age of the workers, when they began work, and their freedom from parental guidance—led social reformers to focus on their plight during the Progressive era. Added to the obvious factors of youth and dependency were economic vicissitudes of the period. Unemployment in the depression of the 1890's may have been as extensive in the manufacturing sector as it was nationwide during the Great Depression of the 1930's (Keyssar, 1986; Lebergott, 1964). Young women workers were viewed by many as marginal laborers whose work depressed the earnings and increased the unemployment of adult male workers, the vital breadwinners of society.

The employment of women in manufacturing since the early nineteenth century was accomplished by the simplification of tasks and the use of various types of machinery. The process of introducing female operatives differed in each industry, while in some—such as foundries, iron and steel, meatpacking, agricultural implements, and, later, automobiles—it rarely, if ever, took place. But in most industries, the division of labor was extensive. The sewing machine revolutionized the production of shoes and factory-made clothing, continuous process machinery lowered skill requirements in the manufacture of cigars and cigarettes, and modern canning and preserving techniques enabled the employment of lesser skilled workers in food processing (Baker, 1964; Brown and Philips, 1986). Enormous incentives existed to manufacture products through a series of minute steps, each capable of being performed by an inexperienced individual. Piece-rate payment accounted for almost one-half (47%) of all female operative positions in 1890 (see Table 3.4), and piece rates were used primarily to pay female workers. Male operatives were paid by piece rate about one-fourth as often (13% in 1890).

As a general proposition, technological advances are accompanied by an increase in the female intensity of an industry or a sector of the economy. Where technological change has been greatest from 1890 to 1980, as measured by total factor productivity increases, women's employment share relative to the average in the economy has increased the most.[10] There are exceptions to the rule, and these have been in traditionally female-intensive industries. In textiles, for example, the reverse process took place over the nineteenth century as the automation of weaving machines enabled workers to operate many looms at once (Abbott, 1910, p. 96). Although technological change does not always lead to the replacement of male workers by females, the instances of men replacing women because of technological change are few compared with those of women replacing men.

Many of the differences, around 1900, between male and female jobs, such as the more extensive division of labor and the use of piece rates for females, owe to the lower number of working years expected from a female worker. With short expected working lifetimes, women (and their families) were not likely to invest in long training programs.[11] That said, it should be emphasized that even though lifetime employment was brief, continuity of employment was considerable for women workers around 1900, as it was in 1939 (see Chapter 2). Indeed, in 1890 the average number of years a female factory or sales worker would eventually spend in the labor force probably exceeded six, even if she did not remain in the labor force after marriage or return to it years later. In 1939, single women were employed for more than 80% of the years since they entered the labor force (see Figure 2.3).

The expected length of employment cannot be directly observed and has been estimated using a theoretical framework and cross-sectional data. Because the available work experience data are cross sectional, and not longitudinal, the mean experience of the working population will not necessarily equal the eventual mean work experience of individuals in the population. The female manufacturing and sales labor force grew rapidly during the period, and large numbers of new workers bias downward the mean level of work experience. The greater the growth rate of a sector, the more the distribution of years experience is weighted toward lower levels of work experience. Statistically, the problem is equivalent to inferring the average life expectation in a society with a high birth rate. The age distribution of a society experiencing a high birth rate will be heavily weighted toward the younger end. There will, not surprisingly, be a large proportion of babies and children, and the average person will be young. More to the point, the average age will be a biased estimate of the average life expectation for the group, just as the average work experience of the working population will not necessarily be a good estimate of the expectation of time in the labor force for an average individual. The methods developed in demography that use cross-sectional age-distribution data to make inferences about death rates can be used for the labor force problem. While the methods are somewhat imprecisely applied to the labor force problem, the estimated experience figure of about six years is reasonably accurate.[12]

Recall from Chapter 2 that even as late as 1940, most young working women exited the labor force on marriage, and only a small minority would return to the labor force. Given that the average woman working in 1900 entered the labor force around age 15, six years of work experience implies that she labored almost continuously from the time she began work to the date of her marriage. Continuity in the labor force does not, however, imply continuity on a particular job. But complementary evidence indicates that young women shifted occupations with considerably less frequency than is generally presumed. Only 14% of the working women the nationwide survey from 1888 stated they held two or more previous occupations; over 50% had no previous occupation, although they may have switched firms with more frequency than they changed occupations. Further, these percentages are invariant to the time workers were employed; the same percentages arise from a sample restricted to five or more years of total work experience.[13]

Even though there was continuity in the labor force and at particular jobs, it is total expected job experience that matters for occupational choice, and total job experience for women was relatively brief. The average male worker had a considerably longer expected lifetime in the labor force, although time with a particular firm may not have been very different between the sexes. The ratio of a woman's expected lifetime work experience to that of a man's was probably less than 15% around 1900, even assuming that the woman worked prior to her marriage.[14]

Work for both men and women in the nineteenth century was arduous, involving long hours, often six days a week, and considerable uncertainty. It is no wonder, therefore, that women, whose relative pay in the market was low, would choose to specialize in the production of family-oriented goods when married. The possible circularity in the reasons for the short duration of women's employment was as clear to contemporaries as it should be to us. "In most cases, probably, woman's expectation of marriage is responsible for her lack of skill, but in some instances, doubtless, her enforced lack of skill is responsible for her longing for marriage as a relief from intolerable drudgery," was the incisive comment of Helen Sumner in her contribution to the Senate report, the source of several of the data sets used here (U.S. Senate Documents, 1910–1911, vol. 96, p. 32).

Whatever the reasons for the brief work expectation of women around the turn of the century, the impact on earnings will be clear from the regression equations of Tables 4.1 and 4.2. Table 4.1 gives earnings functions for four of the data sets described above, and Table 4.2 provides similar information for the fifth, that for married women. The term "earnings function" is used here to describe a relationship between earnings and the various characteristics of individuals that should affect earnings, such as job experience, formal training, schooling, age, health, and marital status. The equations are estimated by regressing individual characteristics on the natural logarithm of earnings. By using that particular functional form, the

TABLE 4.1. Determinants of Earnings Among Working Women, 1888 to 1907

Variable	(1) 1888 Working Women Report	(2) 1907 Single Women Workers	(3) 1907 NYC Women Workers	(4) 1907 Women Adrift
	Annual Earnings [5.58]	Annual Earnings [5.30]	Weekly Earnings [1.76]	Weekly Earnings [1.88]
Constant	5.57 (46.0)	−2.01	1.21 (32.8)	1.52 (12.7)
Job and training characteristics				
Experience	0.087 (10.6)	0.0936 (22.3)	0.0805 (14.3)	0.032 (5.60)
Experience$^2 \times 10^{-2}$	−0.489 (7.87)	−0.293 (14.7)	−0.367 (11.9)	−0.0683 (4.65)
Schooling		0.0345 (3.43)		0.0196 (0.60)
Schooling$^2 \times 10^{-2}$		−0.157 (1.75)		−0.121 (0.52)
Age work began	0.014 (3.32)	0.0295 (9.22)	0.0178[a] (9.04)	
Log days lost	−0.085 (7.78)			
Log days worked		1.22 (73.9)		
Store	0.186 (8.58)		−0.0815 (3.00)	0.0486 (0.72)
Store × experience			0.0214 (3.53)	0.0154 (2.87)
Prior occupations	0.107 (1.97)			
Personal characteristics				
Poor health	−0.314 (2.71)			
Widowed or divorced	−0.076 (0.64)			
Single	0.163 (2.09)			
Does housework	−0.117 (3.50)			
Lives with parents	−0.335 (5.39)			
Born in state	−0.217 (5.48)			
Foreign-born		−0.0216 (0.48)		
Foreign × years in U.S.		−0.0011 (0.79)		
Native-born				0.0749 (1.65)

TABLE 4.1.   (Continued)

Variable	(1) 1888 Working Women Report	(2) 1907 Single Women Workers	(3) 1907 NYC Women Workers	(4) 1907 Women Adrift
Native-born mother	−0.139 (1.85)			
Native-born father	−0.044 (0.56)			
Mother is alive		−0.0419 (1.42)		
R^2	.487	.845	.338	.187
Number of observations	1066	1785	1318	329

aThe variable is age, rather than age work began.

Notes and Sources: See Data Appendix for a description of each sample. The dependent variable is the natural logarithm of earnings. Means are in brackets.

1888 Working Women Report: Experience = age − age work began; Store = 1, if work in store and 0, if factory; Prior occupations = 1 if ≥ 2 occupations prior to present one; Days lost = days not worked due to strikes, factory closing, illness, and so on. All variables are the means of industry-city cells and are either proportions (e.g., single, widowed, poor health) or mean values (e.g., experience, age work began). The regression is weighted by the square root of the number of women in each industry-city category. Other variables entered: three regional dummies.

1907 Single Women Workers: Schooling is months attended divided by 9. Other variables entered: native-born with native parents, city and state dummies.

1907 Women Adrift: Other variables entered: New York City dummy, German parentage, English parentage.

Absolute values of *t*-statistics are in parentheses.

coefficients on experience and education, among others, can be interpreted as returns to investments in training, and the form can be derived from a theoretical framework of investment in human capital (see Mincer, 1974).

EARNINGS OF MANUFACTURING WORKERS

Earnings rose steeply for the first several years of employment in an occupation. In two of the data sets (1888 Working Women Report and 1907 NYC Women Workers sample), earnings rose to about 10 years of work experience. In one of the surveys (1907 Single Women Workers), the peak was attained at 16 years, but rose more rapidly than in the 1888 Report.[15] By estimating the relationship between earnings and experience as a quadratic, additional years of experience appear to decrease earnings beyond about 10 to 15 years, but the effect may simply be a result of the functional form. Other, more flexible, functional forms, such as the Gompertz (double exponential) and the use of dummy variables for years of experience, indicate that earnings rose for about 15 years and then reached a virtual plateau. It is possible, however, and various narrative accounts suggest, that earnings actually did decrease with age at some point.

It should be noted that a term for "maturity" is added to three of the equations in Table 4.1. Because many women in these samples began work at a very young age, a term for the age at which work began has been included. Its coefficient gives the increase in earnings that would have occurred had work been delayed for a year.

TABLE 4.2.   Determinants of Earnings Among
Married Women Workers, 1907

Variable	1907 Married Women Workers
	Annual Earnings [4.84]
Age	0.0270
	(3.32)
$Age^2 \times 10^{-2}$	−0.0447
	(4.26)
Log days worked	0.0327
	(33.7)
Does industrial home work	−0.470
	(11.9)
Husband	
Dead	0.0193
	(0.45)
Away	−0.0436
	(0.64)
Unemployed	0.127
	(1.84)
Native-born	0.285
	(4.55)
Children	
Number ≤ 2 years	0.0538
	(0.67)
Number 3 to 5 years	−0.0487
	(0.65)
Number 6 to 9 years	−0.101
	(0.45)
≤ 2 years × home work	−0.150
	(2.34)
3 to 5 years × home work	0.0304
	(0.54)
R^2	.742
Number of observations	936

Notes and Sources: See Data Appendix for description of 1907 Married Women Workers sample. The dependent variable is the natural logarithm of annual earnings. Mean is in brackets. Variables also entered: interaction between days worked and children ≤ 2, 3 to 5 years; city and state dummy variables. Absolute values of *t*-statistics are in parentheses.

Around the age at which work began (15 years), earnings would have increased between 1% and 3%.

Two occupational groups, manufacturing and sales, are included in the data for three of the samples, and the relationship between earnings and work experience differs somewhat between them. Sales allowed for slightly more advancement with time on the job, but generally entailed lower initial earnings. At four years, the two paid about the same, but sales paid more beyond that point (see results in column 3). The burgeoning sales and, later, clerical sectors were less strenuous, often entailed fewer hours, and would have been preferred by young women who, if they were not dependent on their own earnings, could afford the initially lower pay.

Given the possibility of discrimination in general, it is interesting to explore differences among the earnings of the foreign-born, the daughters of the foreign-born, and those of native-born parents. No one definitive finding results from these data concerning differences in earnings by ethnicity and years in the United States. Although native-born women earned more in the NYC Women Workers sample (by about 4%), they earned less in the 1888 Working Women Report (by 14% had they a native-born mother). Differences in earnings by nativity, however, may reflect intensity of work rather than prejudice on the part of employers. The 1907 Single Women Workers survey shows, for example, that daughters earned 4% less if their mothers were alive, given number of days worked.

The survey from 1888 has considerable detail regarding family background. Those living at home and assisting with housework earned about 40% less than other young working women. In part this may indicate that home responsibilities reduced work intensity. But it is likely, as well, that intensity of work was decreased by an absence of rewards; young women living at home gave almost all their earnings to their families.[16]

The general structure of earnings suggests that most women around 1900 were confined to tasks in which proficiency could be achieved rather quickly. Young women may have been moved around a firm over the years, but promotion within the firm and industry remained extremely limited. The brief and rapid increase in earnings with time on the job reflected some initial learning but no fundamental training. There were, of course, a few exceptions. The sewing trades entailed some opportunity for training, and the 1907 Senate report commented, "Occupational promotion in coat making necessitates changes in the character of the work done and involves a period of reduced productivity and reduced wages" (U.S. Senate Documents, 1910–1911, vol. 87, p. 477). But most female operatives who achieved high earnings with time on the job were those promoted to supervisory capacity.[17] There were virtually no other positions in manufacturing for which earnings were sufficiently high that time on the job could have mattered much beyond the initial increase.

Other studies have added to the findings on the relationship between earnings and experience by separating the components of total job experience into time in an occupation and time with the firm, also called tenure (Eichengreen, 1984). Time with the firm, or tenure, and years on the present job mattered greatly for the earnings of a female worker around 1900. A male worker, however, garnered considerably more from job experience in general, independent of whether work experience was continuous at a given firm or at a particular occupation. These findings are remarkably similar to those observed in later data sets, such as one for 1940 on office workers, to be presented below, and the modern studies discussed above.

The quantitative results reinforce the impression from narrative evidence that little was taught female workers around 1900, and thus that little could be transferred to alternative employments. In some industries, their work was dead-end in the sense that they were hired to perform one task—say, weaving or spinning—and that greater proficiency with time on the job meant they could make more of the product or tend more machines. In other industries—for example, the clothing industry of the above quotation—the work was dead-end in the sense that advancement could proceed from one stage of the sewing process to another. But a clearly defined upper limit existed that could be achieved in a few years and that was a piece-rate operation itself. In sewing, the upper limit for a woman was a buttonhole sewer, the ultimate female trade in apparel.

The returns to formal education, not surprisingly, were low in manufacturing and sales employment. Education, measured by years (or months) of schooling and literacy, was asked in two samples. Years of education had no impact on the earnings of manufacturing workers among women living apart from their families (1907 Women Adrift), and it had no added impact on sales workers in the same sample.[18] Months of education did increase the earnings of young women working in cotton textiles and clothing (1907 Single Women Workers). But literacy, more than months of education, was responsible for most of the increase, and the vast majority of these workers (86%) were literate. Literacy by itself served to increase earnings by 14%.

Women were unable to garner skill through training on the job, and formal education was of little value in their productivity in the manufacturing and sales sectors. It is no wonder, therefore, that the female work force of this era was termed unskilled. Yet the ratio of a worker's wage at her peak in earnings, at 10 years, to her beginning wage was 1.5; by definition, the ratio of an uneducated (but literate) beginner to an educated one was not much more than 1. Almost half the gain in earnings with time on the job was reached after just three years, and about 80% was achieved at five years. The training endowed these workers, therefore, was rapidly learned.[19]

The presence of young, single women in the labor force originally motivated the various labor surveys taken around 1900. Older, married women were still fewer than one-tenth of all employed women in 1900, and it would take another two to three decades for policymakers to focus attention on them. But because the 1907 Senate report was a comprehensive document, married, widowed, and divorced women were surveyed and are the subject of the 1907 Married Women Workers sample. Although the sample reveals less about skills than do the other surveys, it tells more about the nature of industrial home work and the role of the family. Experience and education variables are absent from the survey, but it includes information on the husband, the presence and ages of children, and whether work was performed in the home. The results are shown in Table 4.2.

Women who worked in their homes earned 47% less than did those who worked in factories, holding number of days worked fixed. Those who worked at home and had young children earned 15% less for each child under three years old. Children in general, however, did not affect the earnings of women who worked outside the home. The implication is that children did not alter the number of hours worked or the intensity of work, as long as the woman worked outside her home. Had hours of work been flexible around 1910, women with young children would probably have experienced the same decrease in earnings, given days worked, that married women do in more modern samples, and the number of women who worked would probably have been greater. Days of work differed only slightly by number of children. Women with young children worked about 25 days less in the factory than did those without young children, but they worked the same number of days at industrial home work. The large penalty in earnings for work done in the home, given days worked and family composition, may have been a compensatory differential for the greater flexibility of work and the absence of supervision in the home. But much, it seemed to those who analyzed the survey in 1910, was due to the inability of home-finishers to acquire training and use the machinery of the factory.

"WAGE DISCRIMINATION" IN MANUFACTURING

The circumstances that brought nationwide attention to female workers were virtually absent for the male labor force in the late nineteenth century. Male workers were older, their morals were of less concern, and they were paid considerably more than women. But male workers and their families were the subjects of various statistical surveys, and several were done by the same labor bureaus that surveyed female workers. The nation's concern with working men and their families in the Progressive era stemmed in large measure from the concentration of immigrants in industrial jobs. Surveys of California and Michigan workers by the state labor bureaus cover approximately the same ground as the surveys of female workers used above. These data sets enable the estimation of earnings functions similar to those in Table 4.1 and allow for the construction of the "wage discrimination" measure.

The difference in average (full-time) annual earnings between male and female factory operatives was substantial. Female operatives working full-time across the United States earned 54% of the average male operative in 1890, 55% in 1900, and 56% in 1905 (see Table 3.1). The ratio varies with the industrial composition of the work force as well as by state, and it is, in consequence, somewhat lower in the only state survey that contains both male and female workers, California, for which the ratio is only 46%.[20]

Part of the difference between the earnings of males and females can be attributed to the considerably longer work and occupational experience of the male labor force. Males, on average, had three times the total work experience of females, almost three times the duration in current occupation, and one and one-half times the years with current employer.[21] Much of the difference between the earnings of female and male workers might then be due to the considerably longer lifetime of work for men than women in the late nineteenth century, less so their greater attachment to particular firms. The longer duration on the job and at an occupation may, in turn, have been due to the greater ability of young men to obtain apprenticeships, either formal or informal.

The remaining portion of the difference in earnings would then result from how males and females were paid given their attributes. As is apparent from the discussion of female occupations in manufacturing, their job ladders were relatively short, and even though their wages rose rather steeply at first their earnings reached a plateau early. Males, however, had longer job ladders and garnered skills valued across firms and occupations. Because males and females were rewarded differently for the same characteristics, the resolution of why earnings differ given these characteristics must apply the technique described at the beginning of the chapter.

The measure of "wage discrimination" can be easily applied to the data on male and female earnings in manufacturing for the late nineteenth and early twentieth centuries. In the California sample, for which both female and male earnings are given, mean earnings of a female operative are $6.70 per week and those of a male are $14.69, yielding a ratio of 0.456. Had the average female worker been rewarded for her characteristics as if she were a male, her earnings would have been $8.81. The difference between the earnings of the male, $14.69, and those of the conjectural female, $8.81, is a consequence of his greater job, occupation, and firm experience. The difference between the earnings of a female worker, $6.70, and those of the conjectural female, divided by the difference in the earnings of male and female workers, is a measure of "wage discrimination," and is 35% in this case (using the log values).[22] "Wage discrimination" results from the differential evaluation of equivalent characteristics in the marketplace and from differences in the constant terms, here the earnings of a worker with no job experience. In this case, the measure is largely the result of the difference in earnings when work commenced. Increases in firm experience reduce, rather than widen, differences between the earnings of male and female workers for several years.

The result that firm and total experience reduce earnings differences is in marked contrast to that of modern studies and differs as well from that for clerical work in 1940. It can be understood with reference to Figure 4.2, which shows male and female earnings functions for the manufacturing sector under various assumptions.[23] Because males, but not females, received significantly higher earnings if they were married (17% in this sample), the proportion married is varied in the diagram; it is zero for the M line, and is the mean value in the sample for the M' line. The finding that being married augments the earnings of males, but not females, is consistent with almost all earnings studies using modern data.[24] The magnitude of the coefficient has been virtually stable over time, and is found in studies of all workers, of those in separate sectors, and of those in the United States as well as other countries. But the role of marriage in enhancing the earnings of male workers is still only dimly understood. The premium for modern data increases with duration of marriage and, therefore, has been attributed to greater intensity and effort of individuals with dependents (Korenman and Neumark, 1987). But researchers have not rejected the possibility that employers favor married men and promote them more often, independent of other characteristics. Survey data, presented below, for office workers in the Depression indicate that employers stated they paid married male workers more and promoted them with greater frequency.

The difference between male and female earnings is considerable (about 47%, when both groups are unmarried) at the outset of work experience but narrows until about 10 years. When all work experience is achieved at the same firm and in the same occupation, the difference narrows to 8%, comparing single male and female workers, and 14%, comparing them around the actual means for marital status. The difference is 28% and 34% when half the total work experience is at the current firm and occupation, given the same assumptions for marital status. The convergence of earnings over time occurs because the female earnings function rises steeply for several years, while the male function rises more slowly. Much depends on the

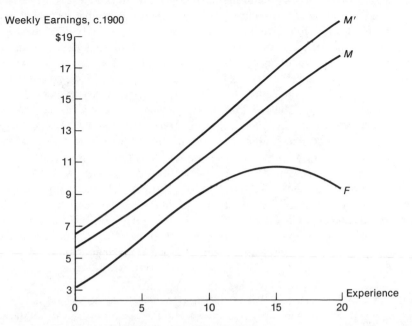

FIGURE 4.2. Earnings Functions in Manufacturing Employment, c. 1900. *Notes and Source:* See text. Line M is $w_m = \exp(1.75 - 0.1663 + 0.0849 \times E - 0.0014 \times E^2)$, where $E =$ years of work experience. Line $M' = [M + 0.1663 - (0.1663 \times \text{proportion single})]$, where proportion single in the sample is .65. Thus M is for unmarried men and M' is for the entire sample. Line F is: $w_f = \exp(1.14 + 0.1646 \times E - 0.0055 \times E^2)$. Other assumptions used are: experience is continuous at the firm and on the job, and all other variables are given by the means in the sample.

division of total work experience among its components. As in modern data, women's earnings rise more steeply within a firm than do men's earnings, but far less rapidly across firms and occupations.

　　With few exceptions, women workers were initially placed in jobs that utilized few prior skills, be they mental, physical, or those acquired at other firms. As they learned, they became more productive. But because their earnings were literally tied to their contemporaneous productivity through the use of piece rates, their earnings were a perfect reflection of their productivity. Males, however, were initially placed in jobs for which, often, brute strength was of importance or for which the job paid a premium to entice them to remain in an apprenticeship. Their earnings, therefore, did not reflect so clearly the learning stage, as did those of females.

　　The most curious finding in the late-nineteenth-century manufacturing data is that earnings differ most between males and females at the commencement of work and decrease with time on the job. The more usual finding since 1940, at least, and particularly for nonmanual jobs is that differences are small initially but widen with time. A central issue to resolve, therefore, is what accounts for the large initial difference in earnings in the manufacturing data.

　　One possibility is that male operatives were on average more productive than females because of greater strength or greater intensity of work in a sector that was still often primitive in its use of equipment. The issue of strength was probably a factor in the initial division of certain industries into the male- and female-intensive categories. Iron and steel, agricultural implements, and foundries began as male-intensive industries, while cotton textiles and apparel began as female intensive. Each may have adopted different types of capital equipment and work organization because of the initial sex composition in the nineteenth century. There were always women sufficiently strong, able, and driven to perform equally to a man in any industry, and the virtual absence of female operatives from certain industries suggests a number of other factors. It is likely that women were barred, in various obvious and subtle manners, from entering certain industries. Molders, for example, took an oath not to train female apprentices in foundries; women workers, prior to the strike of 1904, were prevented from entering slaughterhouses through various means and even after they gained entrance to work in the sausage rooms, they could not work in most others. Thus some of the difference between male and female earnings may be due to occupational barriers, the results of which can be seen in the extraordinary degree of sex segregation of industries and occupations around 1890 (see Chapter 3). But another part of the difference may be due to disparities in average strength and intensity of work.

Given the virtual absence of women in male-intensive industries and the very few occupations in which there were both males and females, it is difficult to judge the returns to strength and work intensity. There is, however, a small group of occupations that paid by the piece and had large groups of male and female workers within the same firm. In a sample of piece-rate occupations, males earned 25% more than females, even when the work was identical, the piece rate was the same, and both worked for the same firm.[25] For the compositors in Table 3.6, the figure is about 35%. But although both males and females in the sample were more than 18 years old, there is nothing else that can be held constant. It is conceivable, therefore, that male workers were better trained and that part of the 25% difference is due to differences in experience and training that should already be accounted for in the "wage discrimination" partition. But even in unskilled, menial work, for which women of greater strength must have been selected and for which training was unnecessary, men earned about 15% more on average than women.[26]

Some of the initial difference in earnings, reflected in the piece rate data, was due to differences in strength. But piece-rate occupations are not well suited to measure differences in strength because occupations relying most heavily on strength were generally male, for reasons of custom, Victorian morality, or real differences in the male and female populations. In consequence, the piece-rate data probably give a lower bound to the actual differential across all jobs.

The 15% figure can be taken as a lower bound for initial differences in productivity in manufacturing. Initial differences are built into the earnings of workers with no work experience, but ought not be blamed on "wage discrimination." Adjusting the constant term for females by 15% raises average earnings in the example above to $7.78 (from $6.70) and narrows the unexplained portion to slightly more than $1.00, or 19.5% of the difference in the logs of male and female earnings.

Even at its initial, unadjusted level of 35%, "wage discrimination" in manufacturing around 1900 was slight in comparison with that found in more recent studies. At its adjusted level of 19.5%, "wage discrimination" in the manufacturing sector was extremely low.[27] Modern, empirical discrimination studies, summarized above, generally find that "wage discrimination" accounts for at least 55% of the difference in the logs of male and female earnings. An unexplained difference of 55% is hard to rationalize by the absence of various factors that are difficult to measure or are unobserved. One of 19.5% seems far easier to explain by such omission, particularly since it is for a sector in which strength demands, intensity of work, and the work environment may have favored male over female workers.

The low ratio of earnings of females to males in late-nineteenth-century manufacturing jobs was due largely to differences in attributes, primarily job experience, despite the extraordinary segregation of industries and occupations between the sexes. But attribute differences may, in turn, be due to discriminatory factors. It has already been noted that young women had few incentives to work hard. They kept very little of their own earnings, they stood almost no chance of being promoted, and their work taught them little of use outside their particular factory. Not surprisingly, they looked to marriage and a home of their own as an escape. Occupational and industrial sex segregation may have had little net effect on the ratio of female to male earnings, but sex segregation may not be as benign as the data on "wage discrimination" imply.

Clerical Sector, 1940

In an autobiographical story written around 1905, Dorothy Richardson described her life as a working girl (O'Neill, 1972; orig. publ. 1905).[28] She began work in New York City at the age of 18, after leaving her home in western Pennsylvania. She worked in a paper-box factory, made artificial flowers, tried to become a sewing-machine operator when the season for flowers ended, worked in a jewelry factory, as a shaker in a steam laundry, and finally as a saleswoman, all in a period of about five years. In each case, "the chief obstacle," she noted, "seemed to be . . . inexperience. I could obtain plenty of work which in time promised to pay five dollars a week, but in the two or three months' time necessary to acquire dexterity I should have starved to death" (pp. 44–45). After several years in manufacturing and sales jobs, which eventually paid her eight dollars a week, she enrolled in night school and became a stenographer. Her 60 weeks of night school gave her commercial skills and general training in spelling and grammar. The payoff was enormous; she became, in her words, "prosperous."

Richardson's story, whether true or not and despite its polemical style, is an almost faithful narrative account of the findings just presented. Her earnings in manufacturing and sales work were low, rose rapidly with job experience, increased with experience at an occupation as opposed to total job experience, but reached an upper limit rather quickly. She had, however, considerably less continuity on the job than women in the various samples. But Richardson lived apart from her family, and her search for housing often disrupted her work. She titled the story "The Long Day" to dramatize the exceptionally long hours and hard labor of factory workers.

Education and the growth of clerical work were her ultimate salvation. Had the story been written 50 years later, it could not have been a more apt parable about the eventual changes in the female labor force and its increase over time.

The character of the story was unique in ambition and ability. Fewer than 20% of the young women in Richardson's birth cohort (presumed to be 1880) eventually completed high school, and their mean education was less than eight years. In the period from 1900 to 1920, the percentage of young women graduating from high school doubled, and the demand for clerical workers in the nation's firms soared. The experience of this one individual was to become that of the entire female labor force; increased education and changes in the sectoral shares of the economy transformed the female labor force. Education and the demand for an educated labor force enabled women workers to increase their earnings and better their working conditions. That, in turn, increased the proportion of women in the labor force and the fraction who would remain in it over the life cycle.

CLERICAL WORK AND CLERICAL WORKERS

The share of all female workers in the clerical sector expanded from just 4% to 21% over the period 1890 to 1930. The clerical sector had been 15% female in 1890 but was more than 50% by 1930, and while male employment in the sector rose as well, the proportion of all employed men in the sector increased trivially, from 3% to 6%. The clerical sector grew primarily by hiring female workers. Many were fresh out of high school and in previous decades would have worked in the nation's factories and retail stores, like the young women in the surveys discussed above. The attraction of the office to young women, or as Sophonisba Breckinridge put it, "the ambition of the school girl to 'work in an office' in preference to work in a factory" (1933, p. 181), is not hard to understand. Factory work was strenuous, confining, often dirty, and frequently hazardous, and it yielded almost no return to education. With the increase in schooling across the United States and with even larger proportions of young women than young men completing high school, there was a large pool of potential clerical workers. If men had a comparative advantage in manufacturing, women possessed it in the clerical sector.

Clerical employment did more than expand during the early twentieth century. It was transformed by a process often likened to the Industrial Revolution. The nineteenth-century clerk was a trusted employee with diverse tasks; a secretary was the confidant of the company president (thus the origins of the word). Both learned the entire operations of the firm, and both could eventually be promoted to head. As firms grew in size, they required larger clerical staffs, and growth encouraged a division of labor reminiscent of that in manufacturing. The division of labor was, in turn, facilitated by the development of machinery beginning with the typewriter. The typewriter, developed in the 1870's, was almost immediately adopted by American businesses, but it was an idea that had been around for some time (Davies, 1982). Bookkeeping, accounting, duplicating, and other machines were invented with the increased demand for mechanization. Mechanization in the clerical sector, as in manufacturing, led to the specialization of tasks and decreased the necessity to hire skilled individuals, capable of learning the firm's entire operation. The growth of commercial schools and commercial classes in high schools allowed firms to hire entry-level personnel who needed little additional training and who could be put to work at a job from which they would never be promoted.[29]

In the early history of the modern office, certain tasks were paid by the piece, as in manufacturing. Typewriters in the Graton and Knight Manufacturing Company, for example, were equipped with cyclometers, "240 depressions of the typewriter keys or space bar [were] equivalent to one point . . . 600 points [were] considered base production and each point produced in excess [was] allowed for at the rate of one and one-half cents a point" (Coyle, 1928, pp. 23–24). But piece rates did not prevail, and their decline was a tribute to the ability of employers to pretest workers whose training in commercial and high-school courses was completed before job entry. Standardization enabled employers to screen workers prior to employment. Commonwealth Edison Company, for example, claimed its stenographers, typists, and dictaphone operators were "classed by temperament and ability. A dictator when he needs a girl telephones to the central bureau and one is sent who is adapted to his kind of work" (Coyle, 1928, p. 23).

Most of the new occupations in the transformed clerical sector were designed for the female employee who had previously been a manufacturing worker. She was young and single, and was presumed to have little interest in remaining in the labor force after marriage. But she now also had a high-school diploma and often commercial courses. Typists, stenographers, and office-machine operators were generally hired directly out of high school, while secretaries and those in the accounting group were frequently selected from among the general clerks. Occupations that hired directly out of high school were predominantly female, while those for which the firm promoted from within were primarily male. Most of the new occupations rapidly became feminized, while many of the older occupations remained in the hands of male workers.

Increased mechanization, greater division of labor, and an expanded supply of educated Americans all served to lower earnings of clerical workers relative to others from 1890 to 1930 and to reduce the gender gap in the sector. The average female clerical worker earned about 1.5 what the average female manufacturing operative did in 1890, but earned 1.25 of the manufacturing wage in 1930 (see Table 3.2). The decline for males is considerably more pronounced. The average male clerical worker earned 1.6 what his manufacturing counterpart did in 1890, but both earned about the same amount by 1930. The ratio of female to male earnings in the clerical sector rose from 0.49 in 1890 to 0.71 by 1930 (see Table 3.2), and the increase served to buoy the average ratio of female to male earnings in the economy. Much of the increase in the economy-wide ratio resulted from a rewarding of individuals more for brains than brawn. These changes appear to signal that the labor market moved in a progressive and possibly emancipating fashion for women. Evidence on the earnings and individual characteristics of clerical workers can assess that notion by computing the degree of "wage discrimination."

EARNINGS OF CLERICAL WORKERS

With the close of the Progressive era, the Department of Labor and its state counterparts discontinued their surveys of the earnings and working conditions of women. The labor of single women and immigrant families was no longer of interest to the nation, and the studies end before the late 1910's and 1920's, when the clerical sector began its rapid rise. The Women's Bureau, established at the close of World War I in 1920, began where the various bureaus of labor left off in a series of important studies of women workers. Two of the studies, one for 1931 and the other for 1940, concern office workers, both men and women, and individual-level schedules survive for the 1940 survey.[30]

A sample of the schedules, called here the 1940 Office Worker Survey, was collected for one city (Philadelphia) and is described in the Data Appendix. It contains more than 1,200 individuals, about 700 women and 500 men. Detailed information was requested by Women's Bureau agents on education, work experience, earnings, occupation, unemployment, and various personal characteristics, such as marital status. Information on occupation and earnings was obtained for both initial and current work status at the firm. The relationship between earnings and individual characteristics is estimated for males and females separately, as in the manufacturing sample, and is given in Table 4.3.

Male clerical workers, like their counterparts in manufacturing, acquired more marketable skills when employed than did their female co-workers. Each year of total experience augmented male earnings more than female earnings, so that a male who changed jobs after five years of employment earned 11% more for his years of prior work than a female, and 19% if he changed jobs after 10 years.[31] The value of the worker to the current firm, however, increased equally for males and females with additional years of experience, although the increase for females depends critically on their continuity with an employer. Education augmented earnings by more than 3% for each year of school. A college diploma yielded 11% for males but 7% for females, and years of college (not shown) yielded 6% per year for males, while females received only 3%. Married men earned on average 12% more than single men, but marital status had virtually no impact on female earnings.

Clerical work was cleaner and less strenuous than manufacturing work and generally paid more (see Table 3.2). It also led to more enduring and transferrable skills and rewarded the increased schooling that had become a national norm. It is understandable why young women preferred office work and why the growth of the clerical sector would lead to the continued employment of women after marriage and childbearing. Recall that manufacturing employment yielded virtually no return to education beyond literacy and that female earnings were heavily penalized for changes in occupation and firm. Female workers in manufacturing who changed both firm and occupation retained only 20% of their increased earnings, but those in the clerical sector kept more than 60%.[32] The average educational attainment of female clerical employees added 22% more to their earnings than had they been manufacturing workers.[33] Finally, the evidence from the 1940 Office Worker Survey indicates that time spent out of the labor force, presumably because of family responsibilities, led to a decrease in women's earnings of 1.6% per year, a figure comparable with that in studies using modern data (Mincer and Polachek, 1974). The penalty was, therefore, somewhat low, particularly in comparison with that implied by the manufacturing data.

If the considerable difference in the earnings of males and females in manufacturing was largely due to rewards to strength, then the replacement of brain for

TABLE 4.3. Determinants of Earnings Among Male and Female Office Workers, 1940

| | Full-time Annual Earnings | | Means | |
| | Male Office | Female Office | Males | Females |
Variable	Workers	Workers	[7.42]	[6.98]
Constant	6.272	6.281		
	(83.1)	(84.2)		
Work experience				
Total experience	0.0521	0.0290	16.0	10.9
	(12.9)	(9.43)		
(Total experience)$^2 \times 10^{-2}$	−0.0864	−0.0441		
	(10.8)	(5.19)		
Current firm experience	0.0156	−0.0025	13.2	8.3
	(3.40)	(0.72)		
Continuity × firm	−0.0032	0.0166	12.5	7.4
experience	(0.80)	(5.99)		
Years laid off	−0.0434	−0.0124	0.10	0.15
	(2.35)	(1.31)		
Years at home		−0.0159		0.51
		(3.35)		
Education and personal				
Married	0.115	0.0225	0.55	0.23
	(3.93)	(1.17)		
Years education	0.0354	0.0305	11.7	11.5
	(5.40)	(4.44)		
High-school graduate	0.0192	0.0151	0.60	0.64
	(0.60)	(0.59)		
College graduate	0.111	0.0688	0.13	0.05
	(2.88)	(1.65)		
R^2	.675	.517		
Number of observations	482	724		

Notes and Sources: See Data Appendix for description of the 1940 Office Worker Survey. The dependent variable is the natural logarithm of full-time annual earnings. Means are in brackets. Full-time earnings are wages paid per last time period worked multiplied by the number of time periods per year. Total experience = experience with current firm + experience at other office jobs + experience at jobs other than offices; Continuity = 1 if work with current firm were continuous; Years at home = years since began all office work − years experience with current firm − years prior office experience. Other variables entered: vocational-school graduate; dummy variable for commercial course taken. Absolute values of *t*-statistics are in parentheses.

brawn work should have evened starting salaries. Beginning salaries were, in fact, narrowed in office work to the point of being indistinguishable statistically. The actual difference in beginning salaries for clerical work, given prior work experience and education, was about 5%.[34] Although the difference in starting salaries implied by the earnings functions between unmarried male and female clerical workers was negligible, it was 47% in manufacturing. While beginning earnings in office work were virtually neutral to sex, the gap widened with every subsequent year, as demonstrated in Figure 4.3. A comparison of the manufacturing and the clerical earnings diagrams reveals dissimilar explanations for differences in earnings between the sexes.

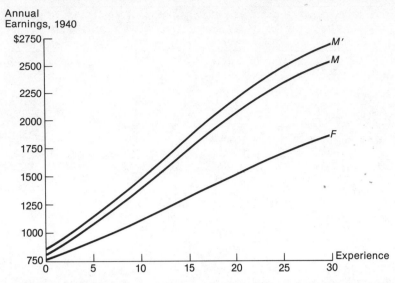

FIGURE 4.3. Earnings Functions in Office Work, 1940. *Notes and Source:* Coefficients are from Table 4.3. Line M is: $w_m = \exp(6.272 + 0.0645 \times E - 0.000864 \times E^2 + 0.0354 \times S)$, where E = years of work experience and S = years of schooling, here 11.5. Line $M' = (M + 0.115 \times$ proportion married), where proportion married in the sample is .55. Thus M is for unmarried men and M' is for the entire sample. Line F is: $w_f = \exp(6.281 + 0.0431 \times E - 0.000441 \times E^2 + 0.0305 \times S)$, where years of schooling is again 11.5. Other assumptions used are: work experience is the same as tenure with the firm; there is continuity on the job; there are no breaks in employment or years at home taken by women; the furlough variable is zero; and the values of all other variables are given by the means in the sample.

Male workers in the clerical survey had approximately the same work experience as those in the manufacturing sample (16 years) but began work at an older age (around 18 years). They also had more continuous time with the current firm than in the earlier sample. Fully 13 of their 16 years in the labor force, or 83%, were spent with their current employer, although the Depression of the 1930's may have served to reduce their mobility across firms (recall that the survey was taken in 1940). Female clerical workers had about 11 years of total work experience on average, of which 75% was spent with their current employer. They had, therefore, almost 70% the total work experience of male employees and 63% of their time with the current firm. Job tenure in clerical work was far more similar between men and women than was work in manufacturing some 30 years earlier. Education was also similar: mean years of schooling were about 11.5 for both, with 62% completing high school; but more than twice as many men than women had college degrees.

"WAGE DISCRIMINATION" IN CLERICAL WORK

Given these similarities, it should not be surprising that adjusting for attribute differences explains only 39% of the initial difference in the log of earnings (an average of 28% and 49%).[35] The value is considerably lower than those of 65% and 81.5% computed using the manufacturing data. The conjectural female clerical worker, paid for her job attributes as a man, would have earned $1,333 per year (in 1940 dollars) rather than the $1,075 she actually did. The average male earned $1,669 per year. The conjectural female, therefore, earned 24% more than she did when rewarded as a woman, and had she been paid as a man the ratio of earnings would have closed to 80% (1,333/1,669) from 64% (1,075/1,669).

Figure 4.3 reveals that two major factors caused female and male earnings to deviate. One is the 12% premium to marriage for men but not women that has already been mentioned. The other is the greater increase in earnings with work experience for men. Men advanced with each passing year more so than women, without any obvious increase in training investment. Earnings were virtually identical for men and women at their initial hire. Men, apparently, did not defer earnings early in their careers to reap higher returns later; they earned higher returns at all levels of work experience.

Women earned 14% less than men of equal schooling and job experience after five years at work, and a single (or married) woman with five years of experience earned 26% less than an equally trained married man. Although years of schooling enhanced earnings about equally for both sexes, college education was worth considerably more for men. The best educated and best trained women earned the least in comparison with their equally trained male counterparts. "Wage discrimination" widened with each year of job experience and each year of education beyond high school. The difference between unmarried male and female college graduates with five years of work experience was 21% and was 33% between a married man and a woman.

Male and female clerical workers began their work careers with apparently similar skills, but males were placed on a different track. The resulting occupational distribution was highly segregated at the upper end, while beginning positions were often integrated. Advancement to secretary for most women clerical workers was the highest achievable rank, and although secretaries earned 40% more than typists, they were paid considerably less than comparably experienced men.

Although the estimates I have produced for the clerical sector around 1940 indicate "wage discrimination" of nearly identical magnitude as found in modern studies, various econometric complications must be acknowledged. In particular, the problem of errors in variables can produce upwardly biased estimates of "wage discrimination." The direction of bias from errors in variables is usually unknown a priori, but in this case it is almost certain to overstate "wage discrimination" (see Hashimoto and Kochin, 1980). The magnitude of the bias will depend on various factors, including the degree to which education, experience, and other relevant variables accurately measure productivity, and the way in which the productivity variables are correlated with sex.

The upward bias to "wage discrimination" could be substantial. But additional evidence indicates that that outcome is unlikely, at least for the period under consideration. There is ample proof that women were excluded by firm policy from virtually all office jobs involving substantial advancement within the firm. Thus the empirical measure of "wage discrimination" is not a statistical artifact of errors in

TABLE 4.4.   Job Restrictions by Sex Among Firms Hiring Office Workers, 1940

Number of Restricted Occupations	Males			Females		
	Firms	Weighted	Average Number of Employees	Firms	Weighted	Average Number of Employees
0	30%	30%	162	26%	21%	191
1	20	11	120	16	13	195
2	21	31	248	21	17	183
3	14	14	207	25	39	211
4	6	6	207	8	4	80
≥ 5	9	7	238	4	6	228

Notes and Sources: 1940 Office Firm Survey. See Data Appendix and Chapter 6. The number of restricted occupations are those listed that were restricted to "men only" or to "women only" on the basis of firm policy. The ≥ 5 row for males also includes the restriction that "all jobs are for men only"; if the firm indicated "all clerical jobs are for women," the restriction for females was set to 3. The weighted columns use the numbers of male or female employees as the weight. The analysis here is limited to the 260 firms with more than 19 employees, having at least 1 female and 1 male worker. Columns may not add to 100% because of rounding error.

variables. Women could not have achieved the male earnings function because they were barred from most jobs with promotional possibilities. The evidence regarding firm-level policies is probably unique to the period examined when discrimination on the basis of sex and marital status was not illegal and when it was often considered public-spirited because of the Depression. It is likely that firms had similar policies before and after the Depression (see also Chapter 6).

Women were prohibited from entering various clerical positions through the personnel policies of most firms, and, as will be detailed in Chapter 6, married women were barred from many of the largest and highest paying firms. The firm-level records of the Women's Bureau study, just used to measure "wage discrimination," termed here the 1940 Office Firm Survey, contain answers to two questions concerning occupations reserved for men and for women by firm policy. The precise questions were "Which [office] jobs are open to men only?" and "Which [office] jobs are open to women only?" The distributions of the number of jobs from which men and women were excluded, among 260 firms with more than 19 employees, are given in Table 4.4.

Across the three large cities in the sample, 74% of all firms had formal policies restricting occupations to "women only," and these restrictions affected 79% of the female employees in the sample.[36] Formal rules concerning the occupations reserved for men were adopted by 70% of the firms sampled, affecting 70% of male employees. Firms generally had both forms of exclusion. Only 13% had just the female exclusion and only 9% had just the male exclusion, while 61% had both and 17% had neither restriction. The exclusions, it appears from the data in Table 4.4, were not related to the size of firm, at least given the stipulation on the minimum number of employees.

Firms often excluded men from the dead-end positions of stenographer, typist, and telephone, switchboard, and comptometer operators, while women were excluded from a variety of occupations. Firms barred women from occupations of authority (executive, department head), and from those for which high skill was required (engineer, draftsman). They often prohibited women from entering the accounting division (accountant, teller, collector, cost controller, paymaster), to which men were often advanced when they demonstrated initiative and drive in the unskilled jobs. But firms also barred women from the unskilled entry-level positions of mail boy, errand boy, and messenger. New York Life Insurance Company considered male office boys a "source of future staff," and Philadelphia Transportation Company likewise hired male messengers "because they are source of raw material" (1940 Office Firm Survey).

Policies that prohibited women from taking positions of authority and those demanding skill might be easily explained, as might those that barred women from certain entry-level positions. But the policy of barring men from dead-end occupations requires further thought. One possibility is that these jobs paid more than many entry-level positions reserved for men (e.g., mail boy, messenger). But because the female occupations were dead-end, management may have wanted to bar men who might become discouraged, demand advancement, and in the process awaken female employees to their lack of mobility. The *Philadelphia Record*, for example, hired only female steno- and bookkeeping-machine operators because "they are not so anxious to get a higher job, they take more interest in the work." The American Baptist Publication Society would not hire males in certain jobs because there was "nowhere for a man to advance" (1940 Office Firm Survey).

Although there were some office jobs that paid women relatively well and that allowed for advancement in the firm and over the life cycle (secretary, bookkeeper), women were virtually barred from advancement in most firms surveyed. At the time of their hire, most female office workers were channeled into dead-end occupations that allowed virtually no progress with time on the job (typist, stenographer, certain clerks). Others began in various clerical positions and would reach their final occupational destination in several years. The end result is the "wage discrimination" computed from the survey data.

The internal labor market mechanism that firms used is partly revealed by considering the earnings equations for men and women in Table 4.5. Two equations are given for men and women in the lower-skilled occupations, the entry points for almost all the men. Another equation is for females in typing and stenography, lesser-skilled jobs only rarely occupied by male employees. The last two equations are for men and women in the higher-skilled occupations, which drew their talents from the lower-skilled pool. Both lower- and higher-skilled occupations gave men about the same rewards for time on the job, in total and with the present firm, and both rewarded education about the same. The movement to the upper-level occupations for the men was a shift upward in the earnings function; a movement in the intercept rather than the slope.[37] For women, however, promotion changed the return to each year of work and involved a higher return to education. Compared with that for the men, the slope of the earnings function is flatter for women in the unskilled occupations, and although the return to experience increases for women in the more skilled occupations, it is still below that for men.

Before promotion, there is a 14% gap between the earnings of single male and female employees with equal job experience and education. Just after promotion, the gap widens to 40%. Thus much of the unexplained difference between the earnings of male and female office workers reflects differences in promotion. And

TABLE 4.5.   Earnings Functions for Unskilled and Skilled Office Workers, 1940

Variable	Lower Skilled Full-time Annual Earnings		Typist, Steno Full-time Annual Earnings	Higher Skilled Full-time Annual Earnings	
	Males	Females	Females	Males	Females
Constant	6.17	6.19	6.48	6.50	5.72
	(69.5)	(52.3)	(69.9)	(58.6)	(34.6)
Total experience	0.0461	0.0287	0.0238	0.0456	0.0384
	(10.1)	(3.59)	(4.22)	(6.86)	(4.19)
(Total experience)^2 × 10^{-2}	−0.0709	−0.0590	−0.0390	−0.0800	−0.0719
	(7.85)	(2.15)	(1.95)	(6.02)	(3.71)
Current firm experience	0.0121	0.0144	0.0134	0.0102	0.0189
	(3.75)	(3.14)	(4.26)	(2.57)	(2.68)
Years education	0.0426	0.0347	0.0205	0.0321	0.0640
	(6.39)	(3.85)	(2.97)	(4.87)	(5.52)
Married	0.083	0.0162	−0.030	0.181	0.134
	(2.34)	(0.41)	(1.14)	(3.94)	(2.38)
R^2	.725	.464	.381	.514	.536
Number of observations	204	187	338	237	121

Notes and Sources: 1940 Office Worker Survey. The dependent variable is the natural logarithm of full-time annual earnings. Full-time earnings are wages paid per last time period worked multiplied by the number of time periods per year. Total experience = experience with current firm + experience at other office jobs + experience at jobs other than offices. Lower-skilled occupations are messenger, mail boy, various lower-skilled clerks, mimeo-machine operators, and so on. The typist-steno column also includes various machine operators. Higher-skilled include professionals, supervisors, those in the accounting group, and so on. The lower-skilled and higher-skilled groups were chosen for comparability between male and female office workers; very few men in the sample were typists and stenographers. Absolute values of *t*-statistics are in parentheses.

much of the difference in promotion reflects barriers to women's occupational advancement.

The Origins of "Wage Discrimination"

Why the clerical sector should reveal substantial "wage discrimination" when the manufacturing sector did not has much to do with changes in the way work was organized from the late nineteenth century to the early twentieth. Manufacturing jobs and many others in the nineteenth century were part of what I shall term the "spot market." Workers were generally paid their value to the firm at each instant, or what economists call the value of labor's marginal product. The easiest illustration of a spot wage is that of the piece-rate worker. There is no clearer case of an individual who is paid her marginal product at every instant in time. Any training undertaken by the worker while on the job reduces the number of pieces made, and thus reduces earnings in exact proportion to product forgone; any time lost due to sickness, absence, or firm closing is also reflected in decreased earnings in a precise relation to the decrease in product. Almost half of all female operatives in manufacturing were paid by piece in 1890, and a large percentage of males in various industries were also piece-rate workers (see Table 3.4). But even those who were paid by time and not by piece were probably "spot laborers." Certainly the large numbers of male day laborers were. With the exception of various highly skilled occupations, such as steel puddlers, most manufacturing jobs were easily learned; with the exception of jobs like supervisor, most could be handled by the average entrant. Firms often hired new entrants on time, and in a week or so the foreman (and often the worker) could assess the worker's ability to handle the job. The incompetent were speedily weeded out from the able, and the novice was quickly trained. Training, moreover, was often paid in its entirety by the worker.

The "spot market" gave way to one of internal labor markets and longer-term implicit contracts characteristic of jobs in the twentieth century.[38] Clerical jobs that emerged in the 1910's and moved into maturity in the 1920's and 1930's were not as simply remunerated as those in manufacturing. The product of individual laborers was less clear, and even when it could be ascertained, as in the use of piece rates in the typing example above, the costs of monitoring output were excessive. Counting cigars, coats, shoes, and glassware was less costly than counting letters typed, transactions handled, and clients serviced. Further, because piece rates encouraged only quantity, even manufacturing jobs that demanded quality rarely paid by the piece (Pencavel, 1977).[39]

Many office skills, such as typing and stenography, were taught off the job in commercial schools, and this allowed the firm to screen applicants easily. But many skills could not be judged in advance. A secretary in the 1920's, for example, used the skills of the typist and stenographer but had to be considerably more competent. Firms, therefore, screened women in lower-level jobs for secretarial positions. The accounting group, primarily male, was selected from a group of undistinguished clerks and office boys, for whom the possibility of advancement increased the effort and intensity of their work.

Firms used promotion to upper-level jobs to elicit optimal effort and loyalty from workers at the lower level. One personnel officer in the 1920's noted, and not facetiously, that when a vice president died, he hired another mail boy. The mail boy may have learned much about the corporation on his way up the ladder, but he also worked harder at each rung knowing that increasingly lucrative rungs lay ahead. The majority of the firms in the 1940 Women's Bureau office survey stated they preferred to hire young, inexperienced workers and to promote from within. Many, like a respondent from Universal Pictures, preferred internal promotion because the policy created "loyal co-operative employees." The carrots of advancement in white-collar jobs replaced the sticks of dismissal in blue-collar jobs.

Another difference between manufacturing and clerical employment was investment in skills. It has already been noted that clerical employment rewarded formal education, while manufacturing employment generally did not. Most learning in manufacturing was on the job, and much was specific to the industry and the job but not to the firm. The returns to occupational experience were substantial, particularly for women, but there were virtually no returns to experience with a particular firm, or what is generally called "tenure." Returns to tenure indicate the existence of skills specific to a particular firm that are nontransferable and thus evaporate when the worker switches firms. Because the skills are unique to a particular firm, they are termed "specific human capital" (Becker, 1975). The costs of specific human capital are often shared between the worker and the firm due to the inherent risks to each in undertaking the investment. An increase in specific human capital, therefore, is another reason why firms would want to increase worker loyalty and decrease turnover. It provides another instance of how the change from the manufacturing jobs of the nineteenth century to the white-collar jobs of the twentieth was a movement from the spot market to the market of longer-run implicit contracts.

The evolution of the modern labor market owes much to the emergence of personnel departments in firms of all types (Edwards, 1979; Jacoby, 1985; Nelson, 1975). Personnel departments wrested control from foremen in manufacturing and from department heads elsewhere. The centralization of hiring, firing, and promotion ensured the long-run objectives of management, often at variance with those of foremen and department heads. Wages, hours, benefits, and the other components of the earnings package were no longer just part of the market-clearing mechanism of the labor market. They were the means by which workers were bonded to firms and were used to sort workers by ability or quit propensity and to elicit appropriate effort by different types of workers.

Personnel departments and various firm policies governing labor relations emerged at the close of World War I for several reasons. Primary among the factors are those that concern general changes in the labor market. The late-nineteenth-century labor market was characterized by periods of substantial unemployment, particularly in the industrial sectors of large American cities. On the eve of World War I, unemployment was 8.5% for the entire nation, and it was considerably higher in cities and industrial areas. But unemployment plummeted after the American entry into the war and remained low for most of the 1920's. Labor in the United States had been plentiful, particularly during periods of rapid immigration, such as between the 1890's and 1914. But the war restricted international movements of labor, and, in its aftermath, the legislation of the 1920's permanently reduced the flow. Turnover rates in manufacturing soared in the extremely tight labor market of the wartime period, and turnover, more than any other single factor, claimed economist Paul Douglas (1919), led to the creation of personnel departments and the wholesale revision of personnel practices. It is likely, however, that the special features of the World War I labor market only hastened change that was already being fostered by alterations in the nature of work and skill.

With the establishment of personnel departments came various work rules and salary schedules. Firms found it profitable to have occupational ladders, within which individuals were promoted when they revealed particular abilities, and the chance of promotion may have altered the effort of workers. Because men and women had different expected lifetimes on the job, firms may have found it profitable to segregate them in different beginning and ending jobs.

Even though many women would eventually be in the labor force for an extensive duration, firms often used sex as a signal of shorter expected job tenure. Employers may have found it difficult to ascertain which women workers would remain for long periods of time and which would quit early. By segregating workers by sex into two jobs ladders (and some dead-end positions), firms may have been better able to use the effort-inducing and ability-revealing mechanisms of the wage structure (see Lazear and Rosen, 1989, for an example of this factor in a model of job investment). But the expected shorter duration of female workers need not have been the only reason for segregating workers by sex and for barring women from entering certain occupations and men from others.

Women may have been barred from managerial and supervisory positions by the prejudices of male workers, employers, and even customers. Because men had dominated occupations in the accounting group prior to the large influx of women, they may have maintained their positions by having firms bar women. A sex-discrimination case brought by the EEOC, and lost by State Farm Insurance Company in January 1988, reveals that barriers to women claims agents in the insurance sector were effective over extensive periods of time (*New York Times*, January 20, 1988). Another possibility, supported by narrative evidence, is that clients, particularly in the banking and insurance sectors, discriminated against female workers. Firms rapidly replaced male bank tellers with female tellers after World War II only after clients realized during the war that women could be trustworthy tellers (Strober and Arnold, 1987).

Women were also barred in the manufacturing sector by subtle as well as by more obvious means, as in the case of the molders described above. But the results of discrimination in manufacturing took the form of differences in the industrial distribution of workers and, to a lesser extent, earnings differences, holding constant individual characteristics. Barriers to the higher-skilled apprenticeships may have had less of an impact on female earnings given their relatively short duration in the labor force. Where wages served primarily to clear the labor market and where individuals were often paid their value to the firm at every instant, "wage discrimination" was less evident.[40]

In the white-collar sector, however, wages and occupations served other purposes and the penalty for short duration in the labor force was more severe. Firms found it advantageous to segment the labor force and create different lifetime jobs for groups with different average lifetime attachments to the labor force. While many young women may have desired positions, such as typist, stenographer, and telephone operator, that required little job investment and had little responsibility, there were others who, it is certain, would have relished the 61% they lost, on average, because they could climb no higher than secretary.

The increase in job experience of women, noticeable across the two periods examined here, may have been due, in part, to the depression economy of the 1930's. The proportion of women who never married soared during the Depression, as did the age at first marriage, while the number of births fell. Even though the age at leaving school increased, so did work experience. Some of the increase may not have been anticipated, and thus some of the measured "wage discrimination" may be due to incorrect job placement given improper work expectations. But because the level of "wage discrimination" found in the clerical sector in 1940 is almost identical to that found in equally rich data sets of the 1970's and 1980's, it is likely that the results reveal more about longer-term change and less about the peculiarities of the 1930's.

Summary: "Wage Discrimination"

"Wage discrimination" rose from at most 20% of the difference in male and female earnings around 1900 in manufacturing to 55% in office work in 1940. The origins of "wage discrimination" are thus to be found in various policies that transformed labor from the spot market of the manufacturing sector to the wage-setting arena of modern firms, in which earnings do not contemporaneously equal a worker's value to the firm. These conscious policies were designed to elicit appropriate effort, to screen for suitable employees, and to bind employees to the firm, among other reasons. Promotion from within, adopted by most large firms in the Women's Bureau 1940 sample, enabled managers to alter worker effort and select for the most able among large groups of workers. There was, as well, real training both on and off the job.

In this newly established labor arena, female white-collar workers were treated differently from men for several reasons. Firms in office work and in manufacturing found it profitable to treat women not as individuals, but as a group. As a group, they were less likely to aspire to positions of responsibility; as a group, they were less likely to remain in the labor force. But because women could conceivably enter the male occupational track in office work—they did, after all, commence work with identical earnings—they would have to be barred from certain occupations if firms (or their employees) did not want them to enter. The situation differed from the manufacturing sector. Formal barriers were infrequently encountered there. Instead, actual requirements, say, strength and various normative influences that defined certain industries as male only, deterred women from requesting entry. The fact that so many entire industries had no female operatives suggests the force of societal norms in the manufacturing sector. In office work, however, such appeal could not be made, and both men and women were instead barred by firm policy from certain occupations.

The overall impact of the new labor policies was to have consciously sex-segregated occupations. Differences in expected tenure on the job may have been responsible for some distinctions in the job ladders offered men and women. But these differences were reinforced by a long history of occupational segregation and by a society that had formed a consensus around the virtue of sex segregation and the appropriateness of differentiating on the basis of sex. They were also enabled by the absence of an opposing ideology that would eventually lead women as individuals to become discontent with their treatment as a group.

Household Production in the Early Nineteenth Century. Spinning and weaving were household crafts that swiftly moved to the factory in the early nineteenth century, along with young women. *(Courtesy of the National Archives)*

Agricultural Labor. "A Negro woman hoeing cotton. She was born a slave two years before the surrender." This timeless photograph could be of a sharecropper, a wage laborer, or a renter, as easily as it could be of a slave a century before. Photograph by Dorothea Lange from the Farm Security Administration collection, Mississippi, June 1937. *(Courtesy of the Library of Congress, USF 34-17324-C)*

Agricultural Labor. "The wife of a farmer picking cotton." Farm women, especially white farm wives, were vastly undercounted in the labor force by the census, even though they produced cash crops. Photograph by Russell Lee from the Farm Security Administration collection, Arkansas, September 1938. *(Courtesy of the Library of Congress, USF 33-11670-M4)*

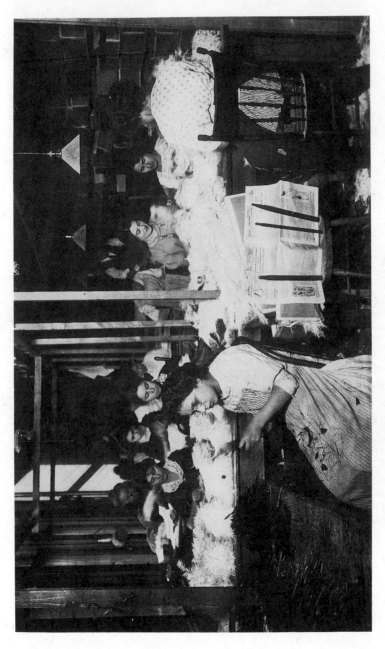

Female-Intensive Industry, c. 1910. Women working in a feather shop. The seasons for artificial flowers and feathers meshed, and workers in this shop probably made artificial flowers in the summer. Both groups served brief apprenticeships after which their earnings often doubled. Experienced feather and artificial-flower workers were paid primarily by the piece, and many did industrial home work. Feather work was dirty, dusty, and probably unhealthy. The median age of single female manufacturing workers in 1910 was about 18; notice the child in the foreground. Photograph by Lewis Wickes Hine. *(Lewis W. Hine Collection, United States History, Local History & Genealogy Division, The New York Public Library, Astor, Lenox and Tilden Foundation)*

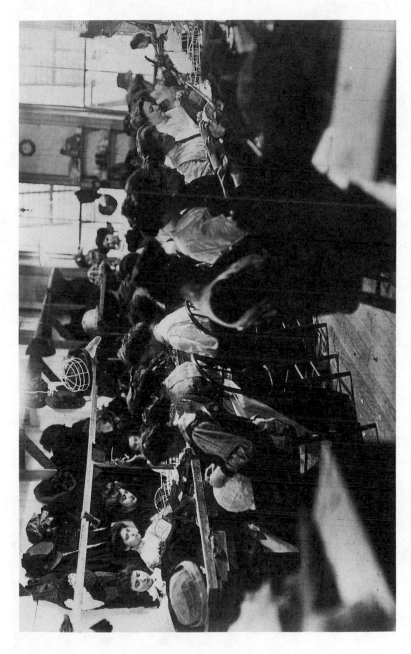

Female-Intensive Industry, c. 1910. Milliners in a small factory. Photograph by Lewis Wickes Hine. (*Lewis W. Hine Collection, United States History, Local History & Genealogy Division, The New York Public Library, Astor, Lenox and Tilden Foundation*)

Male-Intensive Industry, 1905. Men and women making link sausages at Swift and Company, perhaps the only jobs in meat packing that employed women around the turn of the century. This picture was taken just a year after the strike that led to the greater employment of female workers in the meat-packing industry. In 1900, only 5% of all meat-packing workers were women; in 1890, just 3% were. *(Courtesy of the Library of Congress)*

Female-Intensive Industry, 1909. Female spoolers at the White Oak Cotton Mills, Greensboro, North Carolina. "Spoolers where the yarn is wound from bobbins onto spools." About one-third of all female manufacturing operatives worked in the textile industry in 1900. The entire industry was about 50% female; spoolers were almost always women and were generally paid by the piece. *(Courtesy of the Library of Congress)*

Stereographs, depicting exotic scenes as well as more mundane work sites, were extremely popular around the turn of the century. Among the principal publishers was H. C. White Company, responsible for the two shown here.

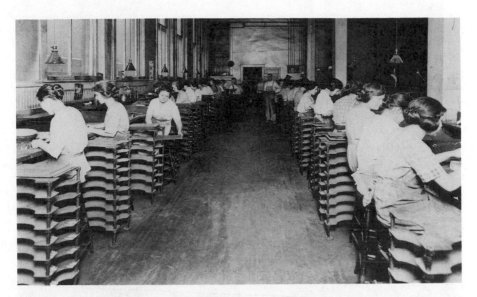

Male-Intensive Industry, c. 1920. "Scene in the core room, Standard Sanitary Mfg. Co. Louisville, KY. Note girl placing plate in core rack without necessity of leaving her seat. Men carry core plates to oven." Metal work did not afford many jobs for women, but the making of small cores was often a female position. The Women's Bureau, which collected this picture, rated the factory as having "good lighting." *(Courtesy of the National Archives)*

Female-Intensive Industry, 1927. "Women laundering and ironing corsets. Seated in large well-lighted room. Royal Worcester Corset Company." *(Courtesy of the National Archives)*

Mixed Industry, 1926. Male and female compositors work on monotype machines in an integrated printing office. Monotype machines operate on a principle similar to that of key-punch machines. Strips of paper are punched and transfer information to the caster machine, which produces type and places it in the galley. The canisters on the machines and the shelf contain right-justification codes. Compositors were among the most educated manufacturing operatives, and were in one of the few integrated occupations in manufacturing. Photograph by D. Sargeant Bell. *(Courtesy of The Historical Society of Pennsylvania)*

World War I, 1918. "Women operatives on punch presses. Large well lighted room. Seats. General Electric Company, Philadelphia." The Women's Bureau, formed during World War I as the Women-In-Industry Service, had a mandate to inspect the working conditions of women in industry. This photograph, taken on the eve of the armistice, shows jobs that were generally atypical for women in peacetime. *(Courtesy of the National Archives)*

World War II, 1941. "Highly efficient as a rivet team are Linnette Laurl and Jean Crowe, of Vultee Field sub-assembly department. Linnette, left, bucks the rivets being driven by Jean, with a light rivet gun during assembly of a fuselage bulkhead." Although the 1940's witnessed a rapid expansion of female employment, riveters like these women generally left the labor force after the war. Much of the increased employment of married women during the 1940's occurred after World War II. *(Courtesy of the National Archives)*

Office Work, Telephone Operators, 1904. Rows of female telephone operators at the Kansas City, Missouri, main home office. Twenty years before, telephone switchboard operators were primarily boys. (*Courtesy of AT&T Archives*)

Office Work, Banking, 1926. A dozen well-dressed young women work under the close supervision of a male clerk in the School Bank Department at the Philadelphia Saving Fund Society. At a time when most bank clerks were male, this department, which dealt only with children, was primarily female. Bags on the floor probably contain deposit books and money collected from various schools. (*Courtesy of Meritor/PSFS Archives*)

Office Work, Comptometer Operators, c. 1925. Rows of comptometer operators, fingers poised, at the Philadelphia Gas Works. Notice several men in the room, apparently clerks but not comptometer operators. Photograph by D. Sargeant Bell. *(Courtesy of The Historical Society of Pennsylvania)*

5

The Changing Economic Role
of Married Women

Of all historical change in the female labor force, the increased participation of married women has been the most meaningful. It has been associated with a decline in the stability of the family, with altered gender relations, and with an increase in the political power of women. The movement of married women from the home to the marketplace has been accompanied by social and political change of enormous consequence. Why their employment increased is the subject of this chapter.

Recall from Chapter 2 that married women's employment is a rather ambiguous economic concept for the earlier part of this century and that preceding. It is likely that an augmented measure of labor force participation, one that includes paid and unpaid work in the home and on the farm, actually decreased before its more celebrated rise. But when the concept of labor force is restricted to work done for pay outside the home, participation rates for white married women increase continuously from 1890 to the present. The rationale, given in Chapter 2, for the more conventional definition is that work for pay, outside the home, alters family relationships and enhances individual productivity far more than other forms of labor and produces more profound social and political consequences. This chapter will address the issue of married women's participation with reference to the more conventional concept of the labor force.

Among married, white women fewer than 5% worked for pay in 1890 and 1900. The figure was equally low for the foreign-born and for those in large urban areas, but was substantially higher among black women, for whom participation was nearly 10 times that among white women in 1890. The figures for white women increase with every decade, and differences emerge around 1920 between city and countryside and across the age distribution. Younger, not older, married women early in this century were first to increase their labor force participation, and the reasons for their lead reveal the importance of increased education and the emergence of white-collar employment.

But until 1950, the increase of married women in the American labor force was slight compared with later developments. Even by 1950, only 21% of all married white women, and 23% of those in urban areas, were in the labor force. After 1950, married women's participation increases by 10 percentage points each decade, and at the time of this writing the rate for married, white women nears 60%. While increases after 1950 were experienced across all age groups, they were greatest initially among older married women, not the younger group as was the case in the 1920's and 1930's. But the reason for the lead taken by the older group in the 1950's and 1960's is related to the earlier phenomenon. Cohorts of older women in the post–World War II period were the younger group of the 1920's and 1930's. Their increased participation after World War II was a continuation through time of their initial role in increasing participation in the earlier period. History is often made, as this example shows, by the movement of cohorts through time. The increase in female labor force participation after World War II was only in part caused by contemporaneous factors, also known as period effects, such as the postwar increase in the demand for labor. Rather, these effects had a notable impact on women because they were more educated and better trained. Thus individual histories or cohort effects matter, and change is often rooted in preceding, and frequently less obvious, events.

I suggested in Chapter 2 that the 1920's were a turning point in the evolution of women's work. The previous period was the era of single working women and witnessed an increasing proportion of young single women working for pay. Public policy and social attention shifted in the 1920's from the protection of women workers and the plight of young working women to the social consequences of married women's paid labor. The attention devoted to employed married women in the decades preceding 1950, however, attests to the actual and imagined consequences of their altered economic role, not to the magnitude of change. Attention was concentrated on a disquieting and growing, but still minor, trend. The rhetoric reveals, as well, the barriers, both tangible and ideological, that would stand in the way of genuine change. In terms of the sheer magnitude, the turning point is clearly 1950. Before 1950, the increase in married women's participation was slow and evolutionary, but after 1950 the process quite simply explodes.

The explosion in the participation of married women is evident in Figures 5.1a and 5.1b, and in Figure 2.1.[1] Figure 2.1 clearly shows that the paid labor of older women increased most rapidly during the 1940's and 1950's, while that of younger women increased greatly in the 1970's and 1980's. The initial rise in the participation of young married women in the 1920's is apparent only in data for large cities (see Table 2.3). The cohort data for white women, Figure 5.1a, and for nonwhite women, Figure 5.1b, are alternative modes of expressing the information contained in Figure 2.1 and thus show the same trends but emphasize the role of cohort. The rapid increase in the participation of older white women is apparent in both Figures 2.1 and 5.1a, particularly among cohorts born between 1906 and 1915, and that for younger women is apparent in the cohorts born since the 1940's. Recall from Chapter 2 that participation rates among black women show movements surprisingly similar to those of white women, but start at considerably higher levels and decline substantially during the Depression.

The explanation offered here for the advance in the participation of married women is accomplished first by using traditional supply and demand analysis, second by estimating a cross-section and time-series model to isolate cohort from

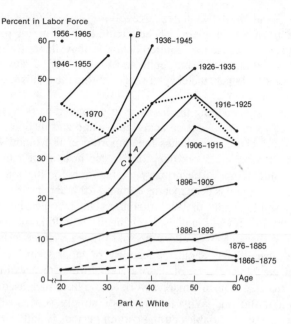

Part A: White

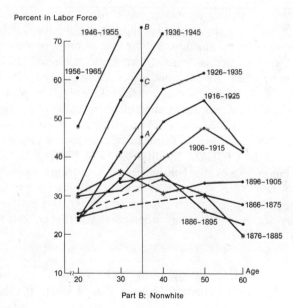

Part B: Nonwhite

FIGURE 5.1. Labor Force Participation Rates by Cohort and Race for Married Women, 1890 to 1980, for Cohorts Born 1866 to 1965. *Notes and Source:* See Figure 2.2 and Table 5.6. Point *A* is the participation rate of 35-year-old-women born between 1920 and 1930; Point *B* is the participation rate of 35-year-old-women born between 1944 and 1954; Point *C* is the response of 14 to 24 year olds asked in 1968 "What would you like to be doing when you are 35 years old?"

period effects, and third by analyzing evolving expectations to assess the less tangible aspects of the problem. The difficult task of a full partitioning is not undertaken, in part because the required data are unavailable for the entire span of history (see Joshi et al., 1985, and Smith and Ward, 1985, for two related methods that could be used). Rather, the chapter sets forth the mechanism that led to the rise of married women's work.

Past attempts at explaining the increase in women's work have applied coefficients estimated from cross-section analyses—wage and income effects—to time-series data. The technique evaluates the importance of women's real wages and family income to women's work decisions to see how much can be explained by these two variables alone. The primary explanation for the long-run increase in married women's work has been that the demand for labor shifted out over an elastic and relatively stable supply of labor function. But income and wage effects, assumed constant in previous analyses, changed over long periods of time, and consideration of these changes alters the role played by female labor supply. The analysis here raises doubts about the stability of labor supply over the long run. Reflection on the broad sweep of history adds further reservations; if the theory were correct, married women's market work would have increased in the nineteenth century, when it did not. Why female labor supply shifted and became more responsive to economic variables during certain periods is addressed by making the cohort a unit of analysis.

In most previous studies of female labor force participation, there are two dimensions to time: a woman's age, yielding life-cycle information, and the date, giving contemporaneous information. But the year of birth, or the cohort, matters as well. Various changes, such as those affecting education and fertility, are carried with cohorts through their life cycle and affect the wages and jobs they are offered and the way they make decisions about work and family. The pooled cross-section and time-series analysis allows a separation of cohort effects from contemporaneous ones. But women born in different years may differ from one another in ways that are less amenable to measurement. Labor force change by cohort probably exhibits "drift" that cannot be explained by differences in observable factors. Younger cohorts may be more able to effect change by circumventing norms that constrained the behavior of their elders. Through their ability to observe past advances in the labor force, they may be in a better position to predict, and thus prepare for, their future. The final section of this chapter considers whether cohorts formed realistic expectations.

Explaining Long-term Trends in Married Women's Labor Force Participation

Supply Versus Demand

Why change occurred in the economic role of married women has been almost as important as the change itself. The idea that married women entered the work force because of a breakdown in social norms and the emergence of a feminist ideology has gained wide acceptance. The timing of the change has contributed to the view.

Vastly increased participation first occurred during and just after World War II, which lessened social norms circumscribing the work of women. Even greater increases since the late 1960's confirm the sense that feminist ideology strongly contributes to economic change. Such an explanation has been interpreted to mean that the supply side of the labor market has been the dominant factor, by the inference that individuals must have changed their preferences for paid work. But it could be viewed alternatively as meaning that the demand side was altered through changed constraints on employers. A competing explanation is that an increased demand for labor, particularly the growth of the clerical and sales sectors whose labor forces have consisted overwhelmingly of women, caused the growth in female labor force participation. The demand-centered explanation has received support in the work of sociologist Valerie Oppenheimer (1970) and from the quantitative analysis of several economists (Mincer, 1962; Smith and Ward, 1984).

Explanations for the increased participation of married women group generally in the two main categories just noted—those that emphasize supply and those that emphasize demand factors. Factors that can shift the supply of labor function include those that change preferences, such as the greater consciousness the feminist movement has brought; family responsibilities, such as the number of children; the time cost of producing household goods, such as food, clothing, and cleanliness; and the income of other family members, as well as the assets of the family. The conditions, hours, and status of work may also affect the position of the supply function. Factors that can shift the demand function include sectoral changes, such as the increase in clerical and sales work, the use of complementary capital, changes in technology that increase the substitutability between male and female labor, formal education that can replace on-the-job training, and the tastes of employers and employees, called discrimination in common parlance.

Although supply and demand are the building blocks of economists, the words here stand for more than just the two sets of factors that determine quantity and price. They also represent the notions of choice and constraint, and the resolution of their relative merit will reveal whether the constraints facing women changed or whether, instead, women modified their behavior. Generally in the labor market, demand-side factors are more reasonably grouped with those altering constraints, while those on the supply side are more reasonably grouped with those affected by choice. For some variables, it is difficult to separate changes in constraints from those of choice. A decrease in fertility, for example, may be considered a change in choice by one group, but a change in constraints by another—say, a cohort living through advancements in contraceptive technology. There is room, as well, for interactions between the two sides. As will be discussed in Chapter 6, married women were barred from clerical employment by many large firms in the 1920's and 1930's. But the bars were abandoned in the 1950's when the supply of young, single workers was markedly reduced and firms turned to older married women as an untapped labor supply. Thus the constraints on married women changed, in part, because single women chose to increase their fertility and because previous generations had, through decreased fertility, altered the age distribution of the population.

There have been many attempts to estimate the relative importance of demand- and supply-side factors (Mincer, 1962; Oppenheimer, 1970; Smith and Ward,

1984). My contribution here is to extend the period to the last century and apply the most general economic model through a well-known technique. Parameter estimates of labor supply from various cross-section studies are applied to data on female earnings and employment from 1890 to 1980. The result is an estimate of the change in supply, on the one hand, and of demand, on the other, that likely produced the observed data on earnings and employment. Although I cannot, without additional parameters, disaggregate supply and demand shifts into their components, the relative merits of the two sets of factors and the way they changed over time can be established. The parameters of labor supply must first be introduced.

Labor Supply: Income, Wage, and Substitution Effects

The number of hours, days, and years individuals choose to work within a given time period and over the life cycle is generally called "labor supply." Economists have studied the determinants of labor supply to understand how public policies, such as taxation and welfare subsidies, affect the amount individuals work. When labor supply is very responsive to changes in the net wage, tax policies can greatly alter the hours, days, and years people work. Economists in the early Reagan administration were concerned with these "supply-side" effects of taxation, and much of (the now-abandoned) supply-side economics was predicated on the sensitivity of labor supply to changes in marginal tax rates. Social concerns of a variety of types have also prompted studies of labor supply. Consideration of the negative income tax in the 1970's and later interest in the effect of Social Security on retirement provided additional reasons to measure labor supply response to changes in wages and assets. Literally hundreds of empirical studies of labor supply, for both males and females, produced parameter estimates to understand and simulate policy change.

In models of labor supply, individuals are assumed to choose hours of work (or days, or participation) by considering their real wage per unit time in relation to the value of their time in alternative activities, including leisure, the production of family services, and education.[2] Assets and other (nonlabor) income also affect the labor supply decision by changing the position of the budget line. An increase in assets and nonlabor income raises the budget line, without altering its slope and by doing so has only an "income effect" on labor supply. (The income effect means the change in, say, hours worked with an increase in income.) The general presumption is that the income effect is negative, and that prediction is usually supported by empirical work. An increase in income will reduce the amount of time individuals want to spend at paid work (and increase the amount of time they spend at leisure and in household production). Further, it is claimed that the income effect has accounted for the decline in hours of work over long periods of time in America and for the secular decline in the age of retirement.

The impact of changes in the wage rate on labor supply is trickier than that of changes in income. The presumption is that increases in the wage rate raise the quantity of labor supplied by making alternative uses of time more expensive. A complication arises, however, because increases in the wage rate also serve to increase income when hours worked is positive. Thus an increase in the wage rate contains two effects: an income effect and a substitution effect (also called the compensated wage effect). The empirical resolution of this aspect of labor supply has led to evidence for and against a "backward bending supply curve." As in all neoclassical economics, however, the uncompensated wage effect (say, the change in hours worked with a change in the wage) can be positive or negative, but the compensated wage, or "own" substitution effect (the change in hours worked due to a change in the wage, holding constant real income or utility), is always positive—in theory, at least.

That takes care of the two primary factors in most models and studies of labor supply: the real wage per unit time and nonlabor income. Note that in the case of married women, nonlabor income can (but need not necessarily) include earnings of other family members, most importantly the husband. There are, however, other factors affecting labor supply. Particularly in the case of women, the number of children and the timing of births may be relevant factors in terms of increased time demands in the home. But fertility may be jointly determined with the work decision. Women who desire careers might reduce their fertility or have children later in life. Their low number of children is not the cause of their greater labor supply. Rather, both are motivated by a similar set of variables, such as career orientation, education, and ability. Whether or not other family members are unemployed is a variable of considerable historical interest and has generated numerous studies of the "added worker hypothesis" (Mincer, 1966). The prices of goods that substitute for those produced in the home (e.g., appliances, frozen foods, day care) and the prices of goods that are complements to leisure (e.g., airplane travel, summer camps for children) are also of interest, but generally do not vary much in cross section.

Among the many relevant variables, some measurable and some not, that can and have been sensibly included in the labor supply function, the real wage and nonlabor income have attracted the most attention. Policy directives, as mentioned above, have often dictated concern with income and wage effects (the coefficients on the income and wage variables). The negative income tax, for example, would have altered both the net wage and nonlabor income and thus the responses to both were of considerable interest. But much of the attention accorded the two parameters of labor supply is generated by a desire to predict the future and explain past trends in labor force participation and hours of work. With the exception of the fertility variable, which has been justifiably omitted from many studies because of its joint determination with labor supply, the real wage and nonlabor income variables are the two main factors that have changed substantially over time and that can be easily measured.

Much of the literature explaining time trends in female labor force participation uses a variant of the framework just outlined. The technique can be understood by reference to the labor supply function, which is a relationship between the real wage and the number of hours, days, or years individuals desire to work, holding other factors constant. The more elastic the function—that is, the larger the wage effect—the more labor supply will expand with an increase in the real wage. The income effect, however, determines the shift in the labor supply function in response to a change in income. Thus the smaller the income effect, the smaller the decrease in labor supply, at all wage rates, for a given increase in nonlabor income. Evidence from cross sections on wage and income effects and from time series on the change in the real wage and nonlabor income is, under certain restricted conditions, all that is needed to predict the change in the quantity of labor supplied in response to these two variables.

The technique just outlined was used by Jacob Mincer (1962) in his pioneering study of female labor supply, later implemented by James Smith and Michael Ward (1984) in a time-series analysis and by others for several countries using post–World War II data.[3] Their findings have had major impact on our understanding of female labor supply and deserve further scrutiny. Both studies find that a simple model of labor supply can explain a large fraction of the change in married women's labor force participation from 1900 to 1950 (in the case of Mincer) and in aggregate hours worked by all (not just married) women from 1950 to 1980 (in the case of Smith and Ward). The simple model includes only the impact of changes in the female wage and the incomes of other family members.[4]

The finding that just two variables can explain so much of the change in participation and hours of work frankly overturns the conventional wisdom that women entered the labor force as a result of a more complex set of factors— changes in social norms, declining barriers to their paid work, increasing work flexibility, smaller numbers of children, and the diffusion of labor-saving devices in the home, to mention a few of the most cited reasons. But according to these and other scholars, increased real earnings of female workers, not a shift in their labor supply function, was of primary importance in the secular increase in female labor force participation and in their hours of paid work. Increased participation within this framework resulted largely from a shift of the demand curve over a rather elastic and relatively stable supply function.

A General Model of the Labor Market for Married Women

The idea behind these frameworks, and a more general model, can be understood by referring to Figure 5.2, which is a variant of the more familiar supply and demand for labor graph. The horizontal axis is the rate of change in labor force participation (or the proportion of available hours spent at work) over time, rather than its static value, and the vertical axis is likewise the rate of change in female (full-time) earnings over time. The slope of the (rate-of-change) supply function is the inverse of the (uncompensated) wage elasticity of supply, and the slope of the demand function is the inverse of the demand elasticity. The intercepts, marked as D^* and S^*, are the shift terms of the demand and supply functions.

Mathematically, these functions can be derived from the static demand and supply functions as follows. Assume the supply of female labor function can be written as

$$\ell_s = [S' \, Y_m^{-\epsilon}] w^{\eta}$$

and the demand function as

$$\ell_d = D w^{-\delta}$$

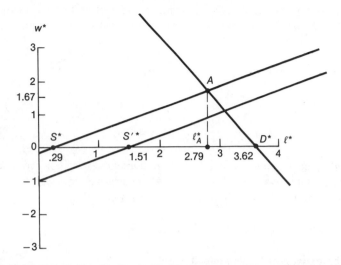

Figure 5.2. The General Model. *Note:* This is a schematic representation of the market for married women's labor, 1890 to 1980. During that time married women's labor force participation (ℓ^*) rose at 2.79% average annually and the full-time real earnings of women (w^*) rose at 1.67% average annually. If the elasticity of supply of female labor were 1.5 and that of demand −0.5, the rate of growth of labor supply (S^*) would have been 0.29% average annually, that of labor supply in the absence of the income effect (S'^*) would have been 1.51%, and the rate of growth of labor demand (D^*) would have been 3.62%. See text for more detail.

where ℓ is the female labor force participation rate, Y_m is family income (other than that of the wife), w is the wife's full-time earnings or wage when employed, S' includes all factors affecting labor supply except Y_m and w, D includes all factors affecting demand except w, and ε, η, and δ are parameters. The parameter ε is the income elasticity, η is the (uncompensated) wage elasticity of supply, and δ is the elasticity of demand. Labor force participation (ℓ), it should be noted, is the dependent variable for both the supply and the demand equations rather than the more conventional number of workers. The reasoning is straightforward. Increasing the relevant population by, say, 10% will increase the supply of (or demand for) labor by 10%; that is, the elasticity of labor supply and demand with respect to the relevant population, here married women, is taken to be one—a reasonable presumption. Taking logs of both sides and totally differentiating yields

$$\ell_s^* = [S' - \varepsilon Y_m^*] + \eta w^* = S^* + \eta w^* \qquad (1)$$

for the rate-of-change supply function, where $S^* = [S'^* - \varepsilon Y_m^*]$, and

$$\ell_d^* = D^* - \delta w^* \qquad (2)$$

for the rate-of-change demand function, where an asterisk (*) beside a variable denotes $\partial \log_e(\cdot)/\partial t$ (t = time).

When supply equals demand (in the usual manner or in rate-of-change form), equations (1) and (2) yield the two familiar reduced forms, again in rate-of-change form:

$$w^* = -[S'^* - \varepsilon Y_m^*]/(\eta + \delta) + D^*/(\eta + \delta) \qquad (3)$$

for the wage, and

$$\ell^* = [S'^* - \varepsilon Y_m^*] \cdot \delta/(\eta + \delta) + D^* \cdot \eta/(\eta + \delta) \qquad (4)$$

for the labor force participation rate. If the demand for labor were infinitely elastic—that is, if the wage (and its rate-of-change transform) were exogenously determined—there would be only one reduced form equation:

$$\ell^* = [S'^* - \varepsilon Y_m^*] + \eta \tilde{w}^* \qquad (5)$$

where $\tilde{w}$ is the exogenously determined wage.

Information is readily available for ℓ, $\tilde{w}$ or equivalently w, and Y_m over time, and cross-section estimates exist for ε and η, the income and wage effects in elasticity form. The logic of the Mincer and the Smith and Ward computations can now be easily demonstrated. If the wage were exogenous, as it is in equation (5), then only $\tilde{w}^*$, Y_m^*, and the factors composing S'^* determine ℓ^*. A large value for η, but a small value for ε and thus εY_m^*, can produce the conclusion that changes in the female wage and in male income "explain" a large fraction of the change in the labor force participation rate and that other factors must be of lesser importance. Both the Mincer and the Smith and Ward estimates of η and ε, together with the rates of change in wages and income, lead to that conclusion. The Mincer parameter estimates applied to the data in Table 5.1 explain 53% of the total change in married women's labor force participation from 1890 to 1960 and 75% of the change using the data originally assembled by Mincer (1962).[5] The model estimated by Smith and Ward explains about 60% of the increase in hours of work for all women from 1950 to 1980.

The framework of these studies is, however, a special case of the more general model, given by the two reduced form equations (3) and (4). Given a value for the elasticity of demand, δ, there are two equations in two unknowns—the shift terms of the supply and demand equations. Even if the value of δ were not known with precision, the relative magnitudes of the supply and demand shifts can still be determined, and a limiting case, $\delta = 0$, will be instructive in the discussion. Therefore, the relative merits of demand and supply factors in increasing the participation of married women can be addressed in the absence of precise information on δ.

The data for the three variables (ℓ, w, and Y_m) are given in Table 5.1. Both the real wage and the labor force participation rate of married women increase substantially over time; thus the equilibrium point (in rate-of-change form) must be contained in the positive quadrant of Figure 5.2, as is point A. The shift term of the

TABLE 5.1. Urban White Female Labor Force and Earnings, 1890 to 1980

Year	Urban White Married Female Labor Force Participation Rate (ℓ)	Full-time Deflated (1967 = 100) Female Earnings (w)	Full-time Deflated (1967 = 100) Male Earnings (Y_m)
1890	4.0%	$1085	$2181
1900	5.1	1216	2556
1910	n.a.	—	—
1920	8.7	1686	3242
1930	12.4	1986	3485
1940	15.2	2060	3387
1950	23.1	3015	5292
1960	31.2	3897	6471
1970	39.3	4760	8123
1980	49.3	4870	8212

Notes and Sources: URBAN FEMALE LABOR FORCE PARTICIPATION RATE: See Tables 2.1 and 2.3 for sources. The 1900 figure was obtained by extrapolation using 1890.

FULL-TIME FEMALE EARNINGS:

1890, 1900, 1930: Computed from Table 3.2 using occupational distributions for white women.

1920: Extrapolated from 1900 using a weighted average of manufacturing and clerical earnings. See description of data underlying C. Goldin, "The Changing Economic Role of Women: A Quantitative Approach," *Journal of Interdisciplinary History* 13 (Spring 1983), table 1.

1940, 1950, 1960: U.S. census data for white female, year-round, full-time workers.

1970, 1980: An average of $(t - 2)$ to (t) for white female, year-round, full-time workers from *Economic Report of the President, 1986.*

FULL-TIME, MALE EARNINGS:

1890, 1900, 1930: Computed from Table 3.2 using occupational distributions for white men.

1920, 1930: Extrapolated from 1900 using Lebergott's data underlying estimates in Goldin (1983).

1940, 1950, 1960: Full-time, year-round white male (median) income from Current Population Reports, P-60 series (January 1962).

1970, 1980: An average of $(t - 2)$ to (t) for white male, year-round, full-time workers from *Economic Report of the President, 1986.*

DEFLATOR: A three-year average, $(t - 2)$ to (t), of the CPI, *Historical Statistics* (1975) and *Economic Report of the President, 1986.*

demand equation must therefore be positive, independent of δ, and must be at least equal to the value of ℓ_A^*. The shift term of the supply function, however, depends on the value of the wage elasticity of supply, η. A large η results in a low and possibly negative value for the shift term, S^*. The lower S^* is, the more changes in the labor force depend on demand factors, given η and ε. Intuitively, and in terms of the more familiar static analysis, the larger the wage elasticity of supply, η, the more likely the increase in participation was caused by an outward movement of a demand function shifting across a relatively stable (and flat) supply function. The factors shifting the demand curve are responsible for the change, but they are aided by the large supply elasticity. The flatter the supply function, the greater the increase in labor force participation with a given change in demand.

By fitting the general framework with the data from Table 5.1, the elasticities of Mincer, and a demand elasticity (δ) of 0.5, it can be demonstrated that the supply function of female labor was relatively stable over the 1890 to 1980 period. The case is depicted in Figure 5.2, where $\ell^* = 2.79$ and $w^* = 1.67$. When $\eta = 1.5$, $\varepsilon = 0.83$, and $\delta = 0.5$, the shift terms are $S^* = 0.29$, and $S'^* = 1.51$, and $D^* = 3.62$. Note that D^* would have been at least 2.79, the value of ℓ^*, had $\delta = 0$, the limiting case. Demand shifted at more than 12 times the rate of supply, which having the value of 0.29 is barely greater than zero. Supply, therefore, was virtually stable. Even in the absence of the negative impact of increased husband's income, the net supply shift, termed here S'^*, is 1.51, less than half the magnitude of demand.

Thus the conclusion of Mincer, from the previous computation of equation (5), is upheld in the more general framework. Increased demand is responsible for more than 90% of the increase in the labor force participation rate. Demand effects far outweigh supply, but only if the parameters were stable over time. That assumption, however, does not appear to be the case.

Mincer had originally estimated income and wage effects to resolve a paradox posed in 1958 by Clarence Long in his volume on the labor force. Long was puzzled that cross-section analyses using individual-level data found considerably larger income than wage effects. Given the slow growth or relative constancy in the ratio of female to male earnings, these findings implied that female labor force participation would have fallen, not increased, over time. Long was thus led to other considerations to explain the increase, such as the diffusion of home appliances during the 1930's and 1940's and other factors that decreased demands on women's household time. Although these considerations moved his results in the right direction, they were, he concluded, far from sufficient in magnitude. The only alternative, he surmised, was that the supply function had shifted for other reasons.

Mincer's solution to Long's paradox was to recognize that the income effect estimated from existing cross-section studies could not be used to predict or explain time series. The income effect from cross-sectional analyses included the impact of transitory changes in income across individuals, while time-series changes did not have a transitory component. To get around the problem, he estimated income and wage effects from aggregated data, a cross section of cities. The estimated income effect then reflected changes in permanent income and could be used to extrapolate time-series trends. Mincer's estimates showed a considerably larger wage than income effect, and thus could easily explain the time-series data.

Since Mincer's study there have been similar cross-section estimations for the periods before and after, and one that reestimated Mincer's coefficients (Cain, 1966). Numerous cross-section estimates using microlevel data have also been produced, most of which have been computed using recent data on hours of work rather than participation (see Killingsworth, 1983; Killingsworth and Heckman, 1986; Smith, 1980, among others, for exhaustive summaries). The conclusion of two recent and comprehensive summaries of the microlevel cross-section (hours) studies is that the estimates range widely and depend more on econometric specification than on time period and data set. The authors of these summaries do give their readers some guidance on the matter. It is that the most reliable estimates for the post–1975 period yield rather small estimates for both the income and the substitution elasticities. (However, see Ben-Porath, 1973, for a cautionary note on comparing estimates from hours and labor force studies.)

Estimates of Income, Wage, and Substitution Effects

Far more can be said, I believe, about parameters from the cross-city studies summarized in Table 5.2, in part because the studies span almost a century, while those on individual-level observations rely primarily on data for the late 1960's and the 1970's. A few caveats concerning the estimation technique must be mentioned. Various econometric problems in the estimation of labor supply functions have been solved since the early 1970's. One of the first problems encountered was that hours of work and labor force participation have obvious bounds; hours, for example, cannot be negative and are often zero, and the participation rate is bounded between zero and one. Standard estimates that do not consider these bounds can be seriously biased. Another problem is that earnings are observed only for individuals who work and have to be estimated for those who do not. Individuals who work, moreover, may not be a randomly selected group with regard to various unobservable characteristics, such as motivation, ability, and drive. The solutions to these estimation problems spawned an entire subfield of econometrics, due largely to the work of James Heckman (see references in Killingsworth and Heckman, 1986), and many of the studies in Table 5.2 do not use the advanced techniques applied to individual-level data.

Despite these cautions, the time series of wage, substitution, and income elasticities in Table 5.2 tell a story about the evolution of paid work of married women that is consistent with much other evidence. The data indicate that income, wage, and substitution elasticities changed substantially over time. A digression, however, is required before proceeding to the evidence.

Most of the studies summarized in Table 5.2 estimate the response, across cities, of women's participation to changes in the female wage and male (or family) income. To achieve comparability, I have translated these responses (that is, the coefficients) into elasticities. That with respect to a change in the female wage is termed the wage elasticity of supply and that with respect to male (or family) income is the income elasticity of supply. Recall that the wage elasticity can be partitioned into an income elasticity and a substitution elasticity, also termed the compensated wage elasticity of supply. The computation of this figure from the other two is not always uncomplicated (see Ben-Porath, 1973).

A problem arises because the various cross-section studies listed in Table 5.2 use labor force participation rates rather than hours worked, and the precise meaning of a change in participation is rather complex. The solution will depend on exactly why participation rates rise with increases in the wage rate, and there are two extreme cases. One is that all working women increase the number of hours they work per year, and the other is that more women enter the labor force. The issue is identical to that raised in Chapter 2 in the discussion of heterogeneity versus homogeneity in labor supply. If working women are homogeneous, all work an identical number of hours (or weeks) per year, differentially allocated over the year due to random factors. The substitution effect under these circumstances is derived using the standard Slutsky decomposition (see Notes to Table 5.2) and is given by the column in Table 5.2 labeled "own-substitution elasticity," (η^s). But if, instead, women are heterogeneous, then those in the labor force work the entire year. An

TABLE 5.2. Labor Supply Elasticities, 1900 to 1980

Year	Source	Wage (Uncompensated) Elasticity (η)	Own-Substitution (Compensated Wage) Elasticity (η^s)	Income Elasticity ($-\varepsilon$)	($\alpha \times -\varepsilon$)
	Cross-City Studies, Married Women's Labor Force Participation Rates				
1900	Fraundorf (1979), working class	0	0.26	-1.32	-0.26
1930	Rotella (1981), white, 25–34 years	0	n.a.	-1.16	n.a.
1940	Bowen and Finegan (1969)	0.60	1.35	-0.60	-0.75
1950	Bowen and Finegan (1969)	0.97	1.55	-0.88	-0.58
1950	Mincer (1962)	1.50	2.03	-0.83	-0.53
1950	Cain (1966), reworking of Mincer	1.30	1.60	-0.47	-0.30
1960	Bowen and Finegan (1969)	0.41	0.67	-0.42	-0.26
1970	Fields (1976)	0.37	0.52	-0.22	-0.15
	Time-Series Study				
1950–1980	Smith and Ward (1984), hours of work	0.82	1.13	-0.52	-0.31

Note: The own-substitution (compensated wage) effect is calculated from the Slutsky equation: $\eta = \eta^s - \alpha\varepsilon$, where $\alpha =$ wife's full-time income (w) divided by husband's (or family's) actual income (Y_m). See the text for a qualification to this procedure. The term ($\alpha \times -\varepsilon$) is also known as the total-income elasticity (see Killingsworth, 1983). All elasticities from cross-city regressions (except 1930) are computed from the coefficients and values for ℓ, w, Y_m in each of the studies. The dependent variable is the percentage of married women in the labor force by city (ℓ). In 1930, the regression was estimated in double-log form. For 1900, "other family income," rather than Y_m, was used. Cain's income data are used to produce Bowen and Finegan's elasticities for 1950 and 1960; census data are used for 1940. Cain (1966, table 11) also presents results for 77 SMAs, rather than the 57 in the Mincer sample. The wage elasticity for a regression containing only the income and wage variables (consistent with the specification used by Mincer) is 0.96, and the income elasticity is -0.22; those for a more extended regression (consistent with specifications used for 1960 and 1970) are 1.06 and -0.72. Neither affects the main conclusions drawn from the table. The 1970 data are for 100 SMSAs.

increase in the participation rate with a rise in the wage must signify that entirely new workers have entered who could not have been working in the immediately preceding period. Under these circumstances, there is no income effect from a wage increase; there is only a substitution effect. The wage elasticity (η) is then identical to the substitution elasticity; in other words, the uncompensated wage effect equals the compensated one. Intermediate cases also exist that are considerably more complex.

Evidence in Chapter 2 suggests the use of the second procedure, because the female labor force has been and is apparently rather heterogeneous in its labor supply. Thus the estimated wage elasticity of supply is the substitution elasticity. But the choice of the two extreme cases is not critical here. As an empirical matter, the results of the analysis in Table 5.2 are remarkably similar for the two extreme cases just outlined. The derived substitution elasticities for both cases are small early in the century, then rise until around 1950, and subsequently decrease in magnitude. Because the discussion is unaffected by which of the two wage elasticity columns is used, the uncompensated one or the compensated one, reference will be made to the "wage elasticity" as a generic term for both.

Returning to the results in Table 5.2, the income elasticity is also not stable over time. At the turn of the century, the income elasticity was large and negative, but the wage elasticity was rather small. The relationship between the wage and income elasticities, therefore, was precisely the reverse of that found by Mincer in his 1950 cross section. A married woman was not easily enticed into the labor force by higher wages, but she was, at the same time, encouraged to leave by higher earnings of her husband and other family members. By 1940, the income elasticity had shrunk somewhat in absolute value, but the wage elasticity had grown considerably. In more recent data sets, both income and wage elasticities are found to be quite small. The question, then, is why the income effect decreased over time while the substitution effect first rose and then fell.

The large, negative income elasticity earlier in the century stemmed, in part, from the sexual division of labor within the home. The higher a husband's income, the greater his demand for his wife's household-production services. But these effects were strengthened by another factor that has diminished over time—the desire to maintain status. A husband whose wife worked could be viewed as indolent, even if he were not.

Recall that around the turn of the century most jobs for women were in manufacturing, agriculture, and domestic service. The clerical and professional sectors were still minor employers of women, and, as will be discussed further in Chapter 6, only a small proportion of school districts and few large offices would hire a married woman. Most employed women were domestic servants and manufacturing workers, although single women were rapidly moving into the clerical, sales, and professional sectors from 1900 to 1920. A white, married woman employed outside her home around 1900 was likely to be a manufacturing worker, and her husband was apt to be low paid, unemployed, sick, or idle for some other reason.

When the work of a married woman was highly circumscribed, her paid labor outside the home was a clear and inescapable signal that her husband had failed to provide for his family. Even in the 1970's the author of a contemporary account of working-class life remarked that "historically, it has been a source of status in [blue-collar] communities for a woman to be able to say, 'I don't *have* to work.' . . . For her to take a job outside the house would be, for such a family, tantamount to a public acknowledgment of [her husband's] failure" (Rubin, 1976, p. 171, emphasis in original).

But a highly educated woman around the turn of this century might have a job because her position would clearly reflect her abilities, not her husband's negligence. There was little chance for error in the message conveyed by an educated wife's working, because highly educated men usually marry highly educated women—that is, "likes marry likes." But the signal provided by a wife's working diminished over time due to changes in education and its value in the economy.

In the early part of the twentieth century, a new array of white-collar jobs emerged that increased returns to education particularly among women with high-school, less so college, education. Thus the laborer's wife in the early twentieth century was offered expanded options and often greater remuneration by the labor market. But for the laborer, the unfavorable signal of her paid employment remained, and her potential earnings were often sacrificed. Thus the social norm produced a smaller measured (positive) substitution effect because it entailed a larger (negative) income effect, at least for the time being.

As more educated women entered the labor force, the signal contained in a wife's employment status accumulated considerable noise. In the 1950's, the occupations of college-educated women were often no different from those of women with high-school diplomas, with the obvious exceptions of teaching and nursing. It became increasingly difficult to infer the economic status and diligence of a husband from his wife's occupation and labor force participation.

The role of norms within the economist's framework of income and substitution effects in affecting the new group of office workers of the 1920's and 1930's was clear to contemporary observers. In a report on clerical workers, Grace Coyle noted that "clerical husbands" are reluctant to "allow" their wives to work, but added that "it is also likely that the more favorable attitude toward the work of married women produced in part by its increase among professional women is having its effect on [the clerical] group" (1929, p. 183). The Lynds, in their famous sociological studies of Middletown, remarked on the emergence of the new middle-class wife and her problems conforming:

> When one speaks of married women's working in Middletown one is talking almost exclusively of Middletown's working class and the lowest rungs of the business class. Among these last . . . the people to whom in a larger and more class-stratified community one might refer as its lower middle-class, there is discernible some tendency for a young wife to retain a clerical job until her husband begins to get established. At the other extreme of the business class, there are one or two young wives of men so wealthy that there can be no question locally of their "having to work," and thus no reflection on their husbands' ability to "provide." (1937, pp. 181–82)

Thus an increase in the employment of married women across the educational spectrum in the clerical and sales sectors tended to reduce the signal provided by a married woman's working. When jobs were less desirable, the only women in the labor force were those pushed in by the low incomes of their husbands. But when jobs were more desirable, working women were employed either because their husbands' incomes were low or because the value of their time was high. As the signal provided by a working wife declined over time, the income effect also dropped. A wife's working no longer provided as strong a signal of an indolent husband as it had previously. Thus the income elasticity declined in absolute value while the measured substitution effect increased. The decline in the income effect was further aided by the greater availability and increased substitutability of market for home-produced goods.

The increase in the substitution effect, and the decline in the power of the income effect, are consistent with advances in the educational attainment of working women compared with all women, over the period from 1890 to 1940. The strong income but weak substitution effect around 1900 meant that working women were less educated than the female population; the weak income but strong substitution effect around 1940 implies just the opposite.

Working women today have higher educational attainment, on average, than women in the entire population. But the female labor force was not always disproportionately drawn from among the most educated in the population. Working women in 1890 came, on average, from the lower portion of the educational distribution. Although precise estimates of their educational attainment cannot be computed, evidence in the 1907 Women Adrift sample indicates that the level of schooling among working women was less than seven years, while that among the entire population of women was almost eight years. By 1940, when data on educational attainment were collected in the population census and when other surveys contained such information, schooling levels among working women were more than a year higher than among the population. Thus the data on the educational attainment show secular improvement in the relative schooling of the labor force, a fact consistent with an increase in the substitution effect and a decline in the income effect.

Completing the historical picture of change in income and substitution effects is the continued decline in the income elasticity from the 1940's to the present and a reversal in the trend for the wage elasticity. As divorce rates have increased and as work in the lives of women has taken on added meaning, the impact of a husband's income on his wife's labor force participation has decreased. Women can no longer assume their lifetime wealth is a function of their husbands' incomes. Further, the increase of nonmanual jobs meant that work began to be more than a means of earning income; it became a way of seeking purpose and status in life. Work also changed in terms of training. Employment at one stage of the life cycle serves now to increase income at another, and the new connections across time have increased the cost of work intermittency. For both reasons the measured substitution effect would be expected to diminish in magnitude. Income and substitution effects estimated for the female labor force in recent years look, not surprisingly, like those estimated for the male labor force. They are rather unresponsive to changes in wages, incomes, and assets (see the estimates using 1975 data in Mroz, 1987).

There is, then, logic to the estimates in Table 5.2, which admittedly come from rather disparate sources. The decreased income effect since 1900 is explained by several factors. Over the first half of the century, women's work began to convey less about a husband's diligence and was, therefore, discouraged less by men. The greater availability and lower price of good substitutes for labor in household production strengthened the downward movement of the income effect over the entire country. Further reinforcement has been recently provided by increased marital instability. With divorce a possible threat to economic security, women have come to base their work decisions less on the adequacy of current family income than they had in the past. The initial increase in the wage effect may be related to the rise in education among women, because increased schooling enabled women to enter more pleasant jobs, not just those that paid more. The effect, however, was delayed by the existence of various barriers to the employment of married women. As women's jobs have become more similar to men's, training considerations, as well as the intrinsic merit of careers, have made the substitution effect smaller. Thus with the decrease in both the income and the wage effects, women, as Henry Higgins once fantasized, have finally become more like men, if only in terms of labor supply parameters.

Applying the General Model, 1890 to 1980

By dividing the entire period since 1890 into three subperiods—1890 to 1930, 1940 to 1960, 1960 to 1980—one can use the cross-section estimates of income and wage elasticities of supply to address the issue raised at the outset: the role of supply and demand factors in the secular rise of married women's labor force participation. The relative merits of the supply- and demand-centered explanations can be assessed using the reduced form equations (3) and (4), the data in Tables 5.1 and 5.2, and a reasonable estimate of the demand elasticity $(-\delta)$. A demand elasticity of -0.5 is assumed. The results for the first two subperiods are robust to values that span the 0 to $-\infty$ range, and the sensitivity of the results for the final subperiod is explored.[6]

From about 1890 to 1930, it is likely that the supply function shifted outward at a rapid rate; that is, S^* was probably quite large and positive during the earliest period. In the absence of the strong, negative impact of the growth of male (husband's) income, the supply function would have shifted out at a rate equal to, or possibly exceeding, that of demand; that is, S'^* was considerably larger than S^* (S^* = 2.8% average annually, and S'^* = 4.3%). Of the three periods considered, the years before 1930 contain the largest absolute increases in the female labor supply function and the largest change relative to demand (D^* = 3.6%). Further, because of the low value of the labor supply elasticity (the wage elasticity of supply was possibly close to zero), the determinants of the growth in the quantity of labor supplied (given by equation 4) consist exclusively of supply-side forces. With a completely inelastic supply function, the equilibrium level of ℓ^* would depend entirely on the shift term of the labor supply function; demand factors, however, would determine w^*.[7] Therefore, not only was supply rapidly shifting outward from 1890 to 1930, but its outward movement was largely and possibly solely responsible for increased participation. Various factors served to shift the supply function outward, that is, to the right, during that period, including the increased level of education, decreased fertility, and changing norms concerning women's work. The situation reverses considerably, though, as one moves to the next subperiod, 1940 to 1960.

During the 1940 to 1960 period, the demand function shifted outward at a rate greatly exceeding that of supply. Indeed, the supply function actually shifted backward during the period ($S^* = -0.56\%$), at least when the negative impact of male incomes is included, and shifted outward at a rather slow rate ($S'^* = 0.94\%$) when the income effect is netted out. All the increase in labor force participation during 1940 to 1960, again using equation (4), comes from demand-side forces that shifted at almost six times those composing S'^* ($D^* = 5.2\%$).[8] Many of the shift variables in the supply function were still operating to increase participation during the period, but they were stifled by the impact of growing family incomes and increased family size. The World War II era and the 1950's were periods of rapid economic growth, particularly among sectors that hired primarily female workers. Demand shifts, therefore, were most responsible for increasing the participation of married women. As will be seen in Chapter 6, the American economy in the 1950's altered aspects of work to accommodate married women workers. Part-time work, shorter hours, and the wholesale eradication of the marriage bar were symptomatic of the desire of American industry to attract a labor force it had never considered significant.

In the final subperiod, 1960 to 1980, it is likely that demand-side forces remained greater in magnitude than those on the supply side ($S^* = 1.9\%$; $S'^* = 2.2\%$; $D^* = 2.9\%$), but their impact in determining labor force participation may have been muted.[9] Because the labor supply elasticity is small, much will hinge on the magnitude of the elasticity of demand, δ. When $\delta = 0.5$, supply-side forces account for about 47% of the change in participation, and demand-side forces account for the remaining 53%; when $\delta = 1$, an upper-bound estimate, supply-side forces increase in their relative importance in determining ℓ^* and account for 60% of the change, with demand-side forces accounting for the remainder. These estimates are within the range of those of Smith and Ward (1984, 1985), who fit a somewhat less general model but take account of the role of fertility and the nature of intertemporal substitution. Over the last two to three decades, married women's participation has again been fostered by factors on the supply side, such as reduced numbers of children, increased probability of divorce, reduced barriers to various occupations, and changes in social norms.

It is now clear that Mincer's explanation for the rise in married women's participation applies perfectly to the period from about 1940 to 1960, less well to the period after, and rather poorly to that before. Recall that Mincer used the simpler expression for the reduced form given by equation (5), which employs the assumption that the wage rate is exogenous. In the analysis above using equation (4) and the elasticities in Table 5.2, "economic" influences, here just the increase in demand factors, were found to explain none of the rise in female labor force participation for the period 1890 to 1930. Demand factors explain virtually all the increase from 1940 to 1960 and about half that from 1960 to 1980. The rather large increase in the demand for labor in the 1940 to 1960 period came at a time when married women's participation was highly sensitive to changes in the wage rate.

Demand factors, in tandem with the large wage elasticity of supply, largely account for the increase in participation during that period. But for the periods both before and after, supply factors may have been of equal or greater importance.

The evolution of married women's labor force participation is therefore a more complex process than one of a (horizontal) demand for labor function tracing out a somewhat elastic, yet stable, supply of labor. Rather, the supply function changed in elasticity over time and supply itself shifted. Consider first change in the responsiveness of labor supply. Most married women in the first subperiod, 1890 to 1930, were less able to respond to greater job availability because they had little previous work experience in the newly emerging sectors. Yet young, single women, during the early decades of this century, experienced substantial increases in schooling and were thus easily absorbed into the burgeoning clerical and sales sectors. In the second subperiod, married women in the older age groups increased their participation, and their greater responsiveness then can be traced to their occupations and enhanced education during the first subperiod. Change, therefore, was effected in two ways: first, by contemporaneous changes in demand factors and, second, by the enhanced responsiveness of women in different age groups. Their greater responsiveness to period effects was accomplished, in part, by the movement of cohorts through time.

The description of the process suggests the merits of a detailed examination of labor force participation by cohort. It also suggests the importance of lags in the historical evolution of female labor that arise from the movement of cohorts through time and from each cohort's expectations about its own future labor force participation. Even more complex are the lags that originate in norms and institutions that inhibit change. The next section examines the first of these issues, that of cohort and contemporaneous change. The following chapter returns to the impediments to change.

A Cohort Approach to Change in Married Women's Labor Force Participation

Cohorts—groups of individuals born in different years (here, decades)—often differ by various endowments, such as education and wealth, and by the socialization each experiences when young. Those that exist simultaneously are affected by common contemporaneous factors, also called period effects, such as unemployment, sectoral shifts in demand, and social upheaval of various forms. One of the central conclusions of Chapter 2 was that the concept of cohort matters in analyzing female labor force participation, particularly that of married women. As suggested there, to be more fully explored below, the reason is that cohorts acquire varying amounts of education, have different numbers of children, accumulate different types of labor market experience, and mature in different social climates. These attributes are then carried with the cohort through time and distinguish it from the others with which it coexists.

What the cohort approach means to the study of the evolution of married women's labor force participation is that two types of variables must be considered simultaneously. The first comprise the more customary factors that affect all cohorts and are termed here contemporaneous factors. An economic boom will usually augment the earnings of all individuals, independent of the cohort in which they were born, although not necessarily (see, for example, Freeman, 1979, on vintage effects). Contemporaneous factors may change over the life of a cohort, but cohort variables, the second set of factors, remain the same.

Three cohort-specific factors can be considered here. One is fertility, measured by the number of children born to ever-married women and by the proportion of married women who never bore children. The second factor is years of schooling, measured by mean or median years attained, the proportion with at least a high-school diploma, and the proportion with at least four years of college. The third factor is the market and home experiences before marriage of a cohort of women. The subject was mentioned in Chapter 2 in the discussion of the proportion of single women who were "at home" during the 1880 to 1930 period, and it is extended here to include the role of the initial occupation.

It will help to reexamine Figures 5.1a and 5.1b, which give cohort participation rates among native-born white and nonwhite married women from 1890 to 1980, covering cohorts born from 1866 to 1965. Certain cohorts, it will be recalled, substantially increased their participation in the years during and just after World War II, while others increased their participation greatly only in the last two decades. Although all cohorts, in the case of white married women, increased their participation relative to previous ones, certain cohorts expanded their work involvement more rapidly than others. As noted before, among cohorts of white women, those born from 1900 to 1910 appear to have set a process in motion that would eventually alter participation rates for decades. Just as many of the cohort lines increase greatly as cohorts move from 1940 to 1950, many increase slowly during other periods. The mothers of the baby boom increased participation only slightly in their younger years. Change during the Great Depression was likewise muted, although there are increases for every cohort of white women.

Cohort Differences in Fertility

Two features of the fertility behavior of American women are striking, one secular and the other cyclical. From the early nineteenth century to the 1930's, the fertility of American women underwent an extended, secular decline. Census data, arrayed in Figure 5.3 by birth cohort, indicate that the average number of births per ever-married white woman was about 5.5 for the cohort born in 1840, and declined to 2.3 for that born around 1910. Evidence from genealogies suggests the fertility decline predates cohorts that can be studied with census data and that it declined even among women born in the late eighteenth century (Wahl, 1986). The decline was more precipitous for certain cohorts, such as those born from 1860 to 1870 and from 1890 to the early part of this century. The process of decline reverses with the cohort born around 1910, and its second feature, that of cyclicity, becomes apparent.

The cyclical nature of fertility has been discussed and analyzed in the many insightful studies of Easterlin (1968, 1978, 1980). The boom period in births begins

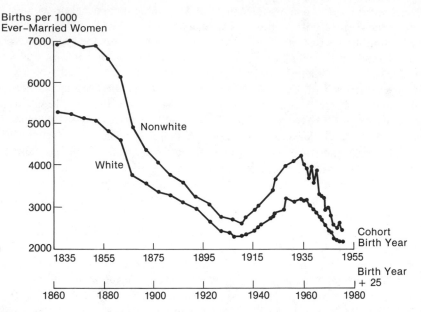

FIGURE 5.3. Births per 1,000 Ever-Married Women by Race and Cohort. *Sources:* Birth cohorts 1835–1924 from *Historical Statistics,* series B 42-48; remainder from U.S. Bureau of the Census, *Current Population Reports, Series P-20, Fertility of American Women,* Nos. 225, 341, 387, 406 (Washington, DC: Government Printing Office, various dates).

with cohorts born around 1910 and continues to those born in the mid-1930's. The process then reverses again, and the baby-bust-generation fertility is revealed in the data for cohorts born after about 1940.

The data for nonwhite women bear a striking resemblance to those for white women, in terms of both secular trends and cyclicity. The levels are higher throughout, particularly for the initial portion of the graph and again for the baby-boom generation. But the turning points and the periods of large decline are virtually identical, suggesting a set of common factors affecting two groups whose labor force characteristics and economic circumstances are extremely different throughout the period.

Many of the common influences are not hard to identify, although not all have been studied in detail. Most can be easily discerned by adding 25 years to the birth year of the cohort, as done in Figure 5.3. The first large decline in fertility, associated with cohorts born between 1860 and 1870, can thereby be traced to the economic depression of the 1890's, although I know of no study that has done so in detail. The movement into the fertility trough begins before the Great Depression, but appears to gain momentum in that decade of economic deprivation.

Easterlin's theory of cyclical fluctuations in fertility, also known as the "relative income" hypothesis, begins with the closing of immigration during the 1920's. Prior to the 1920's, the consequences of economic decline for population change, and therefore the age distribution, were ameliorated by a lessening in immigration.

Likewise, the consequences of periods of economic advance were dampened by an increase in immigration (see Easterlin, 1971). Immigration was pro-cyclical, linked in particular to unemployment in the United States. Its virtual close in the 1920's meant the economic cycle could have a greater impact on fertility in both the short and long runs.

The close of immigration meant that the impact of the business cycle on wages could not be rapidly smoothed. Periods of economic decline resulted in fewer marriages and fewer births rather than less immigration. With a closed population, these fertility changes had long-run effects by changing the age distribution and thus the relative economic rewards of the next generation. Thus fewer births and scant immigration in the depressed 1930's led to higher relative incomes in the 1950's and an increase in family size. This reasoning explains the trough of fertility in the 1930's as well as its subsequent peak in the 1950's. Following the argument one step further, Easterlin connects the next portion of the cyclical path to the decline in relative incomes of the boom generation when it reached maturity. Faced with lower incomes than anticipated, the baby-boom children of the baby-bust generation married late, if at all, and have had the fewest children among all generations of Americans.

Measures of marital fertility other than births per ever-married woman are also relevant to the issue of labor force participation. The distribution of births, here the proportion of ever-married women having no children, is an indicator of the fraction of women who could most easily manage career and home. Figure 5.4 gives the proportion having no births for the white and nonwhite populations of ever-married

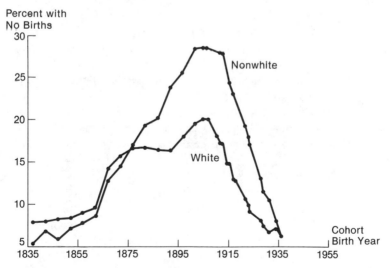

FIGURE 5.4. Percentage of Ever-Married Women with No Births by Race and Cohort. *Sources:* Birth cohorts 1835–1924 from *Historical Statistics,* series B 42-48; remainder from U.S. Bureau of the Census, *Current Population Reports, Series P-20, Fertility of American Women,* Nos. 225, 341, 406 (Washington, DC: Government Printing Office, various dates).

women, scaled once again by the cohort's birth. The proportions can be calculated only for cohorts already beyond childbearing ages and thus end just before 1940, while those for the number of births use measures of birth expectations and end around 1950.

That the proportion of white and nonwhite women having no children bears a resemblance to the data on total births is no accident. Declining fertility is often accompanied by a rise in the proportion with no children. But surprises do appear in the graph. Although the figure for the percentage of white, ever-married women having no births is initially higher than it is for nonwhite women, as it might be expected given the lower fertility of the white population, the nonwhite proportion overtakes the white with the cohort born around 1870. It then remains higher for all subsequent cohorts and reaches a peak with those born around the turn of this century. The peak for white women is reached around the same time, but the percentage for nonwhite women bearing no children is 43% higher.

The extent of childlessness among both white and nonwhite women was considerable. At the peak for white ever-married women, about 20% never had children; and at the peak for nonwhite women, over 28% never had children. The proportions expected to be childless among cohorts born after 1950 are considerably lower than these levels, even across all marital statuses (Bloom, 1986). The data for the most recent cohorts are not found in the diagram because the numbers, extrapolations from various surveys, are subject to considerable debate. But the ranges under consideration are still lower than the levels of these historical cohorts and suggest the merit of further study. The fact that the nonwhite proportion childless among ever-married women born after 1870 exceeds that of whites, while their fertility was also higher, suggests that nonwhite women had considerably greater heterogeneity in their fertility than white women. Many had no births, but among those who did have children, a greater fraction had many.

Thus the fertility and childlessness among cohorts of both white and nonwhite ever-married women varied considerably over time, and both have moved secularly and cyclically. Causes and effects have been mentioned regarding the relationships among fertility, general economic conditions, and the paid labor of women within and across cohorts. Perhaps the most obvious of these is that fertility change affects the subsequent labor force behavior of cohorts of married women, and both baby booms and baby busts can be linked to major economic vicissitudes, such as the depressions of the 1890's and 1930's, the economic revival of the 1950's, and the recession of the 1970's.

Some of the puzzling aspects of cohort labor force participation can now be explained on the basis of the differences among cohort fertility. The increase in participation for cohorts born around the turn of this century appears connected to declines in fertility among both white and nonwhite married women. The slight increase in participation among young married women in the 1950's, in comparison with the large increase among older married women, also seems linked to differences among these two cohorts in their fertility behavior and may, through Easterlin's "relative income" hypothesis, have been the products of earlier changes in fertility.

Cohort Differences in Education

A second factor that distinguishes one cohort from the next is educational attainment. Two measures of educational attainment, the percentage graduating from high school and from college, are given in Figure 5.5 for white and nonwhite females arrayed by birth cohort. Median years of schooling, a measure related to the first two, is given in Figure 5.6.[10] Substantial increases in median years of schooling among white females are apparent for the cohorts born just after the turn of the century. The proportion of young women finishing high school rose rapidly and exceeded one-half by the cohort born in 1910. Thus the median female's educational attainment rapidly increased to 12 years with that cohort. For nonwhite females the increase in high-school completion occurred about 25 years later, and cohorts born around 1935 brought the proportion finishing high school to the 50% mark. The high-school completion figures begin low for both white and nonwhite females born in the late nineteenth century, diverge almost immediately, and then converge with the cohorts born around 1940.[11]

The proportion of white females attending college for four or more years remained roughly constant until the cohorts born around 1930 and then climbed steeply for those born between 1940 and 1950, who finished college between approximately 1962 and 1972. The figures for nonwhite females are about one-half those of white but also begin an ascent with the cohorts born after 1940.

Occupational and Educational Change

The occupational statistics presented in Chapter 3 can now be more meaningfully interpreted in view of educational change by cohort. The transformation of occupations in the economy with the growth of the tertiary or service sector, particularly clerical work, marked the rise in married women's participation across a variety of countries (see, for example, the studies in Layard and Mincer, 1985). That transformation occurred in the United States between 1910 and 1920 when the proportion of white women 20 to 24 years old employed in the clerical sector rose to more than 35%, from a level below 10% around 1900. The proportion in the clerical sector is higher for single than married women at every date, and higher for younger than older women. Of more interest here is that for white women the proportions rise steeply in all relevant years (from 1930 to 1950) with cohorts born after 1900. The feature is apparent in the occupational data in Table 5.3 for all marital statuses, although more so for married women. Among native-white married women in 1930, 27% were clerical workers in the 1906 to 1910 cohort, but only 13% were in the 1886 to 1895 cohort; the figures for 1940 are 34% and 20%, which by necessity include sales workers. Among white married women in large cities, the figures diverge even more, 40% for the 1906 to 1910 group but only 21% for the 1886 to 1895 cohort. The increase in the proportion of employed women in the clerical sector has both period and cohort effects. The percentages increase over time among all cohorts, but the increase is greatest for those born around 1900 for whom, as was shown in the preceding section, schooling advanced most.

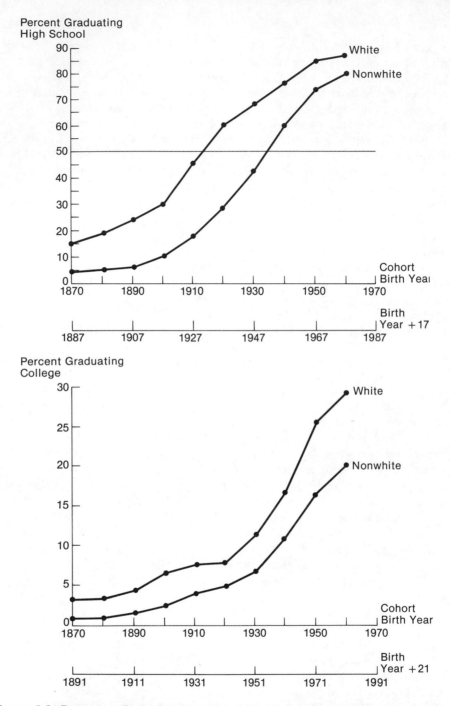

FIGURE 5.5. Percentage Graduating from High School and College by Race and Cohort. *Sources:* U.S. Bureau of the Census, *Current Population Reports, Series P-20, Educational Attainment in the United States,* Nos. 15, 121, 158, 182, 207, 243, 274, 314, 390, 415 (Washington, DC: Government Printing Office, various dates).

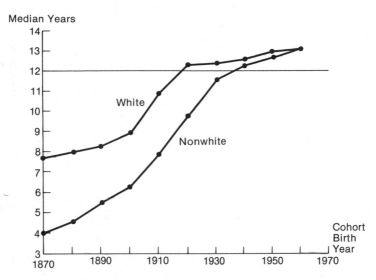

FIGURE 5.6. Median Years Schooling by Race and Cohort. *Sources:* U.S. Bureau of the Census, *Current Population Reports, Series P-20, Educational Attainment in the United States,* Nos. 15, 121, 158, 182, 207, 243, 274, 314, 390, 415 (Washington, DC: Government Printing Office, various dates).

One study has estimated that about one-third of the movement of young women from manufacturing to clerical employment between 1900 and 1930 was due to increased education (Goldin, 1984). The remainder was due to changes in the relative demand for labor in the two sectors and to the preferences of young women for clerical work over manufacturing. As the median educational attainment of white females reached 12 years, the occupational distribution of women moved decisively toward clerical work. Clerical work was, after 1930, the single most important occupational group among white women.

One may question the causality between schooling and the increased proportion of all employed women in the clerical labor force. Increased education could have been the product of the rise in clerical work, not one of its causes. But two further pieces of evidence support the implied assumption here that increased schooling led to the rise in clerical employment and not the reverse. The first is that young men, as well, increased their education in the years considered, and they did not enter clerical work to any great extent. The second is that educational attainment in the United States rose during 1910 to 1930 in urban areas, where clerical jobs were available, as well as in rural areas, where they were not, and it rose at about the same rate among females 6 to 20 years old in both areas.[12]

A similar, but less striking, pattern can be found in the occupational distribution of nonwhite women. There were few nonwhite female clerical workers in 1950, even among the youngest group considered (9.1% of those 20 to 24 years old). But in all subsequent years, the percentage increases, and while it does so among all age groups, the increases are greatest for those born after 1935. As in the case of white

TABLE 5.3. Percentage of Women in Clerical Sector Employment by Cohort and Race, 1930 to 1970

Year	1946 –50	1941 –45	1936 –40	1931 –35	1926 –30	1921 –25	1916 –20	1911 –15	1906 –10	1901 –05	1896 –1900	1891 –95	1886 –90
									Birth Cohort				
White Women													
Married													
1930									26.9	[24.0]	[24.0]	[13.3]	13.3
1940						[35.5]	[35.5]	36.4	34.2	[28.8]	[28.8]	[19.5]	19.5
1940u						[42.2]	[42.2]	43.0	39.6	[31.9]	[31.9]	[21.4]	21.4
All													
1930									33.7	31.9	27.2	21.0	16.7
1940							31.2	30.1	30.2	26.6	21.8	16.9	14.0
1950					48.2	39.0	29.8	[25.9]	[25.9]	[22.7]	[22.7]	17.0	
1960			49.2	40.2	36.2	[32.1]	[32.1]	[27.1]	27.1	24.2			
1970	47.6	37.7	36.7	36.1	36.0	35.5	32.4	29.1					
Nonwhite Women													
1950					9.1	7.2	5.2	[3.2]	3.2	[2.0]	2.0	[0.7]	
1960			16.8	13.1	11.0	[8.5]	8.5	[4.2]	[4.2]	2.8			
1970	39.3	27.0	21.8	17.4	14.9	12.5	10.0	7.3					

Notes and Sources: 1930: White is native-born white. U.S. Bureau of the Census, *Fifteenth Census of the United States: 1930, Population.* Vol. V, *General Report on Occupations* (Washington, DC: Government Printing Office, 1933b).

1940: 1940u is urban; both it and 1940 include sales. *Married:* U.S. Bureau of the Census, *Sixteenth Census of the United States: 1940, Population.* Vol. III, *The Labor Force,* Part 1. *United States Summary* (Washington, DC: Government Printing Office, 1943a). *All:* J. Smith and M. Ward, *Women's Wages and Work in the Twentieth Century* (Santa Monica, CA: Rand Corporation, 1984), table 22.

1950: U.S. Bureau of the Census, *U.S. Census of Population: 1950.* Vol. IV, *Special Reports,* Part 1, Chapter B, "Occupational Characteristics" (Washington, DC: Government Printing Office, 1956).

1960: U.S. Bureau of the Census, *U.S. Census of Population: 1960. Subject Reports: Final Report PC(2)-7A, Occupational Characteristics* (Washington, DC: Government Printing Office, 1963c).

1970: U.S. Bureau of the Census, *Census of Population, 1970, Subject Reports: Final Report PC(2)-7A. Employment Status and Work Experience* (Washington, DC: Government Printing Office, 1973).

Figures in brackets group by necessity two cohorts.

women, nonwhite women moved rapidly into clerical work as median educational attainment by cohort reached 12 years. But neither nonwhite nor white married women, regardless of education, were unconstrained in their occupational choice. The problem was apparently more severe for nonwhite women.

Despite the rapid increase in the employment of single, white women in the clerical sector, married women were barred from clerical positions in large firms across the United States from 1920 to 1950. Single, white women were hired but were often fired when they married, and older married women were often not employed at all by certain firms. These policies predated the depression of the 1930's but were expanded during it. Married white women increased their employment in the clerical sector from 1920 to 1950 by entering small firms and those without the "marriage bar," as it was termed. The reasons for the marriage bar and its eventual impact on labor force participation will be examined in Chapter 6.

Black women, regardless of marital status, education, and other abilities, were barred by a considerably larger fraction of firms' hiring clerical workers than were white married women, according to a 1940 Women's Bureau survey (U.S. Department of Labor, 1942). Chapter 6 uses a sample of firms from this survey to analyze the marriage bar, but its relevance here concerns answers to a question about personnel "policies with reference to race and color." While the marriage bar might be explained on the basis of productivity-related factors, policies that barred the hiring of black women in clerical positions cannot be.[13] They were clearly rooted in personal prejudices, and the source of discrimination appears to lie primarily with white employees.

The policy of not hiring blacks in clerical occupations was so firmly established that most companies surveyed about their policies responded, and with no irony intended, "no colored hired in office, no discrimination as to race," as did Corn Products in Kansas City.[14] Almost 50% of the firms surveyed responded that they had a stated personnel policy prohibiting the hiring of black clerical workers or had instituted an unwritten rule. Included in the remaining group are those that answered "never have had negroes, but don't apply," as did the Federal Reserve Bank of Los Angeles. Several firms gave unsolicited reasons for the policy; one was Security Title Insurance of Los Angeles, which hired "only caucasians . . . for positions which entail meeting the public." Cook Paint and Varnish in Kansas City claimed that "employee attitude prevents effective use of two races," and, similarly, Philadelphia Electric asserted that its "employees refuse to work with colored people in the clerical field."

The marriage bar disappeared as official firm policy in the 1950's, but it is not clear when barriers against black female office workers were dropped. The increase in black female clerical workers with the cohorts born after the mid-1930's suggests that firms responded to an increased supply of educated black women. But firms and employees may also have discriminated more against blacks when average black educational attainment was low.

A central feature of the female labor force, noted in Chapter 2, has been persistence in the labor market, particularly among women who did not quit work at marriage. Working married women remained in the labor force for long periods and accumulated substantial work experience. Persistence, as well as future labor force participation, appear related to the initial occupation of women. Both have been shown to be higher for those who began work in clerical occupations than for those whose first jobs were in manufacturing, given education, age, and the age at which work began. The probability that a married white woman would be in the labor force in 1939 was 13% lower had she begun her work experience in a manufacturing job rather than in a clerical or professional job, given education and other relevant variables (see Goldin, 1989). Therefore, the movement of jobs from the manufacturing to the clerical sector, caused by changes in education and sectoral shifts in the economy, had long-lasting impacts on female work experiences.[15]

Education and occupation were not the only factors that changed with the cohorts born around 1900. Recall from Chapter 2 that advancements in education were accompanied by an increase in labor force participation among young women from 1880 to 1930. With increases in both education and work, very few young women could spend their prenuptial youth "at home" helping their mothers. By 1930 practically all single women were either working or at school, but in 1900 about 35%, among those 16 to 24 years old, were not at either. They were, instead, "at home." The changes in school, labor force, and home time among single women from 1880 to 1930 were reinforcing. Education enabled young women to enter the clerical field, clerical work encouraged their future labor force participation, and the reduction in time spent "at home" reinforced both effects. By 1930 the socialization of young women was accomplished less in the homes of their parents and more in schools and the workplace.

Several variables have been presented that can vary by cohort—education, fertility, and first occupation are among those discussed. How these variables actually changed over time and with cohorts suggests that the labor force participation rates may be a product of factors that vary by both cohort and time, what I have been calling the cohort and contemporaneous factors. Cohorts of white women born around 1900 to 1910 differed from their predecessors in several ways. They experienced a large advance in schooling, they were employed when young in the newly emerging clerical sector, and they spent far less of their youth "at home" than previous cohorts. Their fertility rates were exceptionally low, and a large percentage of them formed childless unions. These cohorts greatly increased their labor force participation rates in the 1950's and 1960's when older and, to a lesser degree, when younger in the 1920's and 1930's. Cohorts born in the 1930's and 1940's had high fertility and experienced small increases in participation rates when young. The youngest cohorts that can be studied here, those born since the 1940's, experienced significant advances in college graduation rates and returned to the low fertility of earlier cohorts. These youngest cohorts have had large increases in participation in the 1970's and 1980's.

The emphasis here on cohort factors is not meant to slight the role of contemporaneous effects and factors that have varied with time. Contemporaneous factors have been central to most analyses of female labor force participation. The female wage, the earnings of married men, the unemployment rate, and the industrial mix or other proxies for the demand for female labor are routinely included in cross-sectional and time-series studies of female labor force participation.[16] These variables do not necessarily vary by cohort, but do vary over time. Other contemporaneous factors include wars, economic depressions, and social upheaval that many cohorts pass through, albeit at different points in their lives.

Cohort effects have been highlighted here because the longer, historical time series has revealed their possible importance. I have emphasized throughout this volume that economic and social change is often carried through time by individuals, and thus a cohort approach can help unravel why economic change often seems delayed. This mode of economic and social change has been termed "the succession of generations" by John Durand (1948, p. 123). Figures 5.3 through 5.6 suggest that some of the large increases in participation rates are related to advances in schooling and that differences across cohorts can be traced to changes in fertility. But because graphical demonstration can be misleading, I consider both the cohort and the contemporaneous variables in a multivariate framework.

A Cross-Section, Time-Series Model

The data of Figures 5.1a and 5.1b yield 37 observations for nonwhite and white married women separately. Each observation is the labor force participation rate of a cohort of married women in a census year. Ten cohorts are contained in Figure 5.1, but because some are too recent to have complete work histories and for others there are gaps in the series, some age groups cannot be included for each cohort. Nine census years are covered from 1890 to 1980; the data for 1910 cannot be used because of the peculiar features of that census discussed in Chapter 2. The data begin with 15 to 24 year olds in 1890 from the birth cohort 1866 to 1875 and end with 15 to 24 year olds in 1980 from the birth cohort 1956 to 1965.[17]

The variables of the preceding discussion can be divided into two groups, those that influence change over time for any particular cohort (what I have termed contemporaneous factors or period effects) and those that differentiate each cohort's experience from that of any other (what I have termed cohort-specific factors). A third variable, that of age, is also included. There are three aspects of time to be considered: one concerns the birth year of the cohort, another is the period or date of an event, and the third is the age of the individual.

The first set of factors, accounting for within-cohort effects, can include the full-time earning capacity of women, the income of other family members, the unemployment rate, and the sectoral mix of the economy. Relative prices for market goods that had been primarily home produced and for labor-saving capital equipment are also key variables, but are not readily available for the full period considered. The data allow for, at most, 10 equations, one for each of the cohorts, expressing the labor force participation rate of cohort i, at time t, (ℓ_{it}), in terms of a vector of period effects, (P_t): $\ell_{it} = f(P_t)$, $t = 1, \ldots, 9$ and $i = 1, \ldots, 10$. Although there are nine years of data, one for each of the census years from 1890 to 1980 (with the exception of 1910), each cohort can have at most five years of data, one for each of the five age groups.

The second set of factors, accounting for cross-cohort effects, includes educational attainment and fertility. Other aspects of early socialization, such as work experience and the amount of time spent at home when young, cannot at present be incorporated. For each nine years of data, the labor force participation rate of cohort i can be expressed as a function of cohort factors (C_i): $\ell_{it} = g(C_i)$. The two sets of equations are pooled to form: $\ell_{it} = h(P_t, C_i, A_{it}, C_i \times A_{it})$, where A_{it} is the age of cohort i at time t, and interaction effects between age and cohort are considered.

A complementary manner of conceptualizing the problem is to return to the simple supply–demand framework introduced above. The labor force participation equation, one of the two reduced forms, is given as equation (4'), and equation (5') gives the reduced form when demand is infinitely elastic:

$$\log \ell = \log S \cdot \delta/(\eta + \delta) + \log D \cdot \eta/(\eta + \delta) \qquad (4')$$

$$\log \ell = \log S + \eta \log \bar{w} \qquad (5')$$

The cohort and contemporaneous variables can be grouped as factors affecting either the supply or the demand side (or both). Most cohort-specific factors (e.g., education and fertility) are generally included on the supply side, and many of the contemporaneous factors (e.g., industrial mix) rightly belong on the demand side. But there are other factors, such as unemployment and the earnings of male workers, that can arguably be included in either camp. Male earnings, for example, are included in the supply function, as in equation (1), to capture the income of the family, but can also be included in the demand for labor function as the alternative input cost of female labor. Because the purpose of the estimation is to find the correlates of labor force participation, rather than to identify labor supply and demand parameters, the variables need not be grouped on one side or the other.

Two equations are estimated, one for white married women and the other for nonwhite married women. The determinants of the labor force participation include the cohort factors described above: births per ever-married woman, the proportion graduating from college, and median education. Two interaction terms are added: between the two youngest age groups and the fertility variable because greater fertility may constrain younger more than older women, and between the college variable and the three oldest age groups because school completion often reduces work among younger women. The contemporaneous factors or period effects include the unemployment rate, a dummy variable for 1950 to account for the residual impact of World War II, full-time (deflated) female earnings, full-time (deflated) male earnings, and the real per capita value of the economy's trade (retail and wholesale) sector to proxy the demand for female labor. The equation for nonwhite women excludes by necessity the income variables, which cannot at present be constructed for them, and the trade variable, which seems less justifiable.[18] Instead, a variable for the percentage of black Americans residing in the South is included to proxy the demand for agricultural labor and the role of lower male incomes in increasing female employment. Three regression equations are presented in Table 5.4. The first two, in columns (1) and (2), are for white women. That in column (1) includes the female earnings variable, justified if their earnings are exogenous, as in equation (5'); that in column (2) excludes the female earnings variable, as in equation (4'). The last equation is for nonwhites and by necessity must exclude all earnings variables.[19]

TABLE 5.4. Pooled Cross-Section, Time-Series Analysis of Married Women's Labor Force Participation by Race, 1890 to 1980

Variable	(1) White	(2)	(3) Nonwhite
Mean of ℓ	[0.237]		[0.382]
Constant	−2.80	−3.41	1.41
	(7.89)	(8.76)	(1.42)
Cohort effects			
Births	−0.383	−0.416	−0.043
	(5.63)	(4.95)	(0.66)
Median years schooling	0.0924	0.129	−0.0612
	(2.79)	(3.26)	(1.23)
Percent graduating college	0.0132	0.00814	0.0622
	(1.51)	(0.76)	(3.35)
Cohort, age interactions			
Births × age groups 1, 2	−0.0436	−0.0855	0.00600
	(1.26)	(2.08)	(0.14)
Percent college × age	0.0273	0.0172	0.100
groups 3, 4, 5	(2.16)	(1.12)	(3.91)
Contemporaneous effects			
Female earnings × 10^{-2}	0.172		
	(3.90)		
Male earnings × 10^{-2}	−0.0929	0.00713	
	(3.42)	(0.64)	
Unemployment	−0.0123	0.0140	−0.0294
	(1.12)	(1.29)	(2.62)
War dummy	0.152	0.0297	−0.338
	(1.82)	(0.31)	(3.03)
Trade × 10^{-2}	0.244	0.308	
	(2.17)	(2.22)	
Percent nonwhite in South			−2.10
			(1.98)
Age effects			
Old	−0.409	−0.381	−0.454
	(4.38)	(3.29)	(3.15)
Adjusted R^2	.986	.978	.871

Notes and Sources: The number of observations for each regression is 37. All are estimated as logistic transforms, $\log_e[\ell/(1 - \ell)]$, where ℓ is the labor force participation rate of married women from Table 2.2 (ℓ from 1890 to 1930 is for white native-born women of native parents and differs slightly from the data in Table 2.2). For the independent variables, Births is for ever-married women and is from Figure 5.3 divided by 1,000; Median years schooling is from Figure 5.6; Percent graduating from college is from Figure 5.5; Female earnings and Male earnings are both full-time equivalents from Table 5.1; Unemployment is the unemployment rate from *Historical Statistics* and *Economic Report of the President, 1980,* and is a three-year average $(t - 2)$ to (t); War dummy is 1 for 1950 and 0 otherwise; Trade is the share of national income accounted for by the trade sector from *Historical Statistics* and U.S. Department of Commerce, Bureau of Economic Analysis, *The National Income and Product Accounts of the U.S., 1929–82: Statistical Tables* (Washington, DC: Government Printing Office, 1986), for 1980; Percent nonwhite in South is from *Historical Statistics* and U.S. census for 1980; Old is 1 for age group 5 and 0 otherwise. Age groups are: 1 = 15–24; 2 = 25–34; 3 = 35–44; 4 = 45–54; 5 = 55–64, and interaction terms are dummy variables equal to 1 if the age group is indicated and 0 otherwise. Absolute values of t-statistics are in parentheses.

The results of the pooled time-series, cross-section analysis for white married women confirm many of the intuitive findings in the discussion of cohort effects. Including or excluding the female earnings variable affects some of the coefficients, but does not alter many of the substantive findings on the role of cohort effects. Even when the growth in the trade sector, the unemployment rate, and the earnings variables are included, cohort effects are important contributors to the participation rate. Indeed, they account for about 35% of the total change over the period for each of the age groups taken separately.

Increases in median years of schooling and in college graduation greatly enhanced the labor force activity of white married women. The elasticity of median years with respect to labor force participation is 0.7, around the means. Further, the coefficient on college graduation triples among the older age groups. Increased college education may have led women to alter their expectations about future work. Although they may have reduced their participation when young, college graduates greatly increased it when older. Evidence in Chapter 7 from a sample of college graduates in 1957 will indicate that while college graduates in the 1950's and 1960's withdrew from the labor force to raise their children, their intent was to return in the future. Increased birth rates decrease labor force activity, not surprisingly, but the effect lasts well beyond the younger age groups. Fertility is only about 10% to 20% more a deterrent to paid work among the younger age groups than it is for the entire cohort.

Greater female earnings increase, while higher male earnings decrease, participation, a finding that accords with the theory of labor supply. The coefficients could be interpreted as income and wage effects, although I have indicated that these parameters probably changed over time. Both income and wage effects implied by the results are substantial, and even in equations that include a time variable, both elasticities are greater than one in absolute value.[20] Higher unemployment rates for the labor force as a whole served to encourage participation of married white women, rather than discourage it, when female earnings are also included in the equation.

The role of World War II in unleashing social change is incorporated in the equation through the inclusion of a dummy variable for 1950. The direct impact of the World War II period varies between the two equations and across others that were estimated. The impact is small, often not statistically significant, but generally positive. Much of the impact of World War II was indirect, rather than direct, and is already incorporated in the consequence of the war on fertility and the postwar increased demand for all workers. The postwar baby boom, earlier marriages, and increased schooling decreased the supply of younger women and led employers to seek older, married women they had hitherto ignored and often barred (see, for example, Oppenheimer, 1970, on demographic effects).

Older, married women were an untapped pool of workers, mobilized in large numbers during World War II. Labor force data, presented in Table 5.5, for the wartime period indicate that from 1940 to the peak of wartime employment of women in July 1944, employment increased most among two groups of women: the very young, 14 to 19 years old, and those older than 45 years. The increase among those 45 to 64 years old was 65% and was 97% among those older than 65 years; it

TABLE 5.5.   The Female Labor Force and World War II

Year	14–19	20–24	Age 25–44	45–64	≥65	Total
			Number of Women in the Labor Force (000)			
1940	1377	2659	6026	2511	271	12845
1940, adjusted	1460	2820	6527	2719	299	13825
1942	2370	2900	7020	3420	400	16110
1943	2930	3120	8190	3970	490	18700
1944	2900	3230	8220	4320	500	19170
1945	2720	3180	8230	4410	490	19030
1946	2160	2780	7370	4020	450	16780
1950	1440	2536	7658	4410	507	16552
(July 1944/1940)	2.295	1.142	1.276	1.651	1.973	
(1950/1940)	1.046	0.954	1.271	1.756	1.871	
			Labor Force Participation Rate			
1940	18.8%	45.1%	30.2%	19.7%	5.9%	
1950	22.6	43.2	33.3	28.8	7.8	

Notes and Sources: 1940: U.S. Bureau of the Census, *Sixteenth Census of the U.S.: 1940, Population.* Vol. III, *The Labor Force,* Part I, *U.S. Summary* (Washington, DC: Government Printing Office, 1943a). The adjusted figures are inflated, on average, by 7.7% for consistency with the Current Population Report figures for March 1940.

1942 to 1946: U.S. Bureau of the Census, Current Population Reports: Labor Force Bulletin, Series P-50, No. 2. *Labor Force, Employment, and Unemployment in the United States, 1940 to 1946* (Washington, DC: Government Printing Office, n.d.).

1950: U.S. Bureau of the Census, *U.S. Census of Population: 1950.* Vol. II, *Characteristics of the Population,* Part 1, *U.S. Summary* (Washington, DC: Government Printing Office, 1953a).

Because the Current Population Report data for the World War II period are not disaggregated by marital status and race, the census data are also given for all women in the labor force. The ratio (July 1944/1940) uses the adjusted 1940 data for consistency with the Current Population Report data, while the ratio (1950/1940) uses the unadjusted numbers for consistency with the 1950 population census. The peak of female employment during World War II occurred in July 1944.

was only 28% among those 25 to 44 years old and 14% among those 20 to 24. Although the 14 to 19 year olds experienced a change exceeding 200%, it was a rather short-lived increase. The ratio of employment in the 1950 census to that in 1940 indicates no growth for the younger age group and a decrease for those 20 to 24 years old. But the increase during the war for women 45 to 64 years old was maintained and even exceeded. Employment for that group rose 76% from 1940 to 1950, and that for those older than 64 years rose by 87%. Some of the change could be due to simple demographics, but labor force participation rates also increase most for the older women, by 46% for the 45- to 64-year-old group and 32% for the very oldest. Although the wartime data cannot be disaggregated by race and marital status, the increase among women in the older age groups suggests that married, rather than single, women were the primary means of bolstering the nation's labor force.

   Much has been written about the participation of American women during World War II and their replacement by men in factories after the armistice (Anderson, 1981; Campbell, 1984; Chafe, 1972). There is still considerable disagreement about whether employed women wanted to remain in the traditionally male industries from which they were eventually displaced. It is clear, however, that older married women were a major resource during the war and continued to be one after, albeit in different employments. A full resolution of the role of World War II must await microlevel data on the employment of women during the 1940's.[21]

The story of long-run economic change that can be told for nonwhite married women from the regression equation is, not surprisingly, less clear than that for white married women. Participation rates for nonwhite married women reflect changes in both the old and the new occupations of women. As late as the 1960's, the majority of black working women were domestic servants and agricultural workers. Thus the participation rate of nonwhite women reflects two opposing trends, the decline in the agricultural sector and the eventual movement of black women from private household work to the clerical, sales, and manufacturing sectors. In the case of white married women, the impact of increased education was translated into higher labor force participation rates through the employment of women in the clerical sector. But in the case of black married women, the increase in education served first to decrease their employment in domestic service but then increase it in various other employments.

Increased education may have had an impact on their occupational mix, but measured as median years of schooling it had little impact on their participation decision over the period considered here and may even have served to decrease paid labor. College graduation, however, had an impact similar to that for white women, and the positive effect is strengthened about threefold when the interaction between the older age groups and college is added. The total impact of college on employment is muted, however, because the proportion of all nonwhite women who completed college among any of the cohorts is rather small. The impact of changing fertility is negative for nonwhite women but not statistically significant. The finding that children have a considerably smaller impact on nonwhite than white participation is consistent with several cross-section studies (e.g., Bell, 1974; Bowen and Finegan, 1969; Cain, 1966; see also Goldin, 1977). In contrast to the results for white women, the unemployment rate has a strong, negative impact on nonwhite women's participation, due almost entirely to the rather large decrease in their participation during the Depression.

Expectations and Cohort Labor Force Participation

Periods of rapid change in any social indicator often complicate the future plans of individuals. The empirical model of the labor force just estimated implies that individuals could have easily extrapolated their future on the basis of a small number of variables. The process of social change, however, is considerably more complex. Because investments in human capital generally occur when individuals are young, adults closest to youth often provide their only guide to an uncertain future. Each generation passes its norms and expectations to the next in a manner that often impedes social progress.

Figure 5.1a helps reveal the revolution in the role of married women that has taken place over the last half-century. The rapid increase in the participation of married women means that cross-section rates by age differ substantially from cohort participation profiles. Thus the dotted line for the 1970 cross section is extremely different from any of the cohort lines. Individuals, however, do not observe their own cohort profiles, except retrospectively. Rather, they often base their judgments about the future on information provided them indirectly by others. That is, they observe the experiences of others in cross section. Because the cohort and cross-section rates differ substantially, expectations and choices made on the basis of cross sections would have been based on rather misleading evidence.

No generation of young women in America could have predicted solely from the experiences of their elders what their own work histories would have been, and most would have been considerably off the mark. In 1930, for example, a cohort of 20-year-old daughters, born in 1910, would have been off by a factor of about 4 in predicting their own participation rates in 25 years had they simply used the experiences of their 45-year-old mothers, born in 1885, as a guide.

But all cohorts were more informed than the method of simple extrapolation suggests. They knew, for example, that their years of schooling were higher than their mothers', and they may have been aware that their present occupations differed from those held by their mothers just before they married. They also may have been able to fill in the gap between their cohort and that of their mothers' by looking at the work activities of their older sisters, their aunts, and others in the intervening cohorts. Knowledge of these differences would have narrowed the gap between the simple extrapolation and the actual value of the daughters' labor force participation. With enough data points for cohorts between theirs and their mothers', they could have predicted their future participation rates with relative ease. Had they access to the data that underlie Table 5.4, they could have made extremely accurate predictions. [22]

Parents, and society in general, however, may reinforce the status quo by socializing daughters to expect the average participation rate of their mothers. Although most individuals revise their expectations with new information, this may not have been possible for many generations of young women.

Empirical evidence on cohorts born between 1944 and 1954 suggests the manner in which expectations were formed and underscores the possibility that many cohorts have vastly underestimated their own future labor force participation. In 1968, the National Longitudinal Survey (NLS) asked their sample of young women, who were then between 14 and 24 years old, what percentage believed they would be in the labor force at age 35. Among white females, 29% responded they would be in the labor force at age 35, and 59% of blacks responded affirmatively (Sandell and Shapiro, 1980). Almost all these young women are now at least age 35, and their labor force participation rate already exceeds 60% if they are married and greatly exceeds it (about 80%) if they are not. The figures reported by white women in 1968 were more in line with their mothers' participation rates in 1968 than with their own 16 years later.

To help visualize the data, the two cohort participation rate graphs, Figures 5.1a and 5.1b, each contain a vertical line at age 35. Point *B* is the actual labor force participation rate of the cohort born from 1944 to 1954 when it reached age 35 (if married), while point *A* is approximately on the cohort line for the group born between 1920 to 1930—the average birth year of the mothers of the young female sample.[23] Point C in Figure 5.1a is 29%, the value given by the young white women as their expected rate, and point C in Figure 5.1b is 59%, the value given by the young black women. Point A is just slightly higher than point C in Figure 5.1a, the proportion of young women who expected to be employed at that point in their life cycle. It may not be a coincidence that the expectation of future labor force activity for these young women at age 35 was approximately equal to their mothers' actual participation rate at age 35. The difference between points A and C is considerably greater among black women.

For white women, at least, the finding that young women's predictions were similar to the actual experiences of their mothers' cohorts might suggest that as individuals their labor force behavior was similar to that of their mothers'. Working mothers, it might be thought, produced working daughters. Mothers with traditional roles, alternatively, reared traditional daughters. Research in this area using the NLS has produced no consensus that individual lives were altered in this manner. Rather, the relationship between maternal labor force behavior and that of daughters is considerably more complex. Two independent studies conclude that while there is an impact of mothers' values regarding paid labor on daughters' work and of mothers' atypical occupations on daughters' occupations, there is no apparent relationship between mothers' labor force behavior and daughters' (D'Amico et al., 1983; Shapiro and Shaw, 1983).

When young women incorrectly assess their future labor market roles, they will probably underinvest in job training and, possibly, formal schooling. The underinvestment could later reveal itself in lower wages for women compared with men, despite similar labor market experience and years of formal education. Lower investments in human capital could, in turn, reduce the rate of increase in the participation rate of adult women.

The young women who vastly underestimated their future labor force participation rates did, according to two researchers, underinvest in job training. Those who claimed they would work at age 35 began work in jobs that initially paid less than the jobs of those who stated they would not work at age 35 (Sandell and Shapiro, 1980). But those who planned more attachment to the labor force eventually earned considerably more. Those who thought they would work when they were 35 years old invested more in on-the-job training than did those who believed they would quickly exit from the labor force. Their earnings were lower initially but rose more rapidly.

Although the expectations of young white women in 1968 were much below their eventual labor force participation, a similar question asked of young women just five years later, in 1973, indicates rapid convergence of expected and actual participation rates. Of those who were 19 to 29 years old in 1973, 60.3% of the white women believed they would be in the labor force at age 35 and 73.8% of the black women did (O'Neill, 1983). Young women across different cohorts and within the same cohort substantially revised their expectations between 1968 and 1973, as can be seen in Table 5.6. In 1968, young white women expected a labor force participation rate when they were 35 years old that was more in line with their mothers' at 35 years old. But by 1973, young women were forming expectations by extrapolating from current conditions rather than by observing current levels.[24]

TABLE 5.6. Expected Labor Force Participation at Age 35 by Race, Age, and Birth Cohort, 1968 to 1979

Age (Year of Survey)	White	Nonwhite
15–19 (1968)	0.29–0.34	0.59
20–24 (1968)	0.29–0.34	0.59
19–24 (1973)	0.562	
25–29 (1973)	0.668	
19–29 (1973)	0.603	0.738

| Cohort Birth Year | White | | |
(Year of Survey)	*15–19*	*20–24*	*25–29*
1944–53 (1968)	[0.29–0.34	0.29–20.34]	
1944–48 (1973)			0.668
1949–53 (1973)		0.562	
1960–64 (1979)	0.74		

Notes and Sources: The 0.29 figure for white 15–19 and 20–24 year olds, as well as the 0.59 figure for nonwhites, in 1968 are from S. Sandell and D. Shapiro, "Work Expectations, Human Capital Accumulation, and the Wages of Young Women," *Journal of Human Resources* 15 (Summer 1980): 335–53, and refer to 14 to 24 year olds. The 0.34 figure is from D. Shapiro and J. Crowley, "Aspirations and Expectations of Youth in the U.S.: Part 2, Employment Activity," *Youth and Society* 14 (September 1982): 45, and is for 14 to 22 year olds. In 1968, the question posed was: "What would you like to be doing when you are 35 years old?" In 1973 and 1979, the question was: "What kind of work would you like to be doing when you are 35 years old?" Although it is possible that the question in the 1970's led a higher percentage to state they would be in the labor force at age 35, Shaw and Shapiro (1987) demonstrate that expectations advanced almost continuously from 1968 to 1978. The percentage answering "don't know" is nearly identical in all years (about 8%), and has been grouped with those in the labor force under the presumption that the respondents did not know their future occupation. Those who responded they would not have an occupation indicated they would be at "home." The data for 15 to 19 year olds in 1979 are those in Shapiro and Crowley (1982, p. 36) for 14 to 21 year olds. The 1973 data are from J. O'Neill, "The Determinants and Wage Effects of Occupational Segregation" (manuscript, The Urban Institute, 1983).

Comparable data on expectations are not available for the period before the NLS data of 1968. But it is reasonable to assume that many previous cohorts of young women also underestimated their actual labor force participation rates, and that the same was true for cohorts of young women since the 1920's. The evidence on expectations provides an additional reason for the finding in Chapter 4 that women earn substantially less than men given their education and work experience. The estimate of "wage discrimination" is a product of many factors, and one could be the early socialization of young women. The evidence on expectations also indicates a sharp break around the time of the feminist revival of the 1970's. The education and training of these cohorts of young women should be more in line with their future labor force experiences, and measures of "wage discrimination" for them should be truer measures of labor market discrimination.

Summary: Married Women in the Labor Force

This chapter has explored the factors serving to increase the participation of married women in the labor force during the past century. The process, it seems, is considerably more complex than an increase in the relative wage of women combined with an elastic supply of female labor. That explanation had been proposed by several scholars to explain recent trends. Although it probably accounts for a substantial amount of the change from 1940 to 1960, it accounts for considerably less before 1940 and for only about half after 1960. Further, it does not explain why certain cohorts were more responsive to change in real earnings than others. I develop a framework to explain change both across and within cohorts that includes three types of variables: cohort effects, period or contemporaneous factors, and age. Cohort effects, which had previously been largely ignored, account for about 35% of the total change over the last century for each of the age groups.

Despite the steady and accelerating increase in labor force participation rates among white married women over the period 1890 to 1980, change was prolonged by various factors. The expectations of women and their employers; constraints, such as those on hours of work, part-time employment, and, more recently, child-care arrangements; "wage discrimination," particularly in the emerging white-collar sector; and barriers erected against the employment of women are among the most important.

There is reason to believe that the process of change in participation was particularly prolonged among older, married women before World War II. I have alluded to the fact that married women, particularly older women, were barred from employment in many of the larger firms hiring clerical workers and from employment as teachers by the vast majority of school boards in the pre-1950 period. The pooled cross-section, time-series estimation presented above contains further evidence to bolster this view. The predicted values for the labor force participation of older, married women (age groups 35–44 and 45–54) are considerably larger than their actual values for 1930, 1940, and 1950. That is, the residuals from the equations are large and negative for these age groups. But the residuals for the same group are positive for 1960 to 1980. Older women had lower participation rates than would be predicted by the model for the period before 1950, suggesting that they were constrained, somehow, in their choice. The estimation can point to the constraint of only one group relative to all others because the mean error around the regression line must be zero. It is also possible that all cohorts and all age groups had lower participation because of constraints, such as discrimination and societal norms against their employment. I turn now to the constraints facing women and how and why they were reduced over time.

6

Why Did Change Take So Long?

Many of the forces that generated change in married women's employment—increased education, a markedly reduced birth rate, and the emergence of the clerical sector, to mention a few—were apparent as early as the 1920's. Yet the process of change in participation and in gender differences in earnings and occupations was extremely protracted. Conditions in the 1930's had much to do with the slow progress in the economic role of women, but the impact of the Depression often worked through preexisting social norms and institutional barriers.

Before 1950, the labor market did little to accommodate married and older women, and many employers barred their hire. Married women were barred from the position of teacher by the majority of local school districts and from clerical work by many large firms. I begin this chapter by discussing prohibitions against the hiring of married women to show how modern personnel practices, social consensus, the Great Depression, and individual expectations acted in concert to delay the emergence of married women in the American economy.

Women with household responsibilities were also hindered by the constraints of the workday. Until the 1930's, the usual work week was 5½ to 6 days and 50 hours long; scheduled part-time work, moreover, was virtually nonexistent before 1950. Even though hours had declined for all Americans from the late nineteenth century to 1940, many women with household responsibilities found hours of work too long in the pre-1950 period to justify paid employment. The chapter ends with the role of hours and part-time work.

The fruits of economic progress are often delayed by institutional constraints, and this chapter discusses two—marriage bars and hours of work. Others have been of equal importance. Discrimination against women in employment, motivated by the concerns of employer and employee alike, surely hindered the achievements of women. Some aspects of discrimination were discussed in Chapter 4, and further evidence is found in the example of marriage bars. Other barriers to change are more elusive, such as the role of norms concerning appropriate occupations for women. Taken together, these constraints and barriers were significant in impeding real change.

The notion that change was impeded prior to the 1950's is often inferred from the slow growth in participation rates of married women before World War II and from the rhetoric of Depression employment policy. Many other factors, however, could have intermediated. Education, first occupation, and fertility, among others, it was shown in Chapter 5, influence the participation of married women, and these cohort effects are maintained throughout one's lifetime. But the analysis in Chapter 5 indicated that even when these factors are considered in a multivariate analysis of cohort and cross-section participation, the residuals are negative and are largest among the older age groups in 1930, 1940, and 1950.[1] Thus these married women had lower participation rates given the other factors considered in the analysis. Why they did is explored here.

Marriage Bars

Discrimination against women is manifested in a variety of ways. In its most typical form, no prescribed barriers exist. Rather, employers, employees, and customers can express their prejudices against women workers by preferring not to associate with them. This form of discrimination is often inferred from its effects on earnings and occupations, as shown in Chapter 4. In other instances, custom and tradition are dominant, and individuals are penalized for deviating. Prescribed barriers against the training and employment of women are perhaps the most easily observed forms of discrimination. Rules have existed barring the education and training of women, as in the professions of law and medicine and among certain medieval guilds and more modern unions (see Morello, 1986, on law; Harris, 1978, on the professions in general). In other circumstances, rules restricted the employment of women, as in the armed forces, post office, local fire departments, and legal profession. The distinction between the two types of discrimination—the more or less subtle revealing of preferences and the rather obvious prohibitions—is often blurred when written rules do not exist but custom dictates the result.

Bars concerning the hiring and firing of married women, termed "marriage bars," arose in teaching and clerical work from the late 1800's to the early 1900's and provide the most numerically important form of all prohibitions in their impact on the employment of married women. In 1920 just 11% of all married women in the labor force were teachers and clerical workers, yet by 1970 the percentage nearly quadrupled, to 41%. The prohibitions covered what were to become the most frequent occupations for married women in the post-1950 era. In contrast, prohibitions against the training and employment of women as doctors and lawyers, probably the best known of all bans, affected a trivial percentage of women.[2] It is also of interest that marriage bars covering clerical and other occupations have existed across a variety of countries and have only recently been prohibited in Japan by its 1985 Equal Employment Opportunity Law.[3]

Prohibitions against the employment of married women consisted generally of two barriers—one against the hiring of married women and the second concerning the retention of existing workers when they married. The first will be referred to as the "hire bar" and the second as the "retain bar." It was uncommon for a firm to hire married women yet fire single women when they married. But firms that banned the hiring of married women often retained single employees when they married. When firms can screen beginners for valued traits or when firms invest considerably in training their workers, firing workers can be costly. Some firms and many school boards allowed women who married in service to remain as temporary workers or as substitute teachers, who could be dismissed at will and whose salaries were not based on tenure. Firms often imposed both the retain bar and the hire bar. It was rare, however, for a firm to impose the same prohibitions on men.[4]

The bar against women who married in service was the more restrictive of the two. In the 1920's, young women were just beginning to extend their working time after marriage. At that time, an older married woman seeking white-collar employment was in the extreme minority, in part because increased education and decreased fertility most affected cohorts born after 1900 (see Table 5.3 on clerical employment by cohort).

The rationale for the marriage bars offered here and elsewhere (Cohn, 1985, 1988) is simply that the policy was profitable, even in the absence of what may be termed clearly prejudicial views about the impropriety of married women's employment. Even though firms lost many trained employees and restricted their labor supply by refusing to hire married women, they gained considerably more. Precisely why they gained is not yet entirely clear, and I offer two complementary reasons that place considerable blame on modern personnel practices, such as fixed salary scales and internal promotion. But the marriage-bar policies also required certain precedents, such as sex-segregated occupations and social consensus.

Discrimination against married women and older workers came rather cheaply to firms in the pre–World War II period: the reduction in labor supply was small, and the loss in training was minimized by the types of occupations routinely offered women. Firms also perceived there were gains to policies that guaranteed homogeneity across sex, race, age, and marital status lines within occupations. But many aspects of this equilibrium were deceptively fragile and would change radically during and after World War II.

By the 1950's, firms could no longer ignore older married women, and certain aspects of the workplace were altered. The marriage bar, which at its height affected 87% of all local school districts and probably about 50% of all office workers, was virtually abandoned in the 1950's. The rhetoric of the workplace changed as well. Where a married woman was once an anomaly, perceived as an inefficient worker, she was now a coveted employee. In the mid-1950's, one personnel director, whose firm had previously barred married women, praised older women's "maturity and steadiness," and another noted that "they are more reliable than the younger ones."[5]

Extent of the Marriage Bar

The extent of the bars across the entire economy has been difficult to assess. These were, after all, the policies of individual firms and, in the case of school districts, individual localities. Prohibitions against the employment of married women teachers have been less difficult to track due to comprehensive surveys of local school districts by the National Education Association (NEA) beginning in the late 1920's.

Marriage bars were instituted in public-school teaching sometime in the late 1800's and were expanded in the early 1900's. Extensive surveys of local school districts beginning with 1928 indicate that 61% of all school systems would not hire

UNDERSTANDING THE GENDER GAP

TABLE 6.1. Marriage Bars Among School Districts, 1928 to 1951,
and Firms Hiring Office Workers, 1931 and 1940

Year	Do Not Retain Single Women When Married		Do Not Hire Married Women	
	Weighted	Not Weighted	Weighted	Not Weighted
	School Districts			
1928	47.3%	52.2%	61.9%	61.0%
1930/31	52.2	62.9	72.2	76.6
1942	58.4	70.0	77.7	87.0
1950/51	9.4	10.0	19.5	18.0
	Firms Hiring Office Workers			
1931 (178)	25.0%	12.0%	36.0%	29.2%
Philadelphia (44)	26.4	14.3	40.4	31.8
1940				
Philadelphia (106)	26.6	23.6	41.1	50.9
Kansas City (83)	28.4	15.7	41.7	31.3
Los Angeles (139)	9.4	8.6	24.4	15.8
	(Policy and Discretionary)		*(Policy and Discretionary)*	
1931	34.7%	27.3%	51.7%	52.8%
Philadelphia	36.9	35.7	60.7	59.1
1940				
Philadelphia	34.5	34.9	58.5	60.4
Kansas City	46.0	30.1	57.8	43.4
Los Angeles	25.1	15.7	38.8	26.6

Notes: School Districts: Weighted figures use city population weights; the unweighted are simple averages by number of school districts. City population weights are from *Historical Statistics*. The "Do Not Retain" case is (1— "may continue to teach"); the "Do Not Hire" case, includes "rarely under special conditions" for 1942 and 1950/51.

Firms Hiring Office Workers: Weighted figures are weighted by the firm's female employment; the unweighted are simple averages across firms in the sample. The 1931 sample includes Chicago, Hartford, New York City, and Philadelphia. Where possible, the responses apply to practices predating the Depression, although the interviews were conducted in 1931 and 1932. The 1940 sample includes Los Angeles, Kansas City, and Philadelphia and refers to practices during the Great Depression. Figures in parentheses are numbers of observations. "Discretionary" means firms stated single women were preferred, married women were placed on special probation, or the policy was up to the department head.

Note that because the 1931 sample has primarily large firms from a limited number of industries and the 1940 sample contains both large and small firms from a wider range of industries, comparisons cannot be drawn between the two years without further statistical work. See text for discussion.

Sources: School Districts: National Education Association (1928, 1932, 1942, 1952), from citations in V. Oppenheimer, *The Female Labor Force in the United States* (Westport, CT: Greenwood Press, 1976; orig. publ. 1970), table 4.5.

Firms Hiring Office Workers: 1931 Office Firm Survey, 1940 Office Firm Survey, see Data Appendix.

a married woman teacher and 52% would not retain any who married while on contract (Table 6.1). Because the data are grouped in the NEA reports by size of locality, Table 6.1 also weights the percentages by population. The unweighted data are generally greater than the weighted data because large cities had proportionately fewer bars. Both types of bars increased during the Depression, and on the eve of American entry into World War II, fully 87% of all school districts would not hire a married women and 70% would not retain a single woman who married. But sometime during World War II, both bars disappeared. By 1951 only 18% of the school systems had the hire bar and 10% the retain bar.

The extent of the marriage bar in office work can be inferred from information in two comprehensive surveys conducted by the Women's Bureau (U.S. Department of Labor, 1934b, 1942), called here the 1931 Office Firm Survey and the 1940 Office Firm Survey (see Data Appendix). A related data set, the employee schedules of the 1940 survey, was used in Chapter 4 to explore differences between male and female earnings in office work. Firm-level manuscripts from these surveys reveal much about the origin and impact of the bars. Although both Women's Bureau surveys were administered in the 1930's, the earlier one, taken in 1931, contains information about the 1920's, and the later one, taken in 1940, reveals the changes that occurred during the Depression.[6] The earlier survey, therefore, will be a guide to whether the bars existed before extensive rationing of jobs during the Depression.

The 1931 survey sampled mainly large firms in seven cities, of which 178 firms in Chicago, Hartford, New York City, and Philadelphia are included here. The 1940 survey was taken in five cities and sampled a wider range of firms; the sample here includes 328 firms in Kansas City, Los Angeles, and Philadelphia. Only Philadelphia is included in both surveys. The firms in the 1931 survey include insurance companies, investment houses, banks, publishing firms, advertising companies, public utilities, and mail-order firms. Added to the 1940 survey are manufacturing firms, retail stores, wholesale outlets, small professional offices, and firms in the transportation and communications sector.[7]

Both surveys contain information of a rather confidential nature regarding firm personnel practices, including occupations offered to either women or men, discrimination against blacks and Jews, the retention of single women when they married, the barring of married women, the use of salary scales, promotion from within, and minimum and maximum age limits. Information of this type would be virtually impossible to obtain in today's litigious environment. But personnel officers and other firm managers interviewed by the Women's Bureau were exceptionally candid, as their remarks below will indicate.[8] The surveys also contain more mundane personnel matters, such as the number of female and male employees, number of new employees, hours of work, personnel benefits (retirement plan, group insurance), union activity, the bureaucratic organization of the firm, and various paternalistic practices. Because the two surveys were executed by the same governmental agency (the Women's Bureau of the U.S. Department of Labor), they are similar in format, although the 1940 survey is more comprehensive.[9]

In 1931, 12% of all firms in the sample had a formal policy of not retaining single women when they married (see Table 6.1), but 25% of all female employees were in firms having such a policy. The policy, therefore, increased with firm size. Some firms did not have a strict marriage bar policy but had discretionary rules allowing them to retain able workers, to hire married women when single were unavailable, or to leave the policy up to department heads. These are termed the "discretionary" cases in the table. About 35% of all female employees were working in firms that would not retain them if they married as a condition of both policy and discretion. Considerably more firms had policies against hiring married women than against the retention of single women who married.[10] About 29% of all firms had such policies in the 1931 survey, and the policies affected 36% of all female employees across these firms. More than 50% of all firms in the sample would not hire married women as a condition of policy and discretion, and more than 50% of all female employees in the sample were employed by those firms.[11]

The policy of firing and hiring married women varies considerably with the type of firm and with firm size (Table 6.2). Insurance offices, publishing houses, banks, and public utilities had the most extensive controls in 1931; insurance offices, banks, public utilities, and the office portion of manufacturing firms had the most in 1940. Large firms, measured by the number of female employees, were more likely to institute such policies than small firms for both years.[12] Although the marriage-bar policy varied considerably by city in the 1940 sample, it did not in the 1931 sample, given the industrial distribution.

Tables 6.1 and 6.2 suggest an increase in the marriage-bar policy during the Great Depression. The data in Table 6.2 that array policies by size of firm show some increase during the 1930's, particularly for the marriage bar as policy. The Kansas City and Philadelphia percentages for the retain and hire bars in 1940 are, with one exception, greater than the average for 1931, but the Los Angeles data are not.[13] The extent and even existence of the increase is difficult to discern because the 1931 survey includes only large firms, and the industrial distribution of firms as well as the cities covered differ across the two surveys.

One way of handling the problem of composition is to pool the two samples and include firm size, industry and city dummy variables, and a year variable to estimate the impact of the Depression. Equations estimated in this fashion exhibit a positive, large, and significant effect for the Depression, in the case of the hire and the retain bar as policy. But the discretionary-policy version of both the hire and the retain bars did not change over time.[14] The Depression, it seems, led firms to extend a discretionary marriage bar into the realm of firm policy. Where firms had exercised discretion in the hiring and firing of married women before the Depression and during its first year, they instituted strict policies not to hire and not to retain married women by 1940.

Philadelphia was the only city sampled in both years and provides further evidence for the extension of the marriage bar during the Depression. Of the 41 firms in the 1931 sample for Philadelphia, 23 were also sampled by the Women's Bureau in the 1940 survey. Of these 23 firms, 11 experienced no change in policy, 2 reversed their prohibitions, and fully 10, or 43%, increased their prohibitions.[15]

Marriage bars have been mistakenly portrayed as originating in the unemployment of the 1930's, but the Depression reinforced and extended already existing bans against the employment of married women.[16] Because the respondents in the 1931 survey often noted that the policy was a Depression measure, and because the data were coded accordingly, the results indicate that the marriage bar, in both the retain and the hire versions, predated the Depression among firms hiring office workers. The precise degree that it did, however, cannot be ascertained with these data. There is, however, ample evidence in Table 6.1 that marriage bars instituted by school districts preceded the Depression, and that the bars in both sectors were expanded during the 1930's. The extensions, however, often took the form of

TABLE 6.2. Marriage Bars by Size of Firm and Sector, Office Work

	Policy		Policy and Discretionary		Distributions of	
	Do Not Hire	Do Not Retain	Do Not Hire	Do Not Retain	Firms	Female Employees
Size of firm in 1931[a]						
11 ≤ 20	0.0%	0.0%	0.0%	0.0%	1.1%	0.1%
21 ≤ 50	25.9	10.9	46.7	21.0	27.5	3.3
51 ≤ 100	40.4	8.4	63.5	28.9	24.2	6.0
101 ≤ 200	17.4	3.5	41.8	26.0	18.5	9.4
201 ≤ 400	31.0	22.2	59.5	47.5	11.8	11.3
401 ≤ 700	39.0	32.2	89.8	45.7	5.1	8.6
≥ 701	39.5	30.4	45.6	33.5	11.8	61.3
Number of observations					178	51597
Size of firm in 1940[a]						
11 ≤ 20	41.0%	17.9%	43.6%	25.6%	24.2%	3.7%
21 ≤ 50	43.6	18.2	49.1	25.5	34.2	11.2
51 ≤ 100	46.9	25.0	65.6	56.3	19.9	15.7
101 ≤ 200	50.0	25.0	75.0	43.8	9.9	13.8
201 ≤ 400	62.5	50.0	62.5	62.5	5.0	12.0
≥ 401	27.3	18.2	54.5	27.3	6.8	43.6
Number of observations					161	25358
					Number of Firms	
Sector in 1931						
Insurance	61.1%	45.7%	73.2%	59.5%	58	
Publishing	37.0	34.7	56.1	36.0	34	
Banking	35.4	21.2	41.9	30.2	27	
Public utilities	32.9	13.5	93.9	42.9	13	
Investment	11.3	1.4	26.6	9.8	27	
Advertising	11.1	0.0	28.2	0.0	13	
Sector in 1940[b]						
Insurance	50.0%	42.3%	53.8%	53.8%	26	
Publishing	33.3	13.3	46.7	33.3	15	
Banking	54.5	9.1	72.7	45.4	11	
Public utilities	50.0	33.3	66.7	50.0	6	
Investment	16.7	16.7	50.0	16.7	6	
Manufacturing	57.6	22.0	67.8	37.3	59	
Sales	17.2	10.3	24.1	13.8	29	

[a]Number of female employees.
[b]Includes only firms in Kansas City and Philadelphia with > 9 female employees for comparability with 1931.
Source: See Table 6.1.

governmental regulations that greatly strengthened preexisting social norms and conventions.

Federal Order 213, passed in 1932 as part of the Federal Economy Act, mandated that executive branch officials, in the face of layoffs, fire workers whose spouses were employed by the federal government. The regulation almost always entailed the firing of married women, although many husbands could have been furloughed. By 1940, 26 states had proposed legislation to restrict married women's employment in state government jobs, and 9 others had some form of restriction already in place (Shallcross, 1940). Similar regulations became effective among various local governments and served to expand the group of affected occupations to include librarians and nurses, although they too were probably covered by prohibitions prior to the Depression.[17]

Federal Order 213 and the actions of state and local governments lent credibility to pre-Depression policies of businesses and local school boards and enabled the extension of a system already in place. The bar was extended to occupations and sectors, such as manufacturing, where it was not extensively found before the Depression. The Depression served to reinforce social norms that kept married women, particularly the emerging middle class, out of the labor force. Because the bars were extended during the Depression, and because they were often justified by the need to ration employment among the most needy, many have thought marriage bars originated in the Depression. But it is inconceivable that marriage bars could have gained such wide acceptance during the Depression had previous policies not existed and had social consensus not been built around them.

Economic recessions are often periods of social recession, when already discarded and outmoded forms of gender relations are extolled. It was no accident, for example, that differences in wages between men and women for similar work were scrutinized in a federal survey taken in 1895–1896 (U.S. Commissioner of Labor, 1897) to establish that women were not taking jobs from men. The report was ordered by Congress during a severe depression when unemployment rates in the manufacturing sector were, for a brief period, as high as they were to be again in the 1930's. The recession of the immediate World War I period also prompted the firing of married women.[18] Similarly, periods of economic expansion often provide an impetus for progressive social change, as happened in the 1950's when the marriage bars vanished.

Firm-Level Evidence, 1931 and 1940

The correlates of the policy of not retaining single women at the time of marriage (Retain Bar = 1) are explored in Table 6.3. A somewhat different set of variables could be included for the more comprehensive survey of 1940. In both 1931 and 1940, there is a positive, yet weak, relationship between the number of employees in the firm and the probability of not retaining women who marry (also see Table 6.2 on the effect of firm size). But in both samples, the impact of firm size declines when factors concerning personnel relations are included. Size, it seems, may be a proxy here for the internal structure of firms and related employee policies. Firms with a policy of internal promotion, fixed salary scales, or regular salary increments with time on the job (Promote) had a higher probability of not retaining single women upon marriage. The probability also increases with policies that set a maximum age for new hires (Maximum age). Firms generally adopted a maximum age policy when they instituted regular internal promotion ladders, and the policy was generally in effect for both men and women. The retain-bar policy increases with the existence of pensions (Pensions), yet decreases with unionization for the 1940 sample (Union). The lower the number of scheduled hours per week (Hours) and the smaller the growth rate of the firm for the 1940 sample (Growth), the greater the probability of not retaining single women.

Another variable related to internal promotion was the existence of certain jobs for which only men would be considered (Male only), and that variable, as well, is positively associated with the retain-bar policy. Although some of these jobs were supervisory and others were professional, the vast majority were entry level, such as messenger, mail boy, and file clerk. The greater the number of these, the more extensive internal promotion was in the firm.[19]

The results indicate that firms with established personnel practices regarding internal promotion and salary increments did not retain single female employees when they married. Their policies, however, were tempered by the tightness of their labor market, so that firms with lower hours, possibly due to work-sharing policies, and lower growth rates were more likely to have the marriage bar.[20]

The coefficients on most variables are sufficiently large to have greatly influenced the marriage-bar policy. In the 1931 data, for example, a firm with 300 employees and a work week of 40 hours would stand a nearly negligible chance, 3.5%, of having the retain bar as policy. But had the firm, in addition, a policy of internal promotion, the probability would rise to 14.9%. If hours fell from 40 to 35, say, because of depressed economic conditions, the probability of the retain bar would rise further to 29.3%. In the 1940 data, the same firm would have a 15.4% probability of the retain bar, increasing to 24.7% with a policy of internal promotion, and to 43.4% with a decrease in hours to 35 from the original 40. Thus the 1940 firms had a much higher chance, from 1.5 to 4 times in these examples, of having the marriage bar independent of their personnel practices and hours. Further, the impact of the Promote variable is less in the 1940 data than the 1931 data. The implied change in the probability of the retain bar with the internal promotion policy is 0.168 for 1931 but 0.076 for 1940, computed around the mean of the dependent variable (0.121 and 0.151, respectively).[21]

All this implies that during the Depression, firms joined a bandwagon that had sanctioned the firing of women who married and their wholesale banning as employees. Some firms in the Depression enacted the bar for reasons similar to those of firms in the 1920's, but many others, particularly in the manufacturing sector, were seeking ways to cope with employment cutbacks. They found precedent and consensus in discrimination against married women.

The presence of the maximum-age policy raises further questions about the hiring of women. In some instances, the policy was related to the existence of pensions or group insurance that were not experience rated, and maximum-age rules shielded the firm from paying out more to employees than had been accumulated.[22] The policy constrained both men and women searching for jobs in their mid-life, but provided greater restrictions for women who lacked continuity in the work force. For men, the new personnel practices often meant that tenure with firms was encouraged and frequently ensured. But for women, the new institutional arrangements became added bars to their reentry at mid-life.

The Women's Bureau schedules contain, in addition to the easily quantifiable

TABLE 6.3.   Explaining Marriage Bars: Logit Regressions for the Retain Bar, 1931 and 1940

Dependent Variable = 1 if Retain Bar is Maintained

Variable	As Policy (1)	(2)	As Policy and Discretionary (3)	Means
		1931		
Number of employees $\times 10^{-3}$	1.00	0.671	0.186	581
	(2.12)	(1.33)	(0.41)	
(Number of employees)$^2 \times 10^{-7}$	−1.26	−0.906	−0.58	
	(1.47)	(1.06)	(0.70)	
Promote	1.58	1.49	1.94	0.536
	(2.40)	(2.18)	(4.27)	
Maximum age		0.775	0.991	0.223
		(1.29)	(2.03)	
Pensions		1.32	0.892	0.289
		(2.32)	(1.99)	
Hours	−0.172	−0.228	−0.225	40.2
	(1.61)	(1.95)	(2.51)	
Constant	3.27	4.91	6.29	
	(0.76)	(1.05)	(1.77)	
Log likelihood ratio	−54.1	−46.1	−78.3	
Number of observations	174	166	166	
Mean of the dependent variable (unweighted)	.121	.120	.289	
		1940		
Number of employees $\times 10^{-3}$	1.90	0.671	0.382	149
	(1.20)	(1.33)	(0.77)	
(Number of employees)$^2 \times 10^{-6}$	−1.41			
	(1.20)			

information just analyzed, comments of personnel directors and agents of the firm revealing their justifications for marriage-bar policies. The reasons elicited for marriage bars often confound the firms' actual constraints, individual prejudices, and societal norms. Some firms expressed concern that women who married in their employ might become less efficient because they would leave in the near future. A personnel officer in a Philadelphia insurance firm noted that although his firm had no official policy, he would prefer that women leave on marriage because "they were less efficient after marriage—too much temporary didn't care attitude."[23] Other agents, concerned that by firing women who married they would lose valued employees, put them on probation. A Philadelphia bank official stated "that those who marry are told that the company reserves the right to dismiss them at any time so that those whose work deteriorates after marriage can be dispensed with."[24] Some firms actually reversed earlier bars, like Provident Mutual Life Insurance of Philadelphia, which had a bar in 1924 but found that "too many valuable [employees] were lost."[25]

Most officers, however, gave no rationale for their policies, and a few offered

TABLE 6.3.   (*Continued*)

Variable	As Policy (1)	(2)	As Policy and Discretionary (3)	Means
		1940		
Promote	0.593	0.155	0.227	0.347
	(1.64)	(0.37)	(0.65)	
Maximum age		1.12	1.03	0.151
		(2.62)	(2.73)	
Pensions		1.11	0.724	0.188
		(2.32)	(1.85)	
Union		−0.845	−1.10	0.074
		(1.01)	(1.54)	
Male only		0.340	0.593	0.450
		(0.90)	(1.93)	
Hours	−0.170	−0.110	−0.093	40.4
	(2.46)	(1.42)	(1.46)	
Growth		−1.93	−2.05	0.162
		(1.20)	(1.61)	
Constant	4.65	2.51	2.67	
	(1.68)	(0.78)	(1.01)	
Log likelihood ratio	−126.7	−99.5	−135.3	
Number of observations	317	271	271	
Mean of the dependent variable (unweighted)	.151	.151	.258	

Notes: Promote = 1 if policy of firm was to promote from within or if there were graded salary steps or annual increases in salary; Maximum age = 1 if the firm had a stated maximum age for new hires; Pensions = 1 if the firm had a pension plan; Union = 1 if the firm's office workers were unionized; Male only = 1 if the firm had at least one job for which women were excluded by policy; Hours = normal weekly hours of office workers; Growth = (new hires in 1939)/(employment in 1939). Means refer to the regression in the last column. Dummy variables for cities and a variable indicating whether salary grades were used were also included in the 1940 regression. Absolute values of *t*-statistics are in parentheses.

Sources: See Table 6.1.

personal reasons. An agent in the publishing industry noted that "men are too selfish and should have to support their wives," and another, employed by the Presbyterian Board of Christian Education, thought "personally that married women should plan to be in their homes if possible."[26] Many personnel officers and other agents appeared to take great pride in answering that their firms gave preference to married men in hiring and in salaries, and to married women whose husbands were unemployable. After all, social consensus in the 1930's labor market was built around rationing jobs by need, the notion that men should earn a "family wage," and norms circumscribing the economic role of married women.

One surprising aspect of the comments is that various firms did mention they gave small dowries or vacations when female employees married, but these were always firms that retained single women and hired married women. In Hartford, where most insurance companies had both the hire and the retain bars, Phoenix Mutual Life, which had no policy, had a "special wedding vacation."[27] The respondent for an investment firm in Chicago, which also did not have the marriage bar, stated the owners "really encourage marriage by giving a present from the company."[28] It does not appear that firms encouraged young women to marry in the same manner that pensions encourage retirement.

Marriage bars, therefore, were instituted by large firms, with centralized hiring, promotion from within, salary schedules that were often fixed and based on tenure with the firm, and other modern employment practices. The evidence suggests that firms may have wanted to encourage turnover when earnings rose more rapidly with tenure than productivity. The experience of local school districts with the marriage bar echoes that of firms hiring clerical workers, although the evidence is at a more aggregated level.

Evidence from Local School Districts

Sometime in the early twentieth century, school districts instituted contractual obligations with teachers and fixed salary schedules. The stated purpose of salary schedules was to elicit appropriate effort from teachers with a minimum of bickering. Although the precise timing is not known, bars against the hiring and retention of married women appear to be linked to these arrangements.[29]

Salary schedules varied widely across the thousands of American school districts by the stipulation of minimum and maximum salaries, salary increments, and thus the number of years of possible increase. Salary schedules, therefore, did not rise limitlessly. By 1923, the vast majority of school districts had adopted a salary schedule, and the average elementary-school teacher would have taken six to eight years to achieve maximum salary.[30] The schedules were further complicated by provisions for increases with training and summer school and for off-scale increments called supermaximum salaries.

As in the case of office workers, the policy of marriage bars was pursued more vigorously when the potential labor supply of already-married women seemed slender and when general economic conditions called for reductions in personnel.[31] It should also be noted that the legality of the marriage bar was often in doubt, and in 1941 alone courts in 22 states ruled the marriage bar "capricious and unjust."[32]

The firing of married schoolteachers was justified by contemporaries in various ways. There was a reason to fit anyone's prejudice, ranging from the moralistic— that married women with children should stay at home and take care of their own —to the Victorian—that pregnant women would be objectionable in the classroom—to the economic—that married women were less efficient than single women and became entrenched.[33] As in the case of office workers, the marriage bar for teachers was successful because most Americans could justify and rationalize it.

Thus the evidence from local school districts and firms hiring office workers suggests that marriage bars are associated with fixed salary scales, internal promotion, and other personnel policies, and that they flourished when the potential sacrifice from limiting labor supply was minimal. The bars, interestingly, were rarely found among firms hiring factory operatives for whom piece-rate payment was often used (47% of all female operatives in the 1890's were on incentive pay, see Table 3.4) and for whom, therefore, the relationship between earnings and productivity was strictly maintained. The only important exception I have encountered is that of electrical machinery operatives (Schatz, 1983) in two large manufacturing firms (General Electric and Westinghouse), both with extensive, modern personnel practices similar to those in office work.[34] The sectoral distribution of the marriage bar creates a prima facie case that it emerged when the relationship between pay and productivity was severed. There were few costs, and much to gain, from both forms of the marriage bar in the 1920's, and the possible benefit grew during the Depression. But increased costs were lurking in the background.

Explaining the Marriage Bar

Social consensus has so often been built around barring the employment of married women that the original reason for the marriage bar has been obscured. A frequently encountered interpretation of these prohibitions involves discrimination against educated, middle-class married women, particularly native-born and white women (see, e.g., Kessler-Harris, 1982). The covered occupations, teaching and clerical work, almost always required high-school education, and thus many have claimed that the bars were intended to limit the employment of educated, middle-class married women. Female operatives in manufacturing, waitresses, and domestic servants, however, were often foreign-born or black, and their positions were generally unaffected by marriage bars. To this way of thinking, the bars served to maintain a threatened status quo, keeping middle-class women in the home to take care of their families. The bars, in this light, were a reaffirmation of a legal and social system characterized by patriarchy.

The personal prejudices of employers, as expressed in the 1940 survey, indicate that certain firms may have passed the marriage-bar policy to limit the employment of middle-class women. But the correlation of the policy with variables concerning personnel policies indicates that, while personal prejudice may have been satisfied, other considerations were paramount.

Another explanation of bars is that employers in firms with rigid wage systems, tied to their workers' seniority, desired a young, inexperienced work force, particularly in times of unemployment. There are two variants of this hypothesis. One applies when managers are unable to set wage scales for separate jobs, as might be the case when there is a strong union, resulting in earnings for certain positions that rise more rapidly than productivity. At some point, therefore, earnings for certain individuals will exceed their productivity, and the firm will want to terminate their employment.[35] Routine clerical work in large firms provides a possible instance in which the job was simple, repetitive, and not accompanied by a continued increase in productivity with experience on the job. The marriage bar was a socially acceptable way of terminating the employment of young women whose wages would eventually exceed their addition to firm revenue.

The position that labor turnover was desired has been convincingly argued elsewhere for the case of two British firms, the Great Western Railway and the General Post Office (Cohn, 1985).[36] Because salary schedules in these firms rose with tenure presumably more than productivity, some experienced workers eventually became too expensive and cheaper beginners were preferred. For reasons that will become clear, it was women, not men, whom these firms wanted to dismiss.

Thus the marriage bar ensured that all women left after a relatively short period and that the firm would not have to support high-priced experienced workers at the expense of cheap beginners. Because the marriage bar did not set a specific age or time period, young women could evade "early retirement" through late marriage. Substantial dowries, according to Cohn, were therefore offered to women who married after at least six years of company service. The dowries were meant to encourage young women to marry and thus leave the firm in the face of their rising real wages but constant productivity.

A related case occurs when firms find it advantageous to pay workers less than their worth at the beginning of their employment, but more later on. Such salary schedules, it is thought, are used to reduce monitoring and supervisory costs and elicit appropriate effort. At some point, say in five years, the (present discounted) value of the payment scheme would just equal one in which the employee were paid her true value to the firm at each date. At five years, then, both firm and employee would be even. But if workers do not leave the firm at the "break-even" point, say at five years, the firm can lose money each day the worker remains. Of course, if the worker leaves before the break-even point, the worker will have lost, and this aspect of the scheme keeps workers in line. Rather than have systematic supervision, a policy of sporadic monitoring with dismissal of unproductive workers will be more effective the heavier the penalty. Under the system of paying workers less at the outset and more later, workers are, in essence, bonded to the firm, and firing compels them to forfeit the bond.

The reasoning is similar that of Lazear (1979, 1981) concerning mandatory retirement and hours restrictions. The problem here, as in the cases examined by Lazear, is that the increased slope to the earnings profile entices the worker to remain beyond the optimum quitting point.[37] Mandatory retirement, hours restrictions, and here marriage bars can all be interpreted as optimum contracts. Workers chose the implicit contract of a sloped profile because it is more lucrative, but they must also agree to the restricted time period of employment.[38] In the case of marriage bars, rather than mandatory retirement, firms want to dismiss workers at a rather early point in their employment. Most young women were hired at around 16 to 18 years old, and most married in their early twenties. Firms, therefore, could treat a five- to seven-year period as the expected tenure for young women, since most would leave at marriage in any case.

While various facts in the American case are consistent with these explanations for the marriage bars, others are not. Marriage bars, it was found, are associated with fixed salary scales, internal promotion, and other personnel practices, and they are not associated with piece-rate work. Severing a strict relationship between productivity and earnings is related, in some manner, to the institution of marriage bars. These facts lend support to the notion that turnover was desired for either of the reasons just outlined.

But firms did not seem to care if single women remained indefinitely with the firm. It was marriage, not age or experience, that mattered.[39] They were also less concerned about retaining women who married in service than about hiring married women. The turnover hypothesis, just outlined, is a theory of the retain bar, not one of the hire bar. But among firms that had some form of the bar in the 1931 sample,

49% had the hire bar but not the retain bar, and thus would not hire a married women but would retain a single women who married.[40]

Barriers to hiring married women, therefore, cannot be attributed to a simple desire to increase turnover. Rather, such barriers can be viewed as reflecting various prejudices concerning married women's employment. Firms may have believed that married women were less productive in general, but that single women could be screened on the job before marriage. Thus it appears that many firms did not want to lose skilled and trusted employees. In fact, the sectors with the most restrictive policies often had female employees with the longest tenure.[41] Further evidence against the turnover thesis is that American firms with dowry arrangements did not institute marriage bars, contrary to the British experience described by Cohn.

Of most significance, the salaries of ordinary female clerical workers (e.g., ordinary clerks, typists) rose by only 1.4% annually with tenure (see Table 4.5).[42] Thus the difference between earnings and productivity could have been increasing at a maximum of only 1.4%. The 1.4% figure is a maximum because part of it may reflect true productivity increases. Further, fixed salary scales, often written into labor contracts and found in personnel brochures, did not rise continually with time and became level at about six years for women.

If the marriage bar were intended to get rid of workers at, say, five years of tenure, then the break-even point between a flat profile and one that rises at 1.4% must be five years. Beyond that point, earnings rise at 1.4% more than does productivity to the firm, assuming the worker's value to the firm does not increase. At six years of service, the employee's cost to the firm would exceed her value by about 3%, and at 10 years the figure would be about 10%, both computed under the assumption that her value to the firm does not increase at all.[43] It is possible that the difference was sufficient to make the marriage-bar policy profitable, but the slow growth in earnings with tenure casts some doubt on the thesis. Although the turnover thesis appears inconsistent with much of the evidence for office workers, it may be more compatible with that for school boards. Earnings data from 1911 to 1917 for Houston schoolteachers indicate that the coefficient on tenure is somewhat larger than in office work and averaged 2.1% per year.[44]

The turnover thesis, therefore, is consistent with the regression results on the retain bar. But it finds less support in the evidence on earnings profiles in office work and in the large proportion of firms having the hire bar but not the retain bar. Further, if the turnover thesis explains marriage bars in the 1920's and 1930's, earnings profiles must have changed radically in the 1950's, when the bars were dropped. But I have encountered no evidence to support that implication. Even though the turnover thesis may not be fully consistent with all the evidence, there is a related possibility.

Employers may have perceived that recently married female employees had reduced productivity but found it costly to supervise, fire, and reduce wages on a discretionary basis. The majority of young women in the 1920's left the work force at the precise time of marriage or soon thereafter; more than 80% did by the estimates in Chapter 2. Firms, therefore, may have been reluctant to retain recently married women who would treat their jobs as temporary positions, be less docile, and be less willing to remain in the dead-end positions to which all were assigned.

Rather, they may have found it more profitable to have rules governing the hiring and retention of married women. The reason that rules, rather than discretion, were preferred concerns a set of related policies instituted by various firms in the 1920's. The policies include rigid salary scales, strict internal promotion lines, and firm paternalism. Thus the rationale here is related to that of Cohn. The personnel policies and salary structures of certain firms caused rules rather than discretion to be most profitable.

Firms often adopt internal promotion, fixed salary scales, and benefit packages to conserve on supervision costs and encourage efficiency and effort among employees (see, for example, Lazear, 1979; Lazear and Rosen, 1981). Discretionary firing could result in greater wage demands to compensate employees for the increased probability of being terminated. In various incentive-based models of the labor market (Bulow and Summers, 1986; Lazear, 1981, 1979), employees base their salary demands on the expected probability of being furloughed. The gains from having rules rather than discretion increase if the reduction in labor supply from curtailing the employment of married women is small.

Therefore, the bar against retaining single women at marriage emerged, in part, from the various policies of modern personnel departments. These policies made discretionary firing costly and resulted in salary scales and promotion procedures that severed the relationship between wages and productivity.

Two complementary reasons have been offered for the benefits of the marriage bar to firms: one involves a reduction in the costs of paying experienced employees and the other, a lowering of the cost to firing workers. But firms also incurred losses from the bar. Trained and trusted employees had to be fired, and no married woman could be hired. Marriage bars were adopted in the 1920's and 1930's because these costs were low. They were minimized by certain features of the labor market. The cost of firing women who married in service was slight because the ancillary rule, the barring of all married women, entailed, at the time, little sacrifice. Costs were further minimized by the type of occupations routinely offered women. In Chapter 4, I discussed how increased education encouraged extensive division of labor in the office and fostered mechanization, both of which increased the value of formal skills and reduced the need for on-the-job training. Experienced female workers, in the majority of offices, were easily replaced by female high-school graduates. Jobs in the clerical sector were highly segregated by sex—men were routinely barred from some occupations, women from others. Firms, therefore, did not lose much by having policies that required them to dismiss women when they married. With little to lose and much to gain, a substantial percentage of firms instituted a marriage bar prior to the Depression, and many extended the bar as a socially acceptable means of rationing employment during the 1930's.

The Decline of the Marriage Bar in the 1950's

The 1950's mark a sharp break in the way the labor market accommodated married women, older women, and women with household responsibilities. Discrimination never disappeared, and child-care centers never flourished. But after 1950, the marriage bar vanished almost entirely (except for flight attendants)[45] and part-time work became widespread. The factors that account for these changes amount to nothing short of a revolution in the demographics of labor supply.[46]

Three-quarters of all female workers in 1900, and more than one-half in the (nonwar) years prior to 1950, were single (see Table 2.4). Not surprisingly, they were exceptionally young. The mean age of single women workers was 20 years in 1900, and that of all working women was 23 years; but by 1950, the mean for all exceeded 36 years. Employers in the 1920's and 1930's routinely hired only inexperienced high-school girls; "younger, untrained people direct from [high] school prove more satisfactory" was the frequent response of personnel officers.[47] They had little reason to look elsewhere. Young, single women flooded the labor market in those years; they were docile, educated, and had few home responsibilities. The labor market for women workers was organized for the young and structured around the presumption that women would remain at work only until marriage.

Demographic shifts of the 1920's and 1930's made many changes inevitable. The decline in the birth rate, evident in Figure 5.3, meant the population had to age substantially in the coming years and that the supply of young women and female high-school graduates had to decline as a proportion of the population. This "labor squeeze" was further exacerbated by several related changes—increased education, the post–World War II decline in the marriage age, and the baby boom.[48] Thus fewer young women were available for employment after the late 1940's, and those who might have been were marrying earlier and having larger families. For all these reasons the supply of young, single female workers simply disappeared. The data in Table 6.4 tell much of the story.

The percentage of the adult female population composed of 16 to 24 year olds was 31% in 1900 but 20% in 1960. The percentage of adult women who were 16 to 24 and single was 21% in 1900 but 11% in 1960, and the proportional decrease is even greater for those 18 to 24 years. The proportion of 16 to 21 year olds at school was 1.7 times as great in 1960 than in 1900. The largest change in Table 6.4 involves combining all three factors—age, marital status, and education—into a

TABLE 6.4. The "Labor Squeeze," 1900 to 1960

Female Population	1900	1920	1940	1950	1960	1900/1960
16–24 years/16–64 years	30.9%	27.0%	29.0%	20.9%	20.3%	1.52
18–24 years, single/ 18–64 years	14.7	12.0	10.9	7.4	6.4	2.30
16–24 years, single/ 16–64 years	20.7	17.0	15.2	10.9	10.8	1.92
16–24 years, single, not at school/16–64 years	14.9	12.9	9.7	5.8	4.1	3.63
						1960/1900
16–21 years, in school/ 16–21 years	27.5	32.9	34.9	37.8	47.4	1.72

Sources: All data are from relevant U.S. population censuses.

single measure: the percentage of adult women composed of those 16 to 24 years old, single, and not at school. The measure is 3.6 times as great in 1900 as in 1960. All three factors point to a decrease in the supply of young, female employees over the first half of this century.

This inversion in labor supply was accompanied by a desire by older, married women to seek gainful employment. The young women of the 1910's and 1920's who left high school and took clerical positions eventually became the older, married women of the 1930's and 1940's. Most were past child-rearing age, and as a cohort they had few children by historical comparison. Further, they had skills and work experience in the emerging sectors of the economy. In the absence of the Depression, they would surely have increased their labor force participation earlier than the 1950's, and their participation during World War II (see Table 5.5) creates a prima facie case for that counterfactual.

Thus the constraints facing firms changed considerably with World War II. No longer did they operate in an environment of unemployment. No longer could they bar the hiring of married women without placing formidable restrictions on their labor supply. Personnel policies quickly reflected these new constraints. The procedures and the rhetoric accompanying them are revealed in original schedules of a 1957 study on personnel policies (Hussey, 1958; called here the 1957 Hussey Report, see Data Appendix).

Older female workers in the mid-1950's were suddenly praised for their maturity, reliability, neat appearance, and less chatty nature. Employers, particularly in the clerical sector, were pleased to "rehire those who . . . previously served in that capacity," as did Penn Mutual Life Insurance, which prior to World War II had a marriage bar. Scott Paper hired married women who could "offer skills gained earlier, before marriage," underscoring the finding that a woman's first occupation altered her chance of future employment (Goldin, 1989).[49] But in retail trades, particularly in the suburbs, the older married woman with absolutely no previous training was now the "ideal employee"; the middle-class woman, "naturally courteous" and "well-bred," who did not have to work was preferred by the major department stores.[50]

Not all personnel officers viewed the hiring of the older married woman with equanimity. There were detractions as well as benefits. In retail trade, one manager remarked that "housewives who have never worked or have not worked for 15 to 20 years are found to be inexperienced in arithmetic and have difficulty in learning to operate the cash registers." In banking, "older women may work more slowly," but most added as well that "the type of service they can give a company is of great value."[51] Firms were still leery of hiring young married women, and some adopted a policy of not hiring those with small children or firing women who became pregnant. The sequel to the marriage bar was the "pregnancy bar." All in all, the best female employee was, in the words of a Sears, Roebuck, and Co. officer, "a married woman with a mortgage on her house and her children partially raised."[52]

By the 1950's, married women were welcomed employees in almost all large, paternalistic companies that just prior to World War II barred their hire. The complete turnaround was a consequence of changed constraints, and these altered constraints may have forced managers to realize married women were actually not less productive than single women. The unemployment of the 1930's, which had compelled firms to ration jobs through means that included the firing of married women, had vanished and in its place was an extremely tight labor market. The young woman of two decades earlier who gave a firm several years before marriage was replaced by one who left school later and married earlier. Firm managers knew the constraints, although they often overstated them: "In the earlier years, the girl of 18 might work until she married at 23 or 24. . . . Now she is more likely to marry within 6 months or a year of starting work and resign within another."[53] But it should also be remembered that the older married woman of the 1950's had been the young woman of the 1920's and 1930's. The point did not escape the attention of firm officers in the 1957 Hussey Report who spoke of women returning to positions they had held decades before. Despite their rusty skills in arithmetic, older married women of the 1950's were considerably more equipped to handle modern clerical and sales work than were their predecessors in the 1920's.

Altered constraints were not the only factors that brought a shift in hiring practices. World War II awakened firms to the fact that bars against hiring married women were lessening their supply of female employees. The number of working women during World War II increased most among those older than 45 years. From March 1940 to July 1944, the peak of the wartime employment of women, those 45 to 64 years old increased in numbers by 165% and those over 64 years by 197%; in contrast, those 25 to 44 years old increased by only 128% (see Table 5.5).

The bars had little impact on potential labor supply in the early 1920's, when the majority of older married women would not have joined the labor force in any event. But the bars became considerably more binding and thus more restrictive as cohorts of educated young women advanced in age. By the 1940's, many in the cohorts who had served as office workers when young were the mothers of grown children, and by the 1950's the vast majority of adult married women had high-school diplomas. It had been easy in the 1920's for firms to issue blanket policies against the hiring of married women, but it was far harder in the 1950's for them to bar certain kinds of married women—those with young children, those with demanding husbands, and so on. So marriage bars were lifted, almost in their entirety, and the participation of married women in the American labor force advanced in the absence of perhaps the most blatant form of employment discrimination in the history of women's work.

The Long-Run Impact of the Marriage Bar

The bars restricted the participation of married women in the American economy in several senses. In the most obvious fashion, they barred married women from employment in a variety of occupations during the first half of this century. But the marriage bars that preceded the Great Depression may have been less overtly and intentionally discriminatory than is apparent. Marriage bars constituted an odd form of discrimination against women. The covered occupations were almost always female-intensive ones, so it cannot be said that women as a group were discriminated against. Social consensus was formed around and fueled the rules, but the dominant underlying rationale was not necessarily a prejudice against middle-class married women's working.

As characterized here and in the work of Cohn (1985, 1988), the bars were initially related to the adoption of tenure-based salary scales and related personnel policies. But they may also have resulted from perceived differences in the efficiency of single and married female employees, and such beliefs may not have been formulated in an unbiased fashion. Discrimination against married women may have caused employers to have a jaundiced view of their productivity. Both reasons offered here for the marriage bars are based on the facts that firm policies segregated office work by sex and routinely placed women in dead-end positions. In Chapters 3 and 4, I discussed the role of discrimination in these related firm policies. But even had marriage bars been motivated entirely by unbiased, but profit-maximizing employers, they encouraged others to find justification for their prejudices. Social norms against the employment of married women that preceded and fostered the bars, and the extension of both the bars and social norms during the Depression, were setbacks to working women.

The immediate impact of marriage bars in the 1920's on married women's employment may not have been substantial, but the longer-range effects were likely of great significance. Young women had little encouragement to invest in skills that were valued in the sectors covered by the bars. They might become typists and possibly machine operators, but they had less incentive to become accountants. The bars also prevented firms from recognizing the hidden labor supply of older married women. As the bars expanded in the late 1920's and during the Depression, many married women, who might otherwise have looked for employment, were discouraged from doing so. As the potential pool of educated and experienced married women expanded, firms may have underestimated the costs of the marriage-bar policy.

The bars in office work both before and during the Depression restricted the employment of married women but did not block their hiring. Smaller firms without modern personnel practices hired married women and did not fire single women when they married. Sectors such as banking, insurance, and public utilities, however, were off-limits to married women, as were a large percentage of local school districts around the country. For office workers, prohibitions often meant that married women were restricted from precisely those firms having internal promotion possibilities. While internal promotion was never substantial for women in any sector, the added restrictions lowered married women's returns to education.

A sample of female clerical workers from the 1940 Women's Bureau survey (the 1940 Office Worker Survey, see Chapter 4) reveals differences between married and single women's earnings, given years with the current employer, total job experience, education, and time spent in the home between jobs, among other relevant factors. Married and single women earned approximately the same on average, but the returns to education varied by marital status. Returns were considerably lower for married women, so that while women with lower than average education received higher earnings if they were married, those with higher than average education received lower earnings. Returns to a year of education were

4.6% for single women but only 1% for married women.[54] The data suggest that married women were channeled into firms, sectors, and jobs in which education was of lower value particularly within the internal promotion scheme.

The extensive movement during the Depression to ration jobs by firing married women can be credited to the marriage bars that preceded 1929. Firms could hardly have built a solid consensus around the firing of married women had it not been for the existence of marriage bars prior to the Depression. The bars, through a peculiar quirk of history, were responsible for the setbacks to women's employment during the Depression. In these ways, marriage bars served to delay the period of increased female labor force participation in America.

Hours of Work and Part-time Employment

Married women returning to the labor force in the post–World War II period found many of its features unchanged. Occupations remained highly segregated by sex, and women received earnings approximately 60% those of men. But they also encountered progressive change; various constraints on older, married women had been loosened. The marriage bar was dropped by most employers, older women became welcomed employees, and women with household responsibilities were accommodated in various ways. Firms began programs to attract married women by offering part-time employment. New York Life Insurance, for example, reported in 1956 that it "now hired married women, although in earlier years it did not, and now employs some women part-time who worked for the company before they started to raise families." Retail establishments were most amenable to part-time work, while manufacturing employers, such as Scott Paper Company, claimed it had "to be more desperate . . . to consider bringing in married women on a part-time schedule."[55]

Hours of Work

The emergence of part-time work in the 1950's is but one element in the changed working hours and days of all Americans over the last century. Nineteenth-century factory work consumed six days per week and more than 10 hours per day. Indeed, many nineteenth-century strikes were provoked by labor's demand for the 10-hour day. Immigrant and female workers were often cited by organized labor as the cause of its inability to reduce hours of work. Immigrants, it was said, were accustomed to long hours, and many came only temporarily to America to earn money. Young female factory operatives were also seen as transient workers who desired to maximize earnings. Legislation was passed in 40 states from the 1850's to 1919 setting maximum hours for female employees in manufacturing and, often, sales work. The legislation played a small role in lowering hours of women's work, but it was often a means for organized labor to gain consensus over the reduction in hours of work for all (see Chapter 7).[56]

Hours and days of work did decline in American factories from the first decade of the twentieth century to 1940. Actual hours of work declined by 2.8 hours from

1900 to 1910 (from 55 to 52.2), then plummeted by 6.1 hours in the turbulent 1910's (from 52.2 to 46.1), and remained fairly steady until the Depression. By the 1920's, the 5¹/₂-day work week was fast becoming the norm, and hours of work had declined to around 48. The Depression, however, catapulted the nation into the 5-day, 40-hour work week of the post–World War II period, from which it has not budged materially.[57] Despite declines in the work week since 1900, scheduled part-time work was virtually nonexistent until the 1950's. Further, the usual workday and work week were extremely long for most of the period considered.

Part-time Employment

Part-time work today is defined as labor force involvement that entails fewer than 35 hours per week. Various empirical and conceptual problems are encountered in tracing the history of part-time work. Data on part-time work have been collected since the 1950's by the U.S. Bureau of the Census as part of the Current Population Surveys for individuals who work at all during the year and since 1940 as part of the decennial population census for individuals who work during the survey week. Data for the pre-1940 period have been culled from various bulletins of the Women's Bureau, which conducted studies to explore women's working hours in the 1920's.

Most hours data for the pre-1940 period refer to scheduled, not actual, hours worked, while hours data for the post-1940 period refer to actual, not scheduled, hours. Both concepts are relevant here. Scheduled hours are often contractual obligations to work a specified amount, while actual hours can reflect temporary losses in work time due to sickness and plant closings, among other factors. Another conceptual issue concerns the cut-off for part-time work. The 35-hour week, today's cut-off point, is 87.5% of the 40-hour week but is only 64% of the 55-hour week, which was the standard earlier in the century.

The increase in part-time work, using the current definition of fewer than 35 hours of actual work, is apparent in Table 6.5, which gives the percentage of female employees who worked part-time from 1920 to 1970. In 1940 only 18% of all women worked part-time, but 31% did in 1970. A far greater increase is discernible in the sales sector, which had on average 7% working fewer than 35 hours per week in the 1920's but almost 50% working part-time in 1970, an increase of seven times. The relevant increase is even greater than sevenfold because most women who logged fewer than 35 hours in the 1920's were not on part-time schedules. Scheduled hours of work among the surveyed mercantile establishments indicate that no woman was hired to work fewer than 44 hours per week—that is, 8 hours per day, 5¹/₂ days per week.[58] Some individuals, even today, who work fewer than 35 hours are actually scheduled to work full-time but cannot, due to involuntary losses in working time. Many women who worked part-time in 1940 and during much of the Depression were constrained to work fewer hours than they desired, particularly in the manufacturing sector.

Two trends, therefore, are apparent in hours and days worked. One is the secular decline in the work week that gained momentum during the World War I and Depression periods. The second is the growth of scheduled part-time work, virtually a post–World War II phenomenon that emerged rapidly during the 1950's,

TABLE 6.5.   Part-time Employment, 1920 to 1970

	Percent Part-time Total Employment	Percent Part-time Sales Sector
1920		
New Jersey		4.3%
Rhode Island		6.1
Illinois		10.1
1940	18.0%	14.3
1950	19.0	24.9
1960	27.7	40.3
1970	31.0	48.3

Notes and Sources: Figures for 1940–1970 are for the entire United States. Part-time work is defined as fewer than 35 hours per week.

1920: U.S. Department of Labor, Women's Bureau, *Women in [New Jersey, Rhode Island, Illinois] Industries: A Study of Hours and Working Conditions,* Nos. 21, 37, 55 (Washington, DC: Government Printing Office, 1922, 1924, 1926), for mercantile establishments. Actual hours distributions are used; no women were scheduled to work fewer than 35 hours per week.

1940: U.S. Bureau of the Census, *Sixteenth Census of the United States: 1940. Population.* Vol. III, *The Labor Force,* Part 1, *United States Summary* (Washington, DC: Government Printing Office, 1943a), table 87, for trade sector workers in general merchandise, variety, apparel, and accessory stores.

1950: See Table 2.1.

1960: U.S. Bureau of the Census, *U.S. Census of Population: 1960, Subject Reports, Occupational Characteristics: Final Report PC(2)-7A* (Washington, DC: Government Printing Office, 1963c), for hours worked of employed individuals with a job and at work.

1970: See Table 2.1.

particularly in the sales sector. Both the secular change in the work week and the increase in part-time work made it possible for women with household responsibilities to enter and remain in the labor force.[59]

It might be countered that increased part-time work was the result, not the cause, of increased labor force participation of married women. Some growth in part-time employment surely reflects a change in the composition of the female labor force. Women who desired part-time employment were more numerous in 1960 than in 1920. But there were, as well, real changes in the menu of hours offered prospective labor force entrants and in the availability of part-time employment. Reasons given by personnel officers for both the initiation of part-time work and the change in marriage-bar policies create a prima facie case that firms, particularly in the sales sector, accommodated married and older women in the face of a declining supply of young, unmarried female workers.

The role that shorter hours of work played in increasing the labor force participation of married women can also be inferred from cross-sectional evidence. One study (Goldin, 1988a) has found a large, negative relationship between the labor force participation rate of women, grouped by nativity and marital status, and mean scheduled hours of work in manufacturing, across 31 large urban areas in 1920.[60] The variation in hours of work across the United States was substantial in 1920; some areas had made the transition from the nineteenth-century norm of 60 hours to that in the 1920's of 50 hours, while others had not. Mean scheduled hours in manufacturing across states was 51.5, with a standard deviation of 2.4 and a range of 10—more than 1 day's labor. Female labor force participation is negatively and strongly correlated with scheduled weekly hours of work for all manufacturing workers. Further, the magnitude of the relationship was greater for married women. Women with home responsibilities increased their labor market work as hours of work declined.

For most of the nativity–marital status groups studied, the elasticity of labor force participation with respect to scheduled work hours exceeded 1 (in absolute value), implying that a reduction of 10% in hours per day would increase labor force participation by more than 10%. The values range from -1.11 for married, native-born women to -2.60 for married, native-born women with foreign-born parents.[61]

According to the estimation, which admittedly does not include many relevant variables, the decrease in hours of work can account for a large fraction of the increase in participation rates among married women over the 1920 to 1940 period. The mean labor force participation rate of married native-born white women living in large urban areas in 1920 was 11%, while mean scheduled hours per week were 51.5. Mean scheduled hours per week fell to about 44 by 1940, while the labor force participation rate rose to 18%. The increase in the participation rate predicted by the decrease in hours worked is almost half the actual change.[62] Similar results have been reported in recent studies, such as one by King (1978) for 1970, which finds higher labor force participation among married women with children in cities where men worked fewer hours.

When hours of work were long and part-time work in the store and factory was unobtainable, women with home responsibilities often made other adjustments. These alternatives, however, were inferior in many respects to the part-time scheduling of work that emerged in the 1950's. There is some evidence (Goldin, 1988a) for the 1920's that women in manufacturing employment worked fewer days per week in states having longer hours per day. A trade-off existed, therefore, between hours per day and days per week. Further, in areas that had seasonal work, such as the canning industry, women often labored excessive hours during the season and had little or no work at other times. The option of working fewer days per week or per year, however, was unavailable to all workers in manufacturing, and it was, most likely, a difficult strategy for those who managed the myriad chores of the home. As Gwendolyn Hughes noted in her study of working mothers: "The ideal arrangement for the mother's employment in many cases would undoubtedly be part-time work . . . but modern industry has thus far developed no technique of adaptation to the social needs of its employees" (1925, p. xiv).

Piece-work may have fostered a more irregular day than strict time payment, and almost one-half of all female manufacturing workers were on some form of incentive pay in 1890. But in many industries, such as textiles, the pace of work was still determined by the speed of the machinery. In others, however, such as apparel, paper, and cigars, the worker had substantial control over the amount produced.[63] Where the fixed costs of capital and supervisory inputs were low, managers may not have cared if workers shortened some days but worked intensively at other times. Many surveys of manufacturing workers did not collect information on hours of work for piece-rate workers because it was thought employers lacked reliable figures on their hours (see, e.g., U.S. Commissioner of Labor,

1905). But most accounts of the nation's larger factories indicate that workers, whether on piece or time payment, kept close to their scheduled hours and thus that part-time work was difficult, if not impossible, to achieve within the confines of the factory.

Outwork, through the laundry (Butler, 1909, p. 195) and garment industries, among others, afforded women the opportunity to earn income while working in their own homes. Boarding housekeeping (see Chapter 2) offered similar flexibility but was often available only to those who owned a home. Earnings data for married women workers, however, demonstrate that the pecuniary penalties for outwork were large. Married women who worked in their homes earned less than half what they could have earned in the factory, and the presence of each child under two years of age depressed earnings by an additional 15% (see Table 4.2). Because the daily earnings of women who worked in the factory were unaffected by the number and ages of a woman's children, factory hours appear inflexible, as suggested above. Part of the 50% penalty for outwork may derive from a decrease in hours of work over the day and suggests that outwork was a form of part-time labor. But the agents of the U.S. government who collected the earnings data suspected otherwise. To them, much of the reduction in earnings was due to the absence of acquired skill because workers could not benefit from using machinery found only in the factory. The substantial learning on the job, described in Chapter 4, that occurred during a short initial period was unattainable by women who worked in their homes.

Married women in the era before 1950 could, therefore, obtain part-time work and work to be done in the home. But the pay was low for various reasons, and the occupations were extremely limited. Women who worked part-time received considerably less per day than did women who worked full-time, and it is likely that they received equally less per hour of work. As the labor market accommodated women who desired to work part-time, the penalty to part-time work also decreased, and women who work part-time today earn about as much per hour as do those who work full-time.[64]

Summary: Easing the Constraints

In sum, marriage bars appeared in white-collar employment sometime before the Great Depression as a response to various personnel policies that severed the relationship between earnings and productivity. The bars therefore had their origins in firm-level policies that were designed to bond workers to firms, create an environment of welfare-capitalism, eliminate opportunistic behavior of supervisors, and reduce turnover. But although the bars had their origins in modern personnel relations, they could never have succeeded without two preconditions. One concerns the supply of labor. Most older married women in the 1920's could not have applied for these jobs because of the vast changes in education during the 1900 to 1930 period. Further, more than 80% of all women who worked before they married dropped out of the work force at the precise time of marriage. The loss in personnel in the 1920's, therefore, was not very great. The second precondition is that social consensus had been built around the necessity for married women to remain in their homes. The great harm done by the marriage bars is found in the Depression. Had it not been for the marriage bars that preceded the Depression, married women could never have been so thoroughly discriminated against during the Depression.

The disappearance of the marriage bars and the increase in part-time work resulted in large measure from a set of related demographic changes that drastically reduced the supply of young female employees. Reinforcing these changes was the increased labor supply of older married women, discussed in Chapter 5, and the decline in hours of work in general. Some employers, respondents in the 1957 Hussey Report, recognized that married older women were "more reliable" and "more dependable" than the younger group they previously hired. The new rhetoric may have been as much a justification for new policies as the old rhetoric was for the marriage bar. But there is a sense that most employers finally realized that marital status and age were unreasonable bars to employment. Yet women were still denied jobs that had promotion possibilities and those that involved substantial learning on the job. They were often treated as a group that had little expected labor force involvement and insignificant desire for rewarding employment. The response that finally erupted in the 1970's was not the evolutionary change that had occurred in the 1950's. Women had finally emerged as a politically influential force in American social policy.

7

The Political Economy of Gender

Women became a major political force in shaping the rules of the workplace long after they gained the vote. More than a half-century separates the Nineteenth Amendment from affirmative action, pay equity legislation, a strong stand by the Equal Employment Opportunity Commission (EEOC) on sex-discrimination cases, and favorable interpretations of Title VII of the 1964 Civil Rights Act. This chapter discusses the history of public policy regarding gender and the sources of the delay.

Until the 1960's, women's discontent with the economic system was not broadly based, although throughout history many have eloquently articulated a sense of injustice. The extreme degree of sex segregation and the "wage discrimination" revealed in Chapters 3 and 4 were often rationalized by employers, society, and women themselves. But discontent widened as women's education and, in turn, their expectations increased. More received college degrees yet found few opportunities commensurate with their training. Like other so-called minority groups, their cause required an ideology and a common voice. The women's movement, born of dissatisfaction with a larger set of issues, finally provided the unity women needed to press forward on economic matters. Thus the delay was due, in part, to women's peculiar position as a majority group, clearly integrated into society, and yet subject to the various forms of discrimination that afflict minorities.

The delay was also due to institutional factors and the original concerns of public policy regarding women's work. In the early twentieth century, women workers, who as a group were young and often easily exploited, were perceived as requiring protection, and legislation was passed to guard women against long hours, night work, low pay, and hazardous conditions. The legislation was championed by many well-intentioned social reformers but was opposed by those committed to equality between the sexes. For the next half-century, the two groups would be at odds over protection and equality. The debate has been recently rekindled in regard to the safety of pregnant women in the workplace and the implications of their protection for Title VII of the 1964 Civil Rights Act.

Before women could become a real force in domestic economic policy, their perceptions of discontent had to be more strongly felt and more widely aired, a common voice and ideology had to be found, and the cause of protective legislation had to be abandoned. They also had to become more significant in terms of their labor force participation, the proportion unionized, and their commitment to longer careers. The recent passage of comparable worth legislation in a large number of states and localities and the call for a national policy on child care are a tribute to the success of women as a political force in shaping the rules of the labor market.

Historical Dimensions of Public Policy

Public policy regarding the work of women in America can be traced back nearly two centuries to the promotion of manufacturing interests in the new nation. As part of a concerted effort to encourage industry, Alexander Hamilton, the first Secretary of the Treasury, entreated the nation and its women in 1791 to participate in these enterprises. Hamilton, and later Gallatin, saw in the factory system a means of utilizing an otherwise underemployed female labor force and of quickening the pace of economic growth in the new nation.

Manufacturing enterprises in the age of Hamilton and Gallatin were thinly scattered across the hinterland. Within the industrial counties of New England and the Middle Atlantic states, young women had substantial labor force participation rates, but working women, in the aggregate, were insufficiently numerous for their employment to be of public concern. The work of women attracted such scant attention in the United States that no population census inquired of their occupations before 1860. And until 1890, published census volumes contain few tabulations of the labor force participation and occupations of women.

By 1880, industrial development had largely shifted from the hinterland to the city, and a wider variety of industries had begun to employ women. Wherever industry and cities appeared in the United States, the labor force participation rates of women, particularly the young and unmarried, increased substantially. Among them were two groups, viewed by many as requiring protection but for different reasons.

One group consisted of young women who had migrated in large numbers from rural areas and small towns to work in the nation's urban centers. By 1900, 25% of all single female workers (16 to 24 years old), excluding servants and waitresses, were living apart from their families in the nation's cities (see Chapter 4). These working women lacked parental guidance and were often dependent entirely on their own support. Unlike mid-nineteenth-century farm girls of New England mill towns who left home only temporarily to work, many of these women migrated to the city permanently. Social reformers had good reason to view them as vulnerable and requiring protection.

Working daughters who lived with their parents are the other group. These young women remitted virtually all earnings to their families (see Chapter 2). Although they were more protected from ruthless employers and the dangers of the city, their schooling, and likely their leisure, suffered from their employment. One study of nineteenth-century families has shown that teenage children gained little from their paid labor (Goldin and Parsons, 1989). Their employment, therefore, could hardly be viewed as their own choosing.

To progressive reformers, therefore, the woman worker was indistinguishable from the more obviously exploited child laborer. Although their labor cut across class lines, the daughters of working-class, immigrant, and black families had the highest participation rates. Reformers accumulated considerable evidence that because they were young, female workers had little bargaining power when accepting a job and were indifferent to the goals of organized labor.[1] Her youth, relative poverty, lack of parental guidance, and possible exploitation by family and employer alike made the female worker a central concern of the reform movement.

An added issue was the economic health of the nation. The late nineteenth century had been punctuated by severe recessions, beginning in the mid-1870's. The depression of the 1890's produced urban unemployment rates that rival even those of the 1930's (Lebergott, 1964). At the same time, the labor force was flooded by unskilled immigrant labor, and while the flow ebbed during periods of high unemployment, the stock was always high (Easterlin, 1971). It is no wonder that the increase of female industrial workers became an issue of concern. Female laborers, it was sensed, were taking jobs from men, lowering their wages, and keeping hours long.

Interest in the employment of women in the Progressive era emerged initially at the state level. Massachusetts established the first Bureau of Labor in the United States in 1873. Under the able direction of Carroll Wright, who would later become the first Commissioner of Labor of the United States, attention quickly centered on the "working girl." Wright's report *The Working Girls of Boston* (1889) served as a model for his more extensive *Working Women in Large Cities* (U.S. Commissioner of Labor, 1889), published in his fourth year as chief of the newly created Bureau of Labor, the year it became the U.S. Department of Labor, although not yet with cabinet rank. Although Wright was concerned with conditions of work he noted that "one of the chief reasons for undertaking this investigation was to determine whether the ranks of prostitution are recruited from the manufactory" (U. S. Commissioner of Labor, 1889, p. 5). Wright endeavored to counter even the most exaggerated and misplaced criticism of female workers.

Public concern about the employment of young women and their conditions of work and home life mounted during the 1890's. The Wright studies provided inspiration for labor commissioners around the country. Within a decade, Illinois, Kansas, Maine, Michigan, Minnesota, Missouri, New York, and Rhode Island followed suit and produced studies similar in spirit and format. Large-scale surveys of wages, work conditions, home life, and labor force experiences were conducted at the state and federal levels. More than 2,000 women were interviewed for *Working Girls of Boston*; over 17,000, across 27 cities, were interviewed for *Working Women in Large Cities*. Culminating the survey reports was the 19-volume Senate *Report on the Condition of Woman and Child Wage-Earners* (1910–1911), which contains information on more than 150,000 female workers, much from personal interviews. Even that study is dwarfed in coverage by Wright's 1895–1896 *Work and Wages of Men, Women, and Children* (1897), which contains data on nearly 245,000 workers gathered from firm records not individuals.

Many of the reports were designed to allay fears that female workers were taking jobs from men. Although the larger threat to native-born male labor was immigration, it was easier to gain consensus on the impropriety of women's work. Further, in the minds of native-born men, male workers of any nationality played by the rules of the workplace, while women did not. Male operatives often complained that women piece-rate workers refused to limit production, disregarding the "stint" (Montgomery, 1987, p. 38). Wright's 1895–1896 study was devised, in part, to evaluate whether women and men earned the same amounts for "equal work"; if they did, Wright could counter criticism that women were undercutting men's wages and supplanting them as workers. To hold productivity on the job constant, Wright strove to find jobs in which men and women worked with the same "efficiency," as measured by employer ratings.[2] Wright's implicit econometric model rivals that of any modern labor economist working on the subject of comparable worth.

Most government reports dealing with female workers of the Progressive era were political documents, but because the data were too extensive to be properly analyzed, the actual surveys were rarely used for any purpose a century ago. Instead, the volumes of state and federal reports often include all the original, individual-level observations, and although the volumes are immense, a mere handful of numbers was selected to support the principal assertions. The legacy of the reports is an abundance of previously unanalyzed data spanning the period 1888 to 1907, many of which were analyzed in Chapters 3 and 4 (see also the Data Appendix).

Wright and his fellow labor commissioners were ideologically united with industrial nationalists, such as Hamilton and Gallatin, who preceded them by almost a century. All defended the freedom of women to labor for pay, although not for egalitarian reasons. Their attention was directed, instead, toward the industrial and economic health of the nation, not the rights of women workers, even though at the time the two issues coincided.

At the close of World War I, public sentiment quickly shifted from young, unmarried women to those with families. The Women's Bureau, founded in 1920 within the Department of Labor (see Sealander's, 1983, fine study of the Women's Bureau), continued to pursue matters begun by state bureaus and Carroll Wright's federal agency. Its primary concern was the work environment—hours, wages, occupational safety, and general sanitary conditions—although it focused as well on the families of women workers—the care of children, the income of husbands, and living arrangements. In its insistence that working women needed to support their families, the Women's Bureau attempted to counter public concern over the encroachment of women in the workplace. It strove to defend female workers against the criticism, directed at them during the Progressive era, as well, that they were taking jobs from male workers and that women, not men, worked for frivolous reasons. The bureau was also involved with the promotion of protective legislation concerning maximum hours, night work, minimum wages, and hazardous conditions of work.

Thus public policy regarding women in the 1920's was a direct extension of the concerns of Wright, and of Hamilton and Gallatin before him. Women were defended as legitimate workers who required the protection of the state. To most nineteenth-century observers, the two goals were harmonious. But to many in the 1920's, even within the Women's Bureau, the twin policies of protection and equality were in direct conflict.[3]

The issues of protection and equality have since been at the center of debates over women's work. At the state and federal levels, the hours, wages, and work conditions of female employees were studied and legislated. But an opposing movement emerged that gained considerable strength and eventually prevailed. A woman's right to a job, equality in pay, and occupational opportunity were all antithetical to her being singled out for protection. Continued tension exists between the goals of protection and equality, as witnessed recently in the "protective exclusion" of pregnant women and those of child-bearing age from certain high-risk jobs.[4]

Gains made at the state level in protective legislation from the mid-nineteenth century to the 1920's prompted many otherwise liberal individuals to oppose legislation, such as the Equal Rights Amendment and related anti-discrimination laws, that would guarantee equality. Eleanor Roosevelt, John Kennedy, Estes Kefauver, and other prominent liberals feared that progress gained through protective legislation would be lost if the equal rights bill were passed (Harrison, 1988).

Society and polity, as late as the 1960's, continued to define women workers as they had been earlier in the century—young, unmarried, exploited, transient, unorganizable, and thus requiring the protection of the state. The eventual consequence was a set of policies that were to be surprisingly and regrettably long-lived and that were to delay a program of ensuring real equality in the workplace. The two originally harmonious goals of the protection of workers and their right to work became incompatible. The episode points to the relevance of institutional constraints and the historical evolution of the female work force in shaping public policy. Thus an analysis of the modern political economy of gender must begin with the origins and the impact of protective legislation.

Origins and Impact of Protective Legislation

Laws regulating the hours, wages, and work conditions of female employees were passed by virtually all states beginning in the mid-nineteenth century (Baer, 1978; Lehrer, 1987; Steinberg, 1982). I deal here with the case of maximum hours legislation, the most extensive and probably most significant form of protective legislation, to show why protective legislation was staunchly defended in opposition to equal rights and anti-discrimination legislation.

State laws regulating daily hours of work appeared in the mid-1800's, and by 1919 all but five states had passed hours restrictions at some time in their histories (Table 7.1). With few exceptions, all laws applied exclusively to female workers in manufacturing and mercantile establishments, although the precise number of hours and other details differed by state. The first law, passed in New Hampshire in 1847, mandated that no manufacturing establishment could compel a woman to work more than 10 hours per day. But it, like the early laws of Maine (1848), Pennsylvania (1848), and Ohio (1852), among others, was unenforceable because the law could not compel female employees to work less than the maximum. Enforceable laws began to be passed in the late 1880's, and, prior to an Illinois law in 1893, most mandated a 10-hour day. The Illinois law provided for an 8-hour day and a 48-hour week but was declared unconstitutional in 1895 by the Illinois Supreme Court (*Ritchie* v. *People*).

By 1909, 20 states had passed enforceable maximum hours laws covering

TABLE 7.1. Maximum Hours Legislation and Scheduled Hours by State, 1909 to 1919

State	First Enforceable Law			Legislated Daily Hours in Manufacturing as of			Scheduled Hours in Manufacturing as of	
	Date	Hours	Coverage	1909	1914	1919	1909	1919
Alabama[a]							10.2	9.4
Arizona	1913	10/56	S,L,T				9.5	8.9
Arkansas	1915[b]	9/54	M,S,L			9	9.9	9.5
California	1911	8/48	M,S,L,T		8	8	9.2	8.0
Colorado	1903	8/	M,S	8	8	8	9.7	8.6
Connecticut	1887	10/60	M,S	10	10	10	9.4	8.6
Delaware	1913	10/55	M,S,L,T		10	10	9.5	8.3
District of Columbia	1914	8/48	M,S,L,T		8	8	9.0	8.2
Florida							10.0	9.3
Georgia							9.4	8.9
Idaho	1913	9/	M,S,L,T		9	9	9.8	8.3
Illinois	1893[c]	8/48	M	10	10	10	9.4	8.3
Indiana							9.6	8.8
Iowa							9.6	8.8
Kansas	1917	9/54	S,L			8	9.7	8.6
Kentucky	1912	10/60	M,S,L,T		10	10	9.5	8.9
Louisiana	1886	10/60	M	10	10	10	10.2	9.3
Maine	1887[d]	10/	M	10	10	9	9.7	8.7
Maryland	1912	10/60	M,S,L		10	10	9.6	8.3
Massachusetts	1879[a]	10/60	M	10	10	9	9.4	8.1
Michigan	1885[f]	10/60	M	9	9	9	9.7	8.6
Minnesota	1895[g]	10/	M	10	9	9	9.5	8.6
Mississippi	1914	10/60	all		10	10	10.2	9.4
Missouri	1909	/54	M,S,L	/54	9	9	9.3	8.5
Montana	1913	9/	M,S,L,T		9	8	9.2	8.6
Nebraska	1899	10/60	M,S,	10	9	9	9.6	8.8
Nevada	1917	8/56	M,S,L			8	9.3	8.5
New Hampshire	1887[h]	10/60	M	9.7	10.25	10.25	9.5	8.3
New Jersey	1892[i]	/55	M		10	10	9.4	8.2
New Mexico	1921[j]	8/56	M,L				9.7	9.1
New York	1886[k]	/60	M	10	9	9	9.3	8.3
North Carolina	1915	11/60	M			11	10.3	9.4
North Dakota	1919[l]	8.5/48	M,S,L,T			8.5	9.4	8.5
Ohio	1911[m]	10/54	M		10	9	9.5	8.6
Oklahoma	1915[n]	9/	M,S,L,T			9	9.6	8.9
Oregon	1903	10/	M,L	10	10	9	9.6	8.0
Pennsylvania	1897[o]	12/60	M,S,L	12	10	10	9.7	8.6
Rhode Island	1885	10/60	M	10	10	10	9.5	8.5
South Carolina	1907[p]	10/60	CW	10	10	10	10.0	9.5
South Dakota	1923[l]	/54	M				9.6	8.9
Tennessee	1908[q]	/62	M	/61	10.5	10.5	9.9	9.1
Texas	1913	10/54	M,S,T		10	9	9.9	8.9
Utah	1911	9/54	M,S,L,T	9	9	8	9.4	8.7
Vermont	1912	11/58	M		11	10.5	9.4	8.7
Virginia	1890	10/	M	10	10	10	9.9	8.8
Washington	1901	10/	M,S,L	10	8	8	9.7	7.8
West Virginia							9.7	8.8
Wisconsin	1911[r]	10/55	M,S,L,T		10	10	9.7	8.9
Wyoming	1915	10/56	M,S,L,T			10	10.3	9.4

TABLE 7.1. (Continued)

	Legislated Daily Hours in Manufacturing as of			Scheduled Hours in Manufacturing as of	
	1909	1914	1919	1909	1919
Number of states with effective hours laws in manufacturing	20	33	40		
Mean scheduled hours					
Weighted by number of employees				9.5	8.5
Unweighted				9.6	8.7

[a]An 8-hour law (unenforceable) was passed in Alabama in 1887 and was repealed in 1894.

[b]Cotton textile firms were exempted.

[c]Declared unconstitutional in 1895; a 10-hour law was passed in 1909.

[d]Maine passed a 10-hour law (unenforceable) in 1848. The 1887 law allowed weekly hours to exceed 60 if workers received overtime pay.

[e]Massachusetts passed a 10-hour law in 1874 that is termed "unenforceable" in the source listed below, but Atack and Bateman (1988) note that at least one case was upheld in court under the law.

[f]The Michigan law was amended in 1893 to apply only to girls under 21 years old; the law again regulated the hours of all women in 1907.

[g]Minnesota passed a 10-hour law (unenforceable) in 1858.

[h]New Hampshire passed a 10-hour law (unenforceable) in 1847.

[i]New Jersey passed a 10-hour law for all workers in 1851, but it carried no fines or penalties. A /55 hour law (applying only in women) was passed in 1892, repealed in 1904, and later followed by a 10/60 hour law passed in 1912.

[j]The 1921 law also provided for a 9/56 maximum for sales workers, and a 8/48 maximum for telephone workers on day and 10/60 on night work.

[k]The law applied only to female workers under 21 years of age, but was extended to all women in 1899.

[l]A 10-hour law (unenforceable) for the Territory of Dakota was passed in 1863. South Dakota passed a law in 1913, but it allowed workers to contract for more than 10 hours a day.

[m]A 10-hour law (unenforceable) was passed in 1852 and was repealed in 1880.

[n]The Territory of Oklahoma passed a 10-hour law (unenforceable) in 1890, which was repealed in 1909.

[o]A 10/60-hour law (unenforcable) was passed in 1848 and applied to all workers in textile and paper factories in Pennsylvania.

[p]The law applied to all persons; a 12/60 law, passed in 1911, applied only to women.

[q]The Tennessee law was passed in 1907 but applied after January 1, 1908. The reduction to 60 hours per week took place by 1910.

[r]Wisconsin passed an 8-hour law (unenforceable) in 1867 that was repealed in 1913.

Notes: Hours: daily/weekly. Coverage: M = manufacturing; S = sales; L = laundries; T = telephone and telegraph; CW = cotton and woolen textiles.

Many early laws (e.g., New Hampshire, 1847; Maine, 1848; Pennsylvania, 1848; Ohio, 1852; Minnesota, 1858) were unenforceable because they allowed workers to contract for more than the maximum number of hours. These laws stated that firms could not "compel" workers to labor over the maximum. Enforceable here also means that the law provided fines and/or jail sentences for violators, and that it was enforceable as a legal document. Legislated daily hours in manufacturing includes only enforceable legislation; weekly maximum is given when there was no daily maximum. For southern states, manufacturing can include only textiles. At one time or another, many states (e.g., Arkansas, California, Delaware, Idaho, Maryland, Minnesota, Nevada, New Jersey, New Mexico, New York, Oregon, and Washington) exempted canning in general or during certain months. Additional, but minor, restrictions applied in various states.

Scheduled hours refers to the average across all workers and is the weekly average divided by 6. See Goldin (1988a) for a discussion of the hours data.

Sources: U.S. Department of Labor, Women's Bureau, *Chronological Development of Labor Legislation for Women in the United States*, Bulletin No. 66-II (Washington, DC: Government Printing Office, 1932); U.S. Bureau of the Census, *Thirteenth Census 1910*, Vol. 8, *Manufactures 1909: General Report and Analysis* (Washington, DC: Government Printing Office, 1913b); U.S. Bureau of the Census, *Population 1920. Fourteenth Census of the United States, Census of Manufactures, 1919* (Washington, DC: Government Printing Office, 1928).

female manufacturing workers, and the vast majority mandated a 10-hour day. Only five states set a maximum below 10 hours. At that time, the average scheduled workday among manufacturing workers, the majority of whom were male and thus not covered by the laws, was 9.5 hours across all states. In 1919, 40 states had maximum hours laws. Of these, 36 had laws mandating no more than a 10-hour day, and eight had laws mandating no more than an 8-hour day. The remaining four states set limits that exceeded 10 hours per day. The average scheduled workday in 1919 was 8.5 hours. The laws, therefore, were rarely extreme in their prohibitions and often coincided with average scheduled hours of all manufacturing workers.

Two contradictory interpretations of protective legislation have emerged. According to one view, the legislation originated in the genuine concerns of reformers about work conditions of all Americans and ultimately benefited women workers. The opposing view is that protective legislation was intended to restrict the employment of female workers and was passed under the guise of reform. Both views find support in the historical narrative.[5]

The Supreme Court, in 1905, found general hours legislation that applied to men and women alike unconstitutional because the laws restricted the right of labor to contract freely (*New York* v. *Lochner*). Various states had previously struck down hours legislation on the same ground even when the law applied only to women, as in the case of the Illinois 8-hour law passed in 1893. But in a now-famous case, *Muller* v. *Oregon* (1908), the Supreme Court upheld the constitutionality of maximum hours restrictions for female workers. According to the Supreme Court, states could pass legislation restricting the hours of women but not those of men. The Oregon law was held constitutional, due, in part, to a brilliant legal brief. The brief became, in the decades following, the legal rationale for the differential treatment of women. *Muller* v. *Oregon* left a legacy that went beyond the decision to uphold the Oregon 10-hour law.

Louis Brandeis, then a young lawyer, and his sister-in-law Josephine Goldmark, working for the National Consumers' League (NCL), wrote the brief for the NCL (Brandeis and Goldmark, 1908). Their defense of the 10-hour law rested on the deleterious effects that work had on women and their future offspring. The brief was predicated on inherent differences between men and women; one bore the next generation, and one did not.[6] It has since exemplified the view that women, because they are physically different from men, require protection. State intervention might be justified on the ground that future lives could be injured by the actions of women and their employers, and that the unborn were insufficiently represented in their actions. Further, women themselves could be coerced into working long hours. The Brandeis–Goldmark brief, however, is a considerably more subtle document than is immediately apparent.

Had women been more powerful as individual workers and as a group, the reform movement would not have had to marshal so radical a case for their protection. But women workers were considerably less organized than male workers. Only 6.3% of all female manufacturing workers were unionized in 1914, while 13.7%, or twice as many, male workers were.[7] And, as I have noted several times before, female workers were often young, poor, foreign-born, transient, and easy to exploit. Social consensus was easily rallied around the need to protect women and their unborn children, and the Supreme Court bought the case as well. Such tactics were fully justified in the minds of many social reformers by the goal of better working conditions for all American workers. After *Lochner*, it was clear that shorter hours could not be won through comprehensive legislation but might be established for certain groups, such as women. The tactic was clearly articulated by many reformers and labor organizers.[8]

The demand for shorter hours was a recurrent feature of labor agitation beginning with the cotton textile mill strikes of the 1830's and 1840's. Despite demands for shorter hours, the work week in manufacturing was long in all states during the nineteenth century. Thus one interpretation of maximum hours laws is that labor saw in it the means to lower hours of work for all workers, and the only constitutional laws were those applying to women. The point was cogently stated by one student of the period, "[A] demand for general legislation to insure shorter hours for all led to the passage of general eight-hour laws. When statutes of such unrestricted application proved unavailing, attempts at hours' regulation concentrated on specific classes of employees" (Cahill, 1932, p. 94).

The precise mechanism by which shorter hours for female workers could reduce hours for all workers is not entirely clear. Most female workers were employed in just two industries, textiles and apparel, while male workers were considerably more dispersed (see Tables 3.4 and 3.5). Because industries and occupations were extremely segregated by sex (see Chapter 3), there was little room, in the short run at least, for substitution against female workers whose hours were constrained. To some reformers, shorter hours for female workers would reduce the work week in female-intensive industries and thus lower hours for male workers in those industries. The position has been embraced by David Montgomery, who notes, in the case of the Massachusetts textile industry, that "because few mills, if any, could function long after the women had gone home, the law effectively established a new standard for textiles" (1987, p. 165). Some reformers thought that a bandwagon effect would ensue and that male workers, particularly in organized industries, might gain concessions for shorter hours. Further, shorter hours in some industries might encourage others in the same city to shorten hours of work.

An opposing rationale for protective legislation is that hours restrictions were supported by native-born white men who feared female workers would usurp their jobs. A mandated limit on the hours of women workers could reduce the demand for their labor.[9] Mechanization in tobacco and canning had reduced the need for skilled male workers, and it was perceived that hours limits would stem the movement from male to female labor in other industries.

The opposing view of protective legislation also finds support in the historical record. Women could not be hired in firms that operated in excess of the hours limit or that required them to work nights in states having night-work laws. The existence of effective constraints is revealed in legal complaints, such as the case of two female box makers who claimed the Illinois 10-hour law restricted their ability to earn income (Kessler-Harris, 1982, p. 190). But restrictions were usually binding only in industries with predominantly male work forces, such as foundries, streetcar railways, and printing and publishing.[10] Most examples of the impact of hours restrictions come from the immediate post–World War I experiences of women workers in nontraditional industries. Hours restrictions were occasionally used to enhance the bargaining power of male workers in unions. In 1919, for example, streetcar conductors in New York City agreed to increase their workday from 10 to 12 hours when the maximum for women was 9 hours, and they eventually persuaded the New York legislature to restrict the employment of women.[11] But the immediate postwar experience served also to reverse previous prohibitions that had severely restricted female employment. Women printers in New York State, for example, who had been constrained in night work and weekly hours eventually won concessions in 1921 that exempted them from certain hours restrictions (Baker, 1925, pp. 362–63).

Florence Kelley, the early-twentieth-century labor reformer, clearly articulated the two opposing notions of protective legislation:

> Statutes restricting the hours of labor of women and children, while enacted in the interest of health and morality, have often been urged by persons animated by two other motives as well. In many cases, men who saw their own occupations threatened by unwelcome competitors, demanded restrictions upon the hours of work of those competitors. . . . In other cases, men who wished reduced hours of work for themselves, which the courts denied them, obtained the desired statutory reduction by the indirect method of restriction upon the hours of labor of the women and children whose work interlocked with their own.[12]

Kelley could not have foreseen that the cause of protective legislation would be advocated for another half-century in opposition to one of true equality between men and women. The resolution of the causes and consequences of protective legislation, therefore, gains new meaning with historical hindsight.

Had protective legislation been championed by those seeking to limit female employment and had they actually achieved their goal, the eventual conflict between protection and equality could reflect continuing desires to restrict female employment and opportunity. But had protective legislation been a net benefit to female workers, and possibly to all labor, a trade-off could have existed between the twin goals of protection and equality.

To assess which of these hypotheses is correct, I explore the impact of protective legislation on hours of work from 1909 to 1919 and on female employment in 1919. The choice of 1919 requires some defense because protective legislation could have reduced female employment in, say, 1900 while having no impact by 1919. The debate over protection and equality arose in the early 1920's after women gained the vote and Alice Paul formed the National Woman's Party (NWP). Only when Alice Paul proposed the Equal Rights Amendment did protective legislation come in direct conflict with an equally lofty goal, although various groups and individual women had previously challenged hours restrictions.

The two opposing views of protective legislation are assessed by estimating the impact of legislation on the hours and employment of women workers in the covered sectors. Although the analysis can resolve the actual impact of maximum hours laws on hours and employment, it cannot settle the reasons for their passage.

Protective legislation may have been motivated by humanitarian concern and the desire for lower hours for both men and women but could, nonetheless, have resulted in reduced female employment. Alternatively, legislation may have been passed to restrict female employment, but could have induced employers to reduce hours of work for all.

Maximum hours laws usually pertained to women in the manufacturing sector, although various states had laws covering mercantile and other employments as well (see Table 7.1). Data on scheduled hours of work are available in the manufacturing censuses for 1909 and 1919, but they aggregate male and female workers by industry or state. In the analysis that follows, various techniques are used to estimate the impact of the law on the working hours of males and females separately.[13]

Hours and Employment Effects of Maximum Hours Legislation[14]

The first issue to be examined is whether maximum hours laws served to reduce hours or, put another way, were associated with reduced weekly hours of female and male manufacturing workers in 1919. The technique used is the estimation of an identity that expresses average hours as a linear combination of those worked by men and those by women.[15] Mean scheduled weekly hours in 1919 (*Hours19*) for all manufacturing workers in each state (and the District of Columbia) are regressed on variables that might cause hours to vary across states such as a South dummy (*South*) and the percentage urban in the state (*% Urban*). Also included is the percent female in manufacturing employment (*% Female*), the maximum hours law in existence, say, in 1914 or 1919 (*Law*), and an interaction between the last two variables (*% Female × Law*). The resulting equation is

$$Hours19 = \underset{(55.7)}{54.7} + \underset{(3.01)}{1.73}\ South - \underset{(3.87)}{0.059}\ \%\ Urban + \underset{(0.48)}{0.041}\ \%\ Female$$

$$- \underset{(1.56)}{1.82}\ Law + \underset{(0.35)}{0.035}\ Law \times \%\ Female$$

$R^2 = .63$; number of observations $= 49$; absolute values of *t*-statistics are in parentheses

where *Law* is defined as of 1914.[16]

Hours legislation is, therefore, associated with a reduction of about 1.8 hours per week for both male and female manufacturing workers. There is no discernible difference in the reduction for male and female workers separately. The relationship between hours legislation and a decline in the work week is not surprising. But the finding that it is associated with a decline in the hours of both male and female workers might be; after all, maximum hours laws applied only to female employees. The results, however, might be biased because male and female hours are aggregated, and the impact of legislation on female hours has been inferred through statistical procedures. It should be emphasized, however, that differences in hours across states in 1909 were not related to the states' eventual laws; that is, states with longer hours did not adopt either stronger or weaker laws, which could lead to a spurious correlation between the law and hours.

Scheduled hours by industry and state are also listed in the manufacturing census, and the decline in hours can, therefore, be estimated for those industries that hired virtually no female operatives. A similar estimation for foundries, an industry that meets this criterion, confirms the findings across all industries. In fact, the reduction in scheduled hours of foundry workers in states with maximum hours laws (once again, that applied only to women) is virtually identical to that from the full estimation. Hours of foundry workers declined by about 1.8 in states having maximum hours laws.[17] The results lend support to the view that protective legislation was passed in states where labor pressed vigorously for general hours reductions. That proposition can be tested directly using disaggregated data by industry for 1914 and 1919, a period of large declines in hours of labor for all Americans.

The two largest female-intensive industries and the two largest male-intensive industries in each state were selected for the analysis. In the case of the two largest female-intensive industries, females were, on average, about 50% of the labor force; in the case of the two largest male-intensive industries, however, they were less than 2% of the labor force. Workers in male-intensive industries, therefore, could not have viewed female labor as a direct threat to their employment; the industries (e.g., lumber, steamcar railroads) never hired but a trivial number of female employees.

The difference in hours of work from 1914 to 1919, among all employees in each of the industries by state, is regressed on the existing weekly hours limit in 1914 and variables to account for differences in hours across states. In most industries and for most states, hours of work declined substantially over the period 1914 to 1919; this was, after all, a period of increased labor demand, a high point in American labor union strength, and a period of decreased immigration. Scheduled hours declined by 3.4 hours in the male-intensive industries and by 4.4 in the female-intensive industries, or by about 7%.[18]

Define (Δ *Male hours*) to be average scheduled hours for males in 1919 minus average scheduled hours for males in 1914, and (Δ *Female hours*) to be the same for females. Let *Limit1914* be the existing weekly hours limit in 1914 (with the zero limit set equal to 66 hours). Then

$$\Delta \text{ } Male \text{ } hours = -20.24 + 0.256 \text{ } Limit1914 + 1.39 \text{ } South$$
$$(3.65) \qquad (3.06) \qquad\qquad\qquad (1.61)$$
$$+ \text{ } 0.0362 \text{ } \% \text{ } Urban$$
$$(1.64)$$

$R^2 = .22$; absolute values of t-statistics are in parentheses

is obtained when estimated across the 49 states (including District of Columbia) and indicates that the 1914 hours limit is positively related to the decline in hours for males from 1914 to 1919. Therefore, the lower the limit, the greater the decline in male hours. However, for females

$$\Delta \, Female \, hours = \underset{(0.85)}{4.27} - \underset{(1.19)}{0.090 \, Limit1914} + \underset{(0.14)}{0.11 \quad South}$$

$$+ \underset{(2.85)}{0.0569 \, \% \, Urban}$$

$R^2 = .17$; absolute values of t-statistics are in parentheses

indicates that the decline in female hours was not related to the existing 1914 limit. These results, taken together, support the hypothesis that labor in male-intensive industries lobbied effectively for hours limits on female workers in states where male laborers ultimately lowered their hours. In many of these states, the dominant male-intensive industry was lumber, in which the Wobblies led successful strike activity in the unique World War I environment (see Hidy et al., 1963, pp. 332–51).

Even though hours restrictions are associated with a decrease in the hours of all workers, males and females, from 1909 to 1919, hours laws may have led to a reduction in female employment. The clearest indictment of maximum hours laws is that they constrained female workers and induced employers not to hire them. Women workers in the printing and publishing industry and on streetcar railways in various large cities were clearly constrained by hours regulations. On average, however, female employment in manufacturing was not reduced. Because female labor force participation is positively associated with lower scheduled hours in a city-wide analysis for 1920 (see Chapter 6), it is even possible that lower hours increased women's employment, perhaps by making work more pleasant, convenient, and compatible with household duties.

To test whether maximum hours legislation reduced female employment in manufacturing, the share of women in manufacturing in 1919 (*Fem1919*), by state, is regressed on factors affecting it as well as aspects of the law. A variable called *Restrictive* measures the extent to which manufacturing laborers in 1909 would have been constrained by the maximum hours legislation in existence in 1914.[19] Thus if 60% of all laborers were working for more than 54 hours per week in 1909 and if legislation were passed in 1911 restricting hours to 54, the variable would equal .60. Also included in the regression are the share of women in manufacturing employment in 1909 (*Fem1909*) to account for previous conditions, a dummy variable for whether the state passed its first maximum hours law between 1905 and 1914 (*Law1905–14*), and the variables *South* and *% Urban*. The results, across all 49 states and the District of Columbia, are

$$Fem1919 = - \underset{(1.28)}{0.013} + \underset{(11.4)}{0.753 \, Fem1909} + \underset{(1.16)}{0.01 \quad South}$$

$$+ \underset{(1.44)}{0.0003 \, \% \, Urban} - \underset{(1.83)}{0.0157 \, Law1905{-}14} + \underset{(1.39)}{0.0181 \, Restrictive}$$

$R^2 = .86$; number of observations $= 49$; absolute values of t-statistics are in parentheses and indicate that the restrictiveness of the law did not have a negative impact, and possibly had some positive effect. The passage of an initial maximum hours law from 1905 to 1914 is associated with a small decrease in the female share of manufacturing employment. A similar estimation for the sales sector indicates an even stronger positive impact of the restrictiveness of the law (see Goldin, 1988a, for details) and a smaller negative impact for the passage of a first law from 1905 to 1914. Thus the restrictiveness of hours laws may be associated with an increase in the share of women in the sales sector and does not appear to be associated with a decrease in the employment share of women in manufacturing.

Protective Legislation Versus Equality

Protective legislation, therefore, had virtually no adverse impact on female employment around 1920, and states with more stringent hours laws had greater declines in hours for all workers than those with less stringent laws. Certain women, to be sure, were constrained by the laws. But from the perspectives of a trade-union leader, a reformer, or a laborer who wanted lower hours, the benefits of maximum hours laws and other types of protective legislation were well worth the costs. Many "social feminists," who in the post-1920's era became involved with "women's issues" in the Department of Labor and elsewhere, had been manufacturing operatives in their youth. Protective legislation was, to them, an indispensable substitute for collective action by women workers. They were probably correct that protective legislation was associated with reduced hours for all workers, although the precise mechanism is not yet clear, and that maximum hours laws resulted in only minor employment effects. But the real costs of protective legislation began to mount almost immediately through opposition to a guarantee of true equality between the sexes. The benefits, though, would remain in the minds of many who fought for shorter hours and better working conditions.

Directly following passage of the Nineteenth Amendment, the National Woman's Party was constituted from the radical wing of the National American Woman Suffrage Association. Under Alice Paul's able leadership, the NWP began its long and still unfinished campaign for the Equal Rights Amendment (ERA). The NWP demanded that "women shall no longer be barred from any occupation, but every occupation open to men shall be open to women, and restrictions upon the hours, conditions, and remuneration of labor shall apply alike to both sexes" (Baker, 1925, p. 432).

The ERA as drafted by Alice Paul read simply: "Men and woman shall have equal rights throughout the United States and every place subject to its jurisdiction" (Becker, 1981, p. 19). In 1923, it fell three states short of ratification but remained a live issue during the Depression and immediately after World War II. In 1971, the House of Representatives finally passed the ERA, as did the Senate in 1972, but the ERA ultimately failed ratification again after being blocked by opposition groups in various states. Opposition to the ERA since the 1970's is clearly identified with conservative interests, but earlier in its history the detractors were a more varied group. Immediately after the initial ratification failure in 1923, groups that supported protective legislation banned together in opposition to the ERA. The finest legal scholars in the 1920's, including Felix Frankfurter, believed that equal rights and protective legislation were incompatible, and that embracing equal rights meant abandoning protective legislation.[20]

From the 1920's to the 1960's, many liberals opposed the ERA, while conservatives often supported it. Professional and business women, who had the most to gain from true equality and the least to lose from terminating protective legislation, generally defended the ERA, while those in opposition were often "social feminists" who perceived women would suffer by forfeiting protective legislation. Liberals continued to define the female labor force in the same terms as did Progressive era reformers—as young, poor, transient, and unorganizable women workers who needed protection more than they needed equality.[21] The cause of protective legislation served to delay a national policy to combat discrimination against women through its definition of women as marginal workers and through the opposition it raised to real equality.

The Federal Government and the Economic Status of Women

Differential treatment of women was legislated by the states and the federal government and sanctioned by the courts. It was one of the many pillars of social and familial stability and, for other reasons as well, was viewed less as discrimination than as paternalism. Harmful discrimination by race was more intelligible to Americans than was discrimination by sex. Until the 1960's, few Americans realized the magnitude and implications of sex discrimination. "[D]iscrimination against Negroes aroused indignation," notes Caroline Bird, "but discrimination against women struck most people as funny" (1968, p. 4). Differences in the incomes, occupations, and educations of white and black men were more reasonably products of differential opportunity than of choice. Equivalent differences between men and women could not, it seemed, be so easily explained. To many Americans, blacks and whites were created equal, but men and women were not.

Numerous factors could be marshaled to explain differences by sex. Men and women chose to have families; children required mothers to remain at home for certain periods, and that, in turn, demanded women's occupations be different from men's. Just how much the observed difference was due to choice and how much to differences in opportunity was not clear. Even statistical measures of discrimination, such as that termed "wage discrimination" in Chapter 4, now admissible evidence in discrimination cases, cannot precisely resolve the reasons for differences. In the 1960's, the movement for equality by sex needed a document that could demonstrate to even the most skeptical observer that women were treated differently from men and that the differences were not entirely due to their choice. That document was provided by the 1963 President's Commission on the Status of Women.

The President's Commission on the Status of Women, 1963

The President's Commission on the Status of Women issued its long-awaited report in 1963. The commission, first proposed in 1946, was formed in 1961 by President Kennedy at the behest of Eleanor Roosevelt. The role of the President's Commission in furthering the causes of feminism and equality is just now being weighed. Although it is perhaps too recent a history, various studies are concluding that the commission's role was major (Harrison, 1988; Mathews, 1982). Its influence worked first through the document itself and second through the many state commissions it initiated that would encourage grass-roots action. Interest here centers on the first influence.

The commission was established by executive order to review progress and make recommendations in six areas, including private employment, protective legislation, and government hiring. It produced a final summary report, *American Women* (1963), and six separate reports of its subcommittees. The subcommittee on private employment was headed by economist Richard Lester, also a member of the commission. As an economist, Lester understood that differences in incomes and occupations between men and women did not constitute prima facie evidence of harmful discrimination, just as differences among men did not. Rather, he and other subcommittee chairs realized that only clear and incontrovertible instances of exclusion and differential treatment would establish that there was harmful discrimination against women.

The final report established various areas of indisputable discrimination against women. Discrimination was evident in the civil service's appointment and advancement policies and practices; those in charge could and did specify the sex of the appointment, even if women and men were equally qualified. Various studies demonstrated that equal pay for equal work was frequently violated in the private sector. State laws mandating maximum hours for women clearly hindered those pursuing professional and managerial careers, as night-work laws did for others. State laws prohibiting women from serving on juries and holding property were also discriminatory.

The document was not a radical statement. Its authors, with only one dissent, voted against endorsing legislation to ensure women equality in employment; they did not want to dismantle the apparatus of protective legislation, and they reaffirmed the importance of the family and women's role in it. The commission, like the majority of Americans, viewed sex and race discrimination as different problems: "The consensus was that the nature of discrimination on the basis of sex and the reasons for it are so different that a separate program is necessary to eliminate barriers to the employment and advancement of women" (U.S. President's Commission, 1963, p. 8).

Yet the report of the President's Commission on the Status of Women established beyond a doubt the existence of harmful discrimination against women in private and public employment and in the laws of various states. The discrimination, moreover, was detrimental to the nation as a whole. The American public needed a statement with force, authority, and clarity to awaken them to age-old discriminatory practices. The commission's report was exactly that.[22]

The 1963 Equal Pay Act and Title VII of the 1964 Civil Rights Act

When first introduced in 1945, the Equal Pay Act was a tactic to defeat the ERA, which had been voted favorably out of the House Judiciary Committee that year (Harrison, 1988). The doctrine of equal pay by sex for equal work was not a new concept in 1963 and had a long and ambivalent history. Equal pay was a frequent demand by unions in peacetime and during both world wars as a guarantee to male workers that their wages would not be depressed by female workers. As early as the 1860's, for example, male printers demanded that their female counterparts receive "equal pay for equal work"—less for the sake of equity than to protect compositors from the low wages of the needle trades (Baron, 1982). The International Association of Machinists decried the practice during World War I of "exploiting women by paying as small a wage as possible" and demanded "equal pay for equivalent work" (New York Department of Labor, 1919, p. 45). During World War II, the National War Labor Board, through General Order No. 16 in 1942, went partway in establishing a doctrine of equal pay for equal work, once again to protect the wages of male workers from encroachment by lower-paid females (see Kessler-Harris, 1982, p. 289).

Yet the doctrine of equal pay was clearly central to a policy of sexual equality in the marketplace. Many liberals, such as John Kennedy, who could not support the ERA because of its conflict with protective legislation, endorsed the Equal Pay Act, which did not endanger existing laws. The original version of the Equal Pay Act used the term "comparable work," but was later changed to "equal work." Given the extreme segregation of occupations across the entire economy, particularly across firms, an act that guarantees "equal pay for equal work" within firms can have little impact on differences in occupations and earnings between men and women. The act, moreover, made no provision for administrative enforcement and covered only jobs under the jurisdiction of the Fair Employment Standards Act. Equal pay for equal work has been, therefore, a rather weak doctrine to combat discrimination.

Just one year after passage of the Equal Pay Act and the publication of the report of the President's Commission on the Status of Women, the 1964 Civil Rights Act was passed. It has become "the most comprehensive and important of all federal and state laws prohibiting employment discrimination" (Babcock et al., 1975, p. 229). Title VII of the Civil Rights Act of 1964 prohibits discrimination on the basis of race, color, religion, sex, or national origin, in hiring, promotion, and other conditions of employment. But until the day before the law was passed, the word "sex" did not appear anywhere in the document. There is considerable disagreement about the facts surrounding the insertion of the word "sex" in Title VII of the act. It is known that Congressman Howard Smith (D-Va.) introduced the word the day before the vote. Some claim he did so to defeat the Civil Rights Act, which he opposed; yet others, including Smith, insist he wanted to protect white women on an equal basis with black women should the bill actually pass. It has been asserted that Smith, as a proponent of the ERA, was influenced by the continued pressure of the NWP, but others contend, despite his assertions to the contrary, that he viewed the entire affair as a joke that would ensure the bill's defeat.[23]

Interesting parallels can be drawn between the Civil Rights Act of 1964 and passage of the Fourteenth and Fifteenth Amendments. Women were asked at both times to postpone their demands so the cause of racial equality could be furthered. At the close of the Civil War, women suffragists and abolitionists pressed that female suffrage be incorporated into the Fourteenth and Fifteenth Amendments, but their cause was abandoned by even their abolitionist friends (see the perceptive discussion in Myrdal, 1944, appendix 5). If not for the curious introduction of the word "sex" in the 1964 Civil Rights Act, women might have lost then as well. In 1964, however, women were told that noninterference not only was in the best interests of the civil rights movement, but also was to their advantage. "Liberals and most of the women's organizations in 1964," writes Caroline Bird, "opposed adding sex to the Civil Rights Bill, primarily because they did not want to endanger protection for Negroes, but also because absolute equality between the sexes before the law might endanger rights and immunities favoring women" (1968, p. 6).

The fact that the inclusion of the word "sex" in the Civil Rights Act of 1964 was an accident, at worst a joke, signifies how difficult it was to mobilize Americans to pass legislation guaranteeing equality by sex. Even after Title VII was passed and the Equal Employment Opportunity Commission was set up to receive and investigate charges of employment discrimination, resources devoted to sex discrimination were severely limited. In its early years, EEOC vigorously investigated newspaper want ads that specified race but would not pursue similar cases in which sex was stipulated. EEOC shied away from cases that might challenge state protective legislation, such as prohibitions against night work for women. Indeed, the National Organization for Women was formed in 1966 to pressure EEOC to deal with these and other aspects of sex discrimination (Harrison, 1988).

Figure 7.1 shows the total number of charges brought to EEOC and the percentage of all categorized on the basis of sex. All EEOC cases grew slowly from 1966 to 1970, and then increased sharply from the early 1970's to 1976, particularly after the Equal Opportunity Act of 1972 bolstered and extended Title VII coverage (see Beller, 1982). One-quarter of all cases were brought on account of sex at the inauguration of EEOC, but the figure decreased in each succeeding year, declining to 18% by 1969. Cases brought on account of sex then surged from the early 1970's to 1973 when they accounted for one-third, and have remained at approximately 30% since.

Origins of Discontent

Few American women before the 1960's would admit that discrimination on the basis of sex affected their earnings and employment. I do not mean that women had not felt discontent with their treatment in the labor market before the 1960's. Educated women, in particular, had often expressed indignity with prohibitions against their employment, particularly in the professions; mass dismissals of women in both post–world war periods were met with outrage; and the marriage bars of the 1930's, certainly the firing of married women by the federal government, led many women to speak publicly about their treatment.[24] Yet most women were silent about

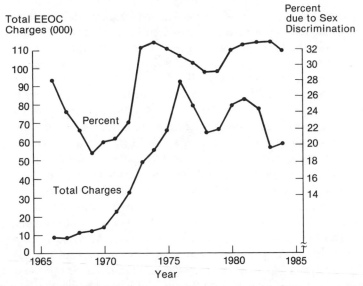

FIGURE 7.1. Complaints Filed with EEOC, 1966 to 1984. *Notes and Source:* Equal Employment Opportunity Commission, *Annual Reports, 1966 to 1984.* Total Charges are all new complaints filed with EEOC during the fiscal year given. The proportion of charges due to sex-related discrimination complaints is derived from a different total. Because EEOC listed the basis of the charges in a manner that involves double-counting, the total here is the sum of all the possible reasons for a complaint. Charges filed on account of age discrimination are removed for 1981 to 1984 due to a change in EEOC's jurisdiction.

their exclusion from promotion and training and about the resulting earnings differences given equal experience and education. Their silence, moreover, was a product of custom and prejudice, just as the silence of black Americans was. Women required a perception of injustice and an ideology to awaken and unify them. Discontent was finally articulated in the 1960's by large numbers of college-educated, middle-class women, and they ultimately produced the feminist revival of the 1960's and 1970's (Freeman, 1975). Although the discontent described by Betty Friedan in her 1963 book was apparent as early as the 1920's (Cowan, 1983a), college-educated women whose expectations greatly exceeded their realizations incited a mass movement.

Perceptions of Discrimination

The use of the word "discrimination" to describe unequal outcomes in earnings and occupations by sex, given identical inputs, is rather recent. In the nineteenth and early twentieth centuries, when most paid labor was in manufacturing and agriculture, inequality of earnings was most commonly viewed as arising from inherent differences between men and women in strength, endurance, drive, and ambition. Butler, for example, notes that "expectation of marriage . . . stunts professional ambition among women. This lack of ambition . . . limit[s] efficiency, and restricts them to subsidiary, uninteresting, and monotonous occupations" (1909, p. 373). Some differences were admitted to have been socially determined; for example, apprenticeships were denied female workers not only because they were not expected to remain with the trade, but also because it was considered socially improper to give or receive training.[25]

The computations in Chapter 4 reveal that differences in earnings between male and female manufacturing operatives around 1900 were slight, given differences in characteristics, compared with the period after 1940. The "wage discrimination" measure showed that the earnings each received were more or less commensurate with the productive attributes each brought to the labor market. There is, perhaps, some truth to the assertions about differences in earnings and occupations between men and women in the nineteenth and early twentieth centuries.

But "wage discrimination" increased considerably with the growth of occupations in the clerical, sales, and professional sectors that substituted brain power for strength and formal education for on-the-job training. Men and women were rather good substitutes at entry-level positions. Recall from Chapter 4 that women in clerical jobs often began in occupations similar to those of men (lower-level clerks), but that men advanced with time on the job and women generally did not. Women who did advance were almost always confined to occupations reserved for women as a matter of stated firm policy. After several years at work, large differences in the earnings and occupations of men and women emerged, even though men and women had virtually the same productive characteristics and the same time on the job and with the firm. Also addressed in Chapter 4 were the reasons why firms found it profitable, even in the long run, to advance men but not women, and why they may also have found it profitable to segregate occupations by sex. At issue here is why women rarely commented on what appears now to be obvious and substantial inequities that widened over time.

Part of the reason concerns norms that define appropriate behavior and that somehow punish deviance. As mentioned in Chapter 4, occupations assume an "aura of gender," informing individuals which should be pursued by each sex. Typing in the late nineteenth century, for example, was deemed too strenuous for women. But it quickly, and with no change in technology, became the quintessential female clerical trade (Davies, 1982). Its necessary qualification became dexterity, not the capacity for arduous labor. Consequently, there may be circularity in the contentment of female workers. Sex-segregated occupations quickly become associated with gender distinctions that are not necessarily part of the original rationale for segregation. For a woman to express dissatisfaction would be to reject one set of traits and embrace another.

The sanctions that secure norms in the labor market often concern another market, that for marriage. The powerful norms that defined appropriate work for women succeeded, in part, because inappropriate behavior entailed severe costs. The most extreme cost for many women was to forgo marriage entirely. Marriage in America was an almost universal institution. The percentage of white women who ever married never dropped below 90% and was generally closer to 95% across cohorts born between 1816 to 1930, a figure that is exceptionally high by European standards. Because marriage was universal, preparing for a life without marriage was considered deviant and was often based on a higher calling, such as scholarship, religion, or humanitarian concern. Occupations with the greatest barriers to women were generally those for which women who gained entry never married. The young woman who entered college or library school in the late nineteenth and early twentieth centuries, for example, might well have entered a convent, so few eventually married (see Garrison, 1979). The woman who worked in or trained for an atypical trade signaled she was deviant. To challenge the norms of the marketplace was often to place at risk other social relationships, such as marriage. Powerful sanctions existed, therefore, that held norms in place and restrained discontent (see Axelrod, 1986, on norms and sanctions).

By 1940, according to the estimates in Chapter 4, 40% of the difference between male and female earnings in office work could not be explained by differences in productive characteristics. The Women's Bureau bulletin (Department of Labor, 1942), which produced the surveys used in Chapter 4 on "wage discrimination," noted wide differences in earnings and occupations of male and female clerical workers. The report commented on the existence of marriage bars and the many occupations reserved for either men or women only. But despite strong evidence that occupational segregation was mandated by firm policy and that firms routinely fired women who married, the words "discrimination," "bias," and "prejudice" were never used to describe the outcomes.

I do not mean that one or several of the meanings of "discrimination" were absent from the discussion. The notion that men and women differ as groups and thus that "statistical discrimination," as defined in Chapter 4, accounts for some of the difference is implicit in documents I have studied. Also mentioned was that custom and tradition may have operated. But there was no clear movement prior to the 1960's to define differences in incomes and occupations between men and women as resulting from discrimination, and history is virtually silent on the impressions of female workers. One reason the voices of history are so mute is that prior to the 1950's most working women were young and unmarried, and most would leave the labor force at the time of marriage. The silence was broken in the 1960's with the increase in adult married women in the labor force, the rise in college education among women, and the emergence of the feminist movement.

As Jo Freeman (1975) and others have noted, college-educated, middle-class women in the 1960's had higher expectations than previous cohorts and compared their achievements with those of their husbands and their male peers. They were likely to find that they, and women as a group, fell far short of them (see also Mathews, 1982; O'Neill, 1969). It was the college-educated woman who perceived and expressed the greatest discontent with labor market outcomes, and it was she who initiated the feminist revival of the 1960's and 1970's. American history had witnessed other periods when educated, middle-class women united to press for equality, but the numbers were now on their side. Not only did the proportion of women with college degrees increase in the 1960's (see Figure 5.5), but the baby boom of the post–World War II period meant there were to be considerably more of them in the 1960's and 1970's.

Discontent Among College Graduates

Much of the widespread discontent among college graduates can be traced to the absence of a wide range of occupations for educated women during the 1950's. As I noted in Chapter 6, the labor market of the 1950's finally accommodated older married women, as it had high-school educated women in the 1920's. But young college-educated women found few openings commensurate with their education in fields other than teaching, nursing, and library and social work.

Several employers in the 1957 Hussey Report (discussed in Chapter 6) commented on the employment of college-educated women. For some, the issue was whether women would remain with the firm long enough to merit additional training, on or off the job. "Most girls who apply," responded the agent for Insurance Company of North America, "don't expect to have a career and of the few who do, many change their plans within a few years. . . . For this reason the company does not recruit women who are college graduates for career jobs" (Sept. 12, 1956). Ironically, others faced the reverse problem; because firms still oriented women's work toward high-school graduates, college-educated women became bored and soon left. Thus the Tradesmen's Bank and Trust Company noted that "the bank has tried to use college women in positions as tellers but . . . after a few months they begin to ask themselves what they are doing counting money all day . . . training a teller is expensive so the personnel department looks for people who will stay longer than . . . college women" (Nov. 19, 1956). In her final report, Miriam Hussey (1958) concluded that "college women still don't have much of a place."

In 1957 the Women's Bureau, concerned with the position of college-educated women in the American economy, undertook a comprehensive and wide-ranging study. Almost 6,000 women, or 7% of all female graduates in 1957, across 153 colleges and universities were surveyed several months after graduation. Information was collected on academic experiences, including major and minor; personal information, such as age, marital status, and number of children; economic information, such as occupation, weeks and hours worked, earnings, and husband's occupation; and other information, such as the woman's expectations about future employment. Women were also encouraged to write longer statements about how their college experiences prepared them for the labor market. Seven years later, in 1964, the Women's Bureau resurveyed these women, and more than 80% of the original group responded. Questions were asked to update information in the original 1957 survey, such as those on marital status, number and ages of children, employment, income, and husband's occupation, and new questions were added, such as husband's attitude toward work. The women were again asked to write longer statements about their work experiences and their attempts to gain employment. Although the bureau had done a similar study in 1945, the 1957/64 College Graduate Survey, as it will be called, was the first large-scale longitudinal survey of college women in America. A sample of about 800 records was culled from the National Archives, and the records were linked across the two surveys (see Data Appendix for more details).

Three months following graduation, 84% were employed. Of these, fully 54% were teachers and 5% were registered nurses.[26] Of the 38% who married, 77% were employed and 10% had at least one child or were then pregnant with their first. Although many planned to take substantial time out of the labor force to raise a family, most, it appears, believed they would return to the labor market at a later date. Only 14% expected in 1957 to pursue a "career," and another 8% indicated they would work continually but without career orientation. Just 8% stated they did not plan to work at all or would work only if the family needed additional income. The vast majority (71%) indicated in 1957 they would stop work when they married or when they had children, or that they would work for only a short period after marriage.

The survey gave them no chance to indicate how long they planned to interrupt their employment. But by cross tabulating the 1964 survey with the 1957 survey, it is found that 77% of those who stated they would stop work in 1957 expressed intentions in 1964 to return at some future date. Therefore, by implication, 77% of the original 71%, or 55%, intended to interrupt their work for an unknown duration, and the remaining 16% did not intend to return to work in the future. Putting the two surveys together, therefore, reveals that in 1957, 21% planned to work continually, 55% intended to work discontinually, and 24% had no intention of working in the future. Most of these women had prepared themselves for fields, such as teaching, that were compatible with interrupted employment and with raising children. By 1964, seven years after graduation, 80% had married and of these 81% had children.

Several months after graduation, most were pleased with how college prepared them for the labor force, although they often lamented the absence of "more practical experience" and "an overabundance of lectures." Some remarked, without further comment, that female college students should "be required to take typing and . . . shorthand." Although the majority were employed in fields, such as teaching and nursing, for which they had been trained, commercial skills were still highly valued, even for college-educated women. Few, however, sensed unfairness in the labor market, although some did; one social-work trainee commented that she "found it very difficult to find a job that would relate to [her] field . . . they are very good in placing men, but very seldom do they have good positions for women." For most, their lives were unfolding, marriages were new, and babies were just being born. It would be fair to summarize their comments as reflecting contentedness with life. But their views change considerably after seven years. Although it is impossible to separate the effects of age from experience, and personal dissatisfaction from discontent with the labor market, the change in their expression is evident.

While the 1957 comments convey complacency, those in 1964 communicate growing frustration: "Past experience in executive training programs . . . shows tremendous barriers against women." "Like many others I feel that the pay is too low for a college graduate." "Unfortunately the school systems have a practice of showing a hiring preference for men over women for Administrative and/or Supervisory jobs." "I have a B.S. in chemical engineering [and] eventually ended up working in a library." "I have experienced some prejudice on the part of employers to hire women in a traditionally man's work," reported a female pharmacist. "I asked the principal why I wasn't considered for the job. . . . He replied that he had asked for a *man*."

The notion that college-educated women perceive employment discrimination to a greater extent than other women receives support in a recent empirical study (Kuhn, 1987). In a 1977 national cross section, 13% of all women responded affirmatively to the question: "Do you feel in any way discriminated against on your job because you are a woman?" But perceptions of discrimination increase nearly threefold, to 35%, when only younger (25- to 34-year-old), college-educated women are considered, and decrease to less than 1% when only older (55- to 76-year-old), high-school educated women are included. About one-quarter of the college-educated women across all ages perceived some discrimination.[27] Perceptions of discrimination by female employees in 1977, therefore, increase markedly with education and decrease with age.

One might suppose from these findings that young, college-educated women were subject to more "wage discrimination" than were older, less-educated women. But that does not appear to be the case. Rather, the study finds that estimates of "wage discrimination," similar to those computed in Chapter 4, are negatively correlated with self-reported discrimination. Those who experience the most discrimination were the least likely to report they encountered prejudice; those subject to the least "wage discrimination"—the younger, most educated group—were most likely to report prejudice. Young, college-educated women may be more likely to encounter other forms of discrimination (termed nonstatistical in the study) or might be more sensitive to and thus more liable to report discrimination.

Both interpretations are consistent with the perception of many labor economists that discrimination cases are most often brought by educated women, and both are also consistent with the notion that college-educated and young women express significantly more discontent with their treatment in the labor market. The evidence from Kuhn's article as well as that from the 1957/64 College Graduate Survey suggest that the increase in college education among women produced a growing recognition that the labor market was somehow unfair to women. The sense that the labor market is prejudiced and that the Equal Pay Act and Title VII have done little to change matters has recently led to a movement for pay equity legislation that has been gaining strength in public-sector employment and within many of the nation's larger establishments.

The New Political Economy of Gender: Comparable Worth and Title VII

Differences in the earnings of men and women are often the result of their different jobs. Office employment in the 1940 surveys analyzed in Chapter 4, for example, was frequently segregated by sex in a deliberate manner, and women's promotional possibilities were severely limited. Several recent studies have demonstrated a negative relationship between the percentage of an occupation's labor force that is female and the wage for female and male workers, holding various individual attributes and industry constant. According to these studies, the sex composition of occupations accounts for between 10% and 30% of the difference between male and female earnings (Johnson and Solon, 1986; Sorensen, 1989).

The Equal Pay Act is unlikely to eliminate differences in pay that arise from differences in jobs because it applies to only payment differences between men and women in the same occupation. Title VII of the 1964 Civil Rights Act has also been weak in counteracting pay inequities that arise from differences in jobs and promotion.[28] Yet the wording of Title VII and the related Bennett Amendment left open the possibility that "equal pay for comparable work" claims were legitimate under the law. The Bennett Amendment was tacked on to Title VII and tied it to the Equal Pay Act in a manner that was, until recently, confusing to most legal scholars. The Equal Pay Act has limited scope in two manners; it applies to only the narrow concept of "equal work" and provides for a number of employer defenses, such as differences in pay due to merit and seniority. In 1981 the Supreme Court, in the landmark case *County of Washington* v. *Gunther*, determined that the Bennett Amendment applied only the defenses of the Equal Pay Act and not its limitations. But the *Gunther* decision did not settle whether Title VII could actually be extended to cover comparable worth claims (see Bureau of National Affairs, 1984).

Comparable worth or work is an extension of the "equal pay for equal work" doctrine.[29] The problem with "equal pay," as Sidney Webb noted in 1891, is "the impossibility of discovering any but a very few instances in which men and women do precisely similar work, in the same place and at the same epoch" (p. 638). Although it is more likely today than in 1891 to encounter men and women working at the same occupation, it is still the case that men and women work in very different jobs. The portion of the difference in earnings due to their distribution across jobs given their characteristics can be eliminated through implementing the doctrine of comparable worth. The doctrine of comparable worth states that jobs of equal or comparable worth should receive equal pay. The problem is determining comparability. There are various methods of judging the difficulty, skill, and responsibility, among other factors, required in a job, and firms routinely hire personnel consultants to evaluate their compensation schedules. Consultants attach scores to each of several types of factors (e.g., responsibility of job, level of skill required), and these scores are then often summed to determine the "worth" of each occupation.

Since the *Gunther* decision, various judges have argued against the extension of Title VII to comparable worth. Instead, 20 states and various localities have passed comparable worth legislation that covers state and local public employees (Cook, 1985). The cases brought under these laws often use the scores for each of the occupations to measure differences in pay among occupations that differ greatly by sex composition but not by test scores. A common guideline is to define a "woman's job" as one that is more than 70% female and a "man's job" as one that is less than 30% female and to equalize pay across these two groups of occupations having the same scores. Also used is a technique that equalizes pay in direct relation to the test scores, that is, in a proportional manner.

Comparable worth became an issue of importance in the 1980's. It emerged from a sense of frustration over the stability in the gap between male and female earnings and occupations. It also gained support from women who were in low-paying jobs, such as typist, secretary, and nurse. But the perception that women's progress was stagnant could never have turned into a call for a new policy without an additional change. While I am neither advocating nor opposing the doctrine of comparable worth, I am suggesting that its adoption is an indicator of women's political power.

With the increase in female labor force participation and the rise of public-sector unions, political power in the labor market shifted. The period since the early 1960's witnessed a continued decline in private-sector unions, which represent primarily male, white, and often blue-collar workers. At the same time, the public sector, which more often contains female, black, and white-collar workers, has surprised observers with its rapid unionization. According to one study (Freeman, 1986), 44% of government employees were represented by labor organizations in 1984 and 36% were members of unions, compared with only 18% in the private sector. But in the early 1960's, public-sector unions were considerably weaker, about one-quarter their 1984 strength. Private-sector unions, however, were twice as strong in 1960, when they contained 35% of the private nonagricultural labor force. Further, the share of women in public-sector unions has risen greatly. In 1984, women were nearly half of all public-sector union members (Freeman and Leonard, 1987); in 1974, only one-quarter of all teachers, a highly feminized occupation, were unionized but more than half were in 1980 (Kokkelenberg and Sockell, 1985).

Summary: Altering the Rules

Women have been able to alter the rules of the labor market because of their enhanced power in the labor market, and they may in the future effect a real change in the distribution of income. Their power was furthered by the relative rise in public-sector unions and the desire of these unions to attract a significant fraction of the work force. One must be cautious, however, about assessing the future political strength of women in altering the rules of the labor market and the economy.

One thing is certain, however. Their newfound political power, whatever its future, was delayed for various reasons. Progressive era concerns with young, single female workers gave rise to protective legislation that eventually retarded the movement for true equality in the marketplace. Despite considerable discrimination, women lacked a common voice and were severely constrained by societal norms. The continued expansion of female labor force participation, the increase in college education among women, and a combination of factors that led to the revival of feminism in the 1960's and 1970's together produced a vast change in the political strength of women that may yet alter the functioning of the labor market. Recent proposals in Congress concerning child-care and maternity leave, and others endorsed by both parties during the 1988 election, suggest that women's issues are finally becoming the nation's issues.

8

Economic Progress
and Gender Equality

Differences between men and women in their earnings, occupations, and economic well-being have probably existed throughout history. The issue I have addressed is whether economic progress serves to foster gender equality. Many doubt that material differences between men and women have been reduced in the past and question whether they will eventually be eliminated. While I do not profess the ability to forecast, I do believe history offers insight.

The Present

There are many sources of skepticism regarding the role of economic progress in producing gender equality. Several find support in the current situation of America's women, as well as in their recent past. A frequently voiced concern, mentioned elsewhere in this volume, is that although women have entered the labor market in impressive numbers over the past several decades, they have not been treated as the equals of men. To many observers, women have been increasingly discriminated against in earnings and occupations while they have attempted to achieve greater equality in labor force participation. Evidence for this view is found in the period from 1950 to 1980. The post-1950's witnessed the greatest advance in the employment of adult women. But the ratio of female to male earnings remained virtually stable at 0.60 during the 30 years after 1950. These facts, in the minds of many, can be explained only by deficiencies in the economic treatment of women. Increased participation with a stable gap in earnings seems paradoxical and led to a call for new policies to combat discrimination in the marketplace.

One cause for optimism is that the ratio of female to male earnings has increased from 1981 to the time of this writing, and differences in occupations have narrowed since 1970. But even though many now see promise for the future in the recent closing of the gender gap, others wonder when setbacks, such as those experienced during the Great Depression, will emerge.

Another source of skepticism is that the personal gains women have made in the labor market are apparently being lost in the home. Women's economic well-being seems to have declined over the past several decades. Women have entered the labor force at an impressive rate. But while their time as paid laborers has increased, their unpaid work as parents and wives has not diminished hour for hour. By one estimate, the hours all women work in the market and in the household increased by 5% from 1959 to 1983, while those for men decreased by 9%. Employed women with families work more hours at home and in the labor market than their husbands (58 versus 53 hours per week in 1975–1976), they work longer hours than wives not employed for pay (58 versus 51 hours), and when employed at full-time jobs, they labor even more (62 hours). Thus the expansion in women's paid employment has led to an overall increase in the hours women work.[1] There are no precise data on consumption within the household, so we do not know whether women's added hours have been fully compensated, and there are no measures of the intensity of housework, so we do not know whether total work effort has increased. But even with these ambiguities, the increase in total hours worked for women and not men is incontrovertible.

Another concern is the increase in divorce and the related rise in paternal default. More women are raising children on their income alone. A mother's income, moreover, is likely to be less than a father's because of her lower past investments in marketable skills. The relationship between the rising divorce rate and the increase in female employment is not yet clear.[2] But whatever the cause, paternal default has been a consequence of both.

As a result of women's lower incomes, more recently combined with divorce and paternal default, considerably more women than men are in poverty. In 1987, women constituted fully 63% of all poor adults and 68% of all poor black adults (U.S. Bureau of the Census, 1988). But despite the widespread perception that women have become a greater fraction of the poor in the past decade, they have not. Women's share of the poor rose somewhat in the 1960's but then decreased in the early 1970's with a general increase in poverty (Fuchs, 1986, 1988). Because women's earnings are on average lower than men's, more are left under a fixed poverty line as all incomes rise. An increase in the percentage of women in poverty, as occurred in the 1960's, may therefore be a statistical artifact of differences in the distribution of earnings between men and women (Fuchs, 1986, 1988). Nevertheless, in 1987 women more than 21 years of age were 1.5 times more likely than men to be in poverty.[3] Poverty has probably not become "feminized" over the past decade, as many have thought. It is more likely that poverty has always been feminized.[4]

The view that economic progress does not engender equality finds considerable support in a growing literature on women in developing countries that contends that the fruits of modern technology are not shared equally by men and women. The consequences of economic development, however, go beyond the economic sphere, and women, it appears, often lose legal, political, and social status in addition to economic goods. Many have searched for a "golden age" of women, for if economic development has often robbed women of their position, then women may have been supreme, at least in a relative sense, sometime in the past. Historical research has uncovered several periods of decline in women's status; for instance, women had once been members of European craft guilds, their paid labor may have been held in higher regard in the early nineteenth century than it was later, and they frequently had legal rights to property later denied them. But no era has emerged when women were unambiguously better off, and a "golden age" for women is not likely to be found.[5]

All the factors just mentioned—economic discrimination against women workers, the "double burden," paternal default, and the proportion of poor adults who are women—have raised concerns that economic progress does not generate economic equality and that the reverse is often the result. Although some of the concerns about the role of economic progress are legitimate, others, I have emphasized here and elsewhere in this volume, are not. Further, many of the rightful concerns expressed today about the ambiguous benefits to women from economic progress have little to do with women's treatment in the workplace. They have far more to do with the division of labor in the home and with the role of the state in enforcing the contractual obligations of fathers.

As long as women bear a disproportionate burden in raising children, the labor market will reflect these differences (see also Fuchs, 1988). And as long as men default on obligations to their children, women and children will be a substantial fraction of the nation's poor. The remedy to the first problem may be tax incentives or subsidies for child care. The justification, however, must be sought in the benefits to the nation from increased population and from the well-being of preschoolers. Policies that require firms to maintain jobs for women with newborns impose greater costs on firms that hire women, and the proper functioning of maternity-leave policies may require tax incentives. The remedy to the second problem, that of paternal default, is far easier than that to the first, in theory at least. It can be found in an aggressive set of legal procedures that mandate child support.

The Past

Despite many of the rightful concerns just mentioned and the impressive historical and development literature on the subject, economic progress over the long run has generated a move to economic equality. Further, there is considerable evidence, presented below, that advances will continue to be made. I have emphasized in this volume that much of the increase in female labor force participation has been the result of economic development—sectoral shifts in demand toward the service sector, increased education, reduced hours, increased real wages, technological change, and decreased fertility. The gap in earnings between men and women narrowed in two periods: during the Industrial Revolution (1820 to 1850) and with the rise of white-collar work and increased education (1890 to 1930). And the narrowing of the gender gap in earnings and occupations during the past decade may be viewed by future economic historians as yet a third period.

But one of the lessons of this history is that progress in the economic sphere is often ambiguous. I have stressed, particularly in the discussion of marriage bars and "wage discrimination," that economic progress often brings advances in some aspects of gender differences while frustrating others. Part of the problem lies in social norms and prejudices that impede change; another is in the dictates of profit maximization in a society that until recently allowed restrictions solely on the basis of sex, among other characteristics.

The rise of the white-collar sector, for example, greatly increased women's labor force participation, expanded women's occupations, and increased the ratio of female to male wages. Office work, teaching, and other white-collar employment offered women better working conditions, shorter hours, and higher pay than manual labor. Yet the unexplained difference between male and female earnings in office work was greater than it was in manufacturing, and office work, rather than manufacturing, developed formal barriers to women's employment. Marriage bars and explicit policies prohibiting the employment of women in particular jobs (and men in other jobs) were found almost exclusively in office work and teaching, prior to the onset of the Great Depression. These barriers, however, do not seem to have emerged from the prejudices of employers or employees. Rather, they originated in the dictates of profit maximization even in the absence of biases toward female employees. These policies may have been fueled by prejudice, but they arose primarily from what is termed "statistical discrimination."

Women were "statistically discriminated" against because as a group they were unlikely, for instance, to remain in the work force long after marriage, and as a group they may have been pleased with jobs that involved a minimum of training. Although the majority of women may have been satisfied with the status quo, an important and growing minority were not. But because the minority could not effect change, the status quo was perpetuated. Another factor in this process was the reinforcement of "statistical discrimination" by a society that has often branded women in atypical occupations as socially deviant.

Another lesson from the economic history of women is that progress frequently appears delayed even when it is not. Real progress may occur but be hidden from view for several decades. I noted in Chapter 2 that work experience among married women has had a large variance. Women were either in the labor force or they were not, for much of their lives. In the 1950's and 1960's, many women, particularly those older than 45 who had not worked for many years, were drawn into the labor force. Thus the increase in their labor force participation served to depress, not increase, the accumulated work experience of the female work force. Other researchers have found, as well, that the large increase in participation depressed the average education level among female workers (Smith and Ward, 1984). Both factors imply that women's earnings, compared with men's, could be stable during periods of growth in the female labor force. Much of the stability in the ratio of female to male earnings during the period from 1950 to 1980 has been attributed to these factors. But because labor force participation rates had climbed sufficiently by 1980, further increases in participation have produced growth in the ratio of female to male earnings.

Another reason why progress often appears hidden is that change frequently proceeds through the aging of cohorts. The young initially receive the fruits of economic progress, through, for example, advances in education, training, revised expectations, and greater control over fertility. But time is required for change to filter through the entire population. At each moment in our history, therefore, we must look to younger women for guidance about our future.

In the 1920's, for example, younger women were finishing high school, getting jobs as office workers, and often extending the period of their employment beyond marriage, as none did before. Thirty years later, they became the older married women in the 1950's who returned to the labor force after their children were grown. The impact of this cohort on the female labor force was delayed until the post–World War II period for reasons given in Chapter 6. But by the 1950's, the labor market had fully accommodated the older married women worker in terms of jobs and hours of work. Several decades were required for these cohorts to influence the participation rates of all married women.

The Future

Just as the past unfolded through the aging of cohorts, the future can be revealed through the experiences of younger women today. Data in Chapter 3 showed that the ratio of female to male earnings is higher among those 25 to 34 years old than those older, and other data indicate that it is even higher for younger and unmarried men and women. Further, during the 1980's the ratio among 25 to 34 year olds increased at a considerably faster rate than that for the entire population (see Table 3.1).

Among the most meaningful changes affecting the young has been the convergence between men and women in the percentage graduating from college, in their college major, and in their choice of postgraduate education (Figure 8.1). In 1960, 38% of all college graduates were female, but the percentage has risen almost steadily since then, reaching 50% by 1981.[6] Only 3% of all first-professional degrees were awarded to women in 1960. But the fraction has climbed rapidly since 1972, and in 1987, 35% were women.[7] In 1975, only 15% of all graduating law students were female; in 1985, 38% were.

The courses of study men and women pursue in college are also converging. Although large differences in various majors still exist (women compose 13% of all engineering majors but 76% of all education majors), there is much similarity in general. In 1985, almost 30% of all female undergraduates majored in business, and the number of male and female business-management and life-science majors were about equal. Even among majors with the greatest differences in male and female enrollment, there has been remarkable change during the past 25 years. In 1960, almost 50% of all female college graduates majored in education, but only 13% did in 1985.[8]

Given the convergence in college graduation rates, college major, and postgraduate education, it is not surprising that women have made rapid advances in the professions. But until the 1990 population census is taken, we will not be able to see how occupational advancement has progressed by detailed age groups.[9] We can, however, discern the impact of educational advance on the younger groups through changes in occupations across the entire population and among those less than 35 years old for certain occupations. Women, for example, were 10% of all lawyers in 1979, but were 15% in 1986 and were 29% among those younger than 35 years old; they were 11% of all physicians in 1979, but 17% in 1986.[10] Considerable advances

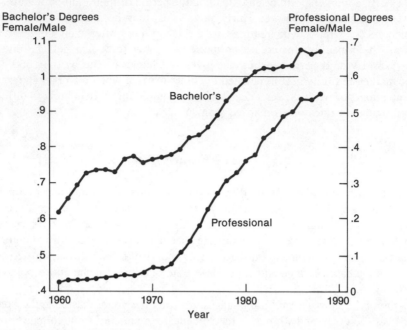

FIGURE 8.1. Bachelor's and Professional Degrees by Sex, 1960 to 1988. *Source:* U.S. Department of Education, *Digest of Education Statistics* (Washington, DC: Government Printing Office, 1988), table 166. Professional degrees are first-professional degrees, primarily in dentistry, medicine, and law.

have been made in other occupations as well, including computer programmers, accountants, and most managerial and supervisory positions. These increases vastly exceed those made in the labor force participation rate of all women during that period.[11]

A primary reason for existing differences in occupations between men and women concerns the time women take from their careers to have and raise children. Recently, the most rapid increase in participation rates among women has been for those with very young children. In 1977, 32% of all mothers with children younger than a year were in the labor force, but 52% were in 1988. Further, a greater percentage of young women are working full-time and year-round today than were 20 years ago. In 1966, 39% of women 25 to 34 years old worked full-time and 50 to 52 weeks per year, but 55% did in 1986. The increase among women 45 to 54 years old was not nearly as large, 52% to 60%. Young women are experiencing considerably more continuity of employment today than they did even a decade ago, and a far greater percentage are working full-time. All this means that their occupations and earnings should be closer to those of comparably educated men.[12]

Another cause for optimism is that women have become better able to predict their futures and thus be more intelligent investors in skills. Recall from Chapter 5 that the vast majority of young women in the 1960's poorly anticipated the large increase in female employment in the 1970's and 1980's. Most may have severely underinvested in skills needed for continued employment. In the early 1970's, however, expectations rapidly converged with reality, and young women began to invest more wisely in skills. One study that traced the cohort of women born between 1944 and 1946 found that in 1968 only 33% of the group expected to be in the labor force at age 35, but by 1975, 57% did. In 1980, when the cohort was 35 years old, 64% were in the labor force (Shaw and Shapiro, 1987). The group was off by 31 percentage points in 1968 but only 7 percentage points in 1975. And as pointed out in Chapter 5, successive cohorts also experienced rising expectations in the 1970's.

Economic progress can generate economic equality between the sexes, but there may be periods of short-run stagnation that are both apparent and real. I have tried in this volume to understand gender differences in today's economy through those of the past. I have also argued that we can forecast the future by observing the experiences of young cohorts today, and these experiences give us ample cause for optimism. If I have assigned a large role to the forces of economic development, it is because, in the long run at least, these factors are preeminent in explaining changes in labor force participation, earnings, and occupations. But I have also recognized that women can achieve real equality only when judged as individuals. Thus gender equality may be fostered by economic progress but must be assisted by legislation and social change.

APPENDIX TO CHAPTER 2

Corrections to the c. 1890 Female
Labor Force Participation Rates[1]

The accuracy and inclusiveness of the pre-1940 census labor force figures have been questioned ever since their collection.[2] Women, it was thought, may have been reluctant to tell
census marshals that they had an occupation when it was not the norm to work for pay or
when the work was done intermittently, over the day and year, within the confines of their
homes. Further, the definition of labor force participation changed in 1940 from the concept
of the "gainful worker" to that of the "labor force," raising the issue of consistency over time.
Numerous criticisms have been lodged against census procedures, but no changes of substantial magnitude have yet been incorporated into the official statistics.[3]

Although data for the entire period, 1890 to 1940, are suspect, those for the earliest years
ought to reveal the most severe biases. I have, for the sake of brevity and because of the
demands of the data, focused only on the interval from 1890 to 1910. Data from turn-of-the-
century surveys at the national level provide independent evidence on the reliability and
consistency of the census and on the possible omission of boardinghouse keepers and home
workers in manufacturing. The censuses from 1890 to 1910 and various time-budget surveys
of the 1920's are used to revise the female agricultural labor force estimates and construct a
value for home-produced goods that were later produced in the marketplace.

There are several conclusions to be drawn from these corrections. The first is that the
gainful worker concept does not necessarily overcount, nor does it necessarily undercount,
female workers in comparison with the labor force construct. Evidence on days worked per
year suggests that the two concepts may have been very close in empirical fact. Female
workers in certain occupations, however, were severely undercounted: boardinghouse keepers were seriously underenumerated in cities, family farm laborers were more than often
omitted in the cotton South, and casual family farm labor was infrequently counted in the rest
of the country. Finally, about 14% of the value of 1890 household production later moved to
the economic marketplace, finding its way into official national income accounts from which
it had necessarily been excluded in earlier periods.

Labor Force Participation

Individuals are counted in the labor force under the gainful worker concept if they were
enumerated with an occupation during the census year. The labor force concept includes
individuals if they are employed for pay during the survey week, are employed for more than
14 hours in unpaid family labor, or are unemployed and searching for work. Durand (1948,

1975) believed that gainful worker estimates always overstated the labor force figures. For the female population, this would imply that the pre-1940 gainful worker estimates are biased upward and that the growth of the labor force is thereby biased downward.

There is, however, no simple theoretical relationship between the gainful worker and the labor force concepts. The precise relationship depends on two factors: the accepted norm for the number of days or weeks worked during the year that constituted having an occupation in the pre-1940 period, and the distribution of actual days or weeks worked during the year.

Suppose all individuals in the pre-1940 reported they had an occupation if they were employed for at least half the year, say, 26 weeks or more. Then 26 weeks would be the accepted norm for the number of weeks worked that constituted having an occupation. In the post-1940 period, a group of individuals each working 26 weeks during the year would have a 50% labor force participation rate under the labor force construct.[4] But each individual working 26 weeks would, given the pre-1940 accepted norm, have a participation probability of 100% under the gainful worker definition. In this case, the gainful worker estimate would be clearly greater than the labor force concept, as was Durand's presumption. If the number of weeks worked was below 26, however, the gainful worker estimate would result in a lower participation rate than the labor force construct. The gainful worker estimate would be zero, and the labor force estimate would be equal to the number of weeks worked divided by 52.

Thus the distribution of weeks (or days) worked across the population will, together with the norm for having an occupation, determine the overall labor force participation rate and the biases in using one construct or the other. A uniform or symmetric distribution around 26 weeks, in the above example, will produce similar estimates under either definition. As a general rule, the concepts will always coincide with a symmetric distribution having as its mean the societal norm for time worked to constitute an occupation. There is, unfortunately, no way of determining what the norm was or whether, indeed, a societal norm ever existed.[5] Various plausible social norms will be used in the examples below, given the actual distribution of days worked from various sources.

The distribution of days worked around the turn of this century was not, in fact, symmetric. It had a long left tail and a substantial mass near the maximum of days worked. The actual distribution of days worked must, therefore, be used to determine whether there is a substantial difference between the gainful worker and the labor force definitions of labor force participation.

A large-scale survey of female manufacturing workers in 1907, *Report on Condition of Woman and Child Wage-Earners* (U.S. Senate Documents, 1910–1911), hereafter the 1907 Senate Report, indicates that mean days worked for single women older than 15 years was 249.[6] Therefore, approximately 83% (249/300, where 300 = maximum days of work per year) of those employed at all during the year would have been counted under the present labor force definition. The gainful worker estimate, as noted above, will depend on the societal norm for days worked during the year and the actual distribution of days. If the norm were half the full year or 150 days, 92% of these women would have been counted (the value was computed from the actual distribution). If the societal norm were 200 days, or 67% of a full year, then 83% of these women would have been counted. The labor force and gainful worker constructs, therefore, coincide with a norm of 67% of a full year, in this specific case. For values below 200 days, the gainful worker estimate will overstate the labor force construct, and for values above 200 days, the gainful worker estimate will understate the labor force construct. Note, as well, that the work force measure is not very sensitive to the societal norm; a decrease of 50 days, for example, increases the absolute number in the work force by only 11% (92/83).

The same report also surveyed married women, working primarily, but not exclusively, as manufacturing laborers in factories and in their homes. The mean for the entire group was

212 days, somewhat lower than that for single women. The labor force definition would have counted as employed 71% of this group. Had those working over 150 days reported an occupation to the census marshal, 73% would have been counted under the gainful worker definition (again, computed using the actual distribution of days worked). The results of the two definitions coincide at 175 days, or 58% of a full year.

Thus it does not appear that the two definitions produce very different labor force results for either single or married women. Further, identical results are produced using another way of conceptualizing the gainful worker concept. Had individuals employed at the precise time of the census enumeration, in the pre-1940 period, reported they had an occupation, the two definitions would always coincide. Under both constructs, the census would be capturing only those individuals engaged in paid employment during the census week.

Intermittent, Part-time, and Home Work

Closely related to the issue of changing definitions is the possibility that a large fraction of working married women a century ago were reluctant to report an occupation or that census takers were biased against reporting a woman's employment.[7] To those who question the census data, such women may have been more hesitant to admit they worked when the work was done at home, regardless of time devoted to paid labors. Those who worked at home may have done so to escape social norms against married women's working. Alternatively, and more probably, married women may not have reported an occupation when the work was done part-time or intermittently through the year, at home or away from home. The issue here is whether these working women were employed a sufficient number of days per year for the gainful worker and labor force constructs to have coincided.

Two surveys exist to address the issue. The *Sixth Annual Report of the Commissioner of Labor* (1890) and the *Seventh Annual Report* (1891), hereafter the 1890/91 Report (see Data Appendix), surveyed industrial families and listed the income earned by all family members, including the wife's earnings and payments from boarders. The 1907 Senate Report contains a survey of married women working in manufacturing both within factories and their homes.

Data from the 1890/91 Report support the official census labor force data for married women in industrial areas. Had census takers included in the labor force all women who earned a positive dollar amount during the year, the percentage of married women (husband present) in the labor force would still have been quite small. In the glass industry, for example, only 2.2% of all wives reported positive earnings; in heavy industries, only 1.3% did; and in textiles, always an anomalous sector regarding female employment, 12.1% did.

These statistics are not surprising, given the nature of the industrial settings and the available work for married women. What is surprising is that among women who did earn a positive dollar amount, earnings were about 50% those of full-time, year-round single women working in industry in 1890. Although there were few married women who worked in industry at that time, these data suggest that those who did work labored for more than half the year.[8]

The data in the 1907 Senate Report, reported above, also bear on the issue of part-time and intermittent work.[9] The proportion of a year worked for the average married women was quite high (212/300 = 71%), and the distribution of days was rather tight around this mean. Thus the gainful worker definition based on these data should have produced a reasonably unbiased estimate of the labor force construct.

Not only did the married women in this sample who worked in manufacturing labor almost full-time, but those working at home tended to work an even greater number of days per year than those in the factories. Those working at home labored for 216 days on average, while those in factories worked 210 days. The work of the industrial home workers was apparently more regular than previously thought. The incomes of industrial home workers in 1907, however, were about half those of women working in factories, after correcting for the number of young children in the household, age, and health of the husband (see Chapter 4). The large difference could be due to a compensating differential, a lower intensity of work, a greater intermittency of work within the day, or less on-the-job training, as suggested by government investigators at the time.

The 1907 Senate Report also surveyed the extent to which home workers, typically finishers in men's ready-made clothing, were helped by family members and friends (U.S. Senate Documents, 1910–1911, vol. 87). Of the 674 home workers interviewed, 176, or 24%, had helpers "with more or less regularity." These helpers were typically young children and, less frequently, the woman's husband. In 36% of the cases, the work involved another adult woman, but in only 19% of the cases did it involve another married or widowed woman. Thus the regularity of industrial home work for these women suggests the census did not undercount them solely because of their intermittent labors, and the nature of their helpers suggests that other adult women were not omitted to any great extent. Further, because home workers were typically of foreign birth, the time series on native-born white women should be less affected.

Undercounts of Female Laborers in Particular Occupations and Sectors

It is frequently asserted that women were undercounted in certain occupations, such as those performed in the home and on the family farm, particularly when the work was unpaid or not remunerated in terms of wages. Three groups of occupations will be considered: boarding-house keepers, unpaid agricultural laborers, and manufacturing workers.

Boardinghouse Keepers

A severe undercount of boardinghouse keepers in late-nineteenth-century cities is suggested by the fact that 14% of all white households in 1880 Philadelphia had boarders (Goldin, 1979), but fewer than 1% of all dwellings in Philadelphia were enumerated in the 1880 U.S. Population Census as containing a female boardinghouse keeper. The adjustment to the labor force figure, however, involves far more than merely including the shortfall in boardinghouse keepers. The data must be made consistent with one of the two employment concepts, and the choice here, as above, is the more modern labor force construct.

Data on income from boarders, as well as the number of boarders, are included in the 1890/91 Report on industrial families (see also Modell and Hareven, 1973). Because the data are presumably gross earnings, not net, the following procedure was used to estimate labor force participation.

1. About 23% of all husband–wife families in the industrial communities surveyed in the 1890/91 Report had at least one boarder or nonnuclear family member (the two were grouped together), and about 16% of all husband–wife families received income from boarders, a figure almost identical to that inferred from 1880 U.S. Population Census data for Philadelphia (Goldin, 1979). Boarding varied by industry, with textile families having the highest percentage with income from boarders. Income from boarding was $201 per year on average across all husband–wife families having positive earnings from boarders.

2. The gross income figure must be adjusted for the additional costs of running a household with boarders to make it comparable with earnings from any other employment. An equation regressing total rent paid on the number and composition of household members

yields only $2.70 for each additional boarder, a mere 3.4% of the total rent. Rent, it appears, was invariant to the presence of boarders, and suggests that boarders occupied rooms that would otherwise have been vacant. Food expenditures, however, were about 29% of average boarding income ($29 × 2/$201, where $29 = average food expenditures per boarder; 2 = average number of boarders; $201 = average gross income from boarders).[10] Net income from boarders was about $140 per year for each boarding household, a figure that translates into 47% of the full-time income of women in comparable geographic areas.[11]

In summary, about 16% of all husband–wife couples and 20% of all female-headed households received income from boarders in industrial areas around 1890, and these figures are consistent with those from studies of cities using the 1880 U.S. Population Census manuscripts. Each boardinghouse keeper earned approximately half the full-time earnings of a female manufacturing worker, a figure comparable with the earnings of industrial home workers.

The distribution of net earnings from boarding indicates that about 37% of all boarding-house keepers should be counted if having an occupation were construed as earning over 50% the full-time yearly income of a female manufacturing worker, one interpretation of the gainful worker concept. The current labor force definition counts home workers if they work 15 hours or more during the survey week or 37.5% of a normal 40 hours work week. By applying the percentage (not the absolute hourly) criterion to earnings, 46% of all boarding-house keepers should be included in the labor force estimate.

These figures and the 16% figure for all husband–wife couples in cities having boarders can be used to construct an upper- and lower-bound labor force estimate. The adjustment for all married women in cities and industrial areas comes to somewhere between 5.9 (= .16 × .37) and 7.4 (= .16 × .46) percentage points, a substantial addition to the 4.0% labor force figure for married white women in cities in 1890.[12]

It might be claimed that all industrial home workers who logged as many days per year as factory workers but earned only 50% of their pay should, on a days-worked-per-year basis, be included in labor force estimates. Using the same logic, all boardinghouse keepers should be included in the labor force as well. Under these conditions, which I believe yield a vast overstatement, the correction for all married women in urban and industrial areas is the full 16%, a substantial addition to the figure for married white women in cities in 1890.

3. These data must still be translated into aggregate statistics. In 1890, 17% of all dwellings were in cities with ≥ 25,000 inhabitants. If the data presented above apply to only such urban areas, the adjustment is somewhere between 1.0 (= .17 × .37 × .16) and 2.7 (= .17 × .16) percentage points for married women and 1.3 to 3.4 percentage points for widows.[13]

The 1900 Public Use Sample indicates that boarding in small cities and nonfarm rural areas was less common than in the larger cities and industrial towns covered in the 1890/91 Report. In areas of < 25,000 persons, 10.6% of all wives and 11.5% of all widows had boarders or lodgers, and in the same areas but among those in farm dwellings, 6.4% of all wives and 7.8% of all widows had boarders or lodgers. Not surprisingly, industrial and densely settled cities contained more extensive boarding than did other areas.[14] The adjust-ment to the female labor force will increase with the addition of values for the smaller cities and rural nonfarm regions, but there is no information on the distribution of income from boarding in those areas. If the distribution were the same as that in the 1890/91 Report, the added amount for wives in the nonfarm areas would be 2.2 percentage points (= 0.106 × 0.37 × 0.558), where 55.8% is the percentage of all nonfarm dwellings in areas of less than 25,000 population.[15] That for widows would be 2.4 percentage points.

The adjustment for boardinghouse keepers in all nonfarm areas, therefore, increases the labor force figure by 3.2 percentage points for married women, 3.7 for widows, and 2.2 for all women. Similar computations for farm households are complicated by adjustments to unpaid family farm laborers (see below). It should be clear, however, that undercounting boardinghouse keepers in small cities, rural areas, and farm communities overstates the later movement of married women into the labor force, particularly in cities, and understates their participation in the market economy in the nineteenth century.

Agricultural Workers

The understatement of female agricultural workers concerns the casual unpaid labor of farm family members. Those who designed the 1910 census were aware of this problem and instructed enumerators that "a woman working regularly at outdoor farm work, even though she works on the home farm for her husband, son, or other relative and does not receive money wages, should be returned . . . as a *farm laborer*."[16] These instructions produced an acknowledged overstatement of the female labor force and later led to the wholesale abandonment of the 1910 census as a source of occupational and labor force data, particularly for women and children.

The 1910 census may be a poor source for labor force estimates consistent with those for adjacent years, but it provides superb data to produce an upper-bound estimate of female employment in the agricultural sector. These data yield a measure of the excess number of female agricultural laborers in 1910 compared with previous censuses and an upper-bound estimate of female agricultural laborers for 1890 and 1900.

The overcount of agricultural workers in 1910 was almost entirely concentrated in the category of unpaid family farm labor in the major cotton-producing states.[17] White families tended to underreport their unpaid family labor far more than did black families, whose wives and daughters were more frequently part of the paid labor force.[18] Because of the different availability of data in the 1890 and 1900 censuses, two complementary procedures have been employed here. Both indicate that the number of female cotton-farm laborers would have been about 50% of the 1910 census estimate had previous census survey procedures been used. Adjusting the undercount of individuals by the number of months worked per year yields an underenumeration of the female agricultural labor force of 1.24 percentage points. To this number must be added the undercount in noncotton regions, which yields a total adjusted figure of about 4.4 percentage points. The details of both adjustments follow.

The first of the two procedures to correct for the undercount in the cotton regions computes the ratio of unpaid female family farm workers to all females in the population in 1910 and compares it with that for 1900. The difference between the two figures is assumed to be the maximum percentage-point undercount of unpaid family farm workers in 1900. In 1910, the ratio was 0.063 for white females older than 15 years. Data from a special report of the 1900 census on working women indicate that only one-quarter of these women had been counted as unpaid family workers in 1900.[19] Thus the undercount is 4.7 percentage points.

The second procedure computes the percentage of women working in agriculture in 1910 and compares it with the figure for 1890, adjusted for the relative decline that sector experienced over the 20 intervening years. In 1890, 8.4% of the white female labor force (older than 14 years) was employed in agriculture; the 1910 census reported 10.5% of the white female labor force (older than 15 years) employed in agriculture. The 1910 figure would have been 5.6% had the relative decline in the male agricultural labor force applied as well to the female labor force and had the 1890 enumeration procedures been followed.[20] The difference between the figure for 1910 and the adjusted figure, 4.9 percentage points, is the shortfall.

The two procedures give almost identical results, a 4 to 5 percentage point shortfall in the labor force participation rate computed for white women older than 15 years in either 1890 or

1900. Using the entire shortfall as the adjustment assumes that all individuals who worked on family farms in 1910 should be included in the labor force estimate. For consistency with both the labor force and the gainful worker concepts, the percentage of a full work year spent in family labor is needed to adjust the shortfall. One study of family cotton-farm labor (Allen, 1931) gives a value of 3.7 months per year as the time women spent working on the farm for their families.[21] A labor force construct would include 31% (3.7/12) of the total number of women working on cotton farms for their families. The adjusted shortfall in the labor force would be 1.24 percentage points for all white female unpaid laborers in the cotton South and 1.33 percentage points for white married women.[22]

Women on farms across America have always worked as unpaid family farm laborers, particularly in dairy, poultry, garden, and orchard activities (see, e.g., Jensen, 1980, 1986). Their labor must certainly have been understated along with that of cotton-farm laborers. Data from time-budget surveys of farm women are used to address the issue. These surveys were conducted in the late 1920's, primarily among western farm families whose daily lives and chores were apparently unchanged in the 30 years that separate them from housewives in 1890.[23] The six surveys that have been consulted yield an average of 9 to 10 hours per week spent by housewives in unpaid family agricultural labor.[24] If each woman performed only 10 hours of unpaid work per week, then none would be counted using the labor force concept employed today.[25] But an expected-value construct might be more appropriate than either the current concept or the gainful worker concept. Given that the average industrial worker's week was 50 hours in the 1920's, another standard would be to include 20% (= 10/50) of the farm wives in the labor force. Multiplying by the appropriate percentages yields an under-count of 5.4 percentage points for all married women.[26] It should be noted that the 1910 census included in the labor force very few farm wives outside cotton areas, and census marshals in 1910 were instructed to count regularly employed unpaid family farm workers.

Manufacturing Workers

A divergence between the late-nineteenth-century manufacturing labor force estimates de-rived from two census sources—population and manufacturing—was noted by Abbott (1910), Rubinow (1907), and Smuts (1960). The problem, quite simply, is that the two numbers differ and differ most substantially for women and children. Abbott (1910) conjec-tured that part of the difference was due to differing definitions of the labor force used in the two censuses. The two definitions differ in exactly the same way the gainful worker concept differs from the labor force concept. The labor force, as defined in the manufacturing census, was a "full-time" equivalent concept; it measures the average number of full-time workers in a firm over the course of a year. The labor force, as defined in the population census, was the gainful worker concept; it measures the number of people who reported an occupation. Given the data presented above on the distribution of days worked in manufacturing, no presump-tion can be made about which definition will produce the upper bound, and the two should have produced nearly similar labor force estimates.

The differences in the two estimates must be traced to aspects of their coverage. The manufacturing census did not survey many of the smaller shops and businesses that employed women in the production of clothing and hats. At the same time, it is possible that the population census undercounted women working for large manufacturing firms. The adjust-ment that will be made to the population census will assume that population census data on women working as dressmakers and milliners are accurate, but that the manufacturing census more faithfully counted women working for the large manufacturing firms. That is, the correction will produce an upper bound by assuming that the maximum of each of the conflicting census figures prevails. Because the labor force figures already include all individuals in the population census, it is necessary to compute only the undercount of workers in large manufacturing firms.

There were 839,952 females (older than nine years) working in manufacturing in 1890 (excluding officers, firm members, and clerical workers), according to the manufacturing census (U.S. Census Office, 1895a). The population census yields 1,027,242 (U.S. Census Office, 1897). Note that the employment of women in manufacturing in 1890 accounted for almost one-third of all women in the labor force. Of the more than 1 million female manufacturing workers in the population census, 602,677 had occupations in the making of clothing and hats. The manufacturing census, however, puts the figure at only 294,194. Given the generous assumption that the population census is more accurate for the occupations in clothing and millinery, but that the manufacturing census is more accurate for the rest, the population census has a shortfall of 121,193 females working in large manufacturing firms.[27] If correct, this number would translate into an increase of 3.1% in the female labor force in 1890, raising the population census estimate by 0.5 percentage point.

Household Production

The most difficult adjustment is the computation of the time spent by women in the household production of goods later supplied by the market. Of the various goods produced in the home around 1890 that later shifted at least in part to the market, clothing, meals, and baked items seem the most important.[28] Time-budgets indicate that about 5 hours per week were spent in the production of clothing by farm wives around the 1920's, and 2.5 hours, at a maximum, were devoted to baking. Total time spent in food preparation and clean-up dominated the time-budgets, accounting for 35% on average. The figure for food preparation is now 23% for full-time housewives. Furthermore, 16% of the total eating time of all family members in the early 1970's was spent consuming restaurant meals (Szalai, 1972, p. 576).[29] Had relative prices enticed families in 1890 to consume the same proportion of their meal time in restaurants as we do today, these families would have saved about 4 hours of meal preparation and clean-up time per week, given the 65-hour household-work week of the 1920 farm housewives.

It seems reasonable to assume that five hours is the combined net addition to household production of clothing and baked goods in 1890, compared with 1980, and that four hours is the saving from restaurant meals.[30] Thus (9/65) or 14% of the time of 1890 wives should be allotted to household production of goods that the market later supplied.

Summary of Adjustments to the 1890 Estimate

Table 2.9 summarizes the various corrections that have been computed. For some, we are on rather firm footing, such as the adjustment to the estimate of boardinghouse keepers. But for others, the adjustments are no more than educated guesses, as is the case for the estimate of unpaid family farm laborers outside the cotton South. The addition of these percentage points to the official census labor force estimates requires further thought in all cases, and only under certain conditions, as noted in the text, would it be correct to use them to augment the original data.

The most significant of the findings is that the labor force participation rate of married women would have to be augmented by about 10 percentage points to account for these unpaid and undercounted activities. The largest adjustments come from the omission of unpaid workers on family farms and the undercounting of boardinghouse keepers. But it should be noted that even though the calculations have used a wide range of data and employed techniques that give reasonable estimates, rather than lower or upper bounds, the nature of the sources must ultimately produce a lower-bound result. Thus the augmented participation rate among white married women in 1890 (2.5 + 10 = 12.5%) may have equaled or exceeded that among white married women in 1940 (12.5%, from Table 2.1). It is likely that participation rates before 1890 exceeded 12.5%, and it is well known that they greatly exceeded 12.5% after 1940. These data, therefore, suggest a U-shape to married women's participation rates over the course of economic development, as discussed in the text.

DATA APPENDIX

Many of the data sets used in this volume were collected from original survey schedules located in the National Archives, Washington, DC. They are described briefly below to alert the reader to their origin, features, and readily available documentation. I will be making these data sets accessible through ICPSR (Interuniversity Consortium for Political and Social Research) at the University of Michigan. I have also included here data that are qualitative in nature. Each has been given a short code name, and they are listed below chronologically by that name. The date listed approximates that of the actual survey, not that of the published report.

1888 Working Women Report: See U.S. Commissioner of Labor, *Fourth Annual Report of the Commissioner of Labor, 1888: Working Women in Large Cities* (Washington, DC: Government Printing Office, 1889); also Goldin (1981). This survey, directed by Carroll Wright, the first U.S. Commissioner of Labor, investigated the conditions of women "who work in great city manufactories upon light manual or mechanical labor and in stores" (p. 9). The study includes 343 industries in 22 regionally dispersed cities and contains information on 17,427 women, of whom 88% were single. Only the 1,148 city-industry averages can be used; the original surveys have never been located. Data were collected on age, work experience, years in current occupation, days not at work during the year, annual earnings, nativity, living arrangements, health, and marital status, among other variables.

1890/91 Report: See U.S. Commissioner of Labor, *Sixth Annual Report of the Commissioner of Labor, 1890*. Part III, *Cost of Living* (Washington, DC: Government Printing Office, 1890), and U.S. Commissioner of Labor, *Seventh Annual Report of the Commissioner of Labor, 1891*. Part III, *Cost of Living* (Washington, DC: Government Printing Office, 1891). Haines (1979) and Goldin and Parsons (1989), among others, have used these data, now available from ICPSR, which give earnings and expenditure information on about 6,000 families in industrial areas. Because I did not collect these data and they are not extensively used in this book, the reader is asked to consult the references given or the ICPSR data listing.

1907 Single Women Workers: See U.S. Senate Documents, *Report on Condition of Woman and Child Wage-Earners in the U.S. in 19 Volumes*, Vols. 86–104 (Washington, DC: Government Printing Office, 1910–1911); also Goldin (1981, 1984) and Aldrich and Albelda (1980). The Senate report, from which these data were taken, is a 19-volume study of 4 primary industries and various related subjects. Information on thousands of workers and their families is included. Several of the volumes give data on single women in Massachusetts, North Carolina, Chicago, and New York City working in the cotton textile and clothing industries. Other industries (silk, glass) were surveyed, but are not in this sample. Also in the sample, but not used here, is related information on young girls and boys working in the same industries. The sample used is restricted to single women workers ≥ 16 years old. Data on occupation, earnings, months schooling, literacy, years since beginning work, days worked, ethnicity, and years in the United States are included. Also available is information on the presence of mother and father, the father's occupation, other children in family, family income, the amount retained by working children, and the rent paid. The Single Women Workers sample contains 1,796 observations; 1,135 children are in the full data set available.

1907 Married Women Workers: See 1907 Single Women Workers for sources. Similar data were collected for married women workers in cotton textiles and clothing in New York City, Chicago, Philadelphia, North Carolina, and Massachusetts (about 15% of the women in the sample were working in other sectors but were included because their children worked in cotton textiles and clothing). The data are identical to those described for single women workers, except that years since work began, literacy, and months schooling are not given. Years married, the condition of the husband (dead, away, unemployed, at work), whether industrial home work was performed, and the number and ages of children are given. The data set contains 936 observations.

1907 NYC Women Workers: See 1907 Single Women Workers for sources. Separate information from the family studies was collected for young women living at home with their parents who worked in factories, stores, and some other enterprises in several large cities. A more limited set of variables exists and includes industry, occupation, ethnicity, age, years of experience, weekly earnings, and weekly contribution to family. The data set contains 1,318 observations for working women in New York City.

1907 Women Adrift: See 1907 Single Women Workers for sources. Somewhat more comprehensive information than that for the NYC Women Workers was collected for women living apart from their families, or "adrift," as the social reform movement termed their state. In addition to the variables mentioned in the NYC Women Workers sample, data on years of schooling, weekly expenditures for car fare, shelter, food, and contributions to needy relatives were collected. There are 393 women in the sample for Philadelphia and New York City.

1931 Office Firm Survey: National Archives, Record Group #86, Boxes 280–281. See U.S. Department of Labor, Women's Bureau, *The Employment of Women in Offices*, by Ethel Erickson, Bulletin of the Women's Bureau, No. 120 (Washington, DC: Government Printing Office, 1934b). Only the firm-level records of this survey survive. The data came from "general interviews with the management on numbers of men and women employed, policies and practices as to hours of work, overtime, vacations, promotions, and welfare activities, restrictions based on age or marital status, kinds of office machines used, and effect of mechanization on employment in the preceding 5-year period" (p. 2). The firms covered in this survey are larger than those in a similar 1940 survey (see below) and include only banks, public utilities, insurance companies, investment houses, publishing companies, and advertising firms. Records for 178 firms in 4 cities (Chicago, Hartford, New York City, and Philadelphia) were used, and information was coded on numbers of female and male office workers, scheduled hours, and personnel policies (whether the firm hired married women, fired women if they married, and had internal promotion, age restrictions, pensions, and group insurance). The comments of the interviewee were also recorded regarding the reasons for various policies and whether policies on marriage were due to the onset of the Depression.

1939 Retrospective Survey: National Archives, Record Group #86, Boxes 446–450. See U.S. Department of Labor, Women's Bureau, *Women Workers in Their Family Environment*, Bulletin of the Women's Bureau, No. 183 (Washington, DC: Government Printing Office, 1941); see also Goldin (1989). Only 532 of the original schedules were found in the archives, although coded cards for others survive. The cards include information on over

2,800 women (including 742 currently married women) working in Cleveland in 1939; the surviving original schedules contain information on 532 married women who were not currently working but who had worked in the past. The Women's Bureau coded work time for the currently working sample in five-year intervals and dropped other information that exists for the sample of women not currently working; thus the samples of working and nonworking women contain somewhat different information. All records were collected. Information was included on marital status, age, foreign birth, education, complete retro-spective work histories, first occupation, last occupation, date at which work began, and, frequently, dates of marriage(s) and pregnancy(ies). It is my belief that this is the first large-scale retrospective survey of women's work patterns in America.

1940 Office Firm Survey: National Archives, Record Group #86, Boxes 496–500. See U.S. Department of Labor, Women's Bureau, *Office Work in [Houston, Los Angeles, Kansas City, Richmond, Philadelphia]: 1940,* Bulletins of the Women's Bureau, Nos. 188-1, 2, 3, 4, 5 (Washington, DC: Government Printing Office, 1942). Both firm- and individual-level records of this survey survive (see below). Information was gathered by the Women's Bureau from payroll records and from interviews with personnel officers and other agents of the firms. Firms of all sizes were surveyed, and include those in the sectors listed for the 1931 survey plus the office portion of the manufacturing, meat packing, petroleum, and transporta-tion and communications industries, nonprofits, government agencies, retail and wholesale businesses, and small offices (e.g., lawyers). The surveys were extensive; for example, fully one-quarter of Philadelphia's office workers were included in the survey (No. 188-5, p. 2). Records for 328 firms in Kansas City, Los Angeles, and Philadelphia were collected, and information was coded on the variables listed above for the 1931 survey, plus new hires in 1939, personnel policies regarding discrimination on the basis of race and sex (whether the firm had policies against the employment of women or men in certain occupations), and the presence of unions. The interviewees often noted whether the firm favored married men in hiring, promotion, and salaries. Only firms with more than 9 female employees and at least 20 total employees were coded in Philadelphia. No government agencies were used in the sample.

1940 Office Worker Survey: National Archives, Record Group #86, Boxes 472–486. See citation above for Office Firm Survey; also Goldin (1984, 1986b). A sample of 724 female office workers and 481 male office workers was collected for Philadelphia. Information was coded for each on age, marital status, education (years and diploma for grade school, high school, college, and various vocational and graduate programs), total work experience, experience with current firm, experience in office work, other experience, current earnings, earnings when worker began at the firm, whether worker had been furloughed, and whether work with the current firm was continuous.

1957 Hussey Report: The files containing these schedules are in box #167 of the (as yet unarchived) papers of Gladys Palmer, generously lent to me by Ann Miller of the Sociology Department of the University of Pennsylvania. They are referred to here as the "Hussey Report," after Miriam Hussey, who, as Gladys Palmer's assistant, conducted the surveys. See Miriam Hussey, *Personnel Policies during a Period of Shortage of Young Women Workers in Philadelphia* (Philadelphia: Industrial Research Unit, Wharton School of Finance and Commerce, University of Pennsylvania, 1958). Approximately 40 complete interviews exist and cover a range of Philadelphia firms and retail stores for 1956 and 1957. Many of the same firms are included in the 1931 and 1940 Office Firm Surveys (see above).

1957/64 College Graduate Survey: National Archives, Record Group #86, Boxes 739–767. See U.S. Department of Labor, Women's Bureau, *College Women Seven Years after*

Graduation: Resurvey of Women Graduates, Class of 1957, Bulletin of the Women's Bureau, No. 292 (Washington, DC: Government Printing Office, 1966). A survey of 6,000 female college graduates of the class of 1957 across 131 institutions was undertaken by the Women's Bureau in the winter of 1957, and about 5,000 women responded to a follow-up survey in 1964. The sample used here contains 763 women surveyed in both years and was randomly drawn. (There are also records for 98 women surveyed in 1957 who did not respond in 1964.) Data were collected in 1957 on college major, marital status, number of children, occupation or continued education, salary, and future employment plans, among other variables. The 1964 resurvey asked age, marital status, husband's employment status and occupation, number of children and exact ages, employment history, hours of work per week, reasons for working, household help, future employment plans, and husband's attitude toward wife's work, among other variables. Both surveys requested additional information on work experience, attempts to obtain jobs, and plans for future employment.

NOTES

PREFACE

1. Among the many book-length and influential studies on female labor force participation are those of economists Bancroft (1958), Bowen and Finegan (1969), Cain (1966), Durand (1948), Easterlin (1980), Long (1958), Mincer (1962, 1966), Smith (1980), and Smith and Ward (1984), and that of sociologist Oppenheimer (1970). See also Blau and Ferber (1986) on summaries of research on gender differences in work and pay.

2. See, for example, the works of historians Campbell (1984), Chafe (1972), Degler (1980), Harris (1978), Kessler-Harris (1982), Lerner (1986), and Tentler (1979); of sociologists Cohn (1985) and Milkman (1987); and of economists Bergmann (1986) and Matthaei (1982).

3. By "wage discrimination," I mean the portion of the difference between male and female earnings that cannot be explained by differences between their productive attributes. See Chapter 4 on the "wage discrimination" concept and the manner in which productive attributes are affected by rewards in the labor market.

CHAPTER 2

1. The computation uses data from *Historical Statistics* (1975) and *Economic Report of the President, 1988*. It assumes that had the female labor force not expanded, 18.2% would have been in the civilian labor force in 1987. The figures for 1890 include those ≥ 14 years old.

2. Cowan (1983b), however, notes that many of the most important changes in household production in the nineteenth century freed men, not women, from household labor.

3. The 10% and 40% figures are derived from the data in Table 2.5 and assume that 15% of urban women were in the labor force at age 45 (40 to 49 years) in 1940 (see Table 2.3 for urban participation rate figures). The figures are upper and lower bounds, respectively, to the true values, because all of the 85% who were out of the labor force had been employed sometime in the past.

4. See Bergmann (1986, pp. 221) on the social consequences of the Social Security system in America.

5. Many economists, among them a recent president of the American Economic Association, Robert Eisner, have suggested including in national income accounts goods produced in the home for the family. Eisner attributes one-third of his extended GNP figure, for 1981, to "nonmarket services produced in households" (1988, p. 1659).

6. Individuals working at least 1 hour per week for pay or 15 hours at unpaid work in the home are included.

7. The Appendix to Chapter 2 and the discussion below will substantiate the assertion that the labor force and gainful worker estimates are comparable.

8. An additional assumption is that employed individuals are in the labor force for the entire year.

9. Research by Johnson and Skinner (1986) indicates that women who work have a higher probability of getting divorced but that the causality runs from the expectation of divorce to work. Data, to be presented in Figure 2.3, indicate that in 1939 women who married early had more years of work experience than single women of the same age. The finding implies that women who married late did not necessarily increase the average participation rate of the cohort and thus bias the cohort profile to be more upwardly sloped.

10. The labor force data in Table 2.3 indicate that the differences between urban areas and the national census data are slight.

11. Robinson (1980) and Smith (1977) have also constructed cohort labor force profiles by marital status.

12. LaFollette (1934, p. 36), for example, in a study of primarily college-educated women, found that 95% had worked before they married.

13. 1957 Hussey Report (see Chapter 6 and Data Appendix for details): Wanamaker's (Philadelphia and Wynnewood).

14. Lynd and Lynd (1937, p. 181). Although the tendency was noticeable in the 1930's in Middletown (Muncie, Indiana), it must have been apparent in eastern cities in the 1920's.

15. The median age for female manufacturing workers around 1890 is from Wright (1889; also U.S. Commissioner of Labor, 1889). The mean age in both samples is around 22.7 years.

16. The median age among the female population, $\geq$ 14 years, in 1960 was 39.8 years. In 1980, as compared with 1960, the median female worker was younger—34.2 years among all working women $\geq$ 16 years, and 38.0 years among all working married women, spouse present; while the median age among the entire population of women $\geq$ 16 years was 40.0 years and was 42.0 years among those married, spouse present.

17. These ambiguities were first pointed out in Ben Porath's (1973) insightful work and were noted as well by Heckman and Willis (1977).

18. The definition of participation applies to the period after 1940 when the official labor force construct was instituted. But the gainful worker construct can be interpreted in a similar manner (see Appendix to Chapter 2).

19. The terms "complete homogeneity" and "complete heterogeneity" appear in Heckman and Willis (1977) and are used here for consistency with their work.

20. The NLS is the National Longitudinal Survey, and the PSID is the Panel Study of Income Dynamics. See Sproat, Churchill, and Sheets (1985), for example, on the NLS.

21. The data include 168 married female office workers who are in the 1940 Office Worker Survey (see Data Appendix; Goldin, 1986b, 1984). The standard deviation of time spent at home is 3.0 years (with a mean of 1.1), suggesting that the vast majority of these women had not left the labor force at all. They were, perhaps, women who had not yet had children or who, like many during the Depression, would never have children (see Chapter 5 on fertility changes over time).

22. See Smith and Ward (1984).

23. Almost all these women had worked sometime prior to marriage, and therefore the degree of continuity within marriage may be understated. Because the date of marriage for those currently working is unavailable, assume these women had, on average, worked for two years prior to marriage and that they all married at age 22. If correct, this implies that 79% of those born around 1905 had worked 75% of the years since marriage. This calculation omits all women who began work after age 20, reducing the sample from 271 women between 30 and 39 years to 184 in the same age group.

24. All the women not at work and not seeking work in 1939 were specifically chosen by the Women's Bureau from among the group who had worked sometime in the past. This biases the results in Table 2.5 against the hypothesis of heterogeneity because it increases years of work experience for the group not currently working.

25. The mean age at beginning work among the nonworkers 40 to 49 years old was 19 years, about 3 years younger than for those currently working. If the mean age at marriage for this group were 22, the average woman in the nonworking group would have worked 20% of the years since marriage and 29% of the time since beginning work.

26. Continuous experience means a break in employment, at any one time, of less than three months (U.S. Department of Labor, 1941, p. 17). Occupational groups used here are similar to one-digit Census Occupation Codes (COC)—for example, professional, technical, and kindred workers; clerical and kindred workers; operatives; service workers; and so on.

27. Among the 111 women (40 to 49 years old) not at work in 1939, 62.1% dropped out at marriage, 4.5% worked only after marriage, and 33.3% worked before and after marriage (see Table 2.6), of whom 86% dropped out at marriage but later reentered. Therefore of those not working in 1939, but who worked when single, (101/106 =) 95% dropped out at the time of marriage. Precise gaps in employment are not available for the 123 who were working in 1939, but at a minimum none left work at marriage. To get the population average, one must weight by the labor force participation rate, or about 15% for those at work in 1939. Thus at a minimum, (.85 × .95 =) 80.8% of the 40- to 49-year-old group who worked when single dropped out of the labor force at the precise time of marriage. The upper-bound figure is 91.1%.

28. The Retirement History Study is discussed in Henretta and O'Rand (1980), Irelan (1972), and Mallen (1974).

29. Changes in the coverage of Social Security will probably understate the finding of persistence. Teachers are probably the largest group of female employees to gain Social Security coverage over time. If a woman employed in a covered occupation then became a teacher in an uncovered district, she would be counted as having left the labor force for the uncovered period. The absence of coverage for domestic workers and the self-employed could go in either direction. The definition of labor market work as two quarters during a year is standard in the literature. It is also similar to that used in analyses of the NLS and the PSID retrospective portions.

30. The year 1951 was selected as the initial date because of the rapid extension of Social Security coverage from its inception to the 1950's. Only the wives of respondents to the Retirement History Study are used.

31. The 3 years were chosen to span the entire 19-year period, and not for any particular aspect of female employment during any of them.

32. The data for women not working in the three years are not given in Table 2.7.

33. Note as well that the simulated data are constructed for a national and not an urban group. The sample data, in Table 2.5, are for a group of urban, married women.

34. The weights used in the calculations that follow are:

Age Distribution of Married Working Women

Age	1930	1940	1950
20–29	.38	.32	.29
30–39	.34	.36	.34
40–49	.19	.22	.25
50–59	.09	.10	.12

Note that the procedure understates the added work experience of many women who were employed during World War II because the cohort labor force data in Figure 2.2 do not include some of the increased participation during the 1940's.

35. The procedure used by Smith and Ward (1984) assumes three groups in the population: S_w = % of the population who stay in the labor force; S_n = % of the population who remain out of the labor force; and $(1 - S_w - S_n)$ who move according to a two-state Markov model. In my framework, the fraction who are homogeneous move in and out, and the fraction who are heterogeneous are either in the labor force or move in as the aggregate participation rate increases.

36. Smith and Ward (1984, table 29, p. 71).

37. Although Smith and Ward (1984) give only the 1950 to 1980 data in their table 29, a set of graphs (figure 11) preceding the table indicates that experience levels for 1940 are approximately the same for women of ages 30 and 40. Therefore, the two years of overlap between my estimates and theirs produce consistent results.

38. Only women <56 years are included in each of the three regressions.

39. The figure of 10.7 uses the labor force weights by marital status for 1940 in Table 2.4.

40. Among female manufacturing workers in California during 1892, the mean number of years since beginning work was 4.95, and years in present employment was 3.76 (Eichengreen, 1984). A similar study across 22 large cities in 1888 yields somewhat higher numbers: 6.95 for years since beginning work, and 4.26 for years in present employment (U.S. Commissioner of Labor, 1889; 1888 Working Women Report). The figure for years since beginning work is an overestimate of mean work experience because employment was discontinuous for some women.

41. Because Smith and Ward (1984) do not present aggregate cross-section numbers, these have been calculated from data in their study using the following procedure. Their work experience data by age (p. 71) are regressed on age; the resulting estimates of work experience for various age groups are then weighted by the age distribution of employed women in each of the years.

42. Ciancanelli (1983) and Bose (1987) have also explored adjustments to participation rates but argue for considerably larger increases. Many of the adjustments make their estimates not comparable with modern labor force data. Ciancanelli, for example, includes all women whose families took in boarders independent of the time they spent at that activity.

43. Using the current concept of labor force participation, for which one has to be employed over 14 hours a week in unpaid family labor, each housewife working 8 hours per week at these activities in 1890 would not increase the labor force participation rate.

44. See Abel and Folbre (1988) for a fine discussion of the historical recognition of the undercount of working women.

45. There is no evidence that the labor force participation rate for black married women in the 1890 census is severely understated.

46. See Durand (1975) and Hill (1983), who analyzes the case of Japanese women choosing among paid employment, family employment, and no employment. Hill finds a negative substitution effect for family employment, but a positive one for paid employment, suggesting that as education and thus earnings increase, paid employment increases and family employment decreases.

47. The published version of the 1790 census of population gives the exact information collected in the manuscripts.

48. The city and business directories of Philadelphia are alphabetical lists of "all business persons and heads of households," together with their addresses. On occasion, they included separate listings of occupations, particularly for doctors, nurses, and midwives, and later for

proprietors of all types. Several early directories, beginning with 1795, listed individuals by city block, creating a virtual walking tour of the city's residences and shops. Distinctions between dwelling houses and places of work can be readily made in the early directories and with a bit more effort in the later ones as well. Because the directories were compiled virtually every year, individuals can be traced through time, yielding information on the occupation of a widow and that of her deceased husband, and on occupational change and geographic mobility for an individual. For more information on city and business directories see Goldin (1986a, pp. 381–82).

49. The data for 1860 were generously made available by the Philadelphia Social History Project.

50. The thesis that women's status deteriorated from a "golden age" in America is best stated by Lerner: "The period 1800–1840 is one in which decisive changes occurred in the status of American women . . . women were by tacit consensus, excluded from the new democracy. Indeed their actual situation had in many respects deteriorated. . . . Women's work outside the home no longer met with social approval . . . many business and professional occupations formerly open to women were now closed. . . . The entry of large numbers of women into low status . . . industrial work had fixed such work by definition as 'woman's work' " (1969, pp. 5, 7).

51. See Goldin (1986a). Labor force participation is defined here, as it is in the gainful worker construct, as having an occupation. An ordinary least squares regression of the labor force participation rate ($LFPR$) on time is

$$LFPR = \quad 0.539 \quad - \quad 0.0028 \; Time$$
$$(16.26) \quad\quad (3.20)$$

$R^2 = .31$, absolute values of t-statistics are in parentheses, and $Time$ begins with $1790 = 1$.

The labor force participation rate of female heads of household varied procyclically with economic fluctuations during the period from 1790 to 1860, and the percentage of all households headed by a woman varied countercyclically.

52. Only 6.4% in 1820 and 7.9% in 1860 lived alone, and only 12.9% in 1820 lived only with children under 16 years old. That is, most female heads of household in both years lived with another adult.

53. Note that blacksmiths, carpenters, and scriveners—among others—did not have wives who carried on their trades after their death. The labor force participation rate of newly widowed women was higher than that of all women, suggesting that some of the inherited trades and businesses were short lived. It is possible that these women took over their deceased husbands' trades for only a brief period, perhaps until their sons became of age to do so. But there is corroborating evidence from wills that widows actually conducted these enterprises. Waciega (1985) has uncovered substantial testimony that wives over the 1750 to 1850 period carried on businesses and trades as silent partners while their husbands were alive and were bequeathed these businesses on their deaths.

54. Norton (1976), in her study of Loyalist women, has concluded that they had little knowledge of family businesses, trades, and general economic management. Loyalist women, however, were considerably wealthier than those in the sample of Table 2.10; many were the wives of prosperous merchants and were probably not involved in daily operations.

55. It is important to realize that the assistance of the wife did not confer independence from her husband during the 1650 to 1850 period. As Ulrich notes, "To talk about the independence of colonial wives is not only an anachronism but a contradiction in logic. A woman became a wife by virtue of her dependence, her solemnly vowed commitment to her husband. . . . The skilled service of a wife . . . also embraced the responsibilities of a

deputy husband. . . . Almost any task was suitable for a woman as along as it furthered the good of her family and was acceptable to her husband. This approach was both fluid and fixed. It allowed for varied behavior without really challenging the patriarchal order of society" (1980, pp. 37–38).

56. These findings are derived from a regression of labor force participation of white female heads of household in 1860 Philadelphia on family composition, wealth, age, ethnicity, and literacy. The mean participation rate among the female heads of household in the sample is 39%. See Goldin (1986a, pp. 394–95).

57. Home-workshop production was mainly the making of palm-leaf hats and straw hats, bonnets, and braids. The percentages given are the total number of females employed in industry divided by the total number of females 10 to 29 years old. If many employed women in industry were older than 30 years, the percentages would be biased upward. Dublin (1979, p. 258, n. 9) reports that for the same period, about 88% of all women working in the large textile mills at Lowell were less than 30 years old, and Wright's (1889) large-scale survey of working women in 1888 shows that, even after manufacturing had become far more concentrated in urban areas, about 86% of all female industrial workers were younger than 30 years. For more detail, see Goldin and Sokoloff (1982).

58. Cott notes that "although Nancy Flynt had to toil to support herself as a single woman, she commented acidly to her married sister on 'the many hours of confinement and other necessary duties that deprive the married woman of a thousand innocent girlish enjoyments'" (1977, p. 54). See also Cott's chapter 2 on domesticity and how marriage altered a young woman's freedom.

59. The percentage never married at age 55 to 64, given below for both the white and native-born white groups, is computed from the censuses of population, 1890 to 1960. This demographic indicator is highly correlated with the age at first marriage but has fewer data requirements.

Percentage Females Never Married at Age 55–64

Birth Cohort	White	Native-born White
1896–1905	8.2%	n.a.
1886–1895	8.2	n.a.
1876–1885	9.4	n.a.
1866–1875	9.3	10.4%
1856–1865	9.7	8.7
1846–1855	7.3	8.2
1836–1845	6.9	7.9
1826–1835	5.9	6.9

Also consistent with the evidence on the proportion never married is that the age at first marriage fell from 1890 to 1970. Yet genealogical records show that the age at first marriage, by birth year of the cohort, rose throughout the eighteenth and nineteenth centuries. I thank Clayne Pope for making these records available to me. See also Preston and Richards (1975) for similar evidence regarding work and marriage rates for a cross section in 1960.

60. Dublin notes that for the nine textile operatives whose letters are reprinted in his volume, all of whom eventually married, their mean age at marriage was 27.5, "considerably higher than usual for women in this period" (1981, p. 31). Further, "the median age at marriage for millhands was 25.2, in contrast to a figure for 22.9 for nonmigrants" (p. 32).

61. Dublin claims that "when Sarah returned home it is likely that she did not turn her savings over to her parents, but spent them as she chose" (1981, p. 22).

62. The sample of female workers living at home is from 1907 NYC Women Workers Report (see Data Appendix). It consists of information on 1,311 women working in factories or stores in New York City in 1907. The following regression explores the relationship among percentage remitted (*Percent*) = (weekly remittance/weekly earnings), age, and earnings.

$$Percent = 1.346 - 0.0261 \ Age + 0.00038 \ Age \ Squared - 0.00875 \ Earnings$$
$$(21.28) \quad\quad (4.78) \quad\quad\quad\quad (3.82) \quad\quad\quad\quad\quad\quad\quad (3.45)$$

where absolute values of t-statistics are in parentheses, $R^2 = .07$, and mean *Percent* = 0.932, mean age = 19.98, and mean weekly earnings = 6.17. Neither the nativity of the worker nor the type of work affects the percentage remitted. The percentage remitted declines to age 34.

63. The urban labor force statistics are not included in Tables 2.1 and 2.2. They have been calculated from data in the 1890 Population Census on the number of women in cities exceeding 100,000 population by age, marital status, and nativity (U.S. Census Office, 1895a, part I, pp. 883–910), and the labor force in these cities by the same variables (U.S. Census Office, 1897, part II, table 118, pp. 630–743), under the assumption that the age–marital status distribution for each nativity was the same for women in the labor force in large cities as it was for all women in nonagricultural occupations (U.S. Census Office, 1897, part II, table 120, pp. 750–51). The resulting figures by age and nativity for single women in 1890 are as follows.

Labor Force Participation Rates,
Single Women in Large Cities

Age	Native-born Native Parents	Native-born Foreign Parents	Foreign-born
15–24	42.9%	54.0%	82.2%
25–34	48.0	62.8	79.0
35–44	43.1	53.3	68.0

64. Data on schooling are presented in Chapter 5.

65. See also the analysis in Rotella (1980), who finds that by 1930 the labor force activity of young, single daughters was not determined by the usual family-economy variables, as it had been earlier in the century.

CHAPTER 3

1. On recent trends in the gender gap in earnings, see Smith and Ward (1984) and O'Neill (1985). Blau and Beller (1988) find the period of narrowing is extended to the 1970's when all workers are considered, not just those working full-time year-round, and hours worked is included in a regression framework.

2. Smith and Ward (1985, table 9) construct earnings ratios by applying earnings for 1970 to occupational distributions from 1890 to the present. Because the ratio of female to males earnings within occupations increased considerably over the period (see Table 3.2), their procedure, which produces ratios more stable over time than are those in Table 3.2, may be misleading.

3. The usual definition of a full-time worker is one who works for pay more than 34

hours per week, and a year-round worker is one who works 50 or more weeks per year. In constructing the estimates for 1890 and 1930, full-time weekly wages are generally used and then multiplied by 52 weeks per year.

4. Goldin and Sokoloff (1984) also explore the degree to which the initial crop facilitates industrialization of a region. Regions with an initially low relative productivity of female (and boy) to male adult labor would be expected to industrialize sooner than would those with a high relative productivity of female (and boy) to male adult labor, when both regions are faced with an increase in the relative price of manufactured to agricultural goods or a (neutral) technical change in manufacturing. The American North had a considerably lower ratio of female to male wages in (grain) agriculture than did the American South (in cotton). The implications of the model for the differential development of the American North and South are also explored. The American South not only industrialized later than the American North, but also had a far lower proportion of its manufacturing labor force that was female (and child) and had smaller firms, given industry composition. Large firms, a high proportion of female (and child) labor, and an intricate division of labor characterized the industrialization of the American North.

5. The relative constancy of the gender gap in earnings within the manufacturing sector for the past century is a topic of current research (Carter, 1988). Carter and Philips (1988), for example, claim the expansion of continuous-process machinery lowered women's employment while raising women's wages. The expansion of these industries relative to others, therefore, could put downward pressure on the ratio of female to male earnings.

6. The ratio of 0.603 in 1970 is a weighted average of the median earnings of various occupational groups. The ratio of the actual medians (for weekly, as opposed to year-round employment, see Table 3.1 for distinction) is 0.623 in 1970 and 0.617 in 1973, the date for which the data in Table 3.2 pertain.

7. The matrix of Table 3.2, Part D, is not a true partitioning of the two factors making up the change in the ratio of female to male occupation-weighted earnings. To get a full partitioning of the ratio, one must use a geometrically weighted average of earnings by occupation for each of the three benchmark years. The use of the geometric mean can be defended on the grounds that the underlying structure of earnings is a function of its log. The partitioning of the change in the ratio of female to male earnings reinforces the results given in the matrix of Part D. Over the entire period 1890 to 1970, the change in the ratio of earnings across occupations encompassed 83% to 111% of the entire change (depending on the weights used), while the change in structure adds only −11% to 17% (the interaction terms add the remainder). The details of the partitioning can be found in Goldin (1987a).

8. See Polachek (1987, table 4) for corrections to the percentages reported in Treiman and Hartmann (1981) using their original data. Aldrich and Buchele (1986), using the NLS, also conclude that sex differences in occupations account for only a small portion of the gap between male and female earnings.

9. Blau (1977) finds that high-wage firms employ proportionally more men than women; Bielby and Baron (1984) demonstrate considerable occupational segregation at the firm level.

10. The full matrix for office workers in 1939 is shown in the table on page 241.

11. The figure is computed from a sample of 15 industries (those from A to C alphabetically). Among all occupations that hired at least one female (375 occupations), one-third (130 occupations) also had at least one male with the same occupational title among the sample of firms in U.S. Commissioner of Labor (1897). Note that this holds even if there were only one male or one female in the occupation and excludes industries that were male-intensive.

Explaining Earnings Among Clerical Workers by Occupations

	w_f	w_m	$\Sigma w_f \phi_m$	$\Sigma w_m \phi_f$	Percent Explained[a]	
Across all occupations	$96.9	$134.0	$95.2	$128.2	−4.6%	15.6%
	(44)	(44)	(44)	(44)		
Occupation-industry cells						
If $f > 1$, $m > 1$	95.7	130.5	101.3	111.1	16.1	55.7
	(31)	(31)	(31)	(31)		
With imputation of w_f, w_m	95.8	136.2	98.8	124.2	7.4	29.7
	(113)	(63)	(60)	(94)		
With imputation and overlap	96.8	134.9	98.8	124.2	5.2	28.1
	(94)	(60)	(60)	(94)		

[a]The first percent explained figure is $(\Sigma w_f \phi_m - \bar{w}_f)/(\bar{w}_m - \bar{w}_f)$, and the second is $(\bar{w}_m - \Sigma w_m \phi_f)/(\bar{w}_m - \bar{w}_f)$.

Notes and Source: $\bar{w}_f$ and $\bar{w}_m$ are mean monthly wages in 1939; the ϕ's give the distribution of male or female workers by occupation. Figures in parentheses are the numbers of occupations or occupation-industry cells that could be used. Even when wages were imputed, 3 cells for the females and 19 for the males could not be because no female or no male was hired in the occupation, independent of industry. The imputation and overlap row uses only the cells that could also be used for the hypothetical figures. There were, for example, 113 cells containing female workers, but only 60 of them also had male workers ($\phi_m > 0$). The source is U.S. Department of Labor (1942).

12. The adjustments can be more clearly understood in terms of the following equations, where F_i, F_s are the number of females in integrated and segregated occupations, M_i, M_s are the same for males, and T_i, T_s are the same for total (male and female) workers. I assume that the 1904 Commissioner of Labor report did not undercount males in segregated occupations, M_s, but that the other three categories were undercounted. From the U.S. manufacturing census, we know the proportion of females in the entire manufacturing labor force:

$$(F_i + F_s)/(T_i + T_s) = .2\text{(}$$

We also know, from the 1895–1896 Commissioner of Labor report, the proportion female in integrated industries:

$$F_i/T_i = .56$$

and both reports concur that

$$F_i/(F_i + F_s) = .72$$

This gives three equations in three unknowns and allows a revision of the 1904 data. The resulting estimates are: $M_s = 104{,}119$ (including male laborers); $M_i = 17{,}151$; $F_s = 8{,}489$; and $F_i = 21{,}829$. Thus the 1904 report undercounted male and female workers in integrated occupations by about one-half and also missed half the female workers in segregated occupations. About 86% of all male workers in the adjusted data are in male-only occupations (compared with 91% in the original data), and 28% of all female workers are in female-only occupations. Of those employed in the integrated occupations, I assume that the distribution of workers across occupations is identical to that in the 1904 report, which gives the value of $\Sigma |f_i - m_i|$ needed to construct the dissimilarity index, where f_i, m_i are the percentages of all female and male workers in occupation i.

CHAPTER 4

1. A release by the U.S. Census Bureau on earnings differences between men and women claimed that "more than half the . . . gap can be explained by differences in such factors as education and work experience. . . . The report said 35% to 40% of the gap in earnings could not be explained by differences in work experience, job tenure, schooling, field of study, or tendency to cluster in certain occupations," implying that the percent female in occupations was added to the regression (*New York Times*, September 4, 1987).

2. *New York Times*, April 17, 1988. The University of Connecticut also seems to have used a version of a comparable worth policy in eliminating pay inequities among professional, nonfaculty positions. In general, employers trying to foster pay equity across a relatively homogeneous group of occupations would probably prefer the "wage discrimination" methods, while those trying to foster pay equity across heterogeneous occupations (e.g., nurses and truck drivers) would probably prefer a comparable worth technique. On comparable worth, see Chapter 7.

3. See Arrow (1972). Lundberg and Startz (1983) consider the case in which innate abilities are identical between two groups but training is acquired and is endogenous. If one group has a more "noisy" acquired-productivity signal than the other, but has a less "noisy" innate-productivity signal, "too little" training will be acquired. In equilibrium, however, average wages for both groups will equal average marginal products.

4. Note that the Equal Pay Act of 1963 prevents firms from paying male employees more to work at the same occupation as women in the same firm.

5. Krueger and Summers (1987) provide recent evidence on the inter-industry wage differential and review material since 1900 contained in Cullen (1956) and Slichter (1950). Raff (1988) provides a historical account of perhaps the best-known example of the payment of an above-equilibrium wage, the case of Henry Ford and the $5 day.

6. The mean increases to 24.3 when the age composition by marital status derived from the 1888 Working Women Report is reweighted by the percentages for each marital group from Table 2.4. Because the 1888 Report is not a microlevel study, but contains city-industry cells, a regression procedure is used to derive the average age for each marital status group. The average age in each city-industry cell is regressed on the marital composition of the cell, yielding

$$Mean\ Age\ =\ \underset{(58.66)}{41.70}\ -\ \underset{(28.06)}{21.26}\ \%\ Single\ -\ \underset{(5.72)}{7.74}\ \%\ Married$$

$R^2 = .47$; number of observations = 1,148; absolute values of t-statistics are in parentheses; regression is weighted by the square root of the number of individuals in each city-industry cell.

The resulting average ages are single, 20.4 years; married, 34.0 years; and other (widowed, divorced, and separated), 41.7 years, which are weighted by the 1890 percentages given in Table 2.4 to get 24.3.

7. The 1907 NYC Women Workers sample presumably contains mainly single women. The mean age for that sample agrees with the mean age of single women computed from the 1888 Working Women Report.

8. U.S. Bureau of the Census (1907a, table 26) contains information on the living arrangements of working women by nativity, occupation, and marital status that reveal the following.

Percentage of Single Women Living Away from Home

	All Occupations	Excluding Servants and Waitresses
All	37.9%	19.8%
Native white	34.4	26.6

Even after deducting servants and waitresses, most of whom boarded with their employers, more than one-quarter of all unmarried, native, white working women lived apart from their families and relatives.

9. Meyerowitz (1988), the first scholarly account of women "adrift," discusses the support networks that emerged to help women in the cities and the culture of the flapper and the liberated woman, which their presence reinforced. See also Vicinus (1985) for a study of working women in England.

10. Goldin (1987b, table 4, p. 203) regresses the relative share of female employment in a sector or industry on the rate of total factor productivity change (the proxy for technological change) for that sector or industry from 1890 to 1980. The relative share of female employment is the share divided by the aggregate female labor force participation rate. Almost all sectors and industries demonstrated the positive relationship between total factor productivity and female intensity, with the exceptions of textiles, food, and apparel—three of the highly female-intensive sectors. Communications, public utilities, finance, and transportation demonstrated large positive effects of technological change on female employment. The clerical and professional sectors could not be included in the analysis.

11. Tentler notes that "investigators found that while parents might sometimes try to establish a son in a promising occupation—one where he could acquire a skill and have a chance at promotion—they rarely gave thought to their daughters' occupations" (1979, p. 104).

12. If there is net growth in employment of $k\%$ per year and if $r\%$ of all employees quit each year, independent of time in employment, the probability density function of work experience in years (x) is given by

$$\lambda \int_0^{\omega} (r + k)e^{-(r + k)x} \, dx = 1 \tag{1}$$

where the expression being integrated is the exponential distribution. The equation can be derived from the cumulative age distribution of stable population with birth rate B, where the net rate of increase, k, is equal to the birth rate minus the death rate, $B - r$. The term $\lambda = 1/[1 - \exp{-(\omega)(r + k)}]$ is a correction factor to ensure that the sum of the distribution of work experience is 1 when the integral is truncated at ω.

The mean of experience (x) in equation (1) is $[1/(r + k)]$ when $\omega = \infty$ and is

$$\frac{1}{r + k} - \omega \left[e^{-\omega(r + k)}/[1 - e^{-\omega(r + k)}] \right] \tag{2}$$

for any value of ω. Notice that equation (2) is the mean of the untruncated distribution $(1/k)$ minus a value that depends on the truncation point.

The growth of female employment in manufacturing between 1880 and 1890 was about 4% average annually and was 4.6% between 1870 and 1880. That for female employment in retailing was probably greater. Using the conservative value of 4% for k, and a value of $\omega = 20$, the distribution of experience for working women in the 1888 sample is reasonably similar to that generated by equation (1) with $r = 0.12$. Mean experience for the cross section, given $r = 0.12$, $k = .04$, and $\omega = 20$ is 5.4. That for the true experience of the individuals, using the same parameters, is 6.3, an increase of 17% over the cross-sectional estimates.

13. The presumption that young working women switched jobs with considerable rapidity and thus experienced much turnover has been formed from the narrative accounts of the period. "The Long Day," for example, is the story of a young woman who worked at more than six jobs in about five years (O'Neill, 1972, orig. publ. 1905). But the average working woman did not change occupations and industries as often.

14. Average expected lifetime work experience for a man is assumed to be 50 years, given that work begins at age 15 and ends at age 65. That for a woman is at least six years if she worked when single. One would have to add to that figure work experience after marriage. The proportion of married women working outside the home around 1890 was very small, but that of widowed and divorced women was between 21% and 46% across all ages (see Table 2.2), or an average of 24% weighted by the age distribution of the labor force. The average age of widows was around 55, and not all women would eventually be widowed. Therefore, the expected work experience of a woman who worked when single would be six years plus some small additional amount, assumed here to be one year.

15. The reasons for the extremely late peak of earnings in the 1907 Women Adrift study may have to do with the heterogeneity of that sample.

16. Montgomery relates that when "Henry Gantt set task quotas for the bobbin winders at the Brighton Mills in New Jersey . . . he found that the older women quickly made the rates, while many young girls failed and quit. . . . Similarly, when Joseph and Feis Company tried to make its Clothcraft Shops in Cleveland a model of modern management, it found that the young women in its employ failed to increase their output in order to earn a bonus. In this case, however, the company probed more deeply and learned that most of the women turned all of their earnings over to their parents. It tried the remedy of sending investigators to the homes . . . to estimate their families' financial needs. Having determined for each woman a specific sum to be deducted from her pay and sent directly to her family, the firm had the rest of her earnings then paid separately to her" (1987, p. 39).

17. The summary of the Senate report, contained in U.S. Department of Labor (1916) noted, "In the factories the highest position to which a woman may aspire is that of forewoman, which is reached by progressive stages, beginning possibly with that of floor or errand girl, but usually as operative" (p. 217).

18. The equation showing the impact of education on sales workers in the 1907 Women Adrift sample is not given in Table 4.1. Even though increased education did not enhance the earnings of workers, sales workers were more educated than those who worked in manufacturing (7.8 versus 6.8 years in the sample). One possibility, supported by the column (3) results, is that sales work did not pay more than factory labor, on average, but had compensatory benefits of nicer working conditions.

19. The data are easily produced from the equations in Table 4.1. Because the dependent variable is the natural log of income, the ratio of earnings after E years to those of a beginner is: $\exp(\alpha E - \beta E^2)$, where E = work experience, α = the coefficient on experience, β = the coefficient on experience squared, and exp is the exponential function.

20. The value of 46% is from Eichengreen (1984) and is consistent with 1890 manufacturing data for San Francisco of 47.5%. The similarity between the survey data and those for the manufacturing census suggests that the survey is not biased. Rather, the composition of

the California work force accounts for the difference between these data and those of the nation.

21. The data from the 1892 California survey (Eichengreen, 1984), the 1888 Working Women Report, and the 1889 Michigan survey are as follows.

	1892 California		1888 Report Females	1889 Michigan Males
	Males	Females		
Years since beginning work	15.02	4.95	6.95	14.30
Years in present employment	10.39	3.76	4.26	6.42
Years with present employer	3.92	2.57		2.98

The Michigan survey data were originally collected by Hannon (1977). The means were generously provided by David Buffum.

22. The calculations use the following data, from Eichengreen (1984, table 3).

Explaining the Log of Weekly Earnings, 1892

	Male		Female	
	Coefficient	Mean	Coefficient	Mean
Constant	1.75		1.14	
Total experience	0.0524	15.02	0.0333	4.95
Total experience^2	−0.0009		−0.0011	
Years in occupation	0.0212	10.39	0.1077	3.76
Years in occupation^2	−0.0004		−0.0030	
Years with firm	0.0113	3.92	0.0236	2.57
Years with firm^2	−0.0001		−0.0014	
Never married	−0.1663	0.65	−0.0005	0.91
Maturity or schooling	0.0247	8.47	0.0195	9.62

The last term is (age − age work began − 6) and was constructed by Eichengreen to proxy schooling, but it also measures a maturity factor. In the earnings functions of Table 4.1, for which actual measures of schooling are available, I find that the age work began has a positive and significant coefficient of about the magnitude found by Eichengreen.

Because these are log earnings equations one can easily construct:

$$w_{m,f} = 2.423 \quad W_{m,f} = \$11.30$$

$$w_{f,m} = 2.176 \quad W_{f,m} = 8.81$$

$$w_m = 2.688 \quad W_m = 14.69$$

$$w_f = 1.902 \quad W_f = 6.70$$

using the shorthand of the section on "wage discrimination" corresponding to the four points in Figure 4.1b. The second column gives the actual dollar values for weekly earnings; the first column is in log form.

It should be noted that even though the example in the text constructs a conjectural female worker who is rewarded for her characteristics as if she were a male worker, the findings are robust to the other extreme method, the creation of a conjectural male worker who is rewarded as if he were a female.

23. Even though the discussion that follows uses the earnings function data from Eichengreen (1984), his data are fully consistent with those of other studies for manufacturing workers around the turn of this century. A comparable earnings function for male manufacturing workers from a 1889 Michigan study differs from that using the California data only by the premium given to married men. The Michigan data yield no premium, while the data for California give one of 17%. The coefficients on the experience and maturity variables are virtually identical, with the exception that returns to experience at an occupation are greater in the Michigan data. David Buffum generously provided me with the earnings equations for the Michigan study.

24. Note, for example, that earnings among single women are greater in the 1888 Working Women Report (Table 4.1). The finding that single women earn more than married women, but that married men earn more than single men has also been found in more modern data.

25. The data are from U.S. Commissioner of Labor (1897) and are for sewing-machine operators, knitters (hosiery), cigar makers, cigar packers, cigar strippers, compositors, carders (cotton), and speeders (cotton).

26. The occupation examined was the bundling of kindling wood, for which there were 246 workers earning piece rates in two firms (U.S. Commissioner of Labor, 1897).

27. Various biases concerning the self-selection of workers may afflict the earnings data for women. Although these cannot be assessed using current data, they do not seem important. The problem, in general, is that individuals who remain on the job for long periods may differ from those who leave early. To the extent that those who leave early are the most productive and able, for which there is no reliable indicator, the earnings function will be biased in favor of discrimination. One possibility is that women who are most able in the labor market are also most productive in the household and, because of this, marry earlier. It seems more likely, from the discussion in Chapter 2, that young women who were highly productive in the labor market married later, not earlier. Thus the possible biases from self-selection do not appear, in this case at least, to have been important. Further, the range of possible occupations for females in manufacturing around the turn of the century was sufficiently limited that biases of this nature could not greatly alter the results presented above.

28. The origins of the short story are still obscure, and its veracity is uncertain.

29. See Rotella (1981) on the economic history of the clerical sector and the female labor force, and Davies (1975, 1982) on the gender-typing of clerical work.

30. Firm-level schedules for both surveys are used in Chapter 6.

31. After five years of work experience, the male worker garners 24% but the female worker, 13%; after 10 years, he receives 44% more, but she 25% more.

32. The 20% figure for manufacturing is computed using the regression coefficients from Eichengreen (1984). Those for the clerical sector use the regression coefficients in Table 4.3.

33. Education adds 36.4% for clerical workers, while literacy adds 14% for manufacturing workers, a value approximately equal to that for schooling around the mean for manufacturing workers using the coefficients from Table 4.1, column (2).

34. The 5% figure is from a regression of deflated beginning salaries on education, marital status, previous employment, and sex. The coefficient on the sex dummy is 0.05.

35. The computation for "wage discrimination" in the clerical sample is as follows. The four points corresponding to those in Figure 4.1b are

$$w_{m,f} = 7.195 \qquad W_{m,f} = \$1333$$
$$w_{f,m} = 7.296 \qquad W_{f,m} = 1474$$

$$w_m \quad = 7.420 \qquad W_m \quad = \quad 1669$$
$$w_f \quad = 6.980 \qquad W_f \quad = \quad 1075$$

where the second column gives annual earnings in dollars, and the first gives the values in log form. The third and fourth numbers in each column are the actual earnings for men and women; the first is the earnings of a man had he been paid as a woman, and the second is the earnings of a woman had she been paid as a man. The two different methods for computing "wage discrimination" give: $[(7.42 - 7.195)/(7.42 - 6.98)] = (.225/.44) = 51\%$, and $[(7.296 - 6.98)/(7.42 - 6.98)] = (.316/.44) = 72\%$. Thus between 28% and 49% is explained by differences in the attributes. Note that less is explained when women are paid as men.

36. One might want to consider a policy that limited occupations to women only as restricting men and vice versa.

37. Marriage for both men and women also increased earnings in the higher skilled occupations.

38. An introduction to internal labor market institutions is Doeringer and Piore (1971). There are three primary strands of the theoretical literature. The first highlights the role of the wage profile in altering worker behavior. By making the wage–experience profile steeper or paying workers on the basis of their performance rank, firms can elicit more effort, tie the worker to the firm, and monitor workers. Lazear and Moore (1984) explore the role of the wage profile in changing employee effort; Malcomson (1984) shows that payment based on employee performance rank dominates even when actual output is not observable by employers; Lazear (1979, 1981) looks at the implications of altering wage profiles on mandatory retirement and hours restrictions; and Lazear and Rosen (1981) examine the implications of a tournament model of payment. A second part of the literature contains models of self-selection, in which wage profiles are used to screen workers. Salop and Salop (1976) consider a framework in which a steeper profile induces self-selection of those with low quit probabilities. Guasch and Weiss (1981) similarly consider a wage profile that includes a payment for a test as self-selecting those with higher ability. A third strand of the literature, drawing on the seminal work of Becker (1975), considers the use of the wage profile to enable both firm and worker to invest in human capital specific to the firm.

In the historical literature, see Sundstrom (1988) and Jacoby (1985). Both discuss the blue-collar labor market, although Sundstrom analyzes the evolution of internal labor markets before the 1920's and Jacoby highlights the period after. Sundstrom concludes that internal labor markets in skilled manufacturing positions evolved before the 1920's due to the demands of job training and firm-specific skills rather than unionization and monitoring. Sundstrom's dating of the emergence of internal labor markets is not inconsistent with the depiction given here of the transition from spot markets to implicit contracts. My interest is in the severing of wages from actual productivity, less with the production of human capital, and with the white-collar, not the blue-collar, sector.

39. Piece-rates and instantaneous monitoring have been instituted recently in various clerical positions through modern computer technology (see Howard, 1985).

40. The point is made forcefully by Rosabeth Moss Kanter in discussing discrimination against women in managerial jobs: "When managerial jobs are routinized and output can be measured, the personal characteristics of the people doing them becomes less important." She discusses a similar role for credentials and formal training: "[A]s training both in the skills and culture of management has been made available such training could begin to substitute for membership in a social group as an assurance of reliability, predictability, and the proper outlook" (1977, p. 55).

CHAPTER 5

1. Figures 5.1a and 5.1b are identical to the left-hand and right-hand panels of Figure 2.2, but each contains a vertical line at 35 years for reasons that will be clear toward the end of the chapter.

2. For an exceptional discussion of the modern labor supply model and literature see Killingsworth (1983).

3. See the papers in Layard and Mincer (1985), particularly that of Joshi, Layard, and Owen (1985) for Britain, which uses a technique similar to that of Smith and Ward (1984, 1985) and the introductory piece by Mincer (1985), which compares results across the various country studies.

4. Smith and Ward (1984, 1985) also include the indirect impact of wages on fertility.

5. The calculation uses the slopes in Mincer's article rather than the elasticities of Table 5.2, although differences in the results are slight. The data for Y_m and w are expressed in 1949 = 100 equivalents when using the slopes, for consistency with Mincer. The results are

$$\Delta\ell(\text{predicted}) = [\Delta(Y_m + w) = 5114]\cdot(-0.53) + [\Delta w = 2025]\cdot(2.05) = 14.41$$

for 1890 to 1960, and 18.41 for 1890 to 1980. The actual $\Delta\ell = 27.2$ for 1890 to 1960 and 45.3 for 1890 to 1980 (see Table 5.1). Therefore, the explanatory power is $(14.41/27.2) = 53\%$ for 1890 to 1960 and $(18.41/45.3) = 41\%$ for 1890 to 1980. Mincer's data (1962, table 10) yield a predicted value for $\Delta\ell$ of 19.20, while the value of $\Delta\ell$, using his calculations, is 25.4; thus 76% is explained. A faster increase in the earnings of both males and females explains the difference between my estimates and those of Mincer. Mincer used data from Long (1958) that imply earnings in 1890 that are far too low for both males and females.

Note that Cain (1966) reestimated Mincer's coefficients and found a minor error. Cain's elasticities in Table 5.2 are these reestimated numbers, and they are used below in a simulation.

6. Hamermesh (1986), in an exhaustive summary of empirical labor demand elasticity studies, shows that almost none is above 1 and very few are above 0.5, in absolute value. Note that a demand elasticity greater than 0.5 increases the shift term of the demand equation but also increases the weight placed on supply-side forces in the determination of ℓ^*, from equation (4).

7. The values for the three variables from 1890 to 1930 (see Table 5.1) are: $\ell^* = 2.8\%$, $w^* = 1.5\%$, $Y_m{}^* = 1.2\%$, all expressed in average annual percentage changes. Given values of $\varepsilon = 1.24$ (the average of 1900 and 1930 from Table 5.2), $\eta = 0$, and $\delta = 0.5$, equations (4) and (5) yield: $S^* = 2.8\%$; $S'^* = 4.3\%$, and $D^* = 3.6\%$. Note that the minimum bound on D^* is 2.8%, the value of ℓ^* when $\delta = 0$. The value of D^* is 4.3% when $\delta = 1$, greatly exceeding most of the estimates in Hamermesh (1986, table 8.2). Thus the finding that supply-side changes were equal to or exceeded those on the demand side is robust to reasonable values of δ. The role of supply in altering ℓ^*, however, is independent of δ when $\eta = 0$.

8. The values for the three variables from 1940 to 1960 (see Table 5.1) are: $\ell^* = 3.6\%$, $w^* = 3.2\%$, $Y_m{}^* = 3.2\%$, all expressed in average annual percentage changes. Given values of $\varepsilon = 0.47$, $\eta = 1.3$ (from Cain, 1966, see Table 5.2) and $\delta = 0.5$, equations (4) and (5) yield: $S^* = -.56\%$; $S'^* = 0.94\%$, and $D^* = 5.2\%$. The minimum bound on D^* is 3.6% when $\delta = 0$. Demand factors are clearly paramount in this case and are thus robust to changes in δ.

9. The values for the three variables from 1960 to 1980 (see Table 5.1) are: $\ell^* = 2.3\%$, $w^* = 1.1\%$, $Y_m{}^* = 1.2\%$, all expressed as average annual percentage changes. Given values

of $\varepsilon = 0.22$, $\eta = 0.37$ (from Fields, 1976, see Table 5.2) and $\delta = 0.5$, equations (4) and (5) yield: $S^* = 1.9\%$; $S'^* = 2.2\%$, and $D^* = 2.9\%$.

10. Mean schooling increases less rapidly than the median, but the acceleration for cohorts born around 1900 is approximately the same in both series. See Smith and Ward (1984) for measures of mean schooling among white women and for a criticism of my use of the median. The use of the median in my work is intended, and highlights the importance of high-school completion and educational norms.

11. Margo (1986) discusses possible biases in estimating black educational attainment from 1940 census data.

12. The percentage attending school among 15 to 20 year olds increased more in urban than in rural areas. But the figures for 15 to 20 year olds aggregate males and females.

13. Marriage bars might be explained on the basis of differences in productivity between single and married women or on the basis of a desire by the firm to increase turnover among lesser-skilled groups. But in the case of race, educational attainment, the single most important consideration in terms of productivity for beginners (see Chapter 4), was observable.

14. Many firm managers indicated that the word "race" meant nativity, not color. Quotations are from 1940 Office Firm Survey (see Data Appendix).

15. Cookingham's study of highly educated women similarly concludes "that the employment behavior of older married women during and after World War II was largely a function of their earlier labor force behavior. Women who worked as young wives were more likely to work after completing their childbearing" (1984, pp. 775–76).

16. For cross-section and time-series studies, see the various entries in Table 5.2. O'Neill (1981) and Clark and Summers (1982) are additional time-series models of labor supply. Clark and Summers find that previous employment affects current employment and that individuals do not intertemporally substitute labor from periods of economic recession toward those of economic boom. This finding complements cross-section evidence (see Chapter 2) that women who are in the labor force tend to remain in for long periods.

17. Joshi, Layard, and Owen (1985) and Smith and Ward (1984, 1985) also estimate similar pooled cross-section, time-series models. Because both studies use annual data, they employ more elaborate econometric specifications to estimate cohort effects and to control for serial correlation, less of a factor here because decadal data are used. Joshi et al. include a set of cohort dummies in a first-stage regression to explain within-cohort effects, and then use the cohort dummies in a second-stage regression to explain across-cohort differences. Smith and Ward estimate a similar first-stage equation in first-difference form, from which they calculate cohort fixed-effects. These are then used in a second-stage regression to estimate across-cohort differences. Neither study clearly differentiates among contemporaneous factors, cohort effects, and cohort "drift."

18. There are no reliable estimates for black female earnings for the period before 1940. Even the 1940 census figure is questionable because most full-time, year-round black female workers were domestic servants who received some income in the form of board and lodging. Almost three-quarters of all full-time, year-round black female workers in 1940 were private service workers who earned, on average, two-thirds the earnings of comparable service workers (data are from the 1940 Public Use Sample tapes). This suggests black female workers earned income in-kind. An additional problem is that if the 1940 ratio of white to black female earnings, even adjusted for the problem just mentioned, is applied to the data for white earnings in 1890 or 1900, the resulting black female earnings are far too low. This implies that the ratio of black to white female earnings must have decreased from 1890 to 1940, an inference that is consistent with the formidable restrictions on black women's employment during the period.

19. Smith (1984) contains the ratio of black to white male earnings for 1890 to 1980.

These are not actual earnings but have been derived from occupational data using earnings by occupation for 1970.

20. The coefficient on female earnings decreases to 0.143 (from 0.172) when time is added to the equation. It decreases to 0.062 when the level of urbanization is added as well. Similar changes occur to the coefficient on male earnings because of multicollinearity among the variables that have a strong time trend.

21. The original schedules from Palmer (1954) have recently been found and are, at the time of this writing, being put in machine-readable form. The Palmer survey will enable a full study of employment transitions from 1940 to 1951.

22. Much will depend on the stability of the coefficients to changes in the period of time considered. When column (1) of Table 5.4 is estimated on data for 1890 to 1960, the coefficients are only slightly different from those of the entire period, but a Chow test cannot be performed because there are too few observations for the 1960 to 1980 period. The actual data and the predicted values from the full model and the subsample are as follows.

Actual and Predicted Married Female Labor Force Participation

Age	Year	Actual ℓ	Predicted ℓ 1890–1980 Model	Predicted ℓ 1890–1960 Model
		Cohort Born in 1940		
15–24	1960	.30	.31	.33
25–34	1970	.36	.37	.40
35–44	1980	.59	.58	.44
		Cohort Born in 1950		
15–24	1970	.44	.48	.56
25–34	1980	.56	.55	.60

Had these cohorts been able to make predictions from the model and the data in Table 5.4, they would have been off by less than 9%. But these young women would not have had the benefit of the full range of data. If, instead, the model is estimated on the 1890 to 1960 period, a cohort born in 1940 would have been off by 11% in 1970, when they were 25 to 34 years old, and by 34% in 1980 when they were 35 to 44 years old. A cohort born in 1950 would have been off by only 7% in 1980, when its members were 25 to 34 years old. Note that although the prediction from the subsample is too low in 1980 for the cohort born in 1940, it is too high for that born in 1950. There is no overall sense that cohorts underestimated their future participation because the basic structure of the determinants of labor force participation changed.

23. The precise mean birth year of their mothers is not known.

24. In a more recent article, Shaw and Shapiro (1987) present additional evidence using the NLS concerning white women who were 34 to 36 years old in 1980. They trace the work expectations of these women from 1968 to 1978 and find that the increase in expectations occurs rather continuously during that decade. There was an initial jump from 1968 to 1969 that may have resulted from a change in the question asked (see Table 5.6). But there were other large increases from 1971 to 1972 and from 1975 to 1977 and smaller ones during other intervals. Over the entire period, the expectations of this group rose from 33% in 1968 to 68% in 1978. In 1980, when they were on average 35 years old, 64% of the group were at work. These numbers are fully consistent with those in Table 5.6.

CHAPTER 6

1. The age groups are 35 to 44 and 45 to 54. The oldest age group, 55 to 64, is not considered because a dummy variable for it was included.

2. In 1980, for example, only 1.4% of all labor force participants were physicians and lawyers.

3. Marriage bars and other discrimination on the basis of marital status are discussed in International Labor Organization (1962). Edwards (1988) analyzes the impact of the Japanese Equal Employment Opportunity Law of 1985. Many Japanese firms, which often have lifetime employment for workers, fired women at marriage.

4. Airlines imposed both forms of the marriage bar in the 1950's that initially affected both male stewards and female stewardesses. Cambridge and Oxford Universities, at one time, mandated that male instructors be unmarried, a continuation of the previous clerical status of professors.

5. 1957 Hussey Report: Penn Mutual Life Insurance Co., August 22, 1956; Brown Instrument, March 29, 1957.

6. The survey was taken in 1931 in the four cities sampled; other cities were surveyed in 1932.

7. Government offices were excluded from the sample because they used civil service procedures.

8. Personnel officers and other agents of the firms freely admitted to having discriminated against blacks in hiring office workers (see Chapter 5). Such candor is echoed in the remarks on sex discrimination.

9. The Women's Bureau also recorded individual-level data from personnel records in each of the firms surveyed. These records do not exist for the 1931 survey but do for the 1940 one and are used in Chapter 4 (see also Goldin, 1984, 1986b).

10. Cross tabulations of the hire and retain bar for the two years yield the following.

1931	1 = bar as policy or discretionary		1940	1 = bar as policy or discretionary	
	Hire Bar			Hire Bar	
Retain Bar	0	1	Retain Bar	0	1
0	45%	27%	0	44%	23%
1	3%	25%	1	3%	30%

11. These summary data are in general agreement with those from a national survey cited in Cohn (1985, p. 99). In that sample, 51% of all offices did not hire married women, and 30% did not retain them in 1936 (when "supervisor's discretion" is treated as no bar). For factory employment, the figures are 39% and 18%; however, there is little evidence that factories had as extensive bars for operatives in the 1920's as they did for clerical workers. Rather, it appears that operatives were almost entirely unaffected by the marriage bar until the Depression.

12. Because the 1931 survey included only firms that had more than 9 female employees, only such firms are included for the 1940 survey information in Table 6.3. Note the limited number of firms in the smallest size group for the 1931 survey and the substantial fraction of total female employees in firms with over 700.

13. The differences between the 1931 and the 1940 data are apparent in Table 6.1. Of the 12 possible cases, the percentages are all greater for Philadelphia and Kansas City in 1940 than for the aggregate in 1931, with the exception of the unweighted, hire (discretionary and policy) case for Kansas City in 1940. The 1940 Philadelphia sample for the weighted, retain

(policy and discretionary) case is just 0.2 percentage point lower than that for the aggregate 1931 sample. It is not clear why Los Angeles is an outlier. It is possible that only large cities in eastern and midwestern states had extensive marriage bars; western cities may have had less restrictive policies, in general, against female employment.

14. The coefficients on the dummy variable for the 1940 sample are: 0.904 ($t = 1.67$) for the case of the retain bar as policy and 0.928 ($t = 2.20$) for the case of the hire bar as policy. An insurance company in Philadelphia with 300 employees, for example, would have had a 23.4% probability of the retain bar in the 1931 sample, but a 43.0% probability in 1940.

15. One firm actually changed each bar in the opposite direction and is included with the group experiencing no net change. Of the 10 that increased the bar, 4 changed the retain bar only, 3 changed the hire bar only, and 3 changed both. The increased bar occurred in three ways: 5 firms moved from a discretionary bar to a bar policy; 2 moved from no bar to discretionary; and 3 moved from no bar to a bar policy. Fully 50% of the increase reflects a change from discretion to rule, providing further evidence to support the pooled regression results that many firms during the Depression merely changed discretionary policies.

16. See the discussion in Scharf (1980), for example.

17. On legislation passed and proposed during the Depression, see Shallcross (1940) and Kessler-Harris (1982); a detailed history of Federal Order 213 can be found in Scharf (1980, chap. 3). See also Wandersee (1981) on the impact of the marriage bar during the Depression, and Pruette (1934).

18. The town of Highland Park, Michigan, in 1921 "decided to strike from its payroll all women employees. . . . The council was prompted in its action by the large number of men out of employment, it is said" (Hughes, 1925, pp. 15–16).

19. A similar variable for "female-only" jobs, those for which men would not be considered, was not significant and was omitted.

20. Note that the 1931 results may reflect the decline in hours during the initial onset of the Great Depression.

21. The computations use the logit regression coefficients in Table 6.3, column (1) Retain Bar "As Policy," for both years. To compute the probability of having the retain bar (P), the coefficients (β) are multiplied by their mean values (X), in this case the 40- or 35-hour week, the 300 employees, and a 0 or 1 for the Promote variable. The equation for the probability (P) in a logit estimation is: $P = 1/[1 + \exp(-X\beta)]$. The computations for the change in the retain bar with the adoption of the internal promotion policy use the formula: $\partial P/\partial \text{Promote} = P(1 - P)\beta$, where β is the coefficient on the Promote variable. The computed data for 1940 implicitly apply to either Philadelphia or Kansas City because of the inclusion of city dummy variables.

22. This discussion raises the possibility that retirement and group insurance policies changed between the 1920's and 1950's and became experience rated. If they did, older women in particular would have benefited. The possibility that some personnel practices changed raises the issue whether tenure-based wage systems and promotion from within were also altered in the 1950's to accommodate the large supply of older female employees.

23. 1931 Office Firm Survey: Indemnity Insurance Co. of North America, Philadelphia.

24. 1931 Office Firm Survey: Provident Trust Co., Philadelphia.

25. 1931 Office Firm Survey: Provident Mutual Life Insurance, Philadelphia.

26. 1931 Office Firm Survey: F. A. Davis Co., Philadelphia; Presbyterian Board of Christian Education, Philadelphia.

27. 1931 Office Firm Survey: Phoenix Mutual Life Insurance, Hartford.

28. 1931 Office Firm Survey: Field Glore and Co., Chicago.

29. Peters (1934, p. 25), in a volume on married women teachers in Virginia, contains the only published evidence I have encountered on the urban–rural breakdown of the mar-

riage bar over time. According to his figures, the majority of urban school boards in Virginia instituted a ban against hiring married women before 1928, while the majority of rural school boards instituted the ban at the start of the Great Depression. About one-third of all urban school boards having a ban after 1932 had one before 1918, while only one-tenth of the rural school boards had such a ban before 1918. This chronology fits that of the institution of fixed salary scales.

30. See National Education Association (1923).

31. Margo and Rotella (1981) consider the case of Houston, in which the marriage bar was established before World War I, then dropped during the war, only to be reinstated after.

32. See Peterson (1987, p. 142), who also notes that in St. Louis, where the bar was established in 1897, no woman challenged it until 1941.

33. See Lewis (1925, pp. 185–88), who lists 31 frequently heard reasons why married women should not be employed as teachers and 31 equally touted reasons why they should.

34. There are probably other exceptions, particularly in manufacturing. Orra Langhorne, for example, in her 1886 volume *Southern Sketches from Virginia* (cited in Scott 1970, p. 122), noted that "married women are not admitted" in the cigarette factories of Lynchburg where white, single women and black women worked.

35. The assumption here is that productivity increases for several years but then levels off. Wages, however, might increase indefinitely with seniority if anchored to a strict salary scale. A related, but somewhat different case, occurs when firms want to increase their workers' earnings at the end of their employment, but withhold payment at the beginning, to elicit appropriate effort or discourage malfeasance. That case is discussed below.

36. See also Cohn (1988), who analyzes one of the surveys used here and finds support for his theory of "synthetic turnover." Although my findings differ somewhat from Cohn's on the details of the marriage bar, our substantive conclusions are quite similar.

37. The optimum quitting point for the worker is when the reservation wage just exceeds the offer wage. The reservation wage might have jumped at the point of marriage, causing most women to leave the labor force. But it might not have increased sufficiently to cause the same women to leave the labor force when the wage profile was artificially sloped.

38. The sloped profile will be more lucrative if the firm can conserve on supervisory costs, elicit more output, or reduce malfeasance.

39. In the case of stewardesses, however, it was often age as well as marriage that was cause for dismissal.

40. The 49% figure includes firms with the bar as policy and the bar as a discretionary course. The figure is 62% for the bar as policy only. In 1940, the same percentages are 42% and 52%, respectively.

41. In New York, for example, 32% of all female office workers had spent five or more years with their present firm; but 44% of those in insurance companies and 38% of those in public utilities had (U.S. Department of Labor, 1934b, p. 27). The evidence for the other cities supports the conclusion here that there is no clear relationship between experience with a firm and the existence of a marriage bar.

42. The 1.4% figure is an average of the coefficients on years of current firm experience for the two lower-skilled female groups in Table 4.5. The coefficient on years of total job experience is larger in magnitude (see Table 4.5), but presumably it is the value of the individual's training to any firm. The notion that firms pay workers less than they are worth at the beginning and more at the end to conserve on supervisory costs pertains to the difference between true productivity and earnings. Thus the coefficient on years with the current firm, also called tenure, is the relevant figure.

43. Typists and stenographers typically began work in 1940 at $70 a month (U.S. Department of Labor, 1942). If earnings rise at 1.4% per year but productivity does not and if

the break-even point is five years, the (constant) value of the worker to the firm is around $73. That is, the present discounted value of $73 over five years is approximately equal to the present discounted value of a stream of earnings that begins at $70 and rises by 1.4% each year for five years. At 10 years of service, for example, the worker costs the firm around $80 a month but is still worth only $73, or 9.6% more than she is actually worth.

44. Earnings functions estimated on the Houston schoolteacher data for the years 1892 to 1922 were generously provided to me by Elyce Rotella and Robert Margo. The equations include total experience, total experience squared, tenure with the school district, and educational levels. The coefficient on tenure varies from about 0.011 to 0.025 over the period 1910 to 1917, but is much smaller for that before and after. The number of observations for the years before 1910 is quite small, and the circumstances of World War I preclude using the data after 1917. Houston revoked its marriage bar sometime during World War I and then reinstated it after the war.

45. United Airlines recently lost a Title VII class action case (*Romasanta* v. *United Air Lines, Inc.*) for firing stewardesses when they married.

46. Oppenheimer (1970, chap. 5) contains such a theory about the evolution of married women's labor market work.

47. 1931 Office Firm Survey: Hartford records.

48. Easterlin (1978, 1980) causally connects the two swings in fertility through a model of relative income. See also the discussion of Easterlin's relative income hypothesis in Chapter 5.

49. 1957 Hussey Report: Penn Mutual Life Insurance, August 22, 1956; Scott Paper, March 28, 1957.

50. 1957 Hussey Report: Lord and Taylor, October 30, 1956.

51. 1957 Hussey Report: Strawbridge and Clothier, November 14, 1956; Central-Penn National Bank, October 19, 1956.

52. 1957 Hussey Report: Sears, Roebuck, and Co., November 7, 1956.

53. 1957 Hussey Report: Fidelity Mutual, August 17, 1956.

54. The sample (1940 Office Worker Survey) is described in the Data Appendix and consists of 724 women, 168 of whom were married. It is discussed at length in Goldin (1984, 1986b). In a regression on the log of full-time yearly earnings, the coefficient on a dummy variable indicating marital status (1 = married) is 0.424, but that on an interaction between the dummy variable and years of education is −.0362. The coefficient on years of education for the entire sample is 0.0458.

55. 1957 Hussey Report: October 8, 1956; August 24, 1956.

56. See also Goldin (1988a) on the period 1909 to 1919, and Atack and Bateman (1988) on hours of work and legislation in 1880.

57. Hours data are actual weekly hours in manufacturing from Jones (1963). Scheduled hours also declined but were higher.

58. The surveys consulted are from Delaware, Illinois, New Jersey, Ohio, and Rhode Island (U.S. Department of Labor, 1922 to 1927).

59. The role of hours in increasing women's employment has been commented on by many others. Bancroft, for example, noted that "the reduction in the scheduled work week in most jobs to 40 hours . . . has permitted many married women to both work and maintain their households" (1958, p. 29).

60. Only one additional independent variable, a dummy variable for southern states, could be included. Wage data are not presently available to be added to the estimation.

61. A 10% reduction of hours from, say, 53.9 to 49.1 is exactly 1 standard deviation around the mean of 51.5 in the 1920 data. A reduction in hours of that magnitude is predicted to increase the participation of married, native-born women from 9.9% to 11.1%, a quarter of

a standard deviation around its mean of 10.6%. A far greater increase in the participation of native-born, married women of foreign-born parents is predicted, from 4.6% to 11.8%, exceeding 1 standard deviation around the mean of 8.2%.

62. The calculation uses an elasticity value of 1.11 for native-born married women. The elasticity for native-born married women of foreign-born parents is more than twice as large (see Goldin, 1988a, p. 203). Use of that elasticity results in a considerable overprediction of the change in participation.

63. Flexibility of hours in cigar making was due to piece-rate payment and the extremely low level of capital used. Patricia Cooper, in her study of cigar makers, remarks that "officially women were allowed to leave anytime, but because they needed the maximum earnings they usually worked steadily" (1987, p. 198). Cooper also notes that this flexibility allowed women with children to be home when they returned from school (pp. 224–25). McGaw (1987), in the case of papermaking earlier in the nineteenth century, also remarks on the flexibility of hours among women workers who almost always worked in the non-mechanized part of the factory and who probably also worked for piece rates.

64. Blank (1987) finds that part-time women workers in manufacturing employments today earn approximately the same per hour as those working full-time. Professional workers on part-time receive a premium, while lower-skilled workers on part-time pay a penalty compared with full-time work.

CHAPTER 7

1. Montgomery (1987, pp. 38–39) concludes that it was age rather than gender that led female workers to ignore output restrictions instituted by labor unions.

2. By joint resolution of the Fifty-third Congress, Wright was "authorized and directed to investigate and make report upon . . . the effect, if any, [the employment of women] has had upon the wages and employment of men" (U.S. Commissioner of Labor, 1897, p. 11). Wright's results did show that women's wages were lower than men's for jobs of the same "efficiency," but he drew no conclusions from that finding.

3. The directors of the Women's Bureau (Mary Anderson and later Frieda Miller) and the more powerful members of the bureau were against the Equal Rights Amendment because they believed it would lead to the erosion of protective legislation. See Harrison (1988) and Rotella (1988) on the conflicts between protection and equality.

4. The *New York Times* reported that many lawyers claim that "'protective exclusion' policies can be a form of illegal sex discrimination" (August 2, 1988).

5. See Baker (1925) for an excellent summary of the evidence pertaining to New York State. She concludes that the positive effects of protective legislation clearly outweighed any negative effects.

6. It is clear from the *Muller* v. *Oregon* brief that government intervention was justified because there was an externality in the form of harm to future generations and because women may have been coerced into working long hours. "[H]er physical structure and a proper discharge of her maternal functions—having in view not merely her own health, but the well-being of the race—justify legislation to protect her from the greed as well as the passion of man. The limitations which this statute places upon her contractual powers . . . are not imposed solely for her benefit, but also largely for the benefit of all" (cited in Babcock et al., 1975, p. 32).

7. Unionization data were generously made available to me by Gerald Friedman.

8. See also Kessler-Harris, who maintains that "Brandeis and . . . Goldmark . . . correctly reasoned that to persuade the court that shorter hours for women were in fact conducive

to the general welfare required evidence that long hours were inimical to health and safety" (1982, p. 187). Brandeis's concern with lowering hours for all workers is clear in his extensive brief for *Bunting* v. *Oregon* (1917), which ultimately served to uphold a general hours law (see Babcock et al., 1975, p. 34).

9. Landes (1980) provides a theoretical model of the impact of maximum hours laws on the employment of women. See also Goldin (1988a).

10. Because hours legislation was justified on the basis of protecting women workers, it may have fostered further restrictions. Ostensibly for health reasons, for example, women were barred in foundries from rooms where cores were baked (Baker, 1925, pp. 367–68). Kessler-Harris (1982, chapter 7), also notes that maximum hours laws led to further restrictions, such as prohibitions of women bartenders, and that restrictions may have had spillover effects.

11. Although legislation was passed that limited the employment of women on streetcars in New York, it was partially repealed after women's groups protested (see Baker, 1925, chap. 7).

12. Quoted in Baker (1925, p. 444).

13. Further, hours of work in the manufacturing censuses are given as scheduled weekly, not actual, hours, and they are listed in groups (e.g., 44 to 48 hours) as a distribution.

14. This section draws heavily on Goldin (1988a).

15. The identity is

$$H = \alpha_f H_f + (1 - \alpha_f)H_m + (\alpha_f \times Law)\beta_f H_f + [(1 - \alpha_f) \times Law]\beta_m H_m$$

where H = mean scheduled hours for males and females aggregated; H_f, H_m = mean scheduled hours for female, males separately; α_f = female share of manufacturing employment; β_f, β_m = the marginal impact of the maximum hours law on mean female, male hours; and $Law = 1$ if the state has a maximum hours law. Rewriting yields the estimated equation:

$$H = H_m + (H_f - H_m)\alpha_f + (H_f\beta_f - H_m\beta_m)\cdot(\alpha_f \times Law) + (H_m\beta_m)Law$$

Thus the constant term equals the hours of men in states without the law, the coefficient on α_f (*% Female*) is the difference between female and male hours in states without the law, that on the existence of a maximum hours law (*Law*) is the decline in hours of males in states having the law, and finally that on the interaction term (*% Female* × *Law*) is the difference in the decline of female and male hours in states with the law.

16. Goldin (1988a) contains further details on the hours and employment data. The year 1914 was originally chosen for consistency with results in Landes (1980). The findings are invariant to using the law as of 1919.

17. The results for the foundry data are

$$Hours = \underset{(61.0)}{54.9} - \underset{(2.70)}{0.046} \text{ \% } Urban - \underset{(0.13)}{0.095} \text{ } South - \underset{(2.18)}{1.80} \text{ } Law$$

$R^2 = .38$; number of observations = 44 (five states had insufficient employment in foundries to be listed in the census); absolute values of t-statistics are in parentheses. Regression is unweighted; weighting by the square root of the number of workers yields a coefficient on *Law* of -1.89. Source is Goldin (1988a).

18. The figures of 4.4 and 3.4 hours for the decreased work week in female- and male-intensive industries are weighted by the number of employees; the unweighted numbers are 3.4 and 3.3 hours.

19. The *Restrictive* variable is almost identical to the variable called *REST* in Landes (1980), and I owe the concept to Landes.

20. Kessler-Harris reports that Felix Frankfurter in 1921 wrote to Ethel Smith, of the Women's Trade Union League, that the ERA "threatens the well-being, even the very life of these millions of wage-earning women" (1982, p. 208).

21. See Becker (1981) on the ERA between the wars, and Harrison (1988) for the period since 1945. Cott (1987, chap. 4) discusses conflicts both within and among individuals identified as social feminists and those associated with the NWP. Becker notes that the U.S. Senate in 1949, 1953, and 1959 passed the ERA with what was known as the "Hayden rider," which exempted all sex-specific legislation, thereby severely weakening the amendment (1981, p. 273).

22. Harrison summarizes the impact of the commission in the following way: "Constrained by its refusal to examine the conflicts in defining roles by sex, its search for unanimity, and its desire for political acceptability, the PCSW often left the hardest problems untackled and forswore the most potent solutions: nevertheless, taken all together, the recommendations of the president's commission broke new ground. . . . It decreed the problem of sex discrimination legitimate, insisting that it hurt not only the individual but also the nation. . . . Although not far ahead of public opinion, the president's commission, by openly acknowledging the legitimacy of the quest for equal treatment, nudged public opinion along . . . the most significant outcome of the commission's existence . . . was unanticipated: a resurgence of a vital, energetic, widespread women's movement, with a coherent feminist philosophy" (1988, pp. 163, 165).

23. See the discussions in Bird (1968), who doubts Smith's seriousness; Harrison (1988), who claims that Smith added the word "sex" to ensure that black women would not receive guarantees denied white women; and Mathews (1982), who discusses the role of Representative Martha Griffiths. See also Livernash (1984, p. 225) for a summary.

24. On the discontent expressed by professional and business women in the 1920's and 1930's, see Cott (1987, chap. 7).

25. See the fine summary in Lundahl and Wadensjö (1984) of the late-nineteenth- and early-twentieth-century literature on differences in pay between men and women in Britain. The economists Cassel, Edgeworth, Fawcett, and Rathbone, as well as Sidney Webb, contributed to a debate that eventually covered the various theories of economic discrimination that now, in more rigorous formulation, are part of the literature on the subject. Thus all the concepts concerning economic discrimination seem to have been understood, but were somehow less strongly appreciated. It is also possible that they were more keenly felt in Britain than in the United States.

26. Only women younger than 33 years old in 1964 are included in the statistics that follow.

27. These numbers have been computed for me by the author of the paper, Peter Kuhn, and hold around the medians (Kuhn, 1987, table 5).

28. Beller (1979, 1982), however, finds that Title VII and related legislation served to reduce the ratio of male to female earnings by 7 percentage points overall and by 14 percentage points in the private sector between 1967 and 1974.

29. See Aldrich and Buchele (1986), who present a possible economic defense of comparable worth and various ways it might be implemented.

CHAPTER 8

1. The change in hours worked from 1959 to 1983 is from Fuchs (1988) and is for all women and all men 25 to 64 years old. Differences in total hours worked between married

men and married women would be even larger. The 1959 and 1983 figures for housework are extrapolations made by Fuchs using 1975/76 data. The data on hours for employed and nonemployed wives are from Cain (1984); the figure for full-time work uses data in Juster and Stafford (1985, p. 148). Cain estimates that employed wives in the 1975/76 survey spent an average of 26 hours in housework, while those not employed spent 51 hours. Employed women also spent on average 32 hours working for pay, giving a total of 58 hours. Their husbands spent about 13 hours in household activities in 1975/76 (Juster and Stafford, 1985, p. 148) and about 40 hours in paid market work, giving a total of 53 hours. Not surprisingly, therefore, employed wives worked more hours than their husbands, and both worked more hours than wives who were not employed. It should be noted that data in Juster and Stafford (1985, p. 310) give a smaller number of hours (45) for "family care" work done by house-wives, and that the hours figure for paid work used here omits the journey to work, second jobs, and so on. See Juster and Stafford for additional data.

2. Michael (1985) presents econometric evidence that divorce "Granger causes" female labor force participation, although his previous work found the opposite, a more historically plausible conclusion. See also Johnson and Skinner (1986), who find that expectations of divorce increase participation in a cross section of married women.

3. The poverty rate for all adult women was 12.2% in 1987 and 8.1% for men, giving a ratio of 1.51.

4. The percentage of all black adults in poverty who are female has risen since 1959 but decreased since 1979. Fuchs (1986, 1988) reports that 59.2% were female in 1959, 69.3% were in 1979, and recent data show 67.9% were in 1987, using the fixed poverty line standard.

In terms of long-run trends, Smith and Ward (1989) report poverty was "sex neutral" in 1940 and 1950, when most families included both husband and wife, but became feminized around 1960. Their data differ somewhat from Fuchs's, although both use the same sources. More women than men were probably impoverished prior to 1940. Hannon (1984) reports data for relief recipients in New York State from 1843 to 1859. Because a husband could receive relief to support his wife and children, the figures greatly understate the proportion of women in poverty. Yet the fraction of women among those getting relief was 44% by the early 1850's and rose to 55% by the end of the decade.

5. The literature on the economic status of women over the course of modernization is extensive and includes Boserup's (1970) pioneering monograph. The historical literature includes Lerner (1969, 1986) and Goldin (1986a), and arguably begins with Engels (1978; orig. publ. 1884).

6. U.S. Department of Education (1988). See also U.S. Bureau of the Census (1988), for data on the percentage of individuals 25 to 29 years old who completed four or more years of college. In the late 1950's, 14% of white men but only 7.5% of white women 25 to 29 years old completed college. By the late 1960's, the figures were 18% and 12%, and by the late 1970's, 27% and 21%. The most recent data indicate virtual equality at 23% for both white men and women 25 to 29 years old.

7. Professional degrees are first professional degrees and are primarily those in medi-cine, law, and dentistry (U.S. Department of Education, 1988, table 180).

8. Data on college majors are from U.S. Department of Education (1988). See also *Economic Report of the President, 1987*, pp. 216–17.

9. "Changes in occupational composition are likely to be more pronounced for younger workers, but because of the limited sample size of the survey, detailed occupation data by age are not available. Data from the next decennial census could be used to examine this issue" (U.S. Bureau of the Census, 1987, p. 4).

10. Data for the entire population are from U.S. Bureau of the Census (1987) and include

only full-time workers. The data for those less than 35 years old are from *Economic Report of the President, 1987*.

11. The labor force participation rate among all women in 1986 was about 55%; in 1979 it was about 51%.

12. Data on labor force participation rates for women with young children are from U.S. Department of Labor, *News*, August 12, 1987 (No. 87-345), and September 7, 1988 (No. 88-431). Those on full-time, year-round work are from Shank (1988). Even though the percentage working full-time and year-round increased from 1966 to 1986, the percentage working full-time, as opposed to part-time, did not. The movement, therefore, was from full-time but intermittently, to full-time and year-round.

APPENDIX TO CHAPTER 2

1. This appendix is derived from material in Goldin (1986c) with minor corrections and additions.

2. Abbott (1910) questioned the occupational information in the late-nineteenth-century population censuses; see Rubinow (1907), however, for a criticism of Abbott. Smuts noted that "the basic criterion, the core of today's labor force concept, was not made explicit until 1910. This is the rule that defines a worker as a person who works for money" (1960, p. 71). He also questioned the 1890 female farm laborer figures (1960, pp. 76–77). Durand, among many others, noted the anomalous 1910 female farm laborer estimates (1948, p. 195). He (1948, pp. 197–200) and Bancroft (1958, pp. 183–97) discuss the implications for the early census data of the change in the definition of the labor force in 1940. Jaffe (1956) argues that the growth in the female labor force was vastly overstated because of omissions in the 1890 and 1900 data. Lebergott (1964, pp. 57–58), however, presents a defense of the census labor force estimates. See also Abel and Folbre (1988), who summarize the problem of under-counting women workers in a historical context, and Conk (1980), who analyzes various issues regarding occupational statistics from 1870 to 1940.

3. Durand (1948, pp. 199, 207) adjusted the 1940 census data for comparability with both the 1930 "gainful worker" estimates and the Current Population Survey data, but the adjustment ratios for females are not substantial. The "gainful worker" adjustment was based on a special survey of the 1930 census and indicated that the "gainful worker" concept overstated the female work force in 1930 by 2.72%. Bancroft (1958) also discusses changes in definition and the comparability of the decennial census with the Current Population Survey data. Lebergott (1964, pp. 71–73) summarizes the debate over the accuracy of the labor force estimates of the female population, particularly the doubts of Smuts (1959, 1960), and concludes by accepting the census figures as the proper standard. More recent works (Abel and Folbre, 1988; Ciancanelli, 1983) contain substantial upward revisions to the official figures, but do not make adjustments consistent with either the gainful worker or the labor force construct. They instead often include in the labor force all women who worked at some time during the census year.

4. This calculation assumes that work is done in weekly intervals.

5. In 1930, the U.S. Bureau of the Census informed enumerators that individuals who worked for wages more than one day per week were to be counted as having an occupation. Had individuals used this rule of thumb in the previous censuses, the norm would have been only 20% of a week (U.S. Bureau of the Census, 1933b, p. 29). There is no indication that such a rule was employed.

6. Some of the variance among these workers in days work stems from the necessary inclusion of those who began work during the year.

7. Conk (1980), for example, presents compelling evidence that census marshals and officials presumed married and adult women were not employed, and often altered data when occupations were unusual and atypical of female jobs.

8. The average married woman working in industry probably worked more than half the year because older women earned somewhat less than experienced younger women in industry (Goldin, 1981). Further, average earnings for married women includes those who began work during the year and for whom days worked that year were artificially low, and those who did industrial home work.

9. It is not possible to distinguish between part-time and intermittent work in the sense of working part of a day. Part-time work usually refers to work performed for fewer than the standard number of hours per week, while intermittent work refers to that done for the full number of hours per week but not the full number of weeks per year.

10. Boarders and other family members were grouped together, and the estimate of two boarders per boarding household is based on only those families reporting income from boarding.

11. Wright (U.S. Commissioner of Labor, 1889) gives a figure of $300 for full-time earnings in manufacturing.

12. Note that I have not subtracted the women already counted as boardinghouse keepers in the census, a procedure that biases upward the estimate. To net out these women would require assumptions concerning their earnings. It is likely that women who reported the occupation of "boardinghouse keeper" earned substantially more than those who reported no occupation yet were receiving income from boarders. If all those who reported the occupation would have been counted under either of the definitions in the text, as was likely, the adjusted percentages must be lowered by exactly the percentage of women already counted. Less than .5% of all married women in cities with ≥ 25,000 people were counted as boardinghouse keepers in the 1900 census.

13. Fully 65% of all manufacturing workers (excluding lumber and flour milling) were in cities with ≥ 20,000 inhabitants. If, instead, the definition of urban and industrial areas includes cities with ≥ 2,500 inhabitants (encompassing 35% of white Americans in 1890), the adjustment is between 2.1 (= .35 × .37 × .16) and 5.6 (= .35 × .16) percentage points for married women and 2.6 and 7.0 for widows. See below, however, for corrections to all nonfarm rural areas.

14. The 1900 Public Use Sample evidence on boarding for cities with ≥ 25,000 persons is 13.7% for wives and 21.0% for widows, or somewhat lower than the 1890/91 Report evidence. The higher figures in the 1890/91 Report probably result from the inclusion of industrial areas.

15. The 1890 population census gives a figure of 17% for the percentage of all dwellings in cities of ≥ 25,000 persons. The 1900 Public Use Sample indicates that 27.2% of all households were farm dwellings. Therefore, the 55.8% figure is a residual. Note that dwellings, not households, are the appropriate unit of analysis.

16. U.S. Bureau of the Census (1914, p. 27). This volume contains few breakdowns of occupational data by age, marital status, race, and region, and therefore the data cannot be corrected for the overstatement of agricultural labor. Smuts, among others, has called for the inclusion of these women in the labor force. He noted that although in 1890 "there were perhaps 4 million married white women living on farms, the census reported only about 23,000 of them in agricultural occupations. In 1950, when the farm population was much smaller than in 1890, nearly 200,000 married white women were counted as unpaid family farm laborers" (1960, pp. 76–77).

17. The proportion of unpaid family workers among all agricultural workers for white females ≥ 15 years old is as follows, by state, in 1910: Alabama (0.507), Arkansas (0.433),

Florida (0.151), Georgia (0.367), Louisiana (0.165), Mississippi (0.507), North Carolina (0.399), Oklahoma (0.177), South Carolina (0.382), Tennessee (0.191), Texas (0.344), Virginia (0.074). All other states had proportions lower than 0.044 (Wisconsin), and averaged 0.007.

18. The lesser underreporting of black female agricultural laborers suggests different norms among the white and black communities regarding the labor of married women. Goldin (1977) discusses the role of slavery in the different responses of black and white households to female labor.

19. U.S. Bureau of the Census (1907a, p. 32) gives 94,601 white female agricultural laborers, of whom 61% were members of farmers' families. Therefore, 57,707 white female family farm workers, or 1.6% of the total female population, were already counted in the 1900 census.

20. The assumption is that the male adult agricultural figures were not affected by the instructions to the enumerators in 1910. The proportion of the male labor force that was in agriculture declined from 0.403 in 1890 to 0.270 in 1920.

21. Allen (1931) surveyed non-Mexican female cotton farm workers in Texas. The number of women interviewed was 664 and included both the unmarried and the married.

22. The 1.24 percentage point figure is: $4.5 \times 0.31 \times 0.89$ (percentage white in the adult female population). The figure for married women multiplies the 1.24 number by the percentage married among the undercounted workers ($\alpha = .624$) and divides it by the percentage married among the entire adult female population ($\beta = .582$). The value for α comes from Allen (1931), and that for β is from the population census for women 15 to 64 years old in 1890.

23. In the South Dakota survey, for example, 50% of the wives reported time for fetching water, 25% had electric lights, and 46% used coal or wood cooking stoves.

24. A listing of these time-budget studies can be found in Vanek (1973). The published reports consulted, together with the mean number of hours worked in unpaid family farm labor and the number of observations, are: Idaho, 1927 (9.74 hours; number of observations = 49); Washington, 1929 (9.9; 137); South Dakota, 1930 (11.55; 100); Montana, 1929-31 (9.12; 48); Oregon, 1929 (11.3; 288); U.S.D.A., primarily California, 1924-28 (8.67; 559). These housewives spent, on average, 65 hours a week on all work, of which 15% was unpaid dairy, poultry, orchard, and garden labor. With the exception of the Montana study, only the records of farm housewives were used. Even though some of these states contained large-scale grain farming and cattle ranching, while others contained mixed farming, the number of hours worked in unpaid family farm labor by wives was fairly constant across states.

25. Only two studies give the distribution of time worked. Using the 15-hour cutoff yields 12% who would have been counted in Montana and 30% who would have been counted in Oregon. It should be noted that a later study, published in 1945 (cited in Abel and Folbre 1988), indicates that 42% of all farm wives surveyed worked $\geq$ 15 hours at unpaid family farm labor. The study, however, was taken during World War II and likely reflects the absence of husbands, farm hands, and sons.

26. This calculation assumes that 40% of the population lived on farms, and 68% of all farms were outside the South.

27. The 121,193 figure is derived as a residual and assumes that 30% of all children working in manufacturing in 1890 were female. There were 545,758 (839,952 − 294,194) women enumerated in the manufacturing census after those in clothing production are subtracted; equivalently 424,565 (1,027,242 − 602,677) remain in the population census after women in clothing production are subtracted. The difference between these figures, 545,758 − 424,565 = 121,193, is the shortfall in the population census of women working in the larger manufacturing firms.

It should be noted that it would be incorrect to adjust or compare the manufacturing employment figures from the two censuses on an industry-by-industry basis, as Smuts (1960) did. The population census lists workers in general classifications, such as "operatives," and does not always associate them with a particular industry.

28. With the exception of meals, these were among the items for which Gallman (1966) computed corrected value-added amounts to augment the pre-1890 national income estimates.

29. It is likely that the time families now spend consuming restaurant meals is considerably higher than the figures reported in Szalai (1972). Therefore, the proportion of the time of 1890 wives that should be allotted to the household production of goods that the market now supplies is probably greater than the 14% figure given.

30. The assumption made in this calculation is that married women currently spend about 2.5 hours per week in the household maintenance and production of clothing and baking.

REFERENCES

Abbott, Edith. *Women in Industry: A Study in American Economic History*. New York: Appleton, 1910.

Abbott, Edith, and Sophonisba Breckinridge. "Women in Industry: The Chicago Stockyards." *Journal of Political Economy* 19 (October 1911): 632–54.

Abel, Marjorie, and Nancy Folbre. "Never Done and Under-Counted: Women's Work and the Pre-1940 U.S. Censuses." Manuscript, University of Massachusetts, Amherst, March 1988.

Aigner, Dennis, and Glen Cain. "Statistical Theories of Discrimination in Labor Markets." *Industrial and Labor Relations Review* 30 (January 1977): 175–87.

Akerlof, George A., and Janet L. Yellen, eds. *Efficiency Wage Models of the Labor Market*. New York: Cambridge University Press, 1986.

Aldrich, Mark, and Randy Albelda. "Determinants of Working Women's Wages during the Progressive Era." *Explorations in Economic History* 17 (October 1980): 323–41.

Aldrich, Mark, and Robert Buchele. *The Economics of Comparable Worth*. Cambridge, MA: Ballinger, 1986.

Allen, Ruth. *The Labor of Women in the Production of Cotton*. University of Texas Bureau of Research in the Social Sciences Study, No. 3. Austin: University of Texas, 1931.

Anderson, Karen. *Wartime Women: Sex Roles, Family Relations, and the Status of Women during World War II*. Westport, CT: Greenwood Press, 1981.

Arrow, Kenneth. "Models of Job Discrimination" and "Some Mathematical Models of Race Discrimination in the Labor Market." In Anthony H. Pascal, ed., *Racial Discrimination in Economic Life*. Lexington, MA: Heath, 1972.

———. "The Theory of Discrimination." In Orley Ashenfelter and Albert Rees, eds., *Discrimination in Labor Markets*. Princeton, NJ: Princeton University Press, 1973.

Atack, Jeremy, and Fred Bateman. "Whom Did Protective Legislation Protect in 1880?" Paper presented at the 1988 Cliometrics Meetings, Oxford, Ohio, March 1988.

Axelrod, Robert. "An Evolutionary Approach to Norms." *American Political Science Review* 80 (December 1986): 1095–111.

Babcock, Barbara Allen, Ann E. Freedman, Eleanor Holmes Norton, and Susan C. Ross. *Sex Discrimination and the Law: Causes and Remedies*. Boston: Little, Brown, 1975.

Baer, Judith A. *The Chains of Protection: The Judicial Response to Women's Labor Legislation*. Westport, CT.: Greenwood Press, 1978.

Baker, Elizabeth Faulkner. *Protective Labor Legislation: With Special Reference to Women in the State of New York*. Studies in History, Economics and Public Law, Columbia University. New York: AMS Press, 1969; orig. publ. 1925.

———. *Technology and Woman's Work*. New York: Columbia University Press, 1964.

Bancroft, Gertrude. *The American Labor Force: Its Growth and Changing Composition*. New York: Wiley, 1958.

Baron, Ava. "Women and the Making of the American Working Class: A Study of the Proletarianization of Printers." *Review of Radical Political Economics* 14 (Fall 1982): 23–42.

Becker, Gary. *Human Capital: A Theoretical and Empirical Analysis, with Special Reference to Education*. 2nd ed. Chicago: University of Chicago Press, 1975.

_____. *The Economics of Discrimination*. 2nd ed. Chicago: University of Chicago Press, 1971; orig. publ. 1957.

Becker, Susan D. *The Origins of the Equal Rights Amendment: American Feminism Between the Wars*. Westport, CT: Greenwood Press, 1981.

Bell, Duran. "Why Participation Rates of Black and White Wives Differ." *Journal of Human Resources* 9 (Fall 1974): 465–79.

Beller, Andrea H. "The Impact of Equal Employment Opportunity Laws on the Male–Female Earnings Differential." In Cynthia B. Lloyd, Emily S. Andrews, and Curtis L. Gilroy, eds., *Women in the Labor Market*. New York: Columbia University Press, 1979.

_____. "The Impact of Equal Opportunity Policy on Sex Differentials in Earnings and Occupations." *American Economic Review* 72 (May 1982): 171–75.

_____. "Changes in the Sex Composition of U.S. Occupations, 1960–1981." *Journal of Human Resources* 20 (Spring 1985): 235–50.

Beller, Andrea H., and Kee-ok Kim Han. "Occupational Sex Segregation: Prospects for the 1980's." In Barbara F. Reskin, ed., *Sex Segregation in the Workplace: Trends, Explanations, Remedies*. Washington, DC: National Academy Press, 1984.

Beney, M. Ada. *Wages, Hours, and Employment in the United States, 1914–1936*. New York: National Industrial Conference Board, 1936.

Ben-Porath, Yoram. "Labor-Force Participation Rates and the Supply of Labor." *Journal of Political Economy* 81 (May–June 1973): 697–704.

Bergmann, Barbara R. *The Economic Emergence of Women*. New York: Basic Books, 1986.

Bielby, William T., and James N. Baron. "A Woman's Place Is with Other Women: Sex Segregation Within Organizations." In Barbara F. Reskin, ed., *Sex Segregation in the Workplace: Trends, Explanations, Remedies*. Washington, DC: National Academy Press, 1984.

Bird, Caroline. *Born Female: The High Cost of Keeping Women Down*. New York: Van Rees Press, 1968.

Blank, Rebecca. "The Effect of Part-Time Work on the Compensation of Adult Women." Manuscript, Princeton University, November 1987.

Blau, Francine D. *Equal Pay in the Office*. Lexington, MA: Lexington Books, 1977.

Blau, Francine D., and Andrea H. Beller. "Trends in Earnings Differentials by Gender, 1971–1981." *Industrial and Labor Relations Review* 41 (July 1988): 513–29.

Blau, Francine D., and Marianne A. Ferber. *The Economics of Women, Men, and Work*. Englewood Cliffs, NJ: Prentice-Hall, 1986.

Blau, Francine D., and Wallace Hendricks. "Occupational Segregation by Sex: Trends and Prospects." *Journal of Human Resources* 14 (Spring 1979): 197–210.

Blinder, Alan. "Wage Discrimination: Reduced Form and Structural Estimates." *Journal of Human Resources* 8 (Fall 1973): 436–55.

Bloom, David. "Labor Market Consequences of Delayed Childbearing." Paper presented at the American Sociological Association, Chicago, 1986.

Bose, Christine E. "Devaluing Women's Work: The Undercount of Women's Employment in 1900 and 1980." In Christine Bose et al., eds., *Hidden Aspects of Women's Work*. New York: Praeger, 1987.

Boserup, Ester. *Women's Role in Economic Development*. New York: St. Martin's Press, 1970.

Bowen, William, and T. Aldrich Finegan. *The Economics of Labor Force Participation*. Princeton, NJ: Princeton University Press, 1969.

Brandeis, Louis D., and Josephine Goldmark. *Women in Industry: Decision of the United States Supreme Court in Curt Muller vs. State of Oregon.* New York: National Consumers' League, 1908.

Breckinridge, Sophonisba P. *Women in the Twentieth Century: A Study of Their Political, Social and Economic Activities.* New York: McGraw-Hill, 1933.

Brissenden, Paul F. *Earnings of Factory Workers, 1899 to 1927: An Analysis of Pay-roll Statistics.* Washington, DC: Government Printing Office, 1929.

Brown, Martin, and Peter Philips. "Craft Labor and Mechanization in Nineteenth-Century American Canning." *Journal of Economic History* 46 (September 1986): 743–56.

Bulow, Jeremy, and Lawrence Summers. "A Theory of Dual Labor Markets with Application to Industrial Policy, Discrimination and Keynesian Unemployment." *Journal of Labor Economics* 4 (January 1986): 376–414.

Bureau of National Affairs. *Pay Equity and Comparable Worth: A BNA Special Report.* Washington, DC: Bureau of National Affairs, 1984.

Butler, Elizabeth Beardsley. *Women and the Trades: Pittsburgh, 1907–1908.* Pittsburgh: University of Pittsburgh Press, 1984; orig. publ. 1909.

Cahill, Marion Cotter. *Shorter Hours: A Study of the Movement since the Civil War.* New York: AMS Press, 1968; orig. publ. 1932.

Cain, Glen G. *Married Women in the Labor Force: An Economic Analysis.* Chicago: University of Chicago Press, 1966.

_____. "Women and Work: Trends in Time Spent in Housework." IRP Discussion Paper No. 747–84, University of Wisconsin, Madison, 1984.

_____. "The Economic Analysis of Labor Market Discrimination: A Survey." In Orley C. Ashenfelter and Richard Layard, eds., *Handbook of Labor Economics.* Vol. 1. Amsterdam: North-Holland, 1986.

Campbell, D'Ann. *Women at War with America: Private Lives in a Patriotic Era.* Cambridge, MA: Harvard University Press, 1984.

Campbell, Helen. *Women Wage-Earners: Their Past, Their Present, and Their Future.* Introduction by Richard T. Ely. New York: Arno Press, 1972; orig. publ. 1893.

Carey, Henry C. *Essay on the Rate of Wages: With an Examination of the Causes of the Differences in the Condition of the Labouring Populations Throughout the World.* Philadelphia: Carey, Lea, and Blanchard, 1835.

Carter, Susan B. "The Gender Gap in Manufacturing Wages, 1885–1935: A Reconsideration." Manuscript, Smith College, April 1988.

Carter, Susan B., and Peter Philips. "Continuous-Process Technologies and the Gender Gap in Manufacturing Wages." Paper presented to the U.C. Intercampus Group in Economic History, Santa Cruz, CA, April–May 1988.

Chafe, William H. *The American Woman: Her Changing Social, Economic, and Political Roles, 1920–1970.* New York: Oxford University Press, 1972.

Ciancanelli, Penelope. "Women's Transition to Wage Labor: A Critique of Labor Force Statistics and Reestimation of the Labor Force Participation of Married Women in the United States, 1900–1930." Ph.D. diss., New School for Social Research, 1983.

Clark, Kim B., and Lawrence H. Summers, "Labour Force Participation: Timing and Persistence." *Review of Economic Studies* 49 (Special Issue, 1982): 825–44.

Cohn, Samuel. *The Process of Occupational Sex-Typing: The Feminization of Clerical Labor in Great Britain.* Philadelphia: Temple University Press, 1985.

_____. "Firm-level Economics and Synthetic Turnover: Determinants of the Use of Marriage Bars in American Offices during the Great Depression." Manuscript, University of Wisconsin, February 1988.

Conk, Margo. *The United States Census and Labor Force Change: A History of Occupation Statistics, 1870–1940*. Ann Arbor, MI: UMI Research Press, 1980.

Cook, Alice H. *Comparable Worth: A Casebook of Experiences in States and Localities*. Manoa: Industrial Relations Center, University of Hawaii, 1985.

Cookingham, Mary E. "Working after Childbearing in Modern America." *Journal of Interdisciplinary History* 14 (Spring 1984): 773–92.

Cooper, Patricia A. *Once a Cigar Maker: Men, Women, and Work Culture in American Cigar Factories, 1900–1919*. Urbana: University of Illinois Press, 1987.

Corcoran, Mary, and Greg J. Duncan. "Work History, Labor Force Attachment, and Earnings Differences between the Races and Sexes." *Journal of Human Resources* 14 (Winter 1979): 3–20.

Cott, Nancy F. *The Bonds of Womanhood: "Woman's Sphere" in New England, 1780–1835*. New Haven, CT: Yale University Press, 1977.

———. *The Grounding of Modern Feminism*. New Haven, CT: Yale University Press, 1987.

Cowan, Ruth Schwartz. "Two Washes in the Morning and a Bridge Party at Night: The American Housewife between the Two Wars." In Louis Scharf and Joan M. Jensen, eds., *Decades of Discontent: The Women's Movement, 1920–1940*. Westport, CT: Greenwood Press, 1983a.

———. *More Work for Mother: The Ironies of Household Technology from the Open Hearth to the Microwave*. New York: Basic Books, 1983b.

Coyle, Grace. "Women in the Clerical Occupations." *The Annals* 143 (May 1929): 180–87.

———. *Present Trends in the Clerical Occupations*. New York: Woman's Press, 1928.

Cullen, Donald. "The Interindustry Wage Structure, 1899–1950." *American Economic Review* 46 (June 1956): 353–69.

D'Amico, Ronald J., Jean R. Haurin, and Frank L. Mott. "The Effects of Mothers' Employment on Adolescent and Early Adult Outcomes of Young Men and Women." In Cheryl D. Hayes and Sheila B. Kamerman, eds., *Children of Working Parents: Experiences and Outcomes*. Washington, DC: National Academy Press, 1983.

Davies, Margery. "Woman's Place Is at the Typewriter: The Feminization of the Clerical Labor Force." In Richard C. Edwards, Michael Reich, and David M. Gordon, eds., *Labor Market Segmentation*. Lexington, MA: Heath, 1975.

———. *Woman's Place Is at the Typewriter: Office Work and Office Workers, 1870–1930*. Philadelphia: Temple University Press, 1982.

Daymont, Thomas N., and Paul J. Andrisani. "Job Preferences, College Major, and the Gender Gap in Earnings." *Journal of Human Resources* 19 (Summer 1984): 408–28.

Degler, Carl N. *At Odds: Women and the Family in America from the Revolution to the Present*. New York: Oxford University Press, 1980.

Doeringer, Peter B,. and Michael J. Piore. *Internal Labor Markets and Manpower Analysis*. Lexington, MA: Heath, 1971.

Douglas, Paul H. "Plant Administration of Labor." *Journal of Political Economy* 27 (July 1919): 544–60.

Dublin, Thomas. *Women at Work: The Transformation of Work and Community in Lowell, Massachusetts, 1826–1860*. New York: Columbia University Press, 1979.

———, ed. *Farm to Factory: Women's Letters, 1830–1860*. New York: Columbia University Press, 1981.

Durand, John D. *The Labor Force in the United States, 1890–1960*. New York: Social Science Research Council, 1948.

———. *The Labor Force in Economic Development: A Comparison of International Census Data, 1946–66*. Princeton, NJ: Princeton University Press, 1975.

Easterlin, Richard. *Population, Labor Force, and Long Swings in Economic Growth: The American Experience.* New York: Columbia University Press, 1968.

———. "Influences on European Overseas Emigration before World War I." In Robert W. Fogel and Stanley L. Engerman, eds., *Reinterpretation of American Economic History.* New York: Harper & Row, 1971.

———. "What Will 1984 Be Like? Socioeconomic Implications of Recent Twists in Age Structure," *Demography* 15 (November 1978): 397–432.

———. *Birth and Fortune: The Impact of Numbers on Personal Welfare.* New York: Basic Books, 1980.

Economic Report of the President. Washington, DC: Government Printing Office, various dates.

Edwards, Linda. "Equal Employment Opportunity in Japan: A View from the West." *Industrial and Labor Relations Review* 41 (January 1988): 240–50.

Edwards, Richard. *Contested Terrain: The Transformation of the Workplace in the Twentieth Century.* New York: Basic Books, 1979.

Eichengreen, Barry. "Experience and the Male–Female Earnings Gap in the 1890s." *Journal of Economic History* 44 (September 1984): 822–34.

Eisner, Robert. "Extended Accounts for National Income and Product." *Journal of Economic Literature* 26 (December 1988): 1611–84.

Engels, Friedrich. *The Origin of the Family, Private Property, and the State.* In Robert C. Tucker, ed., *The Marx–Engels Reader.* New York: Norton, 1978; orig. publ. 1884.

Equal Employment Opportunity Commission (EEOC). *Annual Reports, 1966–1984.* Washington, DC: Government Printing Office, various dates.

Fields, Judith M. "A Comparison of Intercity Differences in the Labor Force Participation Rates of Married Women in 1970 with 1940, 1950, and 1960." *Journal of Human Resources* 11 (Fall 1976): 578–81.

Franklin, Benjamin. *The Autobiography and Other Writings.* New York: New American Library, 1961.

Fraundorf, Martha Norby. "The Labor Force Participation of Turn-of-the-Century Married Women." *Journal of Economic History* 39 (June 1979): 401–18.

Freeman, Jo. *The Politics of Women's Liberation: A Case Study of an Emerging Social Movement and Its Relation to the Policy Process.* New York: Longman, 1975.

Freeman, Richard. "The Effect of Demographic Factors on Age-Earnings Profiles." *Journal of Human Resources* 14 (Summer 1979): 289–318.

———. "Unionism Comes to the Public Sector." *Journal of Economic Literature* 24 (March 1986): 41–86.

Freeman, Richard, and Jonathan Leonard. "Union Maids: Unions and the Female Work Force." In Claire Brown and Joseph A. Pechman, eds., *Gender in the Workplace.* Washington, DC: Brookings Institution, 1987.

Friedan, Betty. *The Feminine Mystique.* New York: Norton, 1963.

Friedman, Milton, and Simon Kuznets. *Income from Independent Professional Practice.* New York: National Bureau of Economic Research, 1945.

Fuchs, Victor R. "The Feminization of Poverty." Manuscript, Stanford University, March 1986.

———. *Women's Quest for Economic Equality.* Cambridge, MA: Harvard University Press, 1988.

Gallman, Robert E. "Gross National Product in the United States, 1834–1909." In Dorothy Brady, ed., *Output, Employment, and Productivity in the United States after 1800.* New York: National Bureau of Economic Research, 1966.

Garrison, Dee. *Apostles of Culture: The Public Librarian and American Society, 1876–1920.* New York: Free Press, 1979.

Goldin, Claudia. "Female Labor Force Participation: The Origin of Black and White Differences, 1870 to 1880." *Journal of Economic History* 37 (March 1977): 87–108.

———. "Household and Market Production of Families in a Late Nineteenth Century City." *Explorations in Economic History* 16 (April 1979): 111–31.

———. "Family Strategies and the Family Economy in the Late Nineteenth Century: The Role of Secondary Workers." In Theodore Hershberg, ed., *Philadelphia: Work, Space, Family, and Group Experience in the 19th Century.* New York: Oxford University Press, 1980.

———. "The Work and Wages of Single Women, 1870 to 1920." *Journal of Economic History* 41 (March 1981): 81–89.

———. "The Changing Economic Role of Women: A Quantitative Approach." *Journal of Interdisciplinary History* 13 (Spring 1983): 707–33.

———. "The Historical Evolution of Female Earnings Functions and Occupations." *Explorations in Economic History* 21 (January 1984): 1–27.

———. "The Earnings Gap in Historical Perspective." In U.S. Commission on Civil Rights, *Comparable Worth: Issue for the 1980's.* Washington, DC: Government Printing Office, 1985.

———. "The Economic Status of Women in the Early Republic: Quantitative Evidence." *Journal of Interdisciplinary History* 16 (Winter 1986a): 375–404.

———. "Monitoring Costs and Occupational Segregation by Sex: A Historical Analysis." *Journal of Labor Economics* 4 (January 1986b): 1–27.

———. "The Female Labor Force and American Economic Growth: 1890 to 1980." In Stanley L. Engerman and Robert E. Gallman, eds., *Long-Term Factors in American Economic Growth.* Studies in Income and Wealth, Vol. 51. Chicago: University of Chicago Press, 1986c.

———. "The Gender Gap in Historical Perspective, 1800 to 1980." In Peter Kilby, ed., *Quantity and Quiddity: Essays in U.S. Economic History.* Middletown, CT: Wesleyan University Press, 1987a.

———. Women's Employment and Technological Change: A Historical Perspective." In Heidi Hartmann, ed., *Computer Chips and Paper Clips: Technology and Women's Employment.* Vol. 2, *Case Studies and Policy Perspectives.* Washington, DC: National Academy Press, 1987b.

———. "Maximum Hours Legislation and Female Employment in the 1920's: A Reassessment." *Journal of Political Economy* 96 (February, 1988a): 189–205. (Longer version originally issued as National Bureau of Economic Research Working Paper, No. 1949.)

———. "A Pollution Theory of Discrimination: Male and Female Differences in Earnings and Occupations." Manuscript, University of Pennsylvania, March 1988b.

———. "Life-Cycle Labor Force Participation of Married Women: Historical Evidence and Implications." *Journal of Labor Economics* 7 (January 1989): 20–47.

Goldin, Claudia, and Donald Parsons. "Parental Altruism and Self-Interest: Child Labor among Late-Nineteenth Century American Families." *Economic Inquiry* (1989, forthcoming). (Revised version of National Bureau of Economic Research Working Paper No. 707.)

Goldin, Claudia, and Solomon Polachek. "Residual Differences by Sex: Perspectives on the Gender Gap in Earnings." *American Economic Review* 77 (May 1987): 143–51.

Goldin, Claudia, and Kenneth Sokoloff. "Women, Children, and Industrialization in the Early Republic: Evidence from the Manufacturing Censuses." *Journal of Economic History* 42 (December 1982): 741–74.

_____. "The Relative Productivity Hypothesis of Industrialization: The American Case, 1820 to 1850." *Quarterly Journal of Economics* 99 (August 1984): 461–88.

Greenwald, Maurine Weiner. *Women, War, and Work: The Impact of World War I on Women Workers in the United States*. Westport, CT: Greenwood Press, 1980.

Gross, Edward. "Plus ça Change . . . : The Sexual Structure of Occupations over Time." *Social Problems* 16 (Fall 1968): 198–208.

Guasch, J. Luis, and Andrew Weiss. "Self-Selection in the Labor Market." *American Economic Review* 71 (June 1981): 275–84.

Haines, Michael. *Fertility and Occupation: Population Patterns in Industrialization*. New York: Academic Press, 1979.

Hamermesh, Daniel S. "The Demand for Labor in the Long Run." In Orley C. Ashenfelter and Richard Layard, eds., *Handbook of Labor Economics*. Vol. 1. Amsterdam: North-Holland, 1986.

Hannon, Joan Underhill. "The Immigrant Worker in the Promised Land: Human Capital and Ethnic Discrimination in the Michigan Labor Market, 1888–1890." Ph.D. diss., University of Wisconsin, Madison, 1977.

_____. "Poverty in the Antebellum Northeast: The View from New York State's Poor Relief Rolls." *Journal of Economic History* 44 (December 1984): 1007–32.

Harris, Barbara J. *Beyond Her Sphere: Women and the Professions in American History*. Westport, CT: Greenwood Press, 1978.

Harrison, Cynthia E. *On Account of Sex: The Politics of Women's Issues, 1945–1968*. Berkeley: University of California Press, 1988.

Hashimoto, Masanori, and Levis Kochin. "A Bias in the Statistical Estimation of the Effects of Discrimination." *Economic Inquiry* 18 (July 1980): 478–86.

Heckman, James J., and Robert J. Willis. "A Beta-logistic Model for the Analysis of Sequential Labor Force Participation by Married Women." *Journal of Political Economy* 85 (February 1977): 27–58.

_____. "Reply to Mincer and Ofek." *Journal of Political Economy* 87 (February 1979): 203–12.

Henretta, John C., and Angela M. O'Rand. "Labor-Force Participation of Older Married Women." *Social Security Bulletin* 43 (August 1980): 10–16.

Hidy, Ralph W., Frank Ernest Hill, and Allan Nevins. *Timber and Men: The Weyerhauser Story*. New York: Macmillan, 1963.

Hill, M. Anne. "Female Labor Force Participation in Developing and Developed Countries—Consideration of the Informal Sector." *Review of Economics and Statistics* 65 (August 1983): 459–68.

Historical Statistics of the United States: Colonial Times to 1970, Bicentennial Edition. Washington, DC: Government Printing Office, 1975.*

Holmes, George. *Wages of Farm Labor*. Bulletin No. 99. Washington, DC: Department of Agriculture, Bureau of Statistics, 1912.

Howard, Robert. *Brave New Workplace: America's Corporate Utopias*. New York: Viking Penguin, 1985.

Hughes, Gwendolyn. *Mothers in Industry: Wage-Earning by Mothers in Philadelphia*. New York: New Republic, 1925.

Hussey, Miriam. *Personnel Policies during a Period of Shortage of Young Women Workers in Philadelphia*. Philadelphia: Industrial Research Unit, Wharton School of Finance and Commerce, University of Pennsylvania, 1958.

*Because of the frequency of citation, I have omitted the agency of publication, U.S. Bureau of the Census.

International Labor Organization. "Discrimination in Employment or Occupation on the Basis of Marital Status." *International Labor Review* 85 (March 1962): 262–82.

Irelan, Lola M. "Retirement History Study: Introduction." *Social Security Bulletin* 35 (November 1972): 3–8.

Jacobs, Jerry. "Long-term Trends in Occupational Segregation by Sex." Manuscript, University of Pennsylvania, May 1988.

Jacoby, Sanford M. *Employing Bureaucracy: Managers, Unions, and the Transformation of Work in American Industry, 1900–1945*. New York: Columbia University Press, 1985.

Jaffe, A. J. "Trends in the Participation of Women in the Working Force." *Monthly Labor Review* 79 (May 1956): 559–65.

Jensen, Joan M. "Cloth, Butter and Boarders: Women's Household Production for the Market." *Review of Radical Political Economics* 12 (Summer 1980): 14–24.

———. *Loosening the Bonds: Mid-Atlantic Farm Women, 1750–1850*. New Haven, CT: Yale University Press, 1986.

Johnson, George, and Gary Solon. "Estimates of the Direct Effects of Comparable Worth Policy." *American Economic Review* 76 (December 1986): 1117–25.

Johnson, William R., and Jonathan Skinner. "Labor Supply and Marital Separation." *American Economic Review* 76 (June 1986): 455–69.

Jones, Ethel. "New Estimates of Hours of Work per Week and Hourly Earnings, 1900–1957." *Review of Economics and Statistics* 45 (November 1963): 374–85.

Joshi, Heather E., Richard Layard, and Susan J. Owen. "Why Are More Women Working in Britain?" *Journal of Labor Economics* 3 (January 1985; supplement): S147–S176.

Juster, Thomas F., and Frank P. Stafford, eds. *Time, Goods, and Well-Being*. Ann Arbor, MI: Institute for Social Research, 1985.

Kanter, Rosabeth Moss. *Men and Women of the Corporation*. New York: Basic Books, 1977.

Kaplan, David L., and M. Claire Casey. *Occupational Trends in the United States, 1900 to 1950*. Bureau of the Census Working Paper, No. 5. Washington, DC: U.S. Department of Commerce, 1958.

Keat, Paul G. "Long Run Changes in Occupational Wage Structure, 1900–1956." *Journal of Political Economy* 68 (December 1960): 584–600.

Kessler-Harris, Alice. *Out to Work: A History of Wage-Earning Women in the United States*. New York: Oxford University Press, 1982.

Keyssar, Alexander. *Out of Work: The First Century of Unemployment in Massachusetts*. New York: Cambridge University Press, 1986.

Killingsworth, Mark. *Labor Supply*. Cambridge: Cambridge University Press, 1983.

Killingsworth, Mark, and James J. Heckman. "Female Labor Supply: A Survey." In Orley C. Ashenfelter and Richard Layard, eds., *Handbook of Labor Economics*. Vol. 1. Amsterdam: North-Holland, 1986.

King, Alan. "Industrial Structure, the Flexibility of Working Hours, and Women's Labor Force Participation." *Review of Economics and Statistics* 60 (August 1978): 399–407.

Kokkelenberg, Edward C., and Donna R. Sockell. "Union Membership in the United States, 1973–1981." *Industrial and Labor Relations Review* 38 (July 1985): 497–543.

Korenman, Sanders D., and David Neumark. "Does Marriage Really Make Men More Productive?" Manuscript, Harvard University, November 1987.

Krueger, Alan B., and Lawrence H. Summers. "Reflections on the Inter-Industry Wage Structure." In Kevin Lang and Jonathan Leonard, eds., *Unemployment and the Structure of Labor Markets*. Oxford: Basil Blackwell, 1987.

Kuhn, Peter. "Sex Discrimination in Labor Markets: The Role of Statistical Evidence." *American Economic Review* 77 (September 1987): 567–83.

LaFollette, Cecile Tipton. *A Study of the Problems of 652 Gainfully Employed Married Women Homemakers.* New York: Teachers College, Columbia University, 1934.

Landes, Elisabeth M. "The Effect of State Maximum-Hours Laws on the Employment of Women in 1920." *Journal of Political Economy* 88 (June 1980): 476–94.

Layard, Richard, and Jacob Mincer, eds. "Trends in Women's Work, Education, and Family Building." *Journal of Labor Economics* 3 (January 1985; supplement).

Lazear, Edward. "Why Is There Mandatory Retirement?" *Journal of Political Economy* 87 (December 1979): 1261–84.

―――. "Agency, Earnings Profiles, Productivity, and Hours Restrictions." *American Economic Review* 71 (September 1981): 606–20.

Lazear, Edward, and Robert L. Moore. "Incentives, Productivity, and Labor Contracts." *Quarterly Journal of Economics* 99 (May 1984): 275–95.

Lazear, Edward, and Sherwin Rosen. "Male/Female Wage Differentials in Job Ladders." In O. Ashenfelter, ed., *Essays in Honor of Albert Rees. Journal of Labor Economics* (1989; supplement, forthcoming).

―――. "Rank-Order Tournaments as Optimum Labor Contracts." *Journal of Political Economy* 89 (October 1981): 841–64.

Lebergott, Stanley. *Manpower in Economic Growth: The American Record Since 1800.* New York: McGraw-Hill, 1964.

Lehrer, Susan. *Origins of Protective Labor Legislation for Women: 1905–1925.* Albany: State University of New York Press, 1987.

Lerner, Gerda. "The Lady and the Mill Girl: Changes in the Status of Women in the Age of Jackson," *Midcontinent American Studies Journal* 10 (Spring 1969): 5–14. Reprinted in Nancy Cott and Elizabeth Pleck, eds. *A Heritage of Her Own.* New York: Simon and Schuster, 1979.

―――. *The Creation of Patriarchy.* New York: Oxford University Press, 1986.

Lewis, Ervin Eugene. *Personnel Problems of the Teaching Staff.* New York: Century, 1925.

Livernash, E. Robert, ed. *Comparable Worth: Issues and Alternatives.* 2nd ed. Washington, DC: Equal Employment Advisory Council, 1984.

Long, Clarence D. *Wages and Earnings in the United States, 1860–1890.* Princeton, NJ: Princeton University Press, 1960.

―――. *The Labor Force Under Changing Income and Employment.* Princeton, NJ: Princeton University Press for the NBER, 1958.

Lundahl, Mats, and Eskil Wadensjö. *Unequal Treatment: A Study in the Neo-Classical Theory of Discrimination.* New York: New York University Press, 1984.

Lundberg, Shelly J., and Richard Startz. "Private Discrimination and Social Intervention in Competitive Labor Markets." *American Economic Review* 73 (June 1983): 340–47.

Lynd, Robert S., and Helen Merrell Lynd. *Middletown: A Study in American Culture.* New York: Harcourt, Brace, 1929.

―――. *Middletown in Transition: A Study in Cultural Conflicts.* New York: Harcourt, Brace, 1937.

Madden, Janice. "The Persistence of Pay Differentials: The Economics of Sex Discrimination." *Women and Work: An Annual Review* 1 (1985): 76–114.

Malcomson, James M. "Work Incentives, Hierarchy, and Internal Labor Markets." *Journal of Political Economy* 92 (June 1984): 486–507.

Malkiel, Burton, and Judith A. Malkiel. "Male–Female Pay Differentials in Professional Employment." *American Economic Review* 63 (September 1973): 693–705.

Mallen, Lucy. "Women Born in the Early 1900s: Employment, Earnings, and Benefit Levels." *Social Security Bulletin* 37 (March 1974): 3–24.

Margo, Robert. "Race, Educational Attainment, and the 1940 Census." *Journal of Economic History* 46 (March 1986): 189–98.

Margo, Robert, and Elyce Rotella. "Sex Differences in the Labor Market for Public School Personnel: The Case of Houston, Texas, 1892–1923." Manuscript, Indiana University, 1981.

Mathews, Jane De Hart. "The New Feminism and the Dynamics of Social Change." In Linda K. Kerber and Jane De Hart Mathews, eds., *Women's America*. New York: Oxford University Press, 1982.

Matthaei, Julie A. *An Economic History of Women in America: Women's Work, the Sexual Division of Labor, and the Development of Capitalism*. New York: Schocken Books, 1982.

McGaw, Judith A. *Most Wonderful Machine: Mechanization and Social Change in Berkshire Paper Making, 1801–1885*. Princeton, NJ: Princeton University Press, 1987.

Meyerowitz, Joanne J. *Women Adrift: Independent Wage Earners in Chicago, 1880–1930*. Chicago: University of Chicago Press, 1988.

Michael, Robert T. "Consequences of the Rise in Female Labor Force Participation Rates: Questions and Probes." *Journal of Labor Economics* 3 (January 1985; supplement): S117–S146.

Milkman, Ruth. *Gender at Work: The Dynamics of Job Segregation by Sex during World War II*. Urbana: University of Illinois Press, 1987.

Mincer, Jacob. "Labor Force Participation of Married Women: A Study of Labor Supply." In H. Gregg Lewis, ed., *Aspects of Labor Economics*. Universities-National Bureau Committee for Economic Research. Princeton, NJ: Princeton University Press, 1962.

———. "Labor Force Participation and Unemployment: A Review of Recent Evidence." In R. A. Gordon and M. S. Gordon, eds., *Prosperity and Unemployment*. New York: Wiley, 1966.

———. *Schooling, Experience, and Earnings*. New York: Columbia University Press for the National Bureau of Economic Research, 1974.

———. "Intercountry Comparisons of Labor Force Trends and of Related Developments: An Overview." *Journal of Labor Economics* 3 (January 1985; supplement): S1–S32.

Mincer, Jacob, and Solomon Polachek. "Family Investments in Human Capital Earnings of Women." *Journal of Political Economy* 82 (March–April 1974): S76–S108.

Modell, John, and Tamara K. Hareven. "Urbanization and the Malleable Household: An Examination of Boarding and Lodging in American Families." *Journal of Marriage and the Family* 35 (August 1973): 467–79.

Montgomery, David. *The Fall of the House of Labor: The Workplace, the State, and American Labor Activism, 1865–1925*. New York: Cambridge University Press, 1987.

Morello, Karen Berger. *The Invisible Bar: The Woman Lawyer in America, 1638 to the Present*. New York: Random House, 1986.

Mroz, Thomas A. "The Sensitivity of an Empirical Model of Married Women's Hours of Work to Economic and Statistical Assumptions." *Econometrica* 55 (July 1987): 765–99.

Myrdal, Gunnar. *An American Dilemma: The Negro Problem and Modern Democracy*. New York: Harper, 1944.

National Education Association. *Teachers' Salaries and Salary Trends in 1923*. Report of the Salary Committee of the NEA, Vol. I, No. 3. Washington, DC: NEA, July 1923.

———. *Practices Affecting Teacher Personnel*. Research Bulletin of the NEA, Vol. VI, No. 4. Washington, DC: NEA, September 1928.

———. *Administrative Practices Affecting Classroom Teachers*. Part I, *The Selection and Appointment of Teachers;* Part II, *The Retention, Promotion, and Improvement of*

Teachers. Research Bulletin of the NEA, Vol. X, No. 1. Washington, DC: NEA, January 1932.

———. *Teacher Personnel Procedures: Selection and Appointment*. Research Bulletin of the NEA, Vol. XX, No. 2. Washington, DC: NEA, March 1942.

———. *Teacher Personnel Practices, 1950–51: Appointment and Termination of Service*. Research Bulletin of the NEA, Vol. XXX, No. 1. Washington, DC: NEA, February 1952.

National Industrial Conference Board (NICB). *Clerical Salaries in the United States, 1926*. New York: National Industrial Conference Board, 1926.

Nelson, Daniel. *Managers and Workers: Origins of the New Factory System in the United States, 1880–1920*. Madison: University of Wisconsin Press, 1975.

New York Department of Labor. *Special Bulletin: The Industrial Replacement of Men by Women in the State of New York*. No. 93. Albany, N.Y. Department of Labor, March 1919.

New York Times. "Women Reduce Lag in Earnings But Disparities with Men Remain." September 4, 1987.

———. "California Women Receiving Millions to Settle Bias Case." January 20, 1988.

———. "Women's Salaries Are Raised by University of Connecticut." April 17, 1988.

———. "Protecting the Baby: Work in Pregnancy Poses Legal Frontier." August 2, 1988.

Norton, Mary Beth. "Eighteenth-Century American Women in Peace and War: The Case of the Loyalists," *William and Mary Quarterly* 33 (July 1976): 386–409.

Oaxaca, Ronald. "Male–Female Wage Differentials in Urban Labor Markets." *International Economic Review* 14 (October 1973): 693–709.

O'Neill, June. "A Time-Series Analysis of Female Labor Force Participation." *American Economic Review* 71 (May 1981): 76–80.

———. "The Determinants and Wage Effects of Occupational Segregation." Manuscript. The Urban Institute, Washington, DC, 1983.

———. "The Trend in the Male–Female Wage Gap in the United States." *Journal of Labor Economics* 3 (January 1985; supplement): S91–S116.

O'Neill, William L. *Everyone Was Brave: The Rise and Fall of Feminism in America*. Chicago: Quadrangle Books, 1969.

———, ed. *Women at Work, Including "The Long Day: The Story of a New York Working Girl"* by Dorothy Richardson. Chicago: Quadrangle Books, 1972; orig. publ. 1905.

Oppenheimer, Valerie Kincade. *The Female Labor Force in the United States: Demographic and Economic Factors Governing Its Growth and Changing Composition*. Westport, CT: Greenwood Press, 1976; orig. publ. 1970.

Palmer, Gladys L. *Labor Mobility in Six Cities: A Report on the Survey of Patterns and Factors in Labor Mobility, 1940–1950*. New York: Social Science Research Council, 1954.

Pencavel, John. "Work Effort, on-the-Job Screening, and Alternative Methods of Remuneration." *Research in Labor Economics* 1 (1977): 225–58.

Peters, David Wilbur. *The Status of the Married Woman Teacher*. New York: Teachers College, Columbia University, 1934.

Peterson, Sharon. "Married Women and the Right to Teach in St. Louis, 1941–1948." *Missouri Historical Review* 81 (January 1987): 141–58.

Phelps, Edmund S. "The Statistical Theory of Racism and Sexism." *American Economic Review* 62 (September 1972): 659–61.

Polachek, Solomon W. "Occupational Segregation and the Gender Wage Gap." *Population Research and Policy Review* 6 (1987): 47–67.

Preston, Samuel H., and Alan Thomas Richards. "The Influence of Women's Work Opportunities on Marriage Rates." *Demography* 12 (May 1975): 209–22.

Pruette, Lorne. *Women Workers through the Depression: A Study of White Collar Employment Made by the American Woman's Association*. New York: Macmillan, 1934.

Raff, Daniel. "Wage Determination Theory and the Five-Dollar Day at Ford." *Journal of
Economic History* 48 (June 1988): 387–99.

Robinson, J. Gregory. "Labor Force Participation Rates of Cohorts of Women in the United
States: 1890 to 1979." Paper presented at the Population Association of America Meetings, Denver, April 1980.

Rotella, Elyce. "Women's Labor Force Participation and the Decline of the Family Economy
in the United States." *Explorations in Economic History* 17 (April 1980): 95–117.

——. *From Home to Office: U.S. Women at Work, 1870–1930*. Ann Arbor, MI: UMI
Research Press, 1981.

——. "Special Protections and Restrictions versus Equal Opportunities for Women in the
Workforce." Manuscript, Indiana University, 1988.

Rubin, Lillian. *Worlds of Pain: Life in the Working-Class Family*. New York: Basic Books,
1976.

Rubinow, I. M. "Women in Manufactures: A Criticism." *Journal of Political Economy* 15
(January–December 1907): 41–47.

Salmon, Lucy Maynard. *Domestic Service*. New York: Arno Press, 1972; orig. publ. 1897.

Salop, J., and S. Salop. "Self-Selection and Turnover in the Labor Market." *Quarterly
Journal of Economics* 90 (November 1976): 619–28.

Sandell, Steven H., and David Shapiro. "Work Expectations, Human Capital Accumulation,
and the Wages of Young Women." *Journal of Human Resources* 15 (Summer 1980):
335–53.

Scharf, Lois. *To Work and to Wed: Female Employment, Feminism, and the Great Depression*. Westport, CT: Greenwood Press, 1980.

Schatz, Ronald W. *The Electrical Workers: A History of Labor at General Electric and
Westinghouse, 1923–60*. Urbana: University of Illinois Press, 1983.

Scott, Anne Firor. *The Southern Lady: From Pedestal to Politics, 1830–1930*. Chicago:
University of Chicago Press, 1970.

Sealander, Judith. *As Minority Becomes Majority: Federal Reaction to the Phenomenon of
Women in the Work Force, 1920–1963*. Westport, CT: Greenwood Press, 1983.

Shallcross, Ruth. *Should Married Women Work?* Public Affairs Pamphlets, No. 49. New
York: National Federation of Business and Professional Women's Clubs, 1940.

Shank, Susan E. "Women in the Labor Market: The Link Grows Stronger." *Monthly Labor
Review* 111 (March 1988): 3–10.

Shapiro, David, and Joan E. Crowley. "Aspirations and Expectations of Youth in the U.S.:
Part 2, Employment Activity." *Youth and Society* 14 (September 1982): 33–58.

Shapiro, David, and Lois B. Shaw. "Growth in the Labor Force Attachment of Married
Women: Accounting for Changes in the 1970's." *Southern Economic Journal* 50 (October 1983): 461–73.

Shaw, Lois B., and David Shapiro. "Women's Work Plans: Contrasting Expectations and
Actual Work Experience." *Monthly Labor Review* 110 (November 1987): 7–13.

Slichter, Sumner H. "Notes on the Structure of Wages." *Review of Economics and Statistics*
32 (February 1950): 80–99.

Smith, James P. "Family Labor Supply over the Life Cycle." *Explorations in Economic
Research* 4 (1977): 205–76.

——, ed. *Female Labor Supply: Theory and Estimation*. Princeton, NJ: Princeton University Press, 1980.

————. "Race and Human Capital." *American Economic Review* 74 (September 1984): 685–98.

Smith, James P., and Michael P. Ward. *Women's Wages and Work in the Twentieth Century*. Santa Monica, CA: Rand Corporation, 1984.

————. "Time-Series Growth in the Female Labor Force." *Journal of Labor Economics* 3 (January 1985; supplement): S59–S90.

————. "Women in the Labor Market and in the Family." *Journal of Economic Perspectives* 3 (Winter 1989): 9–23.

Smuts, Robert W. *Women and Work in America*. New York: Columbia University Press, 1959.

————. "The Female Labor Force: A Case Study in the Interpretation of Historical Statistics. *Journal of the American Statistical Association* 55 (March 1960): 71–79.

Sorensen, Elaine. "The Wage Effects of Occupational Sex Composition: A Review and New Findings." In M. Anne Hill and Mark Killingsworth, eds., *Colloquium on Comparable Worth*. Ithaca: Cornell University–I.L.R. Press, 1989.

Sproat, Kezia V., Helene Churchill, and Carol Sheets. *The National Longitudinal Surveys of Labor Market Experiences: An Annotated Bibliography of Research*. Lexington, MA: Lexington Books, 1985.

Stansell, Christine. *City of Women: Sex and Class in New York, 1789–1860*. New York: Knopf, 1986.

Steinberg, Ronnie. *Wages and Hours: Labor and Reform in Twentieth-Century America*. New Brunswick, NJ: Rutgers University Press, 1982.

Strober, Myra H., and Carolyn L. Arnold. "The Dynamics of Occupational Segregation among Bank Tellers." In Clair Brown and Joseph A. Pechman, eds., *Gender in the Workplace*. Washington, DC: Brookings Institution, 1987.

Sundstrom, William. "Internal Labor Markets before World War I: On-the-Job Training and Employee Promotion." *Explorations in Economic History* 25 (October 1988): 424–45.

Szalai, Alexander, ed. *The Use of Time: Daily Activities of Urban and Suburban Populations in Twelve Countries*. The Hague: Mouton, 1972.

Taussig, F. W., ed. *State Papers and Speeches on the Tariff*. Cambridge, MA.: Harvard University Press, 1892.

Tentler, Leslie. *Wage Earning Women: Industrial Work and Family Life in the United States, 1900–1930*. New York: Oxford University Press, 1979.

Thurow, Lester. *Generating Inequality*. New York: Basic Books, 1975.

Treiman, Donald, and Heidi Hartmann, eds. *Women, Work, and Wages: Equal Pay for Jobs of Equal Value*. Washington, DC: National Academy of Sciences Press, 1981.

Ulrich, Laurel Thatcher. *Good Wives: Image and Reality in the Lives of Women in Northern New England, 1650–1750*. New York: Oxford University Press, 1980.

U.S. Bureau of the Census. *Twelfth Census of the United States, 1900*. Vol. II, *Population*, Part II. Washington, DC: Government Printing Office, 1902.

————. *Twelfth Census of the United States, 1900. Supplementary Analysis and Derivative Tables*. Washington, DC: Government Printing Office, 1906.

————. *Statistics of Women at Work: Based on Unpublished Information Derived from the Schedules of the Twelfth Census: 1900*. Washington, DC: Government Printing Office, 1907a.

————. *Manufactures, 1905*. Part I, *United States by Industries*. Washington, DC: Government Printing Office, 1907b.

————. *Thirteenth Census of the United States, 1910*. Vol. I, *Population, General Report and Analysis*. Washington, DC: Government Printing Office, 1913a.

————. *Thirteenth Census, 1910.* Vol.8, *Manufactures 1909: General Report and Analysis.* Washington, DC: Government Printing Office, 1913b.

————. *Thirteenth Census of the United States, 1910.* Vol. IV, *Population, Occupation Statistics.* Washington, DC: Government Printing Office, 1914.

————. *Fourteenth Census of the U.S.: 1920.* Vol. IV, *Occupations.* Washington, DC: Government Printing Office, 1923.

————. *Population 1920. Fourteenth Census of the U.S. Census of Manufactures, 1919.* Washington, DC: Government Printing Office, 1928.

————. *Fifteenth Census of the United States: 1930. Occupational Statistics, Abstract Summary of the U.S. Census.* Washington, DC: Government Printing Office, 1932.

————. *Fifteenth Census of the United States: 1930. Population.* Vol. II, *General Report, Statistics by Subject.* Washington, DC: Government Printing Office, 1933a.

————. *Fifteenth Census of the United States: 1930. Population.* Vol. V, *General Report on Occupations.* Washington, DC: Government Printing Office, 1933b.

————. *Sixteenth Census of the United States: 1940. Population.* Vol. III, *The Labor Force. Occupation, Industry, Employment, and Income.* Part 1, *United States Summary.* Washington, DC: Government Printing Office, 1943a.

————. *Sixteenth Census of the United States: 1940. Population: The Labor Force, Employment, and Family Characteristics of Women.* Washington, DC: Government Printing Office, 1943b.

————. Current Population Reports, Series P-50, No. 2. *Labor Force, Employment, and Unemployment in the United States, 1940 to 1946.* Washington, DC: Government Printing Office, n.d.

————. *U.S. Census of Population: 1950.* Vol. II, *Characteristics of the Population.* Part 1, *U.S. Summary.* Washington, DC: Government Printing Office, 1953a.

————. *U.S. Census of Population: 1950.* Vol. IV, *Special Reports.* Part 1, Chapter A, "Employment and Personal Characteristics." Washington, DC: Government Printing Office, 1953b.

————. *U.S. Census of Population: 1950.* Vol. IV, *Special Report.* Part 1, Chapter B, "Occupational Characteristics." Washington, DC: Government Printing Office, 1956.

————. *U.S. Census of Population: 1960. Detailed Characteristics. U.S. Summary: Final Report PC(1)-1D.* Washington, DC: Government Printing Office, 1963a.

————. *U.S. Census of Population: 1960. Subject Reports: Final Report PC(2)-6A, Employment Status and Work Experience.* Washington, DC: Government Printing Office, 1963b.

————. *U.S. Census of Population: 1960. Subject Reports: Occupational Characteristics. Final Report PC(2)-7A.* Washington, DC: Government Printing Office, 1963c.

————. Bureau of the Census. *U.S. Census of Population: 1970. Subject Reports: Final Report PC(2)-6A, Employment Status and Work Experience.* Washington, DC: Government Printing Office, 1973.

————. *1980 Census of Population.* Vol. 1, Chapter C: "General Social and Economic Characteristics." Part 1, *United States Summary.* Washington, DC: Government Printing Office, 1983.

————. *Current Population Reports, Series P-20. Educational Attainment in the United States.* Washington, DC: Government Printing Office, various dates.

————. *Current Population Reports, Series P-20. Fertility of American Women.* Washington, DC: Government Printing Office, various dates.

————. *Current Population Reports, Series P-60, No. 161. Money Income and Poverty Status in the United States: 1987 (Advance Data from the March 1988 Current Population Survey).* Washington, DC: Government Printing Office, 1988.

————. *Current Population Reports, Series P-70, No. 10. Male–Female Differences in Work Experience, Occupation, and Earnings: 1984. Data from the Survey of Income and Program Participation.* Washington, DC: Government Printing Office, 1987.

U.S. Census Office. *Report on Manufacturing Industries in the United States at the Eleventh Census: 1890.* Part I, *Totals for States and Industries.* Washington, DC: Government Printing Office, 1895a.

————. *Report on Manufacturing Industries in the United States at the Eleventh Census: 1890.* Part II, *Statistics of Cities.* Washington, DC: Government Printing Office, 1895b.

————. *Report on Population of the United States at the Eleventh Census: 1890.* Part I. Washington, DC: Government Printing Office, 1895c.

————. *Report on Population of the United States at the Eleventh Census: 1890.* Part II. Washington, DC: Government Printing Office, 1897.

————. *Twelfth Census of the United States, 1900. Census Reports.* Vol. VII, *Manufactures.* Part I, *United States by Industries.* Washington, DC: Government Printing Office, 1902.

————. *Twelfth Census of the United States, 1900. Special Reports: Employees and Wages,* by Davis R. Dewey. Washington, DC: Government Printing Office, 1903.

U.S. Commissioner of Labor. *Fourth Annual Report of the Commissioner of Labor, 1888: Working Women in Large Cities.* Washington, DC: Government Printing Office, 1889.

————. *Sixth Annual Report of the Commissioner of Labor, 1890.* Part III, *Cost of Living.* U.S. Congress, House of Representatives, House Executive Document 265, 51st Cong., 2nd sess. Washington, DC: Government Printing Office, 1890.

————. *Seventh Annual Report of the Commissioner of Labor, 1891.* Part III, *Cost of Living.* U.S. Congress, House of Representatives, House Executive Document 232, 52nd Cong., 1st sess., Vols. I and II. Washington, DC: Government Printing Office, 1891.

————. *Eleventh Annual Report of the Commissioner of Labor. 1895–96. Work and Wages of Men, Women, and Children.* Washington, DC: Government Printing Office, 1897.

————. *Nineteenth Annual Report of the Commissioner of Labor. 1904. Wages and Hours of Labor.* Washington, DC: Government Printing Office, 1905.

U.S. Department of Commerce, Bureau of Economic Analysis. *The National Income and Product Accounts of the U.S., 1929–82: Statistical Tables.* Washington, DC: Government Printing Office, 1986.

U.S. Department of Education. *Digest of Education Statistics, 1988.* Washington, DC: Government Printing Office, 1988.

U.S. Department of Labor, Bureau of Labor Statistics. *Bulletin of the Bureau of Labor Statistics, 175.* Women in Industry Series, No. 5, *Summary of the Report on Condition of Woman and Child Wage Earners in the United States.* Washington, DC: Government Printing Office, 1916.

————. *Marital and Family Characteristics of the Labor Force, March 1970.* Special Labor Force Report, No. 130. Washington, DC: Government Printing Office, 1971.

————. *Marital and Family Characteristics of the Labor Force, March 1979.* Special Labor Force Report, No. 237. Washington, DC: Government Printing Office, 1981.

————. *Labor Force Statistics Derived from the Current Population Survey: A Databook.* Vol. I. Bulletin 2096. Washington, DC: Government Printing Office, 1982.

————. *Marital and Family Patterns of Workers: An Update.* Bulletin 2163. Washington, DC: Government Printing Office, May 1983.

————. *News.* No. 87-345, August 12, 1987, and No. 88-431, September 7, 1988. Washington, DC: Government Printing Office.

————. Employment and Earnings series. Washington, DC: Government Printing Office, various issues.

U.S. Department of Labor, Women's Bureau. *Women in the Government Service,* by Bertha M. Nienburg. Bulletin of the Women's Bureau, No. 8. Washington, DC: Government Printing Office, 1920a.

———. *The New Position of Women in American Industry.* Bulletin of the Women's Bureau, No. 12. Washington, DC: Government Printing Office, 1920b.

———. *Women in* [State] *Industries: A Study of Hours and Working Conditions.* Bulletins of the Women's Bureau, Nos. 21 (Rhode Island), 37 (New Jersey), 44 (Ohio), 51 (Illinois), 58 (Delaware). Washington, DC: Government Printing Office, 1922–1927.

———. *Chronological Development of Labor Legislation for Women in the United States.* Bulletin of the Women's Bureau, No. 66-II. Washington, DC: Government Printing Office, 1932.

———. *The Age Factor as It Relates to Women in Business and the Professions,* by Harriet A. Byrne. Bulletin of the Women's Bureau, No. 117. Washington, DC: Government Printing Office, 1934a.

———. *The Employment of Women in Offices,* by Ethel Erickson. Bulletin of the Women's Bureau, No. 120. Washington, DC: Government Printing Office, 1934b.

———. *Women Workers in Their Family Environment.* Bulletin of the Women's Bureau, No. 183. Washington, DC: Government Printing Office, 1941.

———. *Office Work in [Houston, Los Angeles, Kansas City, Richmond, and Philadelphia].* Bulletin of the Women's Bureau, Nos. 188-1, 2, 3, 4, 5. Washington, DC: Government Printing Office, 1942.

———. *College Women Seven Years after Graduation: Class of 1957.* Bulletin of the Women's Bureau, No. 292. Washington, DC: Government Printing Office, 1966.

U.S. House of Representatives, *Documents Relative to the Statistics of Manufactures in the U.S.* 2 Vols. Serial Set Nos. 222 and 223. (Also known as the McLane Report.) Washington, DC, 1833.

U.S. President's Commission on the Status of Women. *American Women.* Washington, DC: Government Printing Office, 1963.

———. *Report of the Committee on Private Employment.* Washington, DC: Government Printing Office, October 1963.

U.S. Senate Documents. *Report on Condition of Woman and Child Wage-Earners in the U.S. in 19 Volumes,* Vols. 86–104. Washington, DC: Government Printing Office, 1910–11.

Vanek, Joann. "Keeping Busy: Time Spent in Housework, United States, 1920–1970." Ph.D. diss., University of Michigan, 1973.

Vicinus, Martha. *Independent Women: Work and Community for Single Women, 1850–1920.* Chicago: University of Chicago Press, 1985.

Waciega, Lisa. "A 'Man of Business': The Widow of Means in Philadelphia and Chester County, 1750–1850." Paper presented at the Philadelphia Center for Early American Studies, March 1985.

Wahl, Jennifer Bourne. "New Results on the Decline in Household Fertility in the United States from 1750 to 1900." In Stanley L. Engerman and Robert E. Gallman, eds., *Long-Term Factors in American Economic Growth.* Studies in Income and Wealth, Vol. 51. Chicago: University of Chicago Press, 1986.

Wandersee, Winifred D. *Women's Work and Family Values, 1920–1940.* Cambridge, MA: Harvard University Press, 1981.

Webb, Sidney. "On the Alleged Differences in the Wages Paid to Men and Women for Similar Work." *Economic Journal* 1 (December 1891): 635–62.

Willard, Frances. *Occupations for Women.* New York: Success, 1897.

Williamson, Jeffrey, and Peter Lindert. *American Inequality: A Macroeconomic History*. New York: Academic Press, 1980.

Wright, Carroll D. *The Working Girls of Boston*: From the Fifteenth Annual Report of the Massachusetts Bureau of Statistics of Labor, for 1884. New York: Arno and the New York Times, 1969; orig. publ. 1889.

Index

Abbott, Edith, 53
added worker hypothesis, 125
age. *See also* older women, in labor force
  at beginning of work, 93, 235n
  labor force participation increasing with, 24
  at marriage, in nineteenth century, 51–52
  maximum, for new hires, 166, 167
  of workers and population, 234n
agricultural labor
  by blacks, 27
  excluded from early census data, 11, 44, 224–25
    adjusting for, 14, 45
  gender gap in (1815–1970), 67–68
Aldrich, Mark, 240n
Anderson, Mary, 255n
apprenticeships, 101, 117
Arrow, Kenneth, 88

Baker, Elizabeth Faulkner, 255n
bank tellers, 117, 206
Baron, James N., 240n
Becker, Gary, 88, 247n
Beller, Andrea H., 75, 239n, 257n
Ben-Porath, Yoram, 234n
Bielby, William T., 240n
Bird, Caroline, 199, 202
black women
  Civil Rights Act (1964) and, 201
  discrimination against, 147, 163
  in labor force
    changing occupations of, 154
    in clerical sector, 145–47
    earnings of, before 1940, 249n
    married, 27–28, 119, 154
    post–World War II increase in, 120
  married, cohorts of, 27–28
    education of, 143
    fertility differences across, 140
    without children, 142
Blank, Rebecca, 255n
Blau, Francine D., 239n, 240n
boardinghouse keepers, 44, 45, 49, 224–25
bookkeepers, 72

Bose, Christine E., 236n
Brandeis, Louis, 192
Breckinridge, Sophonisba, 106
Buchele, Robert, 240n
Butler, Elizabeth Beardsley, 203–4

Cahill, Marion Cotter, 193
Cain, Glen G., 248n
Carey, Henry, 66
Carter, Susan B., 240n
census data
  on cohorts, 17–21
  on earnings, 62
    before 1890, 46, 186
  of 1890, corrections to, 43–46
  on work and occupations, 14–15
children
  in analysis of labor supply of women, 125
  divorce and, 212
  fertility differences across cohorts and, 139–42
  home work, earnings, and (1900), 100–101
  as infants, and women's work, 216
  in labor force
    before 1890, 50
    Hamilton on, 66
  as women's burden to raise, 213
Ciancanelli, Penelope, 236n
Civil Rights Act (1964), 201–2
  Title VII of, 87, 209
  wage discrimination and, 87
civil service, 200
Clark, Kim B., 249n
clerical sector
  education for, 115
  gender gap in, 72
  married women barred from, 123
  occupational and educational change and, 143–47
  wage discrimination in, 105–7, 110–14, 204
    earnings of clerical workers, 107–10
    women barred from occupations in, 111–13, 160
Cohn, Samuel, 172, 178